REMEMBERING THE
FORGOTTEN WAR

A VOLUME IN THE SERIES

Public History in Historical Perspective

EDITED BY
Marla R. Miller

REMEMBERING
THE
FORGOTTEN WAR

THE ENDURING LEGACIES OF THE U.S.–MEXICAN WAR

❖

Michael Scott Van Wagenen

❖

University of Massachusetts Press   AMHERST AND BOSTON

LC 2012022642
ISBN 978-1-55849-930-0 (paper); 929-4 (library cloth)

Designed by Dennis Anderson
Set in Sabon with Goudy Oldstyle display by Westchester Book
Printed and bound by Thomson-Shore, Inc.

Library of Congress Cataloging-in-Publication Data

Van Wagenen, Michael.
Remembering the forgotten war : the enduring legacies of the U.S./Mexican War/
Michael Scott Van Wagenen.
     p. cm. — (Public history in historical perspective)
Includes bibliographical references and index.
ISBN 978-1-55849-930-0 (paper : alk. paper) —
ISBN 978-1-55849-929-4 (library cloth : alk. paper)
1. Mexican War, 1846–1848—Influence.   2. Mexican War, 1846–1848—Public opinion.
3. Collective memory—United States.   4. Collective memory—Mexico.
5. Public opinion—United States.   6. Public opinion—Mexico.
7. Public history—United States.   8. Public history—Mexico.
9. Mexico—Relations—United States.   10. United States—Relations—Mexico.
I. Title.
E404.V35 2012
973.6'2—dc23
                              2012022642

British Library Cataloguing in Publication data are available.

Publication of this book and other titles in the series *Public History in Historical
Perspective* is supported by the Office of the Dean, College of Humanities and Fine Arts,
University of Massachusetts Amherst.

For Monica, Maya, Brodie, Ariana, and Natalia

Haven't you ever thought, you gringos, that all this
land was once ours? Ah, our resentment and our memory
go hand in hand.

Carlos Fuentes, *The Old Gringo*

CONTENTS

Acknowledgments   xi

A Note on Perspectives   xv

Introduction
OF WAR AND SOCCER   I

1   Victory and Dissolution
    THE UNITED STATES, 1848–1865   9

2   In the Shadow of Defeat
    MEXICO, 1848–1866   41

3   Old Soldiers and New Wars
    THE UNITED STATES, 1866–1895   59

4   Creating Heroes
    MEXICO, 1867–1920   81

5   Empire and Exclusion
    THE UNITED STATES, 1896–1929   101

6   Rituals of the State
    MEXICO, 1921–1952   128

7   Good Neighbors and Bad Blood
    THE UNITED STATES, 1930–1965   153

8   Resisting the Gringos
    MEXICO, 1953–1989   174

9   Contesting American Pasts
     THE UNITED STATES, 1966–1989   192

10   Remembrance and Free Trade
     THE UNITED STATES AND MEXICO, 1990–2008   214

     Conclusion
     PUTTING THE SKELETONS TO REST   240

     Notes   247

     Index   315

Illustrations follow page 100

A selected bibliography is available online at scholarworks
.umass.edu/umpress/.

ACKNOWLEDGMENTS

THE PURSUIT of collective memory has been a fascinating journey, one that has taken me throughout the United States and Mexico. Many kind and generous people on both sides of the border have assisted me along the way. At the University of Utah, Robert Goldberg has devoted considerable energy to this project, and I am thankful for his patience, honesty, and wisdom. I am likewise grateful to Eric Hinderaker, Rebecca Horn, Ray Gunn, and Margaret Brady for their guidance. I am also appreciative of Antonio Zavaleta, Philip Kendall, and my former colleagues at the University of Texas at Brownsville for all of their support. A finer group of mentors and friends would be hard to find.

I want to recognize the pioneering work of Robert W. Johannsen, Shelley Streeby, Steven R. Butler, Maria Elena García Muñoz, Ernesto Fritsche Aceves, Pedro Santoni, Enrique Plasencia de la Parra, and Josefina Zoraida Vázquez. The varied perspectives of these gifted scholars provided a firm foundation upon which I built my research. Professors Butler, Santoni, and Vázquez were particularly thoughtful in answering my many queries as I developed this project. I have also benefited greatly from my association with Douglas A. Murphy at the Palo Alto Battlefield National Historical Park and Maritza Arrigunaga Coello at the University of Texas at Arlington. Both generously shared their extensive knowledge and experience with me. My month at the Clements Center for Southwest Studies also had a significant impact on my work. Andrea Boardman, David J. Weber, Benjamin Johnson, and Ruth Ann Elmore made me at home and assisted in my reconceptualization of the U.S.–Mexican War. Professor Weber's death in 2010 is a terrible loss for those of us who had the pleasure of knowing him.

Many other scholars have influenced me during this endeavor. I am particularly grateful to Matthew Bowman, Martha Bradley, Charles Carrillo, John Chávez, Ronald Coleman, Christopher Conway, Natasha Escobar, Richard Francaviglia, Jenkins Garrett, Miguel Ángel González Quiroga, Richard Lowe, Manuel Medrano, Rubén Mendoza, James Mills, Jared Montoya, Alan Morrell, Jon Moyer, Paul Reeve, Clemente Rendón, Miguel Soto, Amanda

Taylor-Montoya, Juan Paco Urrusti, Lola Van Wagenen, Richard Bruce Winders, and David Wrobel for their assistance. In addition, dozens of people have patiently allowed me to pry into their personal lives as I sought to understand the workings of memory. While I am thankful to them all, I owe a particular debt to Oscar Arriola, Rod Bates, Richard Hoag Breithaupt Jr., Christopher Fischer, and Walter Plitt for answering my many follow-up questions.

Several individuals have graciously facilitated my work at museums, historic sites, and archives in the United States and Mexico. They include Donaly Brice, Enriqueta Cabrera, Kathryn Encinas, Sherman L. Fleek, Kristie French, Rolando Garza, Ben Huseman, Hector de Jesus, Brenda McClurkin, Eric Reuther, Kathy Rome, Carlos Rugiero, Richard Schachtsiek, William "Wild Bill" Slaughter, Luis Torres, Karen Weaver, and Lea Worcester. I am also indebted to Hiroko Hashitani, Susan Brusik, and the Interlibrary Loan staff at the Marriott Library at the University of Utah for locating hundreds of rare books for my research. As I worked my way through stacks of Spanish-language sources, it was also reassuring to know that I could count on David Delgado, Esmeralda Polanco, Silvia Vázquez, and Sam Allen for assistance with translations.

I am thankful to the Marriner S. Eccles Graduate Fellowship in Political Economy at the University of Utah for underwriting two years of my work. I am also appreciative of the Clements Center–DeGolyer Library Research Grant at Southern Methodist University, which gave me vital opportunities to conduct archival research. In addition, the Daughters of the Republic of Texas, the Office of External Affairs at University of Texas at Brownsville, the Charles Redd Center for Western Studies at Brigham Young University, and the Tanner Humanities Center at the University of Utah all generously provided funding for my various travels. I am also thankful to the journal *Military History of the West* at the University of North Texas for allowing me to republish my earlier research on U.S.–Mexican War veterans.

My experience with University of Massachusetts Press has been wonderful. I am especially grateful to Marla Miller for being an early supporter of this project. I would also like to thank Amy S. Greenberg and Kirk Savage for reviewing early drafts of my manuscript and providing me with supportive feedback. My editors at the press, Clark Dougan and Carol Betsch, have been kind and patient at every step, and I appreciate their labors on my behalf. I am also indebted to Lawrence Kenney for his skilled copyediting and thoughtful suggestions. Finally, I humbly give thanks for the help and support of my family. My parents, Richard and Sherry Van Wagenen, have always gone beyond the call of duty to assist me in my academic endeavors. My in-laws, David and Marie Delgado, were also very supportive. My children, Maya, Brodie, Ariana, and Natalia, tolerantly weathered this long process and brought me tremendous joy when times were bleak. I could not have even considered such a project without the support of my wife, Monica. Of necessity, she has shouldered many of my responsibilities without complaint. Her hard work, editorial skills, and unfailing faith in me ultimately made this book possible. Unfortunately, the team you start out with is not always the same one with which you finish. I only wish that Ariana and Marie were still with us to celebrate this accomplishment.

A NOTE ON PERSPECTIVES

LIKE MANY authors writing about the U.S.–Mexican War, I am faced with the "American" dilemma. Much to the dismay of the many other nations that share the American continents, residents of the United States have long monopolized the term to describe themselves exclusively. This is particularly galling to Mexicans, who also consider themselves to be American. In the interest of historical context and in keeping with the spirit of this transnational study, I have chosen a compromise. When addressing the war from the perspective of the United States I use "American" to depict only that nation's people. When I approach the conflict from the Mexican viewpoint I use the term "North American." While North America technically includes Canada, Mexico, and the United States, historically Mexicans have used the term to denote the United States and its citizens.

Another difference in the perspectives of the two nations is the many names attributed to the war. There is great power and symbolism in the naming of world events, and both nations have used that authority to their advantage. In the United States the conflict was simply called the Mexican War for many decades. During the 1970s Americans commonly adopted the name Mexican–American War. The Mexican primacy in both of these names implied Mexican belligerence, and they have been phased out. More recently, the term "U.S.–Mexican War" has come to dominate the academic literature. Mexicans originally referred to the conflict variously as La Guerra del 47 (War of '47), Guerra con los Estados Unidos, and Guerra contra los Norteamericanos. By the centennial of the war Mexicans had also adopted the names Intervención Estadounidense en México and Guerra de la Intervención Norteamericana, which continue in common use today. Because of this diverse terminology I use a variety of names, depending on the nation and historical context being addressed.

From the perspective of time, the span of years I selected for the book, 1848–2008, requires explanation. The year 1848 represents the termination of the U.S.–Mexican War. The production of wartime media served a very different end than that created during the subsequent peace. This book therefore excludes the literature, art, music, and other artifacts of memory created during the conflict itself. This is not to say that memory artifacts from 1846–47 are entirely out of bounds: they appear when necessary, especially in the context of comparisons. The book concludes 160 years after the Treaty of Guadalupe Hidalgo, in 2008. This year not only represents a significant war anniversary but also marks a modern crossroads in U.S.–Mexican relations.

Finally, as a U.S. citizen I would be remiss to assert complete objectivity in this book. My ancestors were among the first Americans to settle in the Mexican north as it fell to the United States. Consequently, I have spent the vast majority of my life living in lands that were once part of Mexico, fully enjoying the fruits of conquest. I have also spent many years living in border towns, where my perspective has been indelibly shaped by the culture clash and accommodation that characterize this vibrant middle ground. I have nonetheless sought to maintain a professional distance from my experiences in analyzing and presenting the multiple perspectives of this divisive war.

REMEMBERING THE
FORGOTTEN WAR

Introduction

OF WAR AND SOCCER

❖

THE CLATTER of iron horseshoes on cobblestone echoed through the darkened streets of Mexico City on the morning of September 14, 1847, as U.S. troops cautiously moved toward the great central plaza. The Mexican government had abandoned the capital hours earlier, leaving the colors over the National Palace conspicuously unguarded. North American soldiers entered the deserted building, tore down the flag, and raised the Stars and Stripes over the symbol of Mexico's civil authority. After sixteen months of hard campaigning in northern and central Mexico, the United States had successfully concluded its first war of foreign conquest. Now it was left to the diplomats to negotiate the harsh terms of peace. On February 2, 1848, representatives of the two nations signed the Treaty of Guadalupe Hidalgo, a document which officially ended the U.S.–Mexican War and ceded over half a million square miles of land to the victors. With Texas included, the loss equaled roughly one-half of Mexico's national territory. It was an injury that Mexicans have never forgotten.[1]

A century and a half later, uniformed Americans were back on Mexican soil. This time it was for the Olympic Men's Soccer qualifying match in 2004 in Guadalajara, Jalisco. The soccer rivalry between the two nations had grown increasingly fierce as teams from the United States rose to world prominence during the 1990s. Fearing that a Yankee victory would lead to violence, city officials doubled the security at the stadium and braced for the worst. As the American players ran onto the field escorted by riot police, fans of the Mexican team pelted them with obscenities and debris. When "The Star-Spangled Banner" blared through the public address system, the crowd of sixty thousand drowned out the hated anthem with shouts and whistles.[2]

The mood changed dramatically as the tricolor Mexican flag rose above the stadium and the audience began belting out the *himno nacional*, "Mexicans at the Cry of War." The national anthem was adopted by Gen. Antonio

López de Santa Anna in an attempt to lift his people's sagging spirits when he restored his dictatorship five years after the U.S.–Mexican War. Written by the poet Francisco González Bocanegra, the hymn recalled the recent bloody conflict with the United States. With hands across their hearts Mexican soccer fans pledged through song that "if a foreign enemy dare to profane your soil under his foot, know, beloved fatherland, that heaven gave you a soldier in each of your sons." Later verses promised future invaders (and soccer teams) that the nation would rather see itself destroyed than be humiliated by foreigners again.[3]

The mood grew increasingly tense as the contest progressed and neither side was able to score. Twenty-five minutes into the match several members of the audience took up the chant "Osama! Osama!" evoking the name of the Al Qaeda terrorist Osama bin Laden, who orchestrated the murder of nearly three thousand Americans on September 11, 2001. In spite of showing early optimism, the U.S. team eventually fell behind the Mexicans, losing the game 4–0.[4]

Mexicans had no doubt as to what the soccer match symbolized. Elisabeth Malkin, a Mexican reporter for the *New York Times*, wrote, "To many Mexicans, soccer has become a proxy for all the indignities the country has suffered at the hands of the United States in almost two centuries of independence." First on her list of grievances was the invasion and annexation of Mexican territory by the United States in 1846–48. Confirming Malkin's point, the Mexican newspaper salesman Anselmo Cazares mused about the game, "It's a question of honor, a question of history. . . . We should always beat them, we should always try to humiliate the gringos." In the complex relationship between the United States and Mexico, soccer had transcended sport to become a means of settling old scores.[5]

While it is hardly realistic to expect an international soccer match to be a civil affair, the enduring resentment Mexicans feel toward the United States is quite notable. Equally significant is Americans' incredulity to such an impassioned response. Indeed, most Americans recall only their benevolence to their southern neighbor. "It's a shame," asserted Team USA's Chris Wingert after the match. "We support them, buy a ton of their products, keep their businesses going. We buy . . . more products from them than the rest of the world combined." Back in the United States, Bill O'Reilly, the host of the popular *O'Reilly Factor* on Fox News, scoffed at the Mexican soccer fans, declaring, "I believe there's a growing anti-American sentiment in Mexico. And, you know, for what we've done for this country, it makes me fairly angry."[6]

Why, after so many years, is the memory of the U.S.–Mexican War so indelibly etched in the minds of Mexicans and so easily overlooked by Americans? In many ways this mystery begins and ends at Palo Alto, an open prairie near the confluence of the Rio Grande and the Gulf of Mexico where, on May 8, 1846, U.S. troops faced Mexico's Army of the North in the first major battle of the war. Now part of Brownsville, Palo Alto then stood in the Nueces Strip, territory claimed by both the United States and Mexico. The dispute over this frontier and over the legitimacy of Texas had prompted intermittent warfare between Mexico and the Republic of Texas for nearly a decade. Following the annexation of Texas by the United States in 1845, President James K. Polk sent Rep. John Slidell to Mexico to resolve the border issue and negotiate the purchase of the Mexican province of Alta California. Slidell's failure prompted Polk to order the United States Army into the disputed land to secure American territorial claims as far south as the Rio Grande.[7]

In March 1846 Gen. Zachary Taylor led his troops to the northern bank of the river, directly across from the Mexican city of Matamoros. Local civilians watched nervously as Taylor built a large earthen work named Fort Texas and aimed his cannon at the peaceful town. Responding to the American threat, Mexican forces under Gen. Mariano Arista crossed to the north side of the Rio Grande, where they encountered a company of American dragoons at a small ranch named Carricitos. The resulting skirmish, called the Thornton Affair, led Polk to claim that Mexico had "shed American blood upon the American soil."[8]

While word of the fight worked its way back to Washington, Arista ordered Mexican batteries to fire on Fort Texas. He then led the main body of his army north of the Rio Grande to stop the Americans from resupplying through the Gulf of Mexico. After weeks of posturing, the adversaries finally met on the battlefield at Palo Alto. Although outnumbered, Taylor's tactics and equipment proved superior to those of the Mexican forces. Using the new so-called flying artillery method of firing and quickly moving position, Taylor ordered his officers to rake the Mexican lines with their guns, to deadly effect. By late afternoon the American troops had ravaged the larger Mexican army, prompting Arista to eventually withdraw southward.[9]

The day after the battle, the armies met again at a dry riverbed named Resaca de la Palma. Thick chaparral obscured the battlefield, hindering American artillery and infantry. A charge by American dragoons finally turned the tide of the engagement and forced Arista back across the Rio Grande. With American soldiers massing along the river near Fort Texas, Arista realized he could not hold Matamoros. He ordered a general evacuation and moved his demoralized troops inland toward the city of Monterrey.[10]

These former killing grounds are now part of the Palo Alto Battlefield National Historical Park, the only federally protected site to commemorate the U.S.–Mexican War. Since the inception of the facility in 1992 National

Park Service personnel have developed this land to help visitors interpret the controversial conflict. Today, there is a visitors' center with a museum and screening room for park-approved educational programs. There are paved walkways with cannons and banners marking where major troop maneuvers occurred on the grassy plain. Tourists stroll the uncrowded paths reading bilingual plaques that address the actions of the day in politically neutral language. This thirty-four-hundred-acre park makes for a convenient way to see how the United States chooses to remember its war with Mexico in its most official iteration.[11]

As we shall see, today's tranquility at Palo Alto belies the controversy surrounding this national park. It masks an even larger and long-standing debate in the United States and Mexico over who controls the memory of the war. In the early twentieth century the French sociologist Maurice Halbwachs wrote of "collective memory" as a social construct dependent upon the needs of the group creating it. The historian Michael Kammen expanded upon Halbwachs's conceptualization when he noted an increasing awareness that "societies in fact reconstruct their pasts rather than faithfully record them, and . . . they do so with the needs of contemporary culture clearly in mind—manipulating the past in order to mold the present." Memory is a powerful tool wielded by groups and nations for the attainment of a variety of goals in the present. This book seeks to understand how and why Americans and Mexicans have constructed and reconstructed, time and again, the collective memory of the war in the 160 years after it ended.[12]

The creation of collective memory is a complex process, one that depends on the interactions of three component parts: individual memory, group memory, and public memory. Individual memory signifies the experiences and recollections of a single person. Inherently diverse and intricate in their formation, these remembrances become the building blocks of group memory, or memory rooted in group identity. Whether large or small, every group has a socially negotiated story that defines its past, gives meaning to its present, and shapes its future. Individual memories are contextualized and shaped by the needs of the group to which that person belongs. Individual memories that support the larger goals, values, and beliefs of the group are preserved and perpetuated, while those that threaten these values are rejected, forgotten, and discarded.[13]

The size of a group matters a great deal. Families share a group memory of their lives together. Social clubs, labor unions, religious communities, ethnic groups, and political parties likewise have group memories. Where group boundaries end, the collectiveness of their memories ends. Within national borders, distinct group memories merge and evolve to become the building blocks of a larger public memory. Public memory, by its very nature, acts to reconcile and homogenize varied group memories. In some nations, central authority sanctions a "dominant civil culture." Government funding authorizes and ensures a particular interpretation and meaning. Nevertheless, in this contest for official sanction, groups of differing social, economic, and political power vie for control. The result is a shifting mosaic of memory rather than a static portrait of the past.[14]

Since the mid-1980s no aspect of remembrance has captured the imagination of scholars of American memory more than war. Historians have skillfully shown how the country's past conflicts have become key elements in the formation of national identity. Given this phenomenon, popular commemorations of war provide important insight into how Americans view themselves and their place in the world. In the United States, battlefields have become quasi-religious sites where groups fight to control and define public memory. Motion pictures, war reenactors, artifact collectors, tour guides, and souvenir peddlers further shed light on the commemoration of war and how the past has come to shape the present.[15]

American wars not only have made unique contributions to the development of the nation's identity, but also have served a wide range of political and social agendas. Americans have appropriated the defeat of Texans by Mexican forces at the Alamo and turned their loss into a moral victory for the white race. In the decades after the Civil War, racism and America's fascination with the Confederate Lost Cause worked together to promote white supremacy and segregation. The remembrance of the Second World War, a conflict recalled for unifying the nation, led to contentious debates about how it should be commemorated. The Smithsonian Institution's exhibition of the *Enola Gay,* which dropped the atomic bomb on Hiroshima, and the construction of the National World War II Memorial became ideological battlegrounds that had little to do with the actual combatants. More recently, the divisive war in Vietnam has been harnessed to promote national unity and support for modern-day campaigns in Iraq and Afghanistan. In the United States, as elsewhere, the victors and the vanquished have learned to recast the memory of war to serve their needs long after the guns have gone silent.[16]

In spite of its importance to the expansion of the United States in the nineteenth century, the U.S.–Mexican War is often perceived as being the nation's forgotten war. In the opening words of his popular history *So Far from God: The U.S. War with Mexico 1846–1848* (1989), John S. D. Eisenhower wrote, "Overshadowed by the cataclysmic Civil War only thirteen years later, the Mexican War has been practically forgotten in the United States. Through the years, despite our growing interest in Mexico, it is rarely mentioned. And when the subject comes up, it nearly always deals with the questionable manner in which it came about." Eisenhower is not alone. Many historians believe that the U.S.–Mexican War has slipped from the memory of many Americans because it highlighted their nation's aggression and was then eclipsed by the bloodier Civil War.[17]

Have Americans really forgotten their war with Mexico? The answer, as I will show, is complex. The U.S. invasion of a fellow republic has been embroiled in controversy since the day the conflict began. Modern Americans, like their nineteenth-century compatriots, have struggled to reconcile the gains of the war with the means by which it was initiated. Forgetting the conflict has therefore proven to be a convenient means of easing the national conscience. In spite of this unburdening, the U.S.–Mexican War remains an important, though often unrecognized, component of national remembrance for many people. From the celebrated sideshow attractions of P. T. Barnum's mid-nineteenth-century American Museum to the contemporary religious practices of the Church of Jesus Christ of Latter-day Saints, the war has cropped up in surprising times and places.

In contrast to scholars in the United States, no Mexican would ever claim that their nation has forgotten the war. Historians who study the memory of the nation's military past have largely focused on the creation of myth in Mexico's political culture and examined how rulers have created historic heroes and incorporated them into the civic mythology. The remembrance of revolutionary *caudillos,* for example, has not only established a Mexican standard for *machismo* and manliness but also supported postrevolutionary state building in Mexico. By evoking the memory of these men, Mexico's leaders claimed the inheritance of their revolutionary legacy while actually implementing reactionary social and political programs. The commemoration of other heroes remains equally pliant in the service of the state.[18]

The U.S. invasion has presented an interesting challenge for scholars of Mexican memory, as the dynamics of defeat are vastly different from those of victory. Particularly remarkable is how quickly Mexico's leaders were able to draw from the memory of their battlefield losses to promote national unity and foster support for political reform. Over time Mexicans have learned to reinterpret their humiliation at the hands of their northern neighbor and turn it into a call for obedience to the state. The most potent symbols to emerge from this evolution are the Niños Héroes (Boy Heroes), six military cadets who died in the defense of Mexico City. Through the careful manipulation of memory these obscure young men have been molded into the Mexican archetype of patriotism and self-sacrifice.[19]

While scholars have studied the memory of the U.S.–Mexican War in specific eras, none has comprehensively studied remembrance across time. Moreover, no previous work has crossed the border to recover the memory that both the United States and Mexico have of the conflict. This transnational, comparative analysis offers a unique opportunity to understand fully the making of memory and its consequences. In analyzing the constituent parts of collective memory one can understand better how the past becomes a means to identity, solidarity, and power in the present. The U.S.–Mexican War is fertile ground to recover both past and present meaning and to discover the roots of the two countries' dual, interdependent sense of themselves in the world.[20]

Since 1848 each generation of Americans and Mexicans has attempted to shape a collective memory of the conflict in the context of its ethnic, social, political, and economic environments. From the battlefield to the soccer field, memory has assumed many forms and served a variety of masters. As we shall see, neither the United States nor Mexico has entirely forgotten the war. Remembrance has instead evolved over the past 160 years. The question is, for what purposes? How have immediate political demands harnessed the war's memory? How have the artifacts of memory, including literature, music, film, art, battlefields, historical associations, heritage groups, textbooks, government documents, and museums, shaped the conflict's multifaceted meaning? Further, how do regional, racial, and religious differences influence Americans and Mexicans as they choose how to remember and commemorate the war? What happens when group memories clash and compete in a quest for control?[21]

Ultimately, this book answers the deeper question of how remembrance of the U.S.–Mexican War has shaped the complex relationship between these former enemies now turned friends. The distant violence becomes a new lens through which to view today's rivalries and resentments. Perhaps in this context Americans and Mexicans will come to more fully understand the confusing nuances of war and soccer.

1 Victory and Dissolution

THE UNITED STATES, 1848–1865

❖

On June 25, 1848, the Unitarian minister Theodore Parker took the stage at the famous Melodeon Theater in Boston. Word had arrived a few days earlier declaring that the U.S. Congress had ratified the Treaty of Guadalupe Hidalgo, officially ending the U.S.–Mexican War. Parker had already developed a reputation as a firebrand, and a large crowd packed the floor, anxious to hear his views on the ending of the conflict. Clutching the podium, Parker delivered a diatribe against President Polk, his cabinet, and the Congress for provoking an illegal and unconstitutional war. He reminded his hushed congregation that the nation had invaded Mexico "to dismember her territory, to plunder her soil, and to plant thereon the institution of Slavery." Then, pausing wistfully, he delivered his most damning condemnation: "I wish all this killing . . . could have taken place in some spot where the President of the United States and his Cabinet, where all the Congress who had voted for the war . . . and the controlling men of both political parties, who care nothing for this bloodshed and misery they have idly caused—could have stood and seen it all; and then that the voice of the whole nation had come up to them and said, 'This is your work, not ours. Certainly we will not shed our blood, nor our brothers' blood to get never so much slave territory. It was bad enough to fight in the cause of Freedom. In the cause of Slavery—God forgive us for that!' "[1]

Such impassioned rhetoric seemed more appropriate to Parker's wartime political protests than to a postwar religious sermon. Why did he continue to attack the administration after the violence had ended? His preaching could neither raise a single body from the grave nor alleviate a moment of the suffering he so eloquently described. His stance, with one foot in the past and the other in the present, illustrated the power of memory and the need of individuals and groups to create, control, and contest the ways in which society recalls its history.[2]

9

Parker's criticism of the events of the past two years helped define the struggles of the subsequent twelve years of his life. Slavery had come to represent all that was degrading in the human condition, and Parker used the memory of the dead and maimed in Mexico to undermine the pro-slavery Democratic Party in a critical election year. Believing that his words alone were not enough to end the vile practice, Parker joined the Secret Six, a clandestine group that bankrolled the raid by the radical abolitionist John Brown on Harpers Ferry, Virginia, in 1859. Parker died in exile in Italy on the eve of the Civil War and remains to this day a controversial figure within the Unitarian faith.[3]

More than any other period of U.S. history, the years prior to the end of the Civil War were a time of reflection on the causes and morality of the U.S.–Mexican War. The conflict was never universally popular among Americans. The acclaimed author Henry David Thoreau, for example, famously spent a night in jail for refusing to support the conquest of Mexico with his taxes. In the aftermath of the war, however, no one could dispute the tremendous wealth and territory gained by the invasion. Even so, doubts lingered as to how the nation would reconcile these benefits with its perceived sense of republicanism and fair play. How Americans chose to remember the conflict during this era thus revealed much about their politics, their views on slavery, and their attitudes toward the nation's Manifest Destiny to spread across the continent. Such emotional issues eventually tore the nation asunder, and the struggle to control the memory of the Mexican War played a role in that dissolution.[4]

After the signing of the Treaty of Guadalupe Hidalgo, one of the primary means of creating and contesting memory was the written word. During the war the press had churned out dozens of books celebrating the gallant American fighting man in Mexico. Beginning in 1848, however, Americans recast the war to fit the ideological struggles that were leading the country to civil war. Their first battleground was the presidential election of 1848, in which Whigs and Democrats fought over the public memory of the conflict. The principal debate revolved around the coming of the war itself, with partisans championing or condemning it for their own advantage.[5]

First to do battle were the military men, now turned politicians. After his victories along the Rio Grande, General Taylor became a national hero. Moving inland, he successfully stormed the fortified city of Monterrey, Nuevo León. During this time Gen. Antonio López de Santa Anna returned from a yearlong exile in Cuba and declared himself president once again. Upon hearing of the loss of Monterrey he raised a large army in central Mexico and began a long march to drive the Americans out of the northern frontier.[6]

As Santa Anna maneuvered to retake the north, he met Taylor's troops dug in at a mountain pass called La Angostura, near the Hacienda Buena Vista. When his demands for surrender fell on deaf ears, Santa Anna attacked the American forces in bloody frontal assaults that drove the invaders from several of their positions. Americans then launched successful counterattacks and inflicted terrible casualties on the Mexican troops. After two days of fighting Taylor's hold of the pass proved tenuous. In a move that remains controversial to this day, Santa Anna ordered a retreat southward under cover of darkness, leaving northeastern Mexico to the Americans.[7]

Taylor's celebrated stand against Santa Anna at Buena Vista made him not only a war hero but also the presidential candidate of the Whig Party. Whigs, however, found themselves in the awkward position of stridently condemning the war while simultaneously trying to promote its greatest hero as their candidate. Whig writers implied that Taylor actually disapproved of the invasion of Mexico. *A Review of the Life, Character and Political Opinions of Zachary Taylor* argued that he was merely an obedient soldier executing his sworn duty to the government "notwithstanding that his own private opinions with reference to the war accorded with those of the Whig party." *A Brief Review of the Career, Character and Campaigns of Zachary Taylor* blamed the Democrat Polk for making war "a means of popularity for the administration" while profiting from the conquest.[8]

Democrats immediately attacked Whig duplicity. "A Short Statement of the Causes Which Led to the War with Mexico: Showing the Inconsistent Course of the Whig Party on the Subject" documented how the Whigs had initially voted to support the declaration of war but turned against it when it became politically advantageous to do so. The partisan author lamented sanctimoniously, "Can political inconsistency go further?"[9]

Democrats also deflected blame for their instigating of the war by stressing the hopelessness of diplomacy in achieving peace with Mexico. Statements in *The Democratic Text Book* were typical. This booklet from 1848 described "a glorious War—a war which we were involved by the act of another nation, and justified by the most wanton and unprovoked outrages on the part of our enemy." In the Democratic mind there could be no doubt as to the culpability of Mexico in bringing war to its doorstep. The errant nation failed to negotiate with the United States and chose instead to invade Texas. Such justifications continued beyond the election of 1848 and remained an important part of the Democratic Party's memory of the conflict throughout the rest of the century.[10]

As the power of the Whigs declined in the early 1850s, so did the overtly political nature of their critique of the U.S.–Mexican War. After Taylor's death in 1850, his fellow Whigs took to eulogizing their former champion. Gone were the harsh accusations against their political foes. Thomas D. Anderson's funeral oration in Roxbury, Massachusetts, was representative: "I dare not, without violating the sanctity of the position I occupy, where nothing should be spoken to mar the sympathy of any political party, enter upon the merits of the Mexican War as an act of national justice." Such ecumenism was perhaps more a reflection of growing ideological divisions within the Whig Party than a gesture of goodwill toward its rival.[11] The last feeble Whig attacks against the Democrats for provoking the campaign against Mexico occurred during the presidential election of 1852. During this race the Whigs continued to capitalize on the popularity of Mexican War heroes by nominating the conqueror of Mexico City, Gen. Winfield Scott. The Democrats selected Franklin Pierce, a lesser though not insignificant hero who led their party to presidential victory. In his endorsement of the candidacy of Scott, J. T. Headly wrote that Polk "without forethought or preparation, plunged the nation into a war with Mexico." Even in this example the criticism seemed to be more about the reckless nature of the conflict than about the injustice of its cause.[12]

Electoral politicking was not the only issue on Americans' minds. In the early years following the U.S.–Mexican War, Americans debated its ultimate meaning. For a time it remained unclear if they would remember their hostilities with Mexico as a southern conspiracy to spread slavery, God's divine will for the expansion of the nation, or a manifestation of power and nationalism. All three ideas found their supporters and detractors in the works written immediately after the signing of the Treaty of Guadalupe Hidalgo.

The American Peace Society, a Boston-based organization devoted to pacifism, realized that it could harness the power of the conflict to promote its agenda. Attempting to exert influence over public memory, the members sponsored a writing competition for the "best Review of the Mexican War on the principles of Christianity, and an enlightened statesmanship." Abiel Abbott Livermore won the five-hundred-dollar purse for *The War with Mexico Reviewed,* which the society published in 1850.[13]

Livermore understood the power of memory, stating that "the Mexican war is a new weapon, put into the hands of peace, wherewith to win her bloodless victories." Aside from attacking the evils of the invasion Livermore assailed the perceived slave conspiracy that inspired it. He claimed that "slavery and the war with Mexico have had a cause-and-effect connection. Had slavery not existed in our land, there would have been no annexation." Saving some of his harshest criticism for the government, he stated, "Professing freedom, they waged a war to extend slavery. Calling themselves the friends of the people, they sanctioned and supported a war that loaded their country with a heavy war-debt, and sent misery into multitudes of once happy homes."[14]

Livermore also scoffed at the notion of Anglo-Saxon racial supremacy and Manifest Destiny: "The idea of a 'destiny,' connected with this race, has gone far to justify, if not to sanctify, many an act on either side of the Atlantic; for which both England and the United States . . . ought to hang their heads in shame, and weep scalding tears of repentance." William Jay, another member of the American Peace Society and the author of *A Review of the Causes and Consequences of the Mexican War,* likewise condemned Manifest Destiny. He predicted that the precedent set by this war of "conquest" would have a "durable and disastrous influence on the Republic."[15]

In spite of the lofty goals of the American Peace Society, it was largely ineffectual in creating a memory that most Americans would embrace. Nationalism soared in the late 1840s and 1850s, and readers looked for accounts that inspired a sense of glory and American exceptionalism. Numerous popular histories and soldiers' memoirs rushed to fill the void. Perhaps the most important popular history of the time was Roswell Sabine Ripley's *The War with Mexico* (1849). Controversial for his attacks on General Scott, Ripley, a lieutenant in the war, was the first veteran to publish a satisfactory survey of the Mexican campaign.[16]

As a soldier, Lieutenant Ripley loathed the abolitionist critics of the war, stating that their "crazy philanthropy enabled them to look upon high treason with Mexican eyes." Rather than blaming President Polk or the United States for provoking the conflict, Ripley cited Mexico's hard-line position toward Texas as the ultimate *casus belli*. He wrote that Mexico considered the annexation of Texas to be a tacit declaration of war, and in "thus committing themselves, the Mexican authorities fell into an error which has since been the cause of a foreign war, and of many and continued misfortunes to their country." This idea found fertile ground in the American collective memory.[17]

While peace advocates attacked American atrocities in Mexico, the vast majority of writers praised the army's fighting ability and valor. Celebrated American attributes of humanity also appeared in several accounts. From the earliest writings came stories of American soldiers' mercy toward wounded and captive Mexicans. James Henry Carleton's account of the Battle of Buena Vista, written in 1848, perhaps went furthest in painting this portrait of compassion: "The Mexicans had been taught to believe that the Americans were almost savages; but, when they saw our men kneeling down beside their suffering comrades, grasping them kindly by the hand, giving them water, and all the bread and meat they had brought for themselves, they were affected, even to tears, and feelingly exclaimed, '*Buenos Americanos! Buenos Americanos!*'" These "good Americans" helped ease any sense of collective guilt in the United States about the occupation of Mexico. If American soldiers were behaving nothing like invaders, then the war took on the characteristics of a liberation rather than an exercise in imperialism.[18]

American portrayals of Mexicans also proved important to understanding the written memory of the conflict. Both positive and negative depictions of the enemy in published accounts gave insight into how Americans ultimately viewed themselves. In some cases the strength and gallantry of Mexicans reflected positively on the Americans who defeated them; in others, the portrayal of subhuman Mexicans served as a foil for superior Americans.

The most enduring compliment paid by American writers to the Mexican army dealt with the physical beauty of their forces. Henry Harrison's *Battles of the Republic* (1858) was typical of early accounts in describing the enemy forces as "a thrilling sight. Long rows of bayonets glittering in the sunbeams, together with the lances of the horsemen and hundreds of pennants and national flags, formed a spectacle brilliant and exciting." Surely it took American bravery to stand before this awesome display.[19]

Many authors memorialized the fighting abilities of the Mexican army. Even critics of Mexico grudgingly offered their respect to the "great spirit" manifested by the rank and file. Even the much-feared and oft-maligned Mexican lancer earned the admiration of some writers. In 1865 Albert Brackett's *History of the United States Cavalry,* for example, stated, "Mexican lancers were far from being a contemptible enemy, and many of them were admirable horsemen. Our people had the advantage of larger horses and heavier men as a general thing, but the Mexicans were much more agile, and could handle their horses as well perhaps as any people on earth."[20]

If American authors remembered their rivals positively, they did not do so at the expense of their countrymen. Celebrating the strengths of the enemy served two agendas favorable to the United States. By portraying Mexican forces as being among the best in the world, writers made the contest between the nations seem more equitable. Whether or not the authors viewed the war as an imperialist enterprise, they portrayed the United States as having no advantage on the battlefield. By stressing the strength of the Mexican troops the writers boosted the prestige of the American forces that defeated them. Brackett, for example, complimented the Mexican lancer while enthusiastically lauding the excellence of the American dragoons who ultimately bested them on the battlefield.[21]

The easiest way to celebrate the superiority of American soldiers, however, was through the denigration of Mexican soldiers. This negative depiction was rooted in their supposed brutality, treachery, and cowardice. Such attitudes became apparent in some of the earliest postwar publications. John Scott's account from 1848 of his experience as a prisoner of war in Mexico captured the essence of this negative portrayal: "Hardy, cruel, unrelenting, savage, treacherous, dirty, vulgar, and obscene, the essences of these qualities make up his composition. From such as these are composed the different bodies of the Mexican soldiery, and the numerous guerillas, who infest the country, preying alike on friend and foe. Incited by plunder they are formidable only when booty is to be the reward." John Jenkins's *History of the War between the United States and Mexico* (1850) likewise portrayed a sadistic adversary who "seemed to take great delight in torturing the wounded and the dying." In his autobiography of 1853 George Ballentine remembered that during the Battle of Molino del Rey the "Mexican lancers exhibited most characteristically both their cowardice and cruelty of disposition on this occasion, by riding out and killing the wounded who were lying on the field."[22]

Going beyond conduct on the battlefield, many authors attacked the alleged inferior character of the Mexican people. Much of the criticism was built on the idea that pure, Anglo-Saxon Americans were superior to their mixed-blood rivals. George B. McClellan's wartime journal recorded his contempt for the Mexican people. He claimed that they were "certainly the laziest people in existence—living in a rich and fertile country . . . they are content to roll in the mud, eat their horrible beef and tortillas and dance all night at their fandangos."[23]

Racism toward Mexicans permeated the writings of both supporters and critics of the war. Even the pacifist William Jay fell in line with the popular attitudes of his time. While not specifically mentioning race, he attributed the "extreme feebleness of Mexico" to "the ignorance and superstition of her inhabitants." While Jay loathed the war, he was quick to point out the superiority of American soldiers, noting that "not a battle, not a skirmish occurred in which the Mexicans were not defeated, no matter how vast their superiority in numbers."[24]

Luther Giddings's military memoir of 1853 made no apologies for its white supremacy. Giddings praised the "blue-eyed Saxon—the chosen people of the age" for their conquest of Mexico and predicted that the United States would soon be extended throughout all of Latin America. He indignantly marveled at the vanquished Mexicans, "the majority of whom are so vicious and degraded that one can hardly believe that the light of Christianity has ever dawned upon them."[25]

Celebrating Anglo-Saxon superiority over the Mexican people served another purpose. The historian Amy S. Greenberg found that the years between the U.S.–Mexican War and the Civil War were important to America's evolving attitudes about masculinity. A new "martial manhood," rooted in physical prowess and violence, threatened the established preference for a religious and temperate "restrained manhood." In the midst of filibustering in Latin America and the Caribbean during the 1850s, writings promoting territorial expansion extolled the martial abilities of the American fighting man while feminizing those of the enemy. Manifest Destiny thus became gendered within the varied histories, fictions, travelogues, periodicals, and other writings of the time.[26]

Written accounts of the U.S.–Mexican War played a role in this process. Charles A. Averill's novel *The Secret Service Ship* (1848), for example, followed the romance between the noble Isora la Vega and a dashing American spy named Midshipman Rogers. Although their relationship began with Rogers saving the beautiful maiden from a rapacious Mexican officer, the American invasion of Veracruz placed the erstwhile lovers on opposite sides of the conflict. As Rogers assumed the violent role of conqueror, Isora revealed herself to be a capable warrior in her own right. Donning the disguise of a man, the "Banditti Queen" fought the Americans with more bravery and valor than her male compatriots. In this parable of imperialism Isora represented a nation whose wild passions and people could be tamed only by the masculine American soldier. Confirming the author's message, Rogers embraced Isora at the denouement, declaring, "We shall soon be happy, and you will be all my own, for this war that now divides us for a brief time, must now soon close beyond a doubt, and then there will be no bar of nationality between our union." Assuaging any lingering American guilt, Isora replied, "Ah, dearest, I joy to think how soon we shall be indissolubly united." The consummation of Rogers's and Isora's love served as a gendered symbol of Americans who desired the annexation of the entire nation of Mexico.[27]

The ways in which American authors portrayed themselves and Mexicans proved important to the creation of collective memory. While issues of causation were telling of the political atmosphere in which various writers labored, the portrayal of self and other gave insight into their culture. Images of self reflected the values that Americans wanted to perpetuate. Remembering the acts of gallant soldiers from the past created a society in which militarism, heroism, and masculinity marched hand in hand into the present. Images of treacherous Mexicans, however, revealed attributes that the nation disdained. "Mexican" became an epithet in the national lexicon. By reducing the enemy to a brutal stereotype American writers justified war against their neighbor in ways that politicians alone could not. Ultimately, these accounts denied the nation's guilt by making the war a contest between good and evil. With God's hand on the American shoulder, the nation could bask in the righteousness of its cause.

These written sources were an important early component in the creation of memory, yet they declined in significance after 1849. The 1850s marked a sharp decrease in the number of books printed on the subject, and the onset of the Civil War in 1861 saw publishing about the Mexican campaign nearly cease altogether. After the initial flurry of interest, mostly during the fighting itself, written accounts waned in popularity.[28]

Narratives of the war were not the only printed materials creating memory. Illustrated scenes of combat supplemented the printed word in newspapers, books, and pamphlets. The art of lithography matured in the years leading up to the invasion of Mexico, offering another outlet for visual memory. A number of printers and engravers utilized the latest technology to produce hundreds of affordable lithographs to image-hungry Americans. These prints were often hand-colored with the intention of being displayed as artwork on the walls of American homes of all classes. The prolific engraver Nathaniel Currier alone created some eighty-five of these lithographs. Battle scenes proved especially popular with American audiences. These idealized, fanciful portrayals of combat in exotic climes were often the product of the artist's imagination. Most printers had little interest in historical accuracy and were content as long as the subject was engaging enough to attract buyers.[29]

Vivid scenes of officers dying on the battlefield sold widely throughout the nation. The dramatic death of Col. Henry Clay Jr. inspired many artists to attempt narrative engravings of his final moments. Clay's misfortune began when he was wounded in the thigh while countering a charge of Mexican lancers at Buena Vista. As his men struggled in vain to evacuate him to safety, he ordered them to leave him on the field. Lying prone on the ground with a sword in his hand, he eventually succumbed to a Mexican bayonet charge. In the years after his death Americans could buy prints of Clay in various stages of dying. Currier produced a version with the wounded officer bravely handing his brace of pistols to a comrade. A print published by R. Magee focused on Mexican cruelty by showing the wounded officer being ruthlessly bayoneted to death by two Mexican infantrymen. A third example embellished the story by showing Clay's men carrying away the captured national banner of Mexico before leaving him to his fate.[30]

After the signing of the Treaty of Guadalupe Hidalgo in 1848, the war as a subject began to languish. While prints were still widely available, there were no fresh incidents to inspire new works of art. A handful of exceptions kept the printed image of the conflict alive in the American imagination for a few more years. The popular periodical *Brother Jonathan* released a special pictorial edition on July 4, 1848, to commemorate the American victory over Mexico. Included was a large foldout print entitled *The Storming of the Castle of Chapultepec* by the engraver T. H. Matteson. The editorial staff boasted that the print represented the largest woodcut ever published. In this case, the selling point of the work was as much about the novelty of owning the record-setting print as about the subject matter.[31]

In 1851 George Wilkins Kendall and Carl Nebel published *The War Between the United States and Mexico, Illustrated,* an ambitious three-year project that paired Kendall, one of the conflict's best-known correspondents, with Nebel, one of Europe's foremost illustrators. The collaboration produced a bound portfolio of written accounts and color lithographs of the war's twelve major battles. The volume boasted an unprecedented historical accuracy, as Kendall had witnessed the majority of the battles portrayed in the book. The preface claimed that Nebel had drawn most of the battles "on the spot," but later scholars believed he visited the sites after the fighting ceased. In any case, Nebel had lived in Mexico for years, and the work stood as the best physical representation of the war ever made. The *Boston Atlas* proclaimed, "The battles or armies of no country on the face of the earth have ever been better illustrated." Although spurious details like the presence of mountains near Palo Alto drew some criticism, Kendall's and Nebel's work defined the war for a generation of Americans and continues to be regarded as an important contribution to the visual history of warfare.[32]

Nebel's prints demonstrated the power of memory contained in popular arts. The final print in the book, *Scott's Entrance into Mexico,* for example, helped correct popular American misconceptions about the occupation. The culprit was a lithograph from 1849 by Christian Schuessele that appeared in John Frost's *Pictorial History of Mexico and the Mexican War* and showed Scott leading his army into the great plaza in front of the Cathedral. The print, entitled *The Occupation of the Capital of Mexico by the American Army,* was deceptively placid (see fig. 1). An American flag billowed from a balcony while children played excitedly in the street, and several civilians stood on street corners calmly watching as Scott pranced by on a white horse. Nebel, as noted, was a onetime resident of Mexico, and he felt sincere sympathy for the residents of the capital. His print showed the same scene but with subtle changes. Gone were all signs of a happy reception of the troops, and the American flag was replaced by a striped curtain behind which stood frightened women. Yankee cannoneers manned their guns. Armed Mexican guerillas peered over the tops of buildings, and the streets were nearly empty of civilians. One man was picking up a stone, apparently to throw at a group of American officers nearby (see fig. 2). Nebel's print was more accurate than Schuessele's in portraying the two days of street fighting which actually occurred upon Scott's arrival. More important, it directly challenged popular notions created by Frost and others that the occupation of Mexico City was a peaceful affair. Which version Americans chose to believe no doubt reflected their views on the war.[33]

Lithography may have been the most popular form of combat art, but painters too sought to immortalize events in Mexico. The most important painting of the war was James Walker's *The Battle of Chapultepec*. In 1857 the U.S. Congress commissioned the English-born painter to create a work of art to decorate the new capitol extension. Walker had lived in Mexico City during the war and witnessed the Battle of Chapultepec, a dramatic siege that allowed Americans to breach the capital. His epic canvas was one of the most accurate renditions of a Mexican War battle. Its fate, however, symbolized the declining interest in the war. Originally the painting was to hold a place of honor in the House Military Affairs Committee meeting room, but in the tumult of the Civil War it was moved to the west staircase of the Senate Wing. It hung there in relative obscurity for over a century until it was removed from the Capitol in 1982 (see fig. 3).[34]

Sheet music also proved to be an important outlet for American creativity and entrepreneurship. The same technologies that allowed for inexpensive lithography made the printing of musical scores easy and affordable. Publishing houses throughout the nation printed dozens, if not hundreds, of titles related to battles and heroes of the U.S.–Mexican War. The majority of these were parlor songs for the pianoforte intended for dancing quick steps, polkas, and waltzes. A handful of songs included lyrics celebrating the heroic exploits of American soldiers.[35]

Although the overwhelming majority of war-themed sheet music celebrated American victories over Mexico, at least one composer used his talents to criticize the invasion. As diplomats negotiated the terms of the Treaty of Guadalupe Hidalgo in 1848, Jesse Hutchinson Jr. wrote *Eight Dollars a Day*. The author originally wrote the song to be performed by the Hutchinson Family Singers, a group composed of himself and several of his siblings. This popular lyrical score compared the plight of the common soldier in Mexico, who earned a mere seven dollars a month, to the congressmen "who send the poor fellow there" and banked the title sum. *Eight Dollars a Day* explicitly declared the conflict a "war for slavery on the plains of Mexico." In this critical election year the song warned that "a day of reck'ning's coming on. Behold the gath'ring storm. For the People are the Sovereigns yet, and they demand reforms." Indeed, the Hutchinson family threw their support behind the abolitionist Free Soil Party and performed at its events during the presidential campaign of 1848. The song remained on the family's performance list as late as 1850, when the group went into decline.[36]

One postwar song survived well beyond the others of the genre. J. W. Hewitt published his score for pianoforte *The Maid of Monterey* in 1848. This ballad commemorated the story of a Mexican woman who was killed while aiding wounded American soldiers during the siege of Monterrey in northern Mexico. It bore some similarities to a wartime poem named "The Angels of Monterey" by John Greenleaf Whittier but was published after the war had ended. The song began by describing the Mexican woman as she rushed about among the wounded of the battlefield illuminated by the moonlight:

> She cast a look of anguish on dying and on dead;
> Her lap she made the pillow of those who groan'd and bled.
> And when the dying soldier for one bright gleam did pray,
> He bless'd the senoretta the Maid of Monterey.

The song ended by explaining the anonymous woman's charity toward the American invaders:

> For, tho' she lov'd her nation, and pray'd that it might live;
> Yet—for the dying foemen she had a tear to give.
> Then, here's to that bright beauty, who drove death's pang away,
> The meek-eyed senoretta, the Maid of Monterey.

This ballad remained singular among Mexican War music in that its popularity endured until the beginning of the twentieth century.[37]

One reason for the relative permanence of the song may be its connection to a developing stereotype of Mexican women. From the early days of the conflict American soldiers commented on the kindness, grace, and beauty of the women they encountered on their campaigns, wrote about the "raven tresses" and "pearly teeth" of the *señoritas,* and often imagined themselves the object of their desire. They were frequently portrayed in stark comparison to their "barbarian" men and held aloft as the one redeeming quality of their race.[38]

More subtle factors might have also played a role in the popularity of the song. The American literary scholar Shelley Streeby found that in Mexican War literature "relations between the United States and Mexico were often imagined as relations between male and female." As in the case of Averill's *The Secret Service Ship,* American authors eroticized and romanticized Mexican women in a symbolic exploration of masculinity and the hierarchy between the nations. Andrea Tinnemeyer posited that these interracial relationships also addressed American fears of miscegenation. By elevating the status of Mexican women and in many cases stressing their literal or figurative whiteness, Anglo-Americans could rest assured that their race would not be threatened by the annexation of Mexican lands and people. On the other hand, the denigrating of Mexican women as inferior vindicated the taking of their property. Regardless of the motivation, American memory preserved both the heroic and alluring Mexican woman and the debauched, lascivious Mexican whore for decades.[39]

When peace settled over the country again, the appeal of war music declined. Rising sectionalism and westward expansion turned America's attention toward more pressing issues. Along with war-themed books and art-work, however, music helped make the U.S.–Mexican War the nation's most thoroughly documented historical event prior to the Civil War. The massive scope of this later conflict nonetheless eclipsed the war with Mexico and caused patterns of consumption to change. A new pantheon of heroes and their exploits became the subject of an even larger number of songs, images, and books.[40]

American popular culture was but one element in the creation of the memory of the U.S.–Mexican War. While serving in Mexico, American soldiers also began building the foundations for later remembrance through battlefield pilgrimages, souvenir collecting, honoring of the dead, and the creation of fraternal organizations. American civilians also contributed to the formation of memory through homecoming ceremonies, funeral services, award presentations, and commemorative place names. These activities bound individuals and groups together in a sense of community and gave meaning to the suffering wrought by the war. Memory was not always about unity, however, and for some these activities became the means by which to struggle for power and advantage.

People have long been attracted to the battlefields where their nations' soldiers have fought and died. Referencing the First World War, the historian David W. Lloyd argued that the "appeal of these sites to tourists and pilgrims is indicative of the pervasive presence of the war, and the sense of loss which it engendered in the fabric of life." During the U.S.–Mexican War this impulse first manifested itself among American soldiers who were drawn to the sites of recent combat. What role did this battlefield pilgrimage play in creating a sense of memory for Americans? While it would be impossible to know the impact these visits had on individual soldiers, those who left written accounts of their experiences expressed a variety of emotions ranging from curiosity to horror.[41]

As soon as the end of the first day of the war at Palo Alto the debris-strewn field became a place of pilgrimage for both those who fought in the battle and those just arriving to support the invasion of Mexico. Luther Giddings, an officer of the First Regiment of the Ohio Volunteers, arrived in Texas after the American occupation. He wrote, "The consecrated and still ensanguined fields of Palo Alto and Resaca de la Palma, were not many leagues distant from Camp Belknap; and during our stay there, many of our people took occasion to visit them, in company sometimes with those who had witnessed, and could communicate many thrilling incidents of the battles."[42]

Samuel Curtis, of the Third Ohio Volunteer Regiment, also visited these popular sites while camped in the area. At Resaca de la Palma he described

the "old caps, coats, canteens, and human bones" that were "mouldering together under the green boughs of the musqueets [mesquites]." After briefly
exploring the battlefield, Curtis's party continued on to Palo Alto, where,
among a flock of flamingos, they again found the detritus of war. One volunteer was pleased to find a Mexican musket among the brush. Curtis grimly
noted that the "Mexican line can be traced by the skeletons that lie bleach-
ing on the field."[43]

On June 2, 1846, Christopher Haile, a correspondent for the New Orleans
Daily Picayune, sent a dispatch to the newspaper. He had just returned from
a visit to the battlefields of Palo Alto and Resaca de la Palma, where six dragoons had given him firsthand accounts of their combat. Rather than recount
the battle, he discussed the "feelings of deep sadness" and horror he felt on
visiting these places. Palo Alto turned particularly dramatic when the party
stumbled across the remains of Mexican casualties of Taylor's artillery that
had been mummified by the sun. He spared no detail in describing the man-
gled bodies and the "countenance which their death agonies had stamped
upon them."[44]

Palo Alto and Resaca de la Palma were not the only Texas battlefields visited by American soldiers. The old Spanish presidio at Goliad held an exceptionally poignant place in Texas history. It was here that Santa Anna had ordered the execution of some three hundred captives in the midst of the Texas
War of Independence of 1836. During the U.S.–Mexican War recruiters invoked the memory of that slaughter to inspire enlistment. Members of the
Kentucky Cavalry visited this "eternal monument of the perfidy and cruelty
of Santa Anna" on their way to face the Mexican president at Buena Vista.
The visit proved all the more ominous when the Kentucky volunteers fell captive to Mexican lancers a short time later.[45]

The phenomenon of battlefield pilgrimage was not limited to Texas.
Capt. James Henry Carleton of the First Regiment of Dragoons fought with
distinction at Buena Vista and remained nearby as part of the occupation
force of northern Mexico. Over the ensuing months he eased the boredom
of camp life by visiting the battlefield. His notes and observations later became the basis for a detailed book on the fight that he would publish upon
returning home in 1848.[46]

Lt. Lew Wallace, who would later write the classic novel *Ben Hur,* missed
the Battle of Buena Vista by a matter of days. Unable to contain his curiosity
he ventured out to the foothills under the guidance of friends who had fought
in the two-day struggle. His gifted pen gave horrific life to the aftermath:
"There the wrecks lay in awful significance—dead men and horses, bayonets, accoutrements, broken muskets, hats, caps, cartridge-paper, fragments
of clothing. The earth and rocks were in places black with blood, here a

splotch, there a little rill." The large pit graves of the Mexicans and Americans rounded out an experience of sight and smell he would never forget.[47]

George Rutledge Gibson had a similar experience when he and a small party decided to visit the site of the Battle of Sacramento in Chihuahua. He was horrified to find that five weeks after the battle the wolves were digging up and eating the bodies of the Mexican dead. Gibson noted that the "stench from the dead carcasses both of men and animals made our stay much shorter than it would have been." Declaring that their "curiosity was satisfied," the soldiers left for more inspiring vistas.[48]

This morbid curiosity seemed to drive Americans back to their battlefields throughout the war. One month after the fall of Mexico City a group of the Second Pennsylvania Volunteer Infantry decided to tour the grounds in and around Chapultepec to look for telltale signs of the violence that had recently taken place there. While one of their party noted that the bodies were all buried, they could still see physical signs of the struggle. In Mexico City such battlefield visits were only part of a number of curiosities, including excursions to nearby Indian ruins and museums in the capital.[49]

The few surviving accounts of these soldier pilgrims revealed the emotional impact the battlefield had on their memories. By writing down their impressions they conveyed their sense of wonder, loss, and horror to Americans back home. For the visitors who had not yet seen the actual violence of warfare, the battlefield visit was a place of tutelage where participants could guide them through the experience they must soon endure. For veteran soldiers the battlefield was sacred ground, a place where they could revisit past glories, mourn their dead, and confirm their recollection of the past.

After the war ended, American civilians continued the tradition of battlefield pilgrimage and tourism. During an excursion to southern Texas in 1850 the Presbyterian missionary Melinda Rankin visited the battlefields at Palo Alto and Resaca de la Palma. While she was not the first civilian tourist to visit a Mexican War battle site, she may have been the earliest to publish her thoughts. Considering the land, she wrote, "Although those scenes of blood and carnage are passed by, no one can look upon those interesting battle fields without feelings of deepest emotion; and though time may work its changes, long will it be ere those sacred places lose their power to interest. The soil which has been wet with human blood for the defence of liberty and justice, has become too deeply hallowed, to be soon regarded with careless indifference." In spite of Rankin's call to remember the sites, her compatriots quickly busied themselves with more pressing issues. Nearly fifty years passed before Americans would attempt to honor these sites in any official manner.[50]

Other civilians made pilgrimages to Palo Alto and Resaca de la Palma, among them Teresa Griffen Vielé, who accompanied a party on a visit to the south Texas battlefields in 1852. Unaware that American casualties had been removed from Palo Alto, she sadly mused at the lack of marked graves. Like Rankin, she believed the government should memorialize the field: "If we fail to mark those spots where heroes fall with tablets that tell of their gallant deeds, it is not only wronging them, but wronging generations yet unborn, by allowing them to forget how precious the purchase-money that bought their freedom." Her words spoke to the role of memory in teaching good citizenship to future generations of Americans. She sadly noted that souvenir collectors were removing the last physical reminders of the momentous events that had taken place there.[51]

Like soldiers of all wars, Americans collected relics from the battlefields of the various campaigns in which they participated. Trophies taken from battle sites and removed from dead or captured enemy soldiers played a role in the creation of individual and group memories. These tangible reminders of their experiences served two purposes. The war souvenirs kept soldiers connected to the historic events of their pasts, and, in displaying their trophies informally at home or formally in museums, the soldiers made of these objects a means of conveying memory to those who had not fought.[52]

Flags, uniforms, and weapons of the enemy have long been the souvenirs of choice for American troops. During the U.S.–Mexican War soldiers carried or sent a wide variety of these items back to the United States. Maj. Meriwether Lewis Clark of the First Regiment of Missouri Volunteers captured the guidon of the Mexican lancers at the Battle of El Brazito in New Mexico. He gave the black flag, which bore twin skulls on one side and the slogan *Libertad o Muerte* (Liberty or death) on the other, to his nephew in Missouri. Over the years it was alternately displayed at the Missouri Historical Society and the Museum of Battery "A" in St. Louis, allowing residents of the state to share in their soldiers' victory in New Mexico.[53]

Mexican artillery was the most popular type of trophy collected during the war. The emasculating act of taking and displaying the enemy's cannon was a uniquely powerful symbol of the time. After being displayed at Fort Polk in Port Isabel, Texas, the army shipped the guns captured at Palo Alto and Resaca de la Palma to Trophy Point, adjacent to the Military Academy at West Point, New York. This outdoor exhibit of cannon captured in America's eighteenth- and nineteenth-century wars would eventually be home to over one hundred guns taken during every major campaign in the conflict with Mexico. Many of these cannon remain on display to this day.[54]

Two additional cannons hold a place of honor at West Point. During the Battle of Buena Vista, Lt. John Paul Jones O'Brien and his artillery battery

endured two massive Mexican assaults. Manning his guns until the last possible moment, Jones reluctantly abandoned two brass cannons after both
their crews and horses had been killed. To disguise his defeat Santa Anna
flaunted these captured guns on his retreat southward to Mexico City. Months
later American forces fighting on the outskirts of the capital recaptured the
cannons and sent them to West Point, where they continue to hold a place of
honor on campus.[55]

Not all captured Mexican cannons remained in the hands of the federal
government. Volunteers brought these impressive trophies back to their communities. Soldiers from the Third Regiment of Illinois Volunteers captured a
Mexican six-pound cannon at the Battle of Cerro Gordo. and carried it back
to the United States, where it found a temporary home in the Springfield
Armory in Massachusetts.[56]

Members of the Missouri Volunteers secured eleven Mexican cannons captured during their invasion of New Mexico and Chihuahua. The regiment
paraded the artillery, festooned in garlands, through the streets of St. Louis
upon returning home. One of the cannons, known affectionately as "Old Sacramento" in honor of the battle in which it was captured, served both pro-
and antislavery forces during the Wakarusa War of 1855 in the Kansas Territory. According to one colorful tale, the following year Free Staters took the
ruined type from the abolitionist newspaper the *Herald of Freedom,* which
had been destroyed during the "Sacking of Lawrence," and cast it into grape-
shot. They loaded the improvised ordnance into the cannon and used it
against the "Border Ruffians" at the siege of Fort Titus. During the Civil
War foundry workers in St. Louis likewise reworked three of the Mexican
cannons for use by Missouri volunteers in the Union Army. The barrel of one
of the guns burst in battle, but the two surviving pieces have stood sentinel
over the terrace at the state capitol since being decommissioned.[57]

Some souvenirs had a more personal or even morbid association. When
Col. John J. Hardin of the First Regiment of the Illinois Volunteer Infantry
fell during the second day of the Battle of Buena Vista, his men sought some
token of his bravery. Near Hardin's body lay a dead Mexican lancer with
his weapon apparently cut in half by a sword. The Illinois men, assuming
that their leader had gallantly fought off this attacker in his final moments
of life, packaged up the broken lance and sent it to his grieving family as a
tangible reminder of his bravery and a relic of his perceived martyrdom.[58]

Capt. Robert Anderson of the Third Artillery found himself in the middle
of what could have potentially been the largest trophy taking of the war. Apparently the famous circular Aztec Calendar Stone, which was twelve feet in
diameter, caught the fancy of General Scott. Anderson wrote home that Scott
had ordered him to "collect and arrange all the information I can, relative to

the Zodiacal or Calendrical Stone of the Ancient Mexicans. He thinks somewhat of taking it to Washington, if the Mexicans do not make peace with us."
Fortunately for the future relations of both nations, this treasure of Mexican
patrimony remained behind.[59]

The war trophy which most excited America's public imagination, however, was Santa Anna's prosthetic leg. After subduing the Mexican north,
President Polk sent an amphibious force under General Scott to Veracruz,
the port city on the Gulf of Mexico that offered the easiest path to Mexico
City. Although outnumbered and outgunned, the citizens of Veracruz endured
twenty days of siege and bombardment before surrendering in March of
1847. As the United States Army moved inland from the coast they encountered Santa Anna's forces waiting for them at Cerro Gordo. Scott ordered his
army into the surrounding hills, where they outflanked the poorly defended
Mexican left. The subsequent fight proved a costly rout for Santa Anna, who
abandoned all his personal belongings on the battlefield. Soldiers from Company G of the Fourth Regiment of Illinois Volunteers rifling through the general's carriage found his prosthetic leg and carried it home after the battle (see
fig. 4).[60]

The event prompted American soldiers to compose "The Leg I Left Behind Me," a parody of the popular "The Girl I Left Behind Me." The final
verse proved prophetic:

> But should that my fortune be
> Fate has not quite resigned me
> For in the museum I will see
> The Leg I Left Behind Me

Beginning on June 26, 1847, the great showman P. T. Barnum ran advertisements in the *New York Herald* boasting that "Santa Anna's wooden leg,
taken by the American Army in Mexico," could be viewed at his American
Museum for the admission price of twenty-five cents. There remains serious
doubt as to whether Barnum had the trophy or if it was merely another of
his sensationalized hoaxes. Nonetheless, after the war entrepreneurial veterans of the Illinois Volunteers took the actual leg on a statewide tour, where
curious onlookers paid a fee to gawk at the prosthesis. Symbolic of Mexico's
losses, the disembodied leg was eventually donated to the State of Illinois,
where it became embroiled in controversies that I explore later (see chap. 7).[61]

The first, albeit informal, museum dedicated to the U.S.–Mexican War
was established at Fort Polk in Point Isabel on the mouth of the Rio Grande.
Here General Taylor assigned an officer to take charge of war trophies collected at Palo Alto and Resaca de la Palma. Sergeant Furey of the Second
United States Dragoons delivered up the captured colors of the Mexican

Tampico Regiment to the officer. Soldiers from other units brought in a wide variety of captured Mexican firearms, copper ordnance, lances, drums, saddles, and accoutrements that were exhibited for soldiers and visitors encamped at the fort or arriving by ship from the Gulf of Mexico. The collection was large enough for a correspondent from the *Daily Picayune* to describe Fort Polk as "a complete museum." The Alabama volunteer Alexander Corbin Pickett was one of the many newly arrived soldiers who visited the assemblage. Significantly, the trophy collection was the soldier's first stop on a tour that included a visit to the military hospital to converse with the wounded from the Battles of Palo Alto and Resaca de la Palma and paying respects to the dead. Like the nearby battlefields, the display became a school for those uninitiated in the horrors of war and a site of remembrance for those who had faced combat.[62]

In April of 1864 New York City played host to the Metropolitan Fair. The popular spectacle included a Museum of Flags, Trophies, and Relics in the Union Square Building. The exhibit included over one thousand artifacts of America's wars from the Revolution to the ongoing Civil War. A correspondent covering the event for *Harper's Weekly* was typical in his focus. His report dwelt for a short time on the Revolution before quickly passing the Mexican War trophies to describe recently captured Confederate relics. The reporter summed up the value of the trophies, stating that they "now speak to the fathers and mothers of our brave volunteers of the dangers through which they are passing in defense of liberty and good government." By virtue of their public display these artifacts had become a means of linking civilians attending the fair to their soldiers fighting in the final campaigns of the Civil War.[63]

Like a visit to a battlefield, war trophies emotionally connected people with distant places and times. Civilians could vicariously feel the thrill and danger of combat by viewing and handling objects their troops had used or faced in battle. Soldiers who took trophies symbolically transferred their enemy's power to themselves and imbued the objects with memories of gallant deeds and past victories. These powerful totems held a place of honor alongside the parading troops that carried them home. Certainly soldiers who went through the difficulty of hauling captured cannons and banners back to the United States hoped that their deeds would remain at the forefront of their nation's memory. These tangible reminders of past glories, displayed in public places, offered a hope of immortal remembrance and youth to the graying veterans. Time would tell how successful war trophies were in extending the reach of memory into the future beyond the lives of the combatants.

As the ragged troops returned home from the far-off battlefields of Mexico, communities throughout the nation hosted receptions in their honor. These commemorations served the dual purpose of welcoming soldiers back into civilian life and memorializing the events of the war. The military spectacles, speeches, and honors bestowed on the veterans also created collective memories in the communities that hosted them. Beyond these more obvious roles, the reception of returning veterans allowed for instances of protest and local power struggles. The largest public displays occurred in the southern states, perhaps symbolizing the growing sectional divide now aggravated by events in Mexico.[64]

Varina Howell Davis, the wife of Col. Jefferson Davis, recalled the elaborate festivities surrounding the return of the famed 1st Mississippi Rifle Regiment. These celebrated volunteers had earned distinction at the Battle of Buena Vista, and citizens of the state turned out in large numbers to greet the wounded colonel and his men. Varina Davis recalled, "At Natchez twelve young ladies, holding a garland many yards long, met the regiment at the bluff, and crowned the officers with wreaths. Their banners were also wreathed with bowers. After some preliminary ceremonies there were speeches by the town's-people and officers of the regiment; then, a procession; after which Mr. Davis—who was on crutches—came out in a barouche, nearly hidden with flowers, to take me to the steam-boat. The journey was one long ovation." The people of Mississippi bestowed similar honors on the regiment at every town on the seventy-mile trek between Natchez and Vicksburg.[65]

In Virginia, neighbors of Maj. George H. Thomas turned out to give him a hero's welcome, and South Carolinians flocked to welcome home their returning Palmetto Regiment. Several towns in the state hosted parties for the veterans that included "band music, banners, parades, speeches, toasts, dinners, and large crowds." New Yorkers likewise thronged to greet their volunteers with a parade, reception, and medal ceremony. In contrast, Lieutenant Wallace and the Indiana Volunteers, upon disembarking from transport ships in New Orleans, found themselves the guests of honor at a somewhat dubious gala. Wallace noted that the reception was "a poor affair, indeed, cheap, and unworthy of mention." As he made his way downtown he noted, "The absence of decorations along the streets struck me dismally while passing to the square selected for the ceremony. Cut off for such a time from newspapers, I had failed to appreciate that the war had been discussed with such bitterness that at least half the people viewed it as an unholy invasion. Of course all holding that opinion were unwilling to jubilate. They kept their flags hid and stuck to their shops." Participation in the homecoming commemoration and festivities became a means of expressing both public support and criticism of the war.[66]

In at least one state commemorating and memorializing the service of returning soldiers proved useful in fighting local power struggles. When the South Carolina Palmetto Regiment returned, the cities of Columbia and Charleston bitterly fought for the exclusive right to host their reception. Aggravating a decades-old rivalry, the battle spilled into local newspapers, with angry accusations coming from both sides. To avoid an awkward confrontation the regiment elected to attend commemorative galas in both locations.[67]

A grateful public found other ways to commemorate the service of their returning veterans. Congress bestowed a gold medal on General Scott and presented a sword to General Taylor, while other organizations awarded the two commanders additional medals and swords. A group in California gave Lt. Col. John C. Frémont a presentation sword "of highly wrought and elaborately executed workmanship." The "Ladies of Charleston" then presented the colonel with a "costly gold-mounted belt" on which to hang his new sword. Citizens of Washington bestowed a flag on returning Marines with the legend, "From Tripoli to the Halls of the Montezumas." Pierce, the future president of the United States also received a presentation sword that he proudly wore in a daguerreotype taken soon after the war. Numerous other officers received similar tokens of gratitude.[68]

Scott's gold medal came into play during his bid for president in 1852. A political tract claimed that Scott had deposited the gold medal in the vault of the City Bank of New York. A notorious safe robber reportedly broke into the vault one night and took everything of value except the medal. According to the anonymous author, "Not even a whole life of crime had been able to extinguish in that felon's breast, a feeling of patriotic admiration for his country's best soldier." He then equated the theft of the medal to robbing the old general of his rightful place as president of the United States. The comparison failed to touch the majority of voters, and Scott lost the election.[69]

The story of Major Thomas's presentation sword perhaps best symbolized the politics of U.S.–Mexican War memory during the mid-nineteenth century. By the time he returned to his Virginia home a celebrated hero, Thomas had gained combat experience in places stretching from Florida to Buena Vista. To show their appreciation of his service several of his childhood neighbors in Southampton County commissioned a gold and silver dragoon saber with the names of his campaigns engraved upon the blade. As the nation moved toward Civil War in 1860 Thomas left his treasured sword with his sisters for safekeeping. When he chose to serve the United States in the conflict his Confederate-supporting siblings bitterly gave his sword to the Virginia Historical Society, where it remains on display.[70]

The State of South Carolina was perhaps the most indulgent in heaping tokens of honor upon its veterans. As early as 1847 citizens called for the formation of a cemetery for the war dead in Columbia. The city of Charleston honored its officers with presentation swords and its enlisted men with silver medals. In 1848 the State House of Representatives ordered the minting of gold and silver medallions for the members of the Palmetto Regiment. Unlike presentation swords, these medals were given to both officers and enlisted men, albeit in different metals. In 1856 the legislature further honored its Mexican War veterans by allocating five thousand dollars for a memorial on the grounds of the State House in Columbia. The monument consisted of a large bronze palmetto atop a stone plinth. A plaque on one side bore the inscription, "South Carolina to her sons of the Palmetto Regiment who fell in the War with Mexico." U.S. forces shelling the State House during the Civil War damaged the monument, but the palmetto survived and remains to this day a modest tourist attraction.[71]

The historian David Glassberg discovered that in the wake of the First World War "each town and city became an arena where different memories of war competed for public expression." He found that the commemorative urge originated from within the community rather than being imposed by the federal government. Certainly the same could be said of the U.S.–Mexican War. The violent battlegrounds south of the border evolved into local contests of memory. How communities celebrated or ignored their returning soldiers revealed individual and group political affiliations and feelings about the war. Bestowing swords, medals, and other honors upon officers exacerbated class distinctions among veterans that would later reemerge among their descendants. The building of memorials was an early manifestation of a later impulse to commemorate military service in small towns and big cities throughout the nation. What these diverse expressions had in common was their local focus, as the federal government largely neglected to host homecomings, award medals, or build monuments. As a means of community expression these commemorations were important building blocks of memory. As time passed, conflict would be muted. Still, in antebellum America it was too soon to know what the future held for these memories.[72]

Another way in which states and communities remembered and honored their veterans was by retrieving the bodies of slain soldiers from battlefields and bringing them back to the United States for elaborate state funerals and reinterments. The privilege of an American burial was largely reserved for the wealthiest and most prestigious of officers. Special recovery parties began visiting the battlefields within six months of the beginning of the war and continued their work for several years. At Point Isabel and Palo Alto they collected the bodies of Lt. Jacob Edmund Blake, Maj. Samuel Ringgold, and

Lt. Richard Cochrane. Blake's body found temporary rest at Fort Brown, Texas, before being placed in a mass grave at the National Cemetery in Alexandria, Louisiana, in 1909. Ringgold and Cochrane were returned to their hometowns, where they received full military honors.[73]

Dozens of slain officers were eventually recovered from the battlefields of Mexico and the American Southwest. Each returned body allowed Americans the opportunity to publicly mourn for their fallen countrymen. A handful of extant printed programs offer insight into how these funerals helped create collective memory. As was the case with the written literature of the time, eulogies and sermons given during the war differed in meaning from those that followed the peace. A comparison of the two is helpful in understanding these differences.[74]

After the Battle of Buena Vista, the State of Kentucky paid for the retrieval of the bodies of several officers and enlisted men. All but one of these men were buried in a communal grave near the State House at Frankfort. During a public funeral held on July 20, 1847, the future vice president of the United States, John C. Breckinridge, spoke at length about the sacrifices of the men. He did not condemn Mexico but portrayed the dead men as fighting for the cause of the United States. His impassioned claims of American bravery and honor mirrored his audience's fervent nationalism.[75]

Breckinridge also spoke directly to memory and how it would impact future generations of Americans: "The nation that rewards the devotion of her sons will never want defenders. To the patriot, no consolation can be more precious than the assurance that he will be remembered by his country. On the bloody field it nerves his arm, and at the moment of dissolution soothes his parting spirit." He then called his fellow Kentuckians to visit this hallowed spot to "remember the sacred dust beneath it" and to "turn from the sad but glorious spot, purer men and better citizens." For Breckinridge, maintaining the memory of the war remained intertwined with the survival of the Republic.[76]

Rev. John H. Brown concluded the funeral service by further addressing the importance of memory: "We will *never, no never,* forget their toils and their dangers. We will cherish their memory, onward through life, and in after years, when we visit yonder beautiful cemetery, we will softly draw near to the memorable spot where we deposit their remains, we will lead our infant children to the graves, and while we read the inscription on the marble reared to mark the hallowed place, we will recount to our little ones, the history of their lives, their sufferings and *death* in the memorable victory of Buena Vista." Like Breckinridge, Brown believed memory of the war dead to be a lesson in patriotism and a necessary part of America's civic rituals. While the effect these speeches had on individual mourners cannot be known, the greatest influence seemed to be on Breckinridge himself. Prior to the funeral he had not been a supporter of the war. Perhaps caught up in his own rhetoric, he volunteered for duty in Mexico shortly after the service.[77]

One of the dead Kentucky officers, Capt. George Lincoln, was the son of a former governor of Massachusetts. While technically a member of the regular army, he had been assigned to the Kentucky Volunteers. In gratitude for his service Kentucky sent his body back to Boston for an elaborate state funeral on July 22, 1847. The procession included six hundred soldiers, government officials, and family members. Thousands of spectators watched the somber cortege as it made its way through Boston, boarded special trains, and then continued on through the town of Worcester. Kentuckians even returned the horse the captain was riding when he was killed. The committee of arrangements gave the battle-scarred mount a place of honor, walking empty-saddled behind the coffin.[78]

These two state funerals in late July of 1847 occurred as the United States Army slowly converged on the Mexican capital. Scott's "little army" had cut its direct supply lines with the coast, and the nation was wracked with anxiety over its fate. It would be nearly three months before Americans would capture Mexico City. The eulogies to the Kentuckians slain at Buena Vista spoke to these fears by instilling nationalistic meaning in their sacrifice. While the words spoken by Lincoln's eulogists are lost to history, the dramatic spectacle of his funeral procession became a means of unity and nationalism. In the end, both funerals sought to assuage grief by assuring the mourners that memory would be the path to immortality for the fallen and strength for the future of the nation.[79]

What of postwar funerals? The surviving eulogies reveal that the funerals held both during and after the war served to inspire nationalism and promote memory of the slain. Nonetheless, with nothing more to be gained or lost in Mexico, funeral orators found themselves in new circumstances and addressing new needs. Surviving programs from postwar funerals exemplify how eulogies could be used as platforms addressing the political complexities of the time. They also revealed the growing divide taking place at a local and national level as a result of the successful termination of the war.

Col. Truman B. Ransom died leading the New England Regiment during the assault on Chapultepec. A burial party returned his body to his hometown, Norwich, Vermont, five months later. Officials in Norwich held the funeral on February 22, 1848, twenty days after the signing of the Treaty of Guadalupe Hidalgo and well after hostilities had ended. Gone were the unquestioning calls for national unity in the face of a foreign foe. Ransom's funeral represented instead the political division that began to pull the nation apart in the aftermath of the war.

The service began with a sermon delivered by Rev. James Davie Butler, an old friend and colleague of Ransom at Norwich University. He opened his oration with religious themes but eventually addressed the recently ended war. Glancing over the mourners, he stated, "Seeing before me members of both political parties, I deem this no fitting occasion to blazon abroad the opinions which I, as an individual, hold concerning the Mexican War." True to his word, he never mentioned either political party, but his pointed attack on the Mexican War could have left no one uncertain about his Whig affiliation. Butler criticized the then-prevalent romantic notions of memory, claiming that "Earth hides the slain, and our minds, forgetting the fallen, press onward with the victors." Then he addressed the heavy casualties of the New England Regiment in Mexico by asking the mourners, "Where are the eighty young men who marched forth from this plain last May? They went forth in gay uniform, as victims went to sacrifice garlanded—but shall a tithe of them return to see their native country?" In conclusion he posed a question to the mourners and then answered it himself: "Ransom . . . has lost his life, shall we lose his death? Doubtless we shall, if we look only on the show and pomp of this day."[80]

Following the minister's remarks Gen. Frederick W. Hopkins took the podium. Perhaps feeling awkward after Butler's attack, he characterized the war in part as being the "redress of wrongs unavenged." He defended the army and pronounced that "military art . . . is something more than what the crude notions of the bigoted man, the man of limited views, or the calculating utilitarian would give it credit for being." Although Hopkins identified himself as a Whig, he reminded the audience that Ransom had been a Democrat, "and a noble specimen he was." Hopkins then spent several minutes documenting the many kindnesses and braveries of the deceased before making an appeal to memory by reciting a poem he had written:

> But time's whirling tide, like the deep sea wave,
> Shall not erase from memory the Vermonter's grave.
> O'er mountains and vale, the moon-beams still play,
> And the sun still sheds it ephemeral ray,
> But, brighter, far brighter the star of the brave,
> As its mild luster beams on a Ransom's grave.

The importance of memory was clear to Butler and Hopkins, and they used its complex nuances in burying their friend. Thus was Ransom consigned to the earth, caught between conflicting views of the war in which he perished.[81]

On July 12, 1848, New York sponsored a funeral for six officers who had died in the war. Twenty thousand mourners gathered as the bodies were drawn through the streets of New York City in a "brilliant pageant." John Van Buren, the son of the former president Martin Van Buren, gave the final tributes. In a postwar twist on the funeral eulogy, the abolitionist Democrat did a little political stumping for the Whigs. He praised General Taylor's feats on the battlefield and claimed that his victories, "together with the intelligence, good sense, modesty and humanity of that distinguished commander, have made a wide and deep impression upon the public mind, and secured to him the lasting admiration and gratitude of his country. So conspicuous is this truth that a large number of his fellow-citizens are prepared and anxious to invest him with the highest office." One month later Van Buren officially severed his ties with the Democrats. Rather than supporting the Whigs, however, he helped create the Free Soil Party, which nominated his father as a presidential candidate. Funerals proved to be another battlefield on which memory was contested and mourners enlisted to serve a higher cause.[82]

New Yorkers witnessed an interesting contrast nine years later when their city hosted a belated funeral for Gen. William Jenkins Worth. In addition to his service in the War of 1812 and the Second Seminole War, Worth had distinguished himself in several battles of the Rio Grande and Mexico City campaigns. Cholera in Texas, not bullets in Mexico, cut short his life one year after the war ended. While unquestionably a national hero, Worth was not a martyr. In 1857 the Republican governor of New York, John Alsop King, ordered Worth's remains entombed in a large monument in New York City. With the dissolution of the Whig Party the previous year and passions over Mexico giving way to concerns about Southern secession, the funeral was a politically neutral event. The Democratic mayor, Fernando Wood, eulogized Worth while intentionally avoiding a detailed recounting of the events "so recent and familiar to all." With little to be gained from memorializing the war, the speakers focused on the accomplishments of the man. Nonetheless, the fifty-foot granite monument that tops his mausoleum in Worth Square remains a silent, if not overlooked, reminder of New York's contribution to the U.S.–Mexican War.[83]

For the vast majority of American dead there would be no homecoming or elaborate funerals. Communities in Tennessee, Kentucky, and Missouri erected cenotaphs as places of public mourning and remembrance to loved ones buried in Mexico. Even so, sanitary concerns and the cost of transportation fated most of the dead to lie in little more than an unmarked grave near the spot where they fell. Given that most war deaths were caused by disease, designated burial grounds near military hospitals and camps gave some semblance of reverence, but ultimately these proved to be poor memorials for the dead. Lieutenant Wallace recalled his horror at finding the bodies of his Indiana comrades exposed on the windswept plains of southern

Texas. He personally reburied the remains as best he could. As an old man he looked back on the experience with sadness: "I lingered to take a farewell look at the shifting cemetery, wondering if the government would ever set about bringing the bones of the brave back to Indiana. Fifty years are a long time out of one's life to wait for anything; and now I know that accomplishment will never be."[84]

Not until the twentieth century were American soldiers lost in action on faraway battlefields routinely returned to the United States for burial, yet the U.S.–Mexican War did mark the first time the United States would establish an American military cemetery on foreign soil. Having suffered hundreds of casualties in Mexico City, the army began collecting American bodies in one site. When residents of the capital started using adjacent lands for a garbage dump in 1850, the U.S. Congress allocated funds for the "purchase, excavation, and construction of a burial ground." In 1851 the U.S. government purchased two acres of land in the Colonia San Rafael district on which to establish its permanent burial ground. American officials gathered the remains of approximately 750 soldiers and buried them in a mass grave within the walls of the new Mexico City National Cemetery. An obelisk marking the final resting place of these casualties read, "To the Memory of the American Soldiers Who Perished in this Valley in 1847, Whose Bones, Collected by their Country's Order, Are Here Buried."[85]

The historian Douglas Murphy has argued that Americans helped assuage the grief they felt for the thousands of war dead left in unmarked graves in Mexico through the memorial naming of towns and counties. The preponderance of Mexican War names found across the United States certainly lends credibility to this thesis. Following the outbreak of hostilities on the Rio Grande dozens of counties and towns were named for U.S.–Mexican War battles and heroes, allowing the conflict to become a permanent part of the American landscape. While memory of the war had a perceived immediacy in these communities, changing values and priorities would shroud the popular remembrance of their origins over time.[86]

The practice of naming locations after battles and war heroes in the United States originated with the American Revolution. When the residents of Kansas chose the names Buena Vista and Cerro Gordo for two towns in the early 1850s, they were adding to existing settlements like Bunker Hill and Lexington named after revolutionary battles. After the Civil War, Kansans contributed Shiloh, Bull Run, and Appomattox to the state atlas. What was different about the Mexican War was the unparalleled westward expansion that immediately preceded and followed the conflict. The exploration, settlement, and civic organization of the American West and Midwest necessitated the naming of thousands of municipalities, and the war was a clear inspiration.[87]

Every major campaign became the name of some American city, yet certain battles emerged as more popular choices. The Battle of Buena Vista, for example, had nineteen namesakes, while the siege of Monterrey inspired seventeen. Veterans and supporters of the war created seven Palo Altos, five Cerro Gordos, and four Vera Cruzes. Two cities were named for Churubusco, a hard-won battle on the outskirts on Mexico City. Lesser-known engagements such as El Brazito, Tampico, and Contreras found American counterparts in the remote back roads of the growing nation. Also significant were the number of municipalities named in honor of war heroes. Generals Taylor and Scott were popular inspiration for both towns and counties. More obscure heroes found remembrance as well when names such as Ringgold, Butler, Hardin, and Croghan began to dot the map. Texas, more than any other state, sought to remember the names of soldiers who fought in Mexico. From 1846 to 1859 twenty-three forts and military camps in the state adopted the names of Mexican War heroes.[88]

Although Mexican War names could be found from New York to California, the practice was exceptionally popular in states like Missouri, Illinois, Kentucky, and Indiana, which had sent large numbers of volunteers to fight. Family members who remained behind and veterans returning home were influential in naming communities in these states. Iowa, which received statehood as Taylor marched south from the Rio Grande, named no fewer than nine counties after battles or war heroes. In their enthusiasm to commemorate the role of their volunteers at Buena Vista, Indianans named eight settlements after the popular battle. Given the impact of the war on westward expansion, this naming phenomenon was not surprising.[89]

The names became a means to memory in the communities that adopted them. Many originated with veterans who served in Mexico and wanted to commemorate their deeds for future generations. In some cases they represented the values and priorities of the people of the time. For example, residents of Williamsburg, Kentucky, considered their home a violent place. By renaming their town Monterey in 1847 they drew intentional comparisons to the terrible street fighting that had just taken place in their Mexican namesake. Similar claims were made in the lawless towns of Saltillo, Ohio, and Cerro Gordo, North Carolina.[90]

At other times the naming of towns became part of local power struggles. In 1848 the upstart Leaming family of Hildreth, New Jersey, wrestled political control from the town's namesake family. In renaming the town Rio Grande, the Leamings simultaneously commemorated their family's participation in the U.S.–Mexican War and obliterated their rival's name from the map. In another newly established settlement in Indiana, ethnic rivalries pitted Irish, German, and English settlers in a fight over the town's naming rights. Reportedly each group wanted a name to reflect its country of origin. The would-be neighbors broke the impasse by agreeing to name the town Churubusco, in honor of a battle in which members of all three nations fought for the United States.[91]

In spite of the initial excitement caused by the U.S.–Mexican War, the practice of memorial naming had nearly ceased by the outbreak of the Civil War. A decline in the number of existing towns with Mexican War names followed. Some settlements simply failed to thrive, were abandoned, or merged with larger communities. Other towns decided to change their names—some rather quickly. Buena Vista, Kentucky, adopted the name Mannsville in 1852 to honor a Revolutionary War veteran in the community who had recently died. Two years later Tampico, Illinois, assumed the name Centre when the local railroad announced the town to be halfway between Chicago and Cincinnati. In these cases the nostalgia of the American Revolution and the progress of the railroads trumped the declining attraction of the U.S.–Mexican War.[92]

Another example illustrates how memory and the practice of naming played a role in larger political struggles. In 1847 the town of Lancaster, Missouri, adopted the name Fremont to honor the exploits of Lieutenant Colonel Frémont in California. In 1856 the town's namesake ran as a candidate for president of the United States for the newly organized Republican Party. His abolitionist platform incensed many citizens in the slaveholding state, and the town's residents petitioned for yet another name change to censure Frémont and show their disapproval of his radical ideas. In 1859 the town officially changed its name to Stockton to honor the Democrat Robert F. Stockton, Frémont's commander in California. While the new name perpetuated the memory of the war, it also allowed local residents to express their political ideology in the divisive years leading up to the Civil War.[93]

In Texas most of the twenty-three military installations named for the Mexican War fell into obscurity. A few, however, including Fort Worth and Fort Brown (Brownsville), grew into cities that preserved these names. Around the country a small number of towns continue to perpetuate names related to a war that has largely fallen from national consciousness. If naming these places after people and events of the U.S.–Mexican War was meant to somehow preserve their memory, how effective has this practice been?

While there is no exhaustive research on this subject, the work of social scientists provides some clues. The past several decades have witnessed a growing interest in toponymy, the study of place names in the United States. Toponymists have published numerous regional studies since the pioneering work of George Rippey Stewart in the 1940s. Using a combination of oral history interviews, written surveys, and local archives, researchers explore the derivations of place names. Such studies reveal that many towns named for the U.S.–Mexican War have little or no institutional memory of their origin. This communal amnesia demonstrates the weakening memory of the war over time.[94]

For instance, Larry L. Miller's *Ohio Place Names* listed several towns of Mexican War origin. Miller's study significantly overlooked the town of Comargo, a common American misspelling of the northern Mexican city of Camargo. During the war Camargo served as a large supply depot on the Rio Grande and temporary home for thousands of American troops, including many from Ohio. It is also believed to be the site of an unmarked gravesite of some one thousand Americans. This memory has been lost in Comargo, Ohio, where locals believed the name had some association with the Native American people who formerly lived in the area. The toponymist Robert M. Rennick found a similar situation in Ceralvo, Kentucky. Using county records, Rennick was unable to uncover any information about the etymology of the name and gave possible Scottish, Portuguese, or Spanish roots. In reality Ceralvo is a misspelling of Cerralvo, a Mexican town fifty miles from Camargo. It too was home to an American supply depot during the war and the scene of intense fighting by the Kentucky Volunteers. The connection of Kentucky to this obscure Mexican city has slipped from the state's collective memory.[95]

While the naming of American towns and counties for people and events of the U.S.–Mexican War initially served to memorialize the conflict, the long-term influence on collective memory is dubious at best. Nonetheless, various groups used naming practices during the antebellum period as a way of gaining power and control. Whether fighting local conflicts or making national political statements, the power to name a community played a modest, but not insignificant, role in the struggle to manipulate public memory during this time.

Another way in which veterans preserved the memory of their accomplishments was through fraternal organizations. One month after the fall of Chapultepec several Americans gathered "for the purpose of forming a resort for officers, as a promoter of good fellowship, and of furnishing a home where they could pass their leisure hours in social intercourse." Calling themselves the Aztec Club of 1847, the exclusive group of officers met in an eighteenth-century home in Mexico City. Over the following year of American occupation their numbers grew to 160. Initially the club had no plan to remain active outside of Mexico, but as members returned home many hoped that the group might reconvene in the United States. Aside from a business meeting in 1852, however, the Aztec Club fell dormant until after the Civil War.[96]

Spontaneous reunions naturally occurred whenever old soldiers found excuse to gather or visit one another. In 1849 veterans and civilians met in Philadelphia to hear a commemorative speech on the second anniversary of the Battle of Buena Vista. President Pierce hosted a reunion of his old brigade on the fifth anniversary of the Battle of Churubusco in 1853. Other regional fraternal organizations formed during this time. In 1855 veteran volunteers from South Carolina established the Palmetto Association and began meeting regularly in Columbia. That same year the Montezuma Club convened in New York City in an attempt to reunite former members of the Aztec Club of 1847 into a viable social network in the United States. The sectional divide plaguing the nation, however, doomed the organization to failure in 1859. No one had yet realized the potential power of the veterans, and it would take their being overshadowed by coming events to inspire them to political activism.[97]

At the outbreak of the Civil War in 1861 many former soldiers headed back to duty. When the thirty-eight-year-old Ulysses S. Grant left his family tannery in Illinois to answer President Lincoln's call for volunteers, memory of his former service weighed heavily on his conscience. He later recalled that the "Southern rebellion was largely the outgrowth of the Mexican War. Nations, like individuals, are punished for their transgressions. We got our punishment in the most sanguinary and expensive war in modern times." Indeed, the slavery issue, exacerbated by the soldiers' gains in Mexico, made enemies of former comrades and cast the nation into four years of death and destruction.[98]

On April 9, 1865, Gen. Robert E. Lee, commander of the Army of Northern Virginia, anxiously sat in the McLean home in Appomattox Courthouse, Virginia. He had served the Confederate States of America the entire war, but, his army now shattered and surrounded, surrender seemed his only option. When Grant, now commanding general of the United States Army, arrived at the home, the two men awkwardly faced one another for the first time since 1847. Searching for common ground, they discussed the old army and the days when they had fought under the same flag. These former acquaintances-turned-enemies had served together in Mexico, and both were members of the Aztec Club of 1847. This time of remembrance gave brief respite to their years as deadly rivals and offered hope that enemies might yet become friends. Their meeting would be symbolic of the role the memory of the war would play as Americans struggled to reconstruct their nation and create a new sense of unity.[99]

America's collective memory of the U.S.–Mexican War found many expressions and assumed many forms in the years prior to 1866. As diplomats negotiated an end to the conflict in Mexico City, Americans scrambled to find purpose in the invasion. Whigs and Democrats evoked the hostilities to undermine each other's political platforms. Publishers reaped a harvest of popular histories, war-themed parlor music, and lithographs. American soldiers made pilgrimages to former battlefields, collected trophies from their defeated enemies, and formed fraternal organizations. Some communities honored their returning sons, while others appeared reluctant to commemorate a war whose origins remained steeped in ambiguity. Public eulogies for fallen soldiers served as platforms for militarism, nationalism, pacifism, and even political campaigning. And the naming of towns and counties for Mexican War battles and heroes served the social and political needs of their residents. Each of these modes of conveying memory, so ardently bestowed and so fiercely contested during and after the war, faded in importance as the Union fractured in 1861.

2 In the Shadow of Defeat

MEXICO, 1848–1866

❖

IN DECEMBER 1847 fifteen Mexican military officers met in Santiago de Querétaro, north of Mexico City, to organize a select association. After the American occupation of the capital, Querétaro served briefly as the interim seat of Mexican government. While Antonio López de Santa Anna would later brand the officers' meeting as seditious, the men were neither seeking political power nor plotting against the American occupiers. Rather, these veterans united to write a history of the Guerra de la Intervención Norteamericana (War of North American Intervention). In the ensuing months the men of the association hunted for political and military documents related to their various campaigns and debated and argued about the events they had all participated in but perceived in different ways. During the summer of 1848 they emerged with a manuscript entitled "Notes for the History of the War between Mexico and the United States." Although not the first Mexican history of the war, this well-researched book was the most accurate account of its time.[1]

In the midst of postwar social, political, and economic instability, why would these men devote themselves to writing about the conflict from a Mexican perspective? Although the authors had an eye on the past, they also looked toward an uncertain future. In their opening statements they explained: "It is to be hoped that the hard lesson which we have received will teach us to reform our conduct; oblige us to adopt the obvious precautions against its repetition; benefit us by being made acquainted with its bitter fruits; induce us not to forget the mistakes we have committed; and prepare us to stay the impending blows with which ambition and treachery threaten us." A Mexican version of events was not merely a recounting of historic details; it had a critical didactic function. By analyzing the actions of the previous two years, the men saw in the war profound lessons. If Mexicans could learn from their painful past they could benefit from defeat and rally against future threats to the nation.[2]

41

In the years between 1848 and 1866 Mexico's rulers manipulated the memory of their war with the United States to support their political goals. President José Joaquín de Herrera commemorated the valor of Mexico's National Guard to undermine the influence of the standing army. The return of Santa Anna to power in 1853, however, brought a nationwide ban on such activities. Even after liberal reformers ousted the dictator, the subsequent French invasion and occupation of Mexico pushed the recollection of the North American intervention into the recesses of public memory. The humiliation of defeat not only proved too immediate for popular commemoration but also threatened stable government. As a result Mexico largely repressed the memory of its painful loss for the two decades following the North American invasion.

In the midst of this collective amnesia, however, some Mexicans gave form to their memories. Scholars published occasional treatments of the war, painters and poets found inspiration in the nation's doomed defense, and veterans sought to remember fallen comrades even as they vindicated their conduct on the battlefield. While Mexican commemorations never reached the level of those in the United States during this time, they nonetheless laid the foundation for the vibrant national pageant of memory that eventually blossomed from the ashes of defeat and denial.[3]

Immediately after the signing of the Treaty of Guadalupe Hidalgo, Mexican memory found expression in the written word. Reminiscent of writings from north of the border, Mexican accounts often spoke more to contemporary political needs than to the events of the past. Military treatises were the first Mexican writings about the War of North American Intervention, as army commanders desperately attempted to excuse their losses on the battlefield. Predictably, Santa Anna was the first to seek vindication. His *Detail of the Operations that Occurred in the Defense of the Capital of the Republic* (1848) maintained that Mexicans had unfairly criticized his conduct during the final defense of the country. He rhetorically asked the reader, "Charles XII at Poltava, Alexander I at Austerlitz, and the Great Napoleon at Waterloo—were they criminals?" The former president portrayed himself as having been victimized by "the most unjust of aggressions" of the United States and the inexcusable treason of his own people.[4]

Other disgraced officers took notice, and similar vindications followed. Gen. Anastacio Parrodi explained his loss of a key city on the Gulf of Mexico to the North Americans in his *Memorial of the Military Evacuation of the Port of Tampico, Tamaulipas*. Allies of Mariano Arista printed government proceedings that acquitted the general of charges of cowardice and incompetence in the battles of Palo Alto and Resaca de la Palma and the evacuation of Matamoros. The *Statement of the Secretary of State* declared that Generals

Rómulo Díaz De La Vega and Francisco Garay fought with "ardor and bravery" in defense of Mexican territory. Salvaging or rehabilitating reputations would prove to be vitally important to these early writers, as the political survival of the old guard depended on their persuasiveness.[5]

Opponents of Santa Anna also found voice during this time. One of the deposed president's most articulate critics was Congressman Ramón Gamboa, whose *Impugnation of the Report of General Santa Anna* (1849) justified his attack on the former president's reputation as coming from a desire to return "honor to my fatherland." Gamboa's invective not only focused on the war but also criticized Santa Anna's handling of the Texas campaigns of the 1830s, accusing him even of accepting bribes from North Americans prior to his return from Cuban exile in 1846. Finally, the book disparaged Santa Anna for fleeing the battlefield and abandoning his wounded and dead comrades to the enemy.[6]

Gamboa's attack provoked an immediate response from Santa Anna, who, seeing such indictments as a threat to whatever popular support the old general retained, published within months another vindication specifically to counter Gamboa's charges. His *Appeal to the Good Judgment of Natives and Foreigners* produced additional unpublished documents from the war that he hoped would clear his name. Even so, *Impugnation of the Report of General Santa Anna* haunted the aging dictator throughout his life. Decades later, in his personal memoirs, Santa Anna alleged that Gamboa had recanted his accusations and on his deathbed begged for Santa Anna's forgiveness. While the veracity of this reported confession cannot be confirmed, it demonstrated how profoundly Gamboa's attack had affected him.[7]

Santa Anna was not the only Mexican leader to suffer the anger of the people. In the months leading up to the conflict Gen. Mariano Paredes y Arrillaga forcibly overthrew President José Joaquín de Herrera. Although Paredes's mistakes at the beginning of the war were overshadowed by Santa Anna's greater blunders, he could not escape his critics. In 1852 Mariano Aniceto de Lara wrote *Historical Summary of the Most Notable Deeds of the York, Scotch and Santanista Parties in Mexico*. In this poetic account of the war he scrutinized Paredes's handling of Zachary Taylor's army: "In the meantime the infamous Yankees hastened to capture three cities, while Paredes gloried in his title of invincible. . . . He became the invincible by refusing to fight. Behold the advantage of cowards in turning their backs to the enemy! They neither surrender nor retreat, but simply fall back. Hurrah for Don Mariano!" Paredes died impoverished and disgraced in 1849, unable to defend himself against Lara's accusations.[8]

These charges and countercharges were hardly objective and focused more on the manipulation of the past to support personal agendas. By excusing their battlefield failures Mexican officers could possibly rehabilitate their tenuous careers. Critics of the government could likewise benefit from blaming political leaders like Santa Anna and Paredes for the war. Blaming Mexico's woes on an individual or a small group of men therefore made it possible for these men to bolster their declining status and recover national pride.

In addition to popular histories and vindications, various government commissions examined the war with the primary goal of blaming the United States for initiating the hostilities. *Judgment of the Commission of the Chamber of Senators*(1848) opened by declaring it "would be useless to delve into the origin of the differences that have opened the deep line of separation between the two people that share the North American Empire. . . . The entire world knows which has been the unjust aggressor." The *Statement Directed to the Supreme Government by the Commissioners that Signed the Treaty of Peace with the United States* characterized the conflict as "a war that should never have happened." The commissioners explicitly stated that the conflict was an "unjust war on the part of our enemies" and lamented that justice was not on their side.[9]

These government reports, along with other postwar publications, went beyond merely blaming the United States. In many cases they alleged that North Americans had plotted to steal Mexican lands for generations. Three books published in 1848 demonstrated the depth of conspiracy thinking in Mexican society. *Observations of the Message of the President of the United States* claimed that North Americans had colonized Texas in the 1820s and 1830s as part of a clandestine plan to annex the rich land. Manuel Crecencio Rejón's book *Observations* argued that the United States secretly intended to take northern New Spain in 1803, after it had acquired Louisiana from France. *Notes for the History of the War* claimed that the American conspiracy to acquire all of North America even predated the Louisiana Purchase. The authors reported that the covert scheme reached back to America's founding fathers, exclaiming that "from the days of their independence they adopted the project of extending their dominions, and since then, that line of policy has not deviated in the slightest degree." A novel idea in 1848, this theory dominated later publications.[10]

Mexican writers additionally challenged claims by the United States that the war began with the attack at Rancho Carricitos where "American blood" had been spilled allegedly on "American soil." An almanac by Antonio Rodríguez from 1848 argued that the war actually commenced with Taylor's invasion of Point Isabel several weeks earlier. *Notes for the History of the War* considered the hostilities to have been initiated by Capt. John C. Frémont and his "band of adventurers," who wreaked havoc in California "under the pretext of a scientific commission" in the months leading up to the official declaration of war. While largely ignored by North American writers, these incursions into Mexican territory pushed the onset of the conflict to an earlier date. In Mexican eyes, this nullified American claims of self-defense, justified the actions of Mexican troops at Rancho Carricitos, and expunged any doubt that the United States had begun the war.[11]

Mexicans also considered aggression by the United States proof of the nation's inherent deceitfulness and malice. *Judgment of the Commission of the Chamber of Senators* portrayed the United States as unethical and beyond appeals to common decency, concluding regretfully that in dealings with the United States "their right is in their sword." While Gamboa detested Santa Anna, he was nonetheless critical of the invading U.S. military. He quoted a contemporary newspaper account of the invading North Americans that described them as "harrowing in appearance, poorly uniformed, many of them in shirts, armed with sabers, carbines, and pistols of low quality, and their horses were very fat, slow, and ungraceful like all of their race, poorly saddled, and for a harness a pack saddle and a bridle without ornaments or any kind of adornment." To Mexicans, these *Yanquis* resembled common brigands and highwaymen more than disciplined soldiers.[12]

The Americans' unkempt appearances notwithstanding, Mexicans recognized the deadly nature of these soldiers. *Notes for the History of the War* reported that civilians in the newly occupied capital became enraged at "the haughtiness of the North Americans." A spontaneous uprising took place among the poor, many of whom bravely died "in defense of their liberty," resisting the invaders with clubs and stones. General Scott adopted a merciless policy of retribution to subdue Mexico City. The authors recalled how "Americans penetrated through the streets . . . bringing cannon, breaking down doors, sacking houses, and committing a thousand other excesses." The "unbridled soldiery" looted, raped, and murdered. As street fighting continued a second day, any house suspected of harboring snipers was "demolished by the artillery and its inhabitants killed."[13]

According to Mexican authors, these treacherous North American invaders also brought crime, anarchy, and fear to their once-peaceful nation. The *Manifesto of the Municipal Government of the Inhabitants of the Capital* (1848) described a postwar Mexico in chaos: impassable roads clogged by the foul detritus of the invading army; jails, hospitals, and schools lacking in basic necessities; civilians retreating to their homes to escape endemic crime and violence. While Mexican guerillas continued to fight the occupation, North American antipartisan campaigns terrorized innocent civilians.[14]

Mexicans considered the greatest treachery of the United States, however, to be its theft of the northern half of the nation in the treaty forced upon them at Guadalupe Hidalgo. This loss profoundly injured national pride and left many Mexicans demanding to know why the United States annexed Nuevo México and Alta California when it claimed to want only to secure the southern boundary of Texas. Rejón's *Observations* mourned the Treaty of Guadalupe Hidalgo and feared a future of landlessness and poverty. The authors of the *Statement Directed to the Supreme Government by the Commissioners that Signed the Treaty of Peace with the United States* saw the separation of Mexican citizens in Nuevo México and Alta California as the "most keenly felt loss that a people can feel."[15]

In dealing with their defeat Mexican authors had to explain how a degenerate, duplicitous, and godless people could achieve such an overwhelming victory. Taking the offensive, authors championed the reputation of their army and found consolation in the valor of the soldiers, who bravely faced overwhelming odds. Mexico had lost the war, they claimed, not because of cowardice but because of a lack of modern technology, arms, and soldiers before a numerous, powerful foe. By depersonalizing their losses, the writers set about salvaging honor from defeat.[16]

Mexicans frequently wrote about the inferior quality of their ordnance. Parrodi's *Memorial of the Military Evacuation of the Port of Tampico, Tamaulipas* was typical in stating that the North American army had "much larger forces with better artillery." A government report of 1851 entitled *Documents Related to the Meeting Convened in the Capital for the Governors of the States* argued that North American soldiers enjoyed superior weaponry, including percussion rifles, while Mexican soldiers fought with outdated flintlock muskets. The account also blamed Mexico's losses on cannons that were "poorly constructed and poorly mounted"—a factor that contributed to confusion on the battlefield. Lest anyone attribute Mexican military defeat to a lack of fighting spirit, the report lauded the Mexican officer corps, "which were well comported with instruction that was always dignified and praiseworthy." It lauded the rank and file of the Mexican army with a clear message: if Mexico had enjoyed the technological advantages of the United States, the nation could have withstood the foreign invasion.[17]

Parallel to this sentiment was the idea that Mexico had won a moral victory by merely resisting the more powerful United States. Authors extolled the indomitable Mexican spirit that rose above their devastating losses on the battlefield. *Observations of the Message of the President of the United States,* for example, declared, "American artillery has destroyed our soldiers, but it can never destroy our history." Considering how future generations perceived Mexico's military defeat, the book stated, "The justice of the cause will wash away the dishonor." Ultimately, Mexicans understood that in North America's war of aggression they would always hold the moral high ground.[18]

Moral loftiness aside, Mexicans had to confront the humiliation of losing every major campaign against the North Americans. While the symbols of defeat are powerful forces of memory, a single victory can become a nation's rallying cry even in the midst of an otherwise devastating war. Mexican authors of necessity conjured up both literal and symbolic victories. The *Definitive Failure of the Supreme Tribunal of War* (1850), for example, declared that Mexico had won the Battle of Palo Alto, arguing that at the end of the day "Mexican troops remained in their positions, owners of the field, and without having lost a single span of land." While technically accurate, Mexican forces had suffered heavy casualties and had been halted by North American artillery. Unable to hold the field, General Arista retreated southward the next morning. Addressing this ambiguity, the authors wrote, "While not decisive for our troops, it was not won by the Americans either." Few Mexicans, however, truly considered Palo Alto a victory.[19]

More persuasive were Mexican claims that they had won the Battle of La Angostura (Buena Vista). By all accounts, after two days of fighting General Taylor's lines were near collapse, yet just short of success Santa Anna declared victory and withdrew from the field, leaving the battered Americans the uncontested possessors of the Mexican north. The United States quickly claimed success and turned Buena Vista into its greatest triumph. Ignoring the ramifications of his retreat, Santa Anna paraded captured North American cannons and flags as proof of his conquest. While many Mexicans saw through his haughty display, the nation largely accepted his boast.[20]

Mexican authors found consolation in their lone putative victory. Rodríguez's pocket almanac celebrated Santa Anna's war trophies as proof of the "terrible injury" inflicted upon the invading Americans. Lara's *Historical Summary* likewise touted the supposed Mexican triumph at La Angostura. *Notes for the History of the War* declared that the Mexican army had defeated the North Americans at La Angostura but recognized that Santa Anna's retreat left the ultimate outcome ambiguous. The book stated that the North Americans "feigned the glory of having conquered, on our part the army was proclaimed victorious, alleging in proof the trophies captured, the positions taken, and the divisions vanquished. The truth is, our arms routed the Americans in all the encounters, and so far the issue of the battle was favorable to us. There had been three partial triumphs, but not a complete victory." The authors sadly offered the opinion, shared by the entire nation, that their troops "had displayed a valor worthy of a better fate."[21]

In addition to claiming a literal triumph at La Angostura, Mexican commentators forged a powerful symbolic victory from the fall of Chapultepec Castle. The castle was essential to the defense of Mexico City, and its fall on September 13, 1847, allowed American troops to occupy the capital. In this case, however, unlike that of La Angostura, Mexicans never disputed their loss. Rather, they hailed the heroism of the young cadets who defended the military academy housed in the castle. This tragic defeat became a Mexican Thermopylae or, perhaps more appropriately, a Mexican Alamo, and in later generations a myth would arise about the role the Niños Héroes (Boy Heroes) played in the defense of their country.

While the legend had yet to take root in the Mexican collective memory, early accounts of the battle laid the foundation on which the great stories of the cadets were constructed. *Notes for the History of the War* gave Mexicans one of their first glimpses of the brave students: "In the corridor, converted into a surgical hospital, were found mixed up the putrid bodies, the wounded breathing mournful groans and the young boys of the college." The historians reported that during the night before the assault many soldiers deserted their posts, leaving the castle in jeopardy. At daylight the North Americans overwhelmed the garrison at the base of Chapultepec and, using assault ladders, scaled the hill and breached the castle walls: "The advance continued to the rampart, where our defenders, astounded by the bombardment, fatigued, wanting sleep, and hungry, were hurled over the rocks by the bayonets or taken prisoners. A company of the New York Regiment ascended to the top of the building, where some of the students still fired, [students] who were the last defenders of that Mexican flag which was quickly replaced by the American."[22]

Significantly, this account described Mexican soldiers falling from the walls of the castle to the rocks below. While later legends alleged that at least one of the cadets jumped from the precipice rather than surrender the Mexican flag, the authors of *Notes for the History of the War* believed that the defenders were forced over the wall at bayonet point during the fighting. The anonymous Mexican author of the *Observations of the Message of the President of the United States* gave yet another explanation of the incident. He openly criticized the troops at Chapultepec and bemoaned the fact that his country was "defended by soldiers who prefer to throw themselves from the heights than to fight, like Chapultepec." North American sources likewise confirmed that Mexican soldiers jumped from the castle but attributed these desperate acts to the confusion of their retreat.[23]

North Americans contributed to the developing myth of the Boy Heroes. In his translation of *Notes for the History of the War between Mexico and the United States* into English in 1850 Albert C. Ramsey added a lengthy footnote to the Mexican account of the Battle of Chapultepec. As a colonel in the Eleventh United States Infantry, Ramsey had participated in the battle and was a firsthand witness of the day's events. He wrote, "The little boys, students of Chapultepec, took their first lessons in real war at the same school where they studied their books. They fought manfully, bravely, and with heroism. One of them was told by his mother that he must never return if not with honor, that she would rather see his dead body than him living disgraced. This spirited little fellow stood to his gun in the assault, and when some retreated and were killed, he would not yield an inch. He was captured where he stood, and his heroism saved both his honor and his life. There is no doubt of this fact. He was brought to the United States and is now finishing his education." While the story of the valiant young cadet cannot be verified, it pointed to a literal co-opting of the Boy Heroes legend by North Americans. To Ramsey the boy embodied attributes best nurtured in the United States. Spirited and unyielding, he had the makings of a Mexican Horatio Alger.[24]

The Battle of Chapultepec was profoundly embarrassing for Santa Anna. Gamboa, his principal critic, blamed the fall of the castle on the president's failure to reinforce the small garrison. From the perspective of many Mexicans the blood of the martyrs of Chapultepec stained the president's hands. During Santa Anna's return to power in 1853 the memory of the battle temporarily disappeared from public consciousness. Rather than remembering the dead of Chapultepec, official discourse excused the president and vindicated his guilt in the affair.[25]

In 1856 the Mexican general-turned-historian Joaquín Rangel published the first post–Santa Anna history of the conflict by revising and reprinting a report he wrote about the Battle of Chapultepec in 1847. Rangel identified some of the officers and cadets killed at the castle, helping to popularize their names. He wrote, "Glory and honor to the heroes who sacrificed themselves for the fatherland! The 13th of September is also the same day that the brave [Lt. Col. Felipe Santiago] Xicoténcatl presented himself at the head of his battalion to hold the hill of Chapultepec from the charge of the enemy. There he died with the valiant Cano, the cadets Suárez, Melgar, Montes de Oca, and many others whose fame we should exalt posthumously with the prize of their blood and their lives." Rangel then published an open letter to the new, reform-minded president, Ignacio Comonfort, petitioning him to memorialize the fallen cadets with a monument. This would not be done for thirty more years. Indeed, another generation passed before Mexicans would popularly commemorate the battle in any meaningful way.[26]

Rangel encouraged other Mexican writers to take advantage of the new freedom of the press enjoyed under President Comonfort's administration to challenge the more numerous North American histories. He wrote, "It's very discouraging that only in these works can one find details of this very interesting war, that generally disturbs the Republic, and for many individuals cost them the sacrifice of their finances and interests." Rangel, pleading with his countrymen to write and publish competing perspectives, admonished, "Now is the time for Mexican writers to occupy themselves with writing this important history." In spite of such calls the War of North American Intervention proved a difficult subject for the first postwar generation of Mexicans.[27]

Unfortunately, the ouster of Santa Anna in 1855 did not bring an end to strife in Mexico. Social and political turmoil after 1857 explains the relative dearth of writings about the War of North American Intervention. The Reform War of 1857–61 was a civil war incited by Mexican conservatives opposed to the liberal administration of Benito Juárez. After a brief respite Mexico faced yet another protracted war when France invaded the country in 1862, an intervention that would end five years later with the execution of the puppet monarch Maximilian of Habsburg. Years of violence disturbed the social order, tapped scarce financial resources, and distracted the Mexican public from the wrongs inflicted by the United States.

Like North Americans, Mexicans of this postwar era found ways beyond the written word to express memory. Art and music, for example, played roles in creating remembrance of the War of North American Intervention. Although the conflict raged in the midst of Mexico's "golden age" of lithography, battle scenes were unpopular subjects for Mexican artists. The shame of defeat contributed to Mexicans' reluctance to memorialize the North American invasion, and, further, most lithographers worked for publishing houses creating illustrations for books. At the onset of war the practice of selling individual prints as artwork was not yet popular in Mexico. After the fall of Mexico City, however, a handful of engravers and printers working in the capital realized the market potential of selling images to the occupying North American troops and began to vend loose-leaf prints as souvenirs.[28]

The few surviving examples of Mexican lithographs of the war often demonstrated a carelessness in production expected in inexpensive keepsakes. An engraver known only as Reinaldo created several crude images that compromised artistic skill in the rush to produce prints for the souvenir market. The printer Joaquín Heredia, in his cartoonlike portrayal of the Battle of Contreras with English and Spanish titles, featured U.S. Dragoons prominently in the foreground in an obvious appeal to a North American audience. The engraver H. Mendez also created images for sale to North Americans that included bilingual titles and captions, among them his *View of Cerro Gordo,* which offered an expansive battle panorama of Gen. David Twiggs's final assault on the hill. While giving detail to natural features such as mountains, the artist simplified his human subjects by placing the combat in the extreme background of the artwork. Mendez also skewed the perspective of the scene, giving his work an amateurish appearance.[29]

Not all Mexican artwork was of poor quality. Unlike his primitive portrayal of Cerro Gordo, Mendez's *View of Chapultepec and Molino del Rey* was a skilled treatment of the subject and caught the attention of the American engraver Nathaniel Currier, who copied it for the market in the United States (see fig. 5). Currier also sought out and duplicated other higher quality Mexican lithographs. In 1848 the Mexican publisher Ignacio Cumplido printed *Garita de Belén* to celebrate his countrymen's final defense at the gates of the capital. The scene highlighted the bravery of Mexican soldiers as they faced the crushing onslaught of North American troops. Mexican women and children were shown fleeing as the invaders fired artillery indiscriminately into the city. In spite of its sympathetic portrayal, it is unlikely that this print was popular among Mexicans, but it did appeal to Currier, who duplicated the image almost exactly for his American clientele.[30]

After the occupation Mexican engravers continued to create illustrations for books. Authors of this era produced few popular histories of the war, so demand for combat-themed art remained small. One exception was Julio Michaud y Thomas's *Colorful Album of the Mexican Republic*, printed in 1850. In this beautifully illustrated volume the engraver Ferdinand Bastin created a scene from the Battle of Cerro Gordo as viewed from the Americans' battle lines. Although the Mexicans had lost this battle, the image showed the Yanqui invaders being halted at a ravine. Several American soldiers lie dead or wounded as their charge falters against a wall of Mexican musket fire. While Mexican readers were painfully aware of their ultimate loss, the book's illustration made it clear that their soldiers fought a brave campaign.[31]

In addition to engravers, painters created images of the war for the Mexican public. The most famous works of the time were oil paintings of the six Niños Héroes. In an attempt to immortalize his dead comrades, the former cadet Santiago Hernández y Ayllón painted portraits of the slain young men from memory in the years after the war. Today, these works hang in the Museo Nacional de Historia in Chapultepec Castle, where they remain at the center of the cult of the Boy Heroes. The War of North American Intervention also became a subject for religious ex-voto paintings that commemorated events in which Mexican soldiers survived terrible ordeals. Local folk artists created these small paintings to be placed in Catholic churches, where they bore solemn witness to the intervention of a saint or deity on behalf of a faithful soldier. In one surviving example, the votive painting portrayed a Mexican lancer named Antonio Pliego being pursued by thirty-five American soldiers. Underneath the painting Pliego offered written thanks to the Black Christ of Esquipulas for the miracle of his escape (see fig. 6). This art form was unknown in the United States and offered a Mexican Catholic expression of the war's memory. Other examples may have been created in the years following the conflict, although their relative impermanence has doomed them to obscurity.[32]

In Mexico there was no boom of war-themed sheet music as in the United States. There is anecdotal evidence of traditional borderlands *corridos*, or folk ballads, composed in the conquered New Mexican Territory or possibly even in the Lower Rio Grande Valley of Texas, but these too have slipped from memory. Perhaps the war's greatest influence on popular music was the composition of the national anthem, *Mexicanos, al grito de guerra* (Mexicans at the cry of war). When Santa Anna returned to power in 1853 he attempted to boost the nation's morale by adopting a national anthem. A poem written by Francisco González Bocanegra recalled the recent bloody struggles to maintain Mexican sovereignty, and four verses of his original ten-stanza poem were selected as the official *himno nacional*.[33]

The entire anthem dealt with war, but certain lines alluded to the unfortunate events that had just occurred in Mexico. The first verse, for example, explicitly addressed foreign invasion:

> But if a foreign enemy
> Dare to profane your soil under his foot
> Know, beloved fatherland, that heaven gave you
> A soldier in each of your sons.

Focusing on the pain of recent events, verse three described the prospect of losing the war. Still, González Bocanegra portrayed not a surrender but a conflict fought to the last soldier:

> Fatherland, before your children become unarmed
> Beneath the yoke their necks in sway,
> May your countryside be watered with blood,
> On blood their feet trample.
> And may your temples, palaces, and towers
> crumble in a horrid crash,
> and their ruins exist saying:
> The fatherland was made of one thousand heroes here.

At this time North Americans expressed interest in acquiring territory in northern Mexico to build a railroad. If Mexico refused to negotiate, another war with the United States seemed possible. This threat of crashing ruins made clear Mexico's resolve to see itself destroyed rather than be occupied again.[34]

The final verse of the anthem is similar to contemporary North American war eulogies. Like northern tributes to the dead, the lyrics promised the soldiers of Mexico that they would not be forgotten:

Fatherland, oh fatherland, your sons vow
To give their last breath on your altars,
If the trumpet with its warlike sound
Calls them to valiant battle.
For you, the garlands of olive,
For them, a glorious memory.
For you, the victory laurels,
For them, an honored tomb.

In fulfillment of this promise, a century later the Mexican government would build a towering memorial and tomb to the martyrs of Chapultepec called the Altar to the Fatherland. As I explore in later chapters, this monument would become central to Mexico's public memory of the war.[35]

Why would Santa Anna have selected a national anthem that recalled the U.S. invasion? While the poem clearly had allusions to the past, it demanded that Mexicans look to the present and the future. In addition to the interest in Mexican lands shown by the United States, European powers were considering occupying the resource-rich nation, and, indeed, within a decade France had invaded Mexico for the second time in twenty-five years. The war imagery of the anthem galvanized Mexicans in national defense and promised invaders a devastating and bloody fight. Like the rhetoric of North Americans at that time, *Mexicanos, al grito de guerra* promised the soldiers of Mexico immortality in the "glorious memory" of the national consciousness. Perhaps, too, in a war of heroic defense Santa Anna may have hoped to reclaim his dignity.[36]

Art and music were not the only means through which Mexicans expressed their remembrance of the war during this era. Similar to their northern enemies, Mexican troops collected war trophies as evidence of their battlefield exploits, although the lack of combat victories limited their opportunities to capture the coveted souvenirs. The most important war trophies were the North American cannons and flags taken at La Angostura. Santa Anna paraded his prized relics along his retreat route to prove he had achieved a great victory. As he passed through San Luis Potosí he presented one of the flags to the state legislature and carried the remaining two back to the capital. Although North American troops recaptured two of the artillery pieces at the Battle of Cerro Gordo a few months later, one cannon, the flags, and a number of small arms remained in Mexican hands. When the government moved its headquarters to Querétaro after the fall of Mexico City it brought the valued trophies with it. These reminders of Mexico's glory remained proudly on display in the museum of the Maestranza de Artillería de México (Artillery School of Mexico) into the twentieth century.[37]

As another way of commemorating battlefield accomplishments Mexico bestowed medals on veteran officers. Beginning in December of 1847 the Mexican government commissioned nine awards for specific campaigns and battles, three commendations of merit, and a medal for survivors of the San Patricio Battalion. These decorations, unlike North American medals, which were distributed at the local level, were issued in the name of the Mexican Republic, thus putting control of the bestowing of honors in the hands of the central government. Such tokens have great symbolic value for soldiers and civilians and granted an official endorsement of bravery in the face of defeat. Most important, they bore witness that the wearer was not responsible for Mexico's loss.[38]

As North American troops prepared to evacuate Mexico City during the spring of 1848, the Congress of Mexico elected José Joaquín de Herrera to the presidency. Herrera, who had also served as president before the war, was a moderate politician who was interested in reunifying Mexico in the wake of the social and ethnic turmoil of the North American invasion. Under his administration the government sponsored an annual memorial ceremony at Churubusco, where an old Franciscan convent had become a makeshift fortress for the undersupplied Mexican troops guarding the passage to Mexico City. On August 20, 1847, these soldiers faced a blistering North American assault, and the fierce fighting that ensued proved costly to both sides. Deserters from the U.S. Army, fighting under the Mexican flag as the Batallón de San Patricio, kept the battle raging hours after Mexican attempts at surrender. Mexican forces capitulated only after having run out of ammunition. The president was particularly interested in commemorating the role of Mexico's National Guard in the defense of Churubusco and the capital because he had previously been deposed in a military coup and believed that the standing army was too easily manipulated by autocrats. Citizen-soldiers were therefore the key to preserving the nation's struggling democratic institutions. Mexico's regular army resented the slight and sought ways to reassert its place of honor in national memory.[39]

State funerals were one of the battlegrounds on which the National Guard vied with the Mexican army. As in the United States, there were few public services for the country's war dead. Indeed, the returning of soldiers' bodies was a luxury that only the wealthiest citizens could afford. Most Mexican casualties were left on the battlefield, where North Americans disposed of them in mass graves. Even officers remained anonymous in death. Battles that took place near Mexico City, however, allowed some Mexican war dead to be identified and interred in modest burials.[40]

As the one year anniversary of the invasion of their capital neared, Mexicans took a number of steps to honor their slain militia troops. First, the

Nuevo México Theater hosted a play entitled "When There Are No Parties, Mexico Will Gain Immortality." The production dramatized the doomed defense of Mexico City and praised the sacrifices of the nation's National Guard battalions. Three weeks later, survivors of the Batallón Independencia gathered at the former convent at Churubusco to mourn their dead comrades and pay tribute to the sacrifices of the citizen soldiers.[41]

Mexico's irregular troops had fought tenaciously alongside the regular army in the battles near the capital. Among the National Guard officers killed during the campaign were Lt. Col. Francisco Peñúñuri and Lt. Col. Lucas Balderas. President Herrera realized that state funerals for these men would enhance the prestige of the National Guard and aid in his efforts to enlarge the organization. He consequently procured plots and sponsored elaborate reburials for the men at the celebrated Panteón de Santa Paula in Mexico City. When officers from the Mexican army tried to provide similar honors for four of their fallen comrades the government demurred, stating that the exhumation might spread disease. The officers protested on the grounds that the government was discriminating against the army and eventually prevailed in securing their funerals.[42]

Surviving accounts of these official army funerals testified to the symbolic importance of such gestures at a time when President Herrera sought to weaken the power of the regular military. The ceremony began with carriages drawing the disinterred bodies of Lt. Col. Juan Cano, Lt. Col. Felipe Xicoténcatl, Gen. José Frontera, and Gen. Francisco Pérez through the streets of the capital. A large procession of soldiers, military cadets, and invalid veterans escorted the remains. The cadets carried a black banner that read, "To Those That Died for the Fatherland" and draped the hearse with a standard reading, "Those of All the Battles of the War against the United States." Individual soldiers trailing behind the hearse carried placards bearing the names of each of the battles along with the number of Mexicans killed in them. The somber cortege finally arrived at the Panteón de Santa Paula, where tombs had been prepared for the men. At the chapel, a cadet stepped forward with a banner and laid it in Lieutenant Colonel Xicoténcatl's tomb, exclaiming, "The Military College sends me here to place this flag here so no one may lay hands upon it." The ceremony ritually bound the nation's future officers to those of the past and celebrated the preeminence of the Mexican army.[43]

Upon returning to power Santa Anna initially attempted to use the war's memory to undo Herrera's reforms and bolster the reputation of the army to strengthen his tenuous hold on the government. He tried to appropriate the growing authority of the National Guard by posthumously awarding regular army commissions to its slain leaders. Santa Anna also considered plans to rebury additional high-profile officers and construct monuments in their honor, but by 1855 he realized that such observances would draw attention to his failed defense of the capital. Accordingly, he abandoned his planned memorials, repealed the law honoring the Battle of Churubusco, and forbade the annual services at the former convent. To focus instead on his victories, Santa Anna replaced the Churubusco commemoration with a celebration of his defeat of the Spanish at Tampico in 1829.[44]

After Santa Anna was yet again driven from office Mexicans once more sought public means of remembering their fallen heroes. In the 1856 edition of his *Detail of the Operations that Occurred in the Defense of the Capital of the Republic* Rangel appealed to President Comonfort to undo Santa Anna's legacy. He wrote, "I raise my voice in supplication, asking that you not leave them in darkness and without reward, and if in this year it is not possible to erect a monument to these heroes who well deserve the deep gratitude of our citizens, declare by the end of the coming year that you eternalize the names of those who had the noble resolution to die for the fatherland!!" President Comonfort, a veteran of the war himself, responded by repealing Santa Anna's prohibitions and personally attended the commemorations at the convent that year alongside military dignitaries. Presidents Benito Juárez, Sebastián Lerdo de Tejada, and Porfirio Díaz continued the tradition by being present at the annual observances until 1899. In spite of the government-sponsored events at Churubusco, public commemorations of the war remained modest throughout this period.[45]

Comonfort's most enduring influence on the memory of the North American invasion was the erecting of memorials to soldiers killed defending Mexico City. In February of 1856 the president commissioned the sculpting firm of Hermanos Tangassi to build two matching marble monuments at the sites of the battles of Churubusco and Molino del Rey (see fig. 7). He further commanded that the remains of several slain officers be reinterred in the base of the structures. Honoring both the dead and his precarious presidential authority, Comonfort ordered his name engraved prominently on both monuments. These gestures proved ineffectual, as conservatives drove the president from office the following year.[46]

Mexico's early commemorations revealed a burgeoning cult of martyrs associated with the North American intervention. Similarly, literature focused not on the survivors but on those who had died or been disabled. These men paid the highest price for the fatherland, and in subsequent decades they were the center of their nation's memory. Rangel, for example, exonerated the dead and wounded, alleging that the defeat was "not on account of the loss of glory of those who died heroically for their fatherland and those who lost limbs or who can show the wounds they received defending the national territory." While this trend of exalting the fallen took root during this early period, it became more apparent in later generations.[47]

Before hostilities began, the Mexican government made provisions for soldiers wounded or killed during their service. On paper at least volunteers and draftees could expect a minimum of protection for themselves and their families. Service contracts promised that if a recruit should "become disabled in service or will die in action or as a result thereof, he and his family will receive the pensions assigned them by existing laws." Apparently, "existing laws" fell short of providing the necessities most families required. After the war, the Congress passed a law that promised pensions to the wives and children of casualties of the regular army, a law soon expanded to include National Guard forces and militia troops. In 1849 the Mexican secretary of state reaffirmed that the government would care for its wounded and disabled veterans. Declaring that "these distinguished veterans gave commendable service and are loyal and dutiful," he proposed the construction of a Hotel de Inválidos, or soldiers' home, to house those unable to care for themselves. Santa Anna's return to power certainly placed such plans in jeopardy, and the ultimate status of the institution remains unclear.[48]

Like American soldiers, Mexican veterans united for mutual support and to commemorate their deeds during the war. The first group to organize was composed of the surviving cadets of the Military College. Initially the young men gathered informally as an unofficial association dedicated to preserving the memory of their classmates who perished at Chapultepec. Beginning on September 13, 1848, the cadets observed a moment of silence on campus. In 1851 and 1852 survivors of Chapultepec held ceremonies to honor their dead. At this time there remained some confusion as to the number, names, and ages of the cadets who died. By 1852 Mexicans referred to them as children, a not entirely accurate description but one that imbued the cadets with innocence and bravery beyond their years.[49]

The Mexican government feared the grass-roots commemoration at the college would conflict with its officially sanctioned ceremonies at Churubusco and prohibited the cadets from publicly honoring their slain comrades. In subsequent years they met in private homes and cafes in silent tributes. As all memorials ceased after Santa Anna's final return to power, the director of the college received orders forbidding the cadets from honoring their fallen brothers in any manner. Still, they persevered by holding clandestine commemorations at which they would gather to make speeches and toasts to honor the six young men.[50]

By the end of the 1850s the former cadets of the Military College had grown to adulthood. Those who remained in the army again faced foreign invasion. When President Juárez temporarily suspended repayment of loans to Spain, England, and France in 1861, the European powers threatened to declare war. Taking advantage of the distraction of the Civil War in the United States, France made good on its threat. In 1862 it landed a large amphibious force at Veracruz, and, employing a strategy reminiscent of the North American one in 1847, French troops marched along the National Road toward the Mexican capital. On May 5 Mexican forces made a stand at Puebla and decisively defeated the invaders. Although the battle gave Mexico a national holiday—Cinco de Mayo—it proved to be only a temporary setback for the army of Napoleon III: two years later Emperor Maximilian I sat as France's puppet monarch in Mexico City.[51]

The years between 1848 and 1866 were marked by political instability and intermittent warfare, preventing Mexicans from widely remembering and commemorating their conflict with the United States. The grass-roots manifestations that did emerge were, at times, dominated by political authorities, highlighting a growing tension between popular and official forms of memory. In spite of these challenges some groups persisted in memory making. Basic forms of postwar recollection, in Mexico as in the United States, included printed material, music, lithographs, funeral rites, and military rituals. Mexicans also found culturally unique forms of remembrance such as ex-voto paintings. The most notable difference in how the two nations expressed their memories was in the role played by their governments. Beginning with President Herrera's attempt to bolster the reputation of the National Guard by creating a commemoration at Churubusco, Mexico's rulers exerted control over the conflict's memory. Unlike the United States, where memorialization occurred at state and local levels, in Mexico the federal government took an active role in creating, regulating, and repressing memory. Remembrance, nonetheless, persisted, even in the face of official suppression, demonstrating the resilience of the collective consciousness.[52]

As Robert E. Lee surrendered to Ulysses S. Grant at Appomattox Courthouse, Virginia, Mexican liberals were embroiled in war with France and its collaborators. Commemoration of the War of North American Intervention had always been tenuous, but during this latest threat to Mexican sovereignty the conflict largely disappeared from the nation's memory. In 1867, however, Mexico defeated the French, drove out their army, and executed their would-be emperor. The way was cleared for the nation to again find symbol and meaning in its defeat by the United States.

3 Old Soldiers and New Wars

THE UNITED STATES, 1866–1895

✣

IN 1884 Ulysses S. Grant retired from public life to write his memoirs. This final endeavor was a race against time as throat cancer steadily closed off his airway. Poor financial investments had left Grant impoverished, and his manuscript offered him a last opportunity to reverse his declining fortunes. As he wrote, memories of Mexico haunted his mind and pen. Since fighting there under Zachary Taylor and Winfield Scott, Grant had maintained a keen interest in his Mexican adversary. In 1865 he unsuccessfully pressed for an invasion of Mexico to drive out the French and restore the government of Benito Juárez. After his presidency Grant served as head of the speculative Mexican Southern Railroad and helped broker a free trade treaty with the Mexican government. He counted Mexico's minister to the United States, Matías Romero, among his closest friends. During Grant's desperate final years Romero's generosity helped stave off the former president's bankruptcy.[1]

Given his history, Grant's condemnation of the U.S.–Mexican War was not surprising. In his memoirs the old soldier angrily attacked the Polk administration, writing, "We were sent to provoke a fight." He continued his critique of the American occupation of southern Texas: "I was bitterly opposed to the measure, and to this day regard the war which resulted as one of the most unjust ever waged by a stronger against a weaker nation. It was an instance of a republic following the bad example of European monarchies, in not considering justice in their desire to acquire additional territory." While some have charged Grant with writing post-Reconstruction Republican political propaganda, there is little doubt of his sincerity. His memoirs echoed sentiments he had expressed publicly and privately ever since his service in the Mexican War.[2]

What does the writing of a dying veteran reveal about the memory of the U.S.–Mexican War in the thirty years after the Civil War? At first glance

Grant's memoir appeared to perpetuate the themes of previous decades. Certainly his attack on the expansionist Democratic Party closely paralleled the condemnations made by Whigs and Republicans during the antebellum and Civil War years. The timing of his writings, however, points to a critical difference. With death approaching, Grant, knowing he would not live long enough to benefit politically from his manuscript, hoped mainly that his final testament instead would shape how the world remembered him. He also hoped that the work might prove to be a financial windfall for his family. Grant's writings embodied the two greatest desires of Mexican War veterans in the decades after the Civil War. The grizzled warriors wanted future generations to remember them favorably; many also expected compensation for their past service to offset the poverty of old age.

The organization and politicization of veterans in the period between 1866 and 1895 mark a shift in the memory of the U.S.–Mexican War. Previously, the veterans had celebrated their valor in fighting the Mexican War, but now, in their waning years, the old soldiers hoped to earn service pensions from the government. Lingering sectional divisions and the fear that former Confederates might receive federal annuities turned the issue into a contentious war of words that would rage for years. This forced soldiers of the U.S.–Mexican War, more than any other group of U.S. veterans, to prove their loyalty to the country they had served. As advocacy for pensions moved to the forefront of the veterans' agenda, they focused on the financial windfall that the war had brought the nation. These economic gains would become the primary focus of pension supporters throughout their long fight in Congress.[3]

The driving force behind the organizing of Mexican War veterans was a Virginian named Alexander M. Kenaday. While he was still a young man Kenaday's family moved to Missouri, where he spent his adolescence on the Mississippi River working as a steamboat steersman and newspaper apprentice. At the outbreak of hostilities he joined a volunteer company in New Orleans and shipped out to Matamoros, Tamaulipas. Disappointed because, like many late arrivals to the Rio Grande, his unit failed to see action before their ninety-day enlistments expired, he returned to New Orleans and promptly enlisted in the Third United States Dragoons. His new unit offered the young man no shortage of action as it engaged the enemy in battles all the way from Veracruz to Mexico City. In the assault on the Churubusco convent, Sergeant Kenaday distinguished himself by jumping into a burning munitions wagon and tossing out bags of black powder, averting a potentially disastrous explosion.[4]

After the war Kenaday set off for the gold fields of California. Finding no success in mining, he returned to the newspaper business and in 1851 helped organize and lead the Eureka Typographical Union, which established minimum pay standards for the state's typesetters. After the Civil War Kenaday learned that medical schools were collecting the corpses of indigent veterans in San Francisco for dissection. He shuddered at the thought of his comrades facing such an "ignoble desecration." Kenaday was determined to put the skills he had learned in union organizing to good use by creating an association of fellow Mexican War veterans to care for their elderly brethren and provide them proper burials.[5]

The opportunity presented itself in 1866 when members of the First New York Volunteers living in San Francisco requested that their fellow Mexican War veterans join them for the Fourth of July parade. At the reunion that followed Kenaday stood before the veterans and proposed that they form an organization named the Society of Veterans of 1846. His emotional speech inspired some two hundred former soldiers and sailors to join his ranks. Notwithstanding his central role in organizing the group, Kenaday preferred that men of national repute front the organization while he worked behind the scenes recruiting and fundraising.[6]

The Society of Veterans of 1846 immediately set about soliciting money to care for the aged and dying. Need soon outweighed the group's meager coffers, forcing Kenaday to search for new funding sources. He drafted a petition to the U.S. Congress asking it to allocate monies to build a soldiers' home on the Pacific Coast similar to one the government had built in Washington, D.C., in 1851. The original home had been established with reparations collected in Mexico City, and Kenaday believed that Mexican War veterans living in the West should have access to similar services.[7]

Serious illness prevented Kenaday from undertaking his mission to the nation's capital until the summer of 1868. The strong-minded veteran lobbied Congress for the next six months, and finally, in January 1869, the Senate approved the petition and sent it to Secretary of War John Aaron Rawlins. Unfortunately, Rawlins died before acting on the proposal, and his successor, William Worth Belknap, who had little interest in the measure, returned the unsigned petition to the War Department, where it was buried and forgotten. Undaunted, Kenaday spent the next four years unsuccessfully attempting to raise support for his soldiers' home in the West.[8]

With the proposal at an impasse Kenaday decided to pressure Congress by forming another veterans' organization in Washington. His first step was to seek national exposure for his fledgling group, and President Grant's second inauguration in March of 1873 gave him the opportunity to do just that. Kenaday successfully petitioned the planning board to include a group of Mexican War veterans to honor the president's service in the conflict and then placed advertisements in the local newspapers asking for support from local veterans. On Inauguration Day approximately thirty former soldiers participated in the ceremonies.[9]

Shortly after Grant's inauguration, James S. Negley, a member of the House of Representatives and president of a Pennsylvania veterans' group named the Scott Legion, contacted Kenaday about service pension legislation he wished to present to Congress. Negley's bill proposed an annuity similar to that offered to veterans of the War of Independence and the War of 1812. While the Soldiers' Home could care only for men wounded in battle, a pension would assist all veterans in their old age. Negley, a general in the Civil War, had begun his military career fighting under Scott in Mexico. Having served in volunteer units in both conflicts, he was especially interested in the care of irregular troops, who at times fell outside the jurisdiction of the federal government. Negley suggested that Kenaday use his network to create a national organization of Mexican War veterans to support his pension legislation.[10]

Kenaday realized that a pension could provide a viable alternative to his soldiers' home and embarked on the project with his characteristic zeal. After two months of planning and promotion he convened the first meeting of the National Association of Veterans of the Mexican War. During its initial gathering in Washington in May of 1873 the group elected Gen. James W. Denver as president. Denver, the man for whom the capital of Colorado was named, was a shrewd choice. He had diverse political experience, including public service as a congressman, a commissioner of Indian Affairs, and the governor of the Kansas Territory. After its modest first meeting the group planned to reconvene in Washington the following January.[11]

The national convention in 1874 was a great success. The three-day affair included more than 250 delegates from nearly all the states and territories in the nation. The one threat to the group's unity was that many of the men had been enemies during the Civil War. On the opening day General Denver addressed the assembled veterans in an attempt to soothe the rivalries between Northern and Southern factions. Obliquely referencing the Civil War, Denver stated, "I trust that none of these differences will be brought into this Convention, and that no question of politics or other disturbing matter will be alluded to, but that our deliberations may be confined entirely to the events and consequences pertaining to the time when all were actuated by the single motive, as one man, to uphold the honor and glory of our common country and the actors in those great events." Denver's appeal appeared to work, as the delegates put aside their differences to address more immediate issues.[12]

Denver's opening speech furthermore laid out the political agenda of the group. After lauding the contribution of the war to the "business pursuits" of the United States, he reminded his comrades that their service had "furnished capital for the most gigantic commercial operations" in the decades since hostilities had ended. He mourned the fact that a number of their fellow veterans remained in "indigent circumstances" despite their incalculable financial contributions to the United States. He concluded his remarks by insisting that "the country ought to take care of them. Their services entitle them to consideration, and it ought not to be withheld from them." The solution the group proposed was the sponsorship of a pension bill.[13]

To succeed with their pension legislation Denver and Kenaday needed to control how the public remembered the veterans. This was no easy task considering the nation's focus on the more devastating Civil War. While the antebellum memory of the soldiers stressed their gallantry, new memories incorporated their changing goals. As petitioners to Congress, the men had to appeal to the sympathies of the lawmakers and the country at large. New visions collided with old as the national association honored the soldiers' former glory while emphasizing their loss of status, declining age, and poverty. They were no longer the robust men of 1846 but the deserving poor who warranted the nation's pity.

The national association unanimously supported the drafting of a pension bill to be submitted to Congress immediately. The proposed legislation, "An Act granting Pensions to certain Soldiers and Sailors of the War of eighteen hundred and forty-six with Mexico, and the Widows of deceased Soldiers and Sailors," was more commonly referred to as the Mexican Pension Bill. The bill promised a monthly payment of eight dollars to any man who had served honorably in Mexico for at least sixty days or to his surviving widow. The group also agreed on several secondary goals related to memory formation, including writing an official history of the war, building a national monument to honor their accomplishments, marking the graves of American casualties in Mexico, and other activities meant to celebrate the "names and fame" of soldiers, both living and dead.[14]

Politicking was not the only activity at the reunion. Veterans also heard speeches, poems, and musical tributes celebrating their exploits on Mexican battlefields. Perhaps most gratifying, they basked in their memories and rekindled old friendships. The highlight for many attendees was President Grant's invitation to them to visit the White House and meet with him. During Grant's administration the popular former general was inundated with requests to attend veterans' reunions across the country, but his busy schedule prevented him from attending the vast majority of these meetings. His hosting of the national association at the White House therefore spoke to his great affection for his Mexican War comrades. Reversing the tradition that called for official visitors to file in front of the president, Grant personally walked the line of his fellow veterans, introducing himself and shaking each man's hand. He then accompanied them to the Masonic Temple, where they continued the festivities. In high spirits the veterans adjourned with a well-defined political strategy and an eagerness to meet again the next year.[15]

Nine days after the convention two Mexican War veterans presented the pension legislation to both houses of Congress. Congressman Negley tendered the bill to the House of Representatives, while John A. Logan, a Republican from Illinois, delivered it to his colleagues in the Senate. Although the congressmen showed an early interest in the Mexican Pension Bill, they eventually focused on its fiscal feasibility. Critics of the bill initially stressed the fact that Congress had previously awarded bounty land warrants of up to 160 acres to the returning veterans as a reward for their service. One "high standing" senator allegedly told the veterans that they had "received a land warrant . . . and that is enough!" When the Bureau of Pensions submitted a report that thirty-nine thousand of the original fifty-eight thousand veterans were still living, congressional support evaporated.[16]

Perhaps expecting the bill to pass without delay, delegates to the national association had failed to develop an effective means of fundraising to sustain their petition. This omission might have doomed the legislation had not Kenaday devoted himself full time to the work. In 1875 the group assessed fees to each state delegation to offset the cost of lobbying. Still, Kenaday had to front much of the money, hoping that the group would eventually reimburse him. One year later only six states and territories had fulfilled their financial obligations, and internal bickering over money prompted the New York delegation to threaten to withdraw from the national association. Kenaday and Denver were able, however, to ease the anger and keep the organization together.[17]

As their legislation met resistance in Congress, members of the national association turned their attention to other goals. In addition to supporting a pension, the mission statement of the organization included the charge to "rescue from oblivion the memory of their comrades who died and were buried on the battle-fields of Mexico . . . and proper care bestowed on their resting place." As the years passed, most Americans forgot about their war dead buried across the Rio Grande. Even family members resigned themselves to never seeing the places where their loved ones fell.[18]

In 1875 a former army surgeon named A. G. Carothers visited the old army cemetery near Monterrey, Mexico, to pay his respects to his fallen comrades. At a place the Americans called Walnut Spring, burial parties had gathered many of the remains of soldiers killed in the siege. They painstakingly marked each grave with a headstone, but they failed to purchase the land from its Mexican owner. After the occupation force left, the owner had parceled out the cemetery stones to building projects and plowed the field for cultivation. Carothers was horrified to find the burial ground obscured by a cornfield.[19]

The desecration moved Carothers to action. He approached representatives of the Mexican government in Saltillo about securing title to the field and proposed that they allow him to place a monument over the burial ground. An unnamed Mexican official encouraged his plan as long as the monument did not "offend the sentiments of the Mexican people by reference to their discomfiture in the battle." Upon returning to the United States, Carothers petitioned Secretary Belknap to purchase the cornfield and erect a suitable monument, but, again demonstrating the little interest he had in the Mexican War veterans, Belknap took no action, and the cemetery remained unmarked. Belknap forwarded the petition to the national association with the recommendation that it ask Congress to build instead a U.S.–Mexican War memorial in Washington, D.C.[20]

President Denver understood that the relative dearth of Mexican War monuments had troubled many veterans, who jealously watched as the nation lavished honors on the returning soldiers of 1865. Accordingly, another goal of the national association had been to rectify this imbalance. Denver proposed that the organization support "the erection of a suitable monument at the Capital of the United States, dedicated to the achievement of American arms in Mexico." Unfortunately, finding congressional support for the project proved even more difficult than passing the Mexican Pension Bill, and, in spite of the national association's lobbying for a federal memorial it never materialized.[21]

The closest the federal government came to honoring the veterans' service was through the commissioning of a statue of General Scott to be placed in Washington. The equestrian bronze, marked only with his surname, was dedicated in 1874 as one of a series of monuments paying tribute to the commanders of the nation's conflicts from the Revolution through the Civil War. No mention was made of the general's service in Mexico, however, and, given Scott's fifty-three-year military career, the casual observer might assume the statue commemorated his role as commanding general at the beginning of the Civil War. This is not surprising in light of the overall lack of memorials recalling American imperialism and Manifest Destiny in the capital. The historian Kirk Savage found that, with the exception of a relief sculpture of a mournful Native American family on the U.S. Capitol Building, there are no tributes to the nation's conquest of indigenous people, Mexicans, or Spaniards. Americans prefer to celebrate less controversial events in the seat of their democracy.[22]

Other officers who earned distinctions beyond the U.S.–Mexican War were also honored with memorials during this era. Monuments to Nathaniel

Lyon in St. Louis and in Eastford, Connecticut, for example, evoked not only his heroism in Mexico, but also his unfortunate distinction of being the first Union general killed during the Civil War. In 1883 the State of Kentucky erected a fifty-foot obelisk to General Taylor near his tomb in Louisville. While the memorial's lateral inscriptions named the many battles in which Taylor fought, the face recalled his more important role as president of the United States. Indiana and Ohio included modest mention of their soldiers in Mexico on larger monuments dedicated to the Civil War. In these examples the U.S.–Mexican War was merely a component of one's greater service to the nation.

During this time California and the Utah Territory took steps toward erecting war memorials exclusively commemorating the U.S.–Mexican War, but these, as we shall see, would not be completed until the twentieth century. Pennsylvania, on the other hand, was successful in dedicating a monument to its Mexican War dead on the grounds of the capitol in Harrisburg in 1868. The seventy-five-foot marble sculpture would be the largest monument to exclusively honor the conflict until the twentieth century. Its completion after the Civil War, however, owed more to its legislative commission and funding in 1858 than to any postbellum commemorative impulse.[23]

Finding itself at an impasse in creating a federal monument, the National Association of Veterans of the Mexican War helped honor former soldiers on a more personal level by awarding medals. In 1875 Kenaday proposed casting bronze medals from cannons captured in Mexico and asked Congress to furnish him with the guns. Once again lawmakers blocked Kenaday's plans. Always sympathetic toward his Mexican War comrades, Grant bypassed Congress and ordered the secretary of war to give the veterans four cannons (see fig. 8). Beyond symbolizing bravery, the medals had a very practical purpose for members of the national association. Beginning in 1876 several railroads offered members of the organization free passage to their annual reunions. Apparently men posing as veterans took advantage of the policy, and the problem increased as pretenders grew hopeful that they might be able to secure pensions. Aware of the imposters, Kenaday carefully monitored the distribution of the medals, which bestowed a literal stamp of legitimacy upon the wearer. In terms of sectionalism, the medal symbolically united veterans regardless of their Civil War service. Although issued by a private organization, the national association badge was the only decoration available to all participants in the conflict.[24]

Putting aside the distraction of the war memorial and the medals, Kenaday focused most of his energy on the Mexican Pension Bill. Committing himself to work "with vigor in sunshine and storm," Kenaday tirelessly hunted down veterans around the country, added them to the rolls of the national association, and solicited their financial support. Locally, veterans worked with their states to pass resolutions encouraging senators and representatives to approve the pending legislation. As the fight for the service pension continued into the 1880s more state legislatures submitted petitions to Congress urging its passage.[25]

The protracted congressional debate allowed both allies and enemies of the Mexican Pension Bill to manipulate memory to conform to their respective agendas. Throughout the 1870s and 1880s two vastly conflicting images of the veterans evolved in Congress. The bill's opponents portrayed them as vigorous, wealthy southerners who deserted their former flag to secede from the Union. Supporters, on the other hand, portrayed the old soldiers as ailing, impoverished patriots who hailed from all parts of the nation. Caught in the middle, the veterans were unwilling to remain passive pawns. Through their comrades and allies in Congress veterans' organizations took an active role in crafting a group memory to support their quest for a pension.[26]

Prior to the Civil War written accounts of American soldiers in Mexico stressed their battlefield bravery and exploits. As the pension issue moved to the forefront of the veterans' agenda they focused increasingly on the financial windfall the war had brought the nation. Within weeks of introducing the Mexican Pension Bill congressional supporters submitted a report to their colleagues that asked:

> For what consideration would the General Government part with this 937,785 square miles, with its two millions of people and untold resources, and commanding position in the continent, holding in its arms the great gateway to the great empires of the East? No money consideration could buy it at all; its value is beyond price; we could not do without it; we can see in it a bright and glorious future of a dense population, containing all the true characteristics of wealth, refinement and a high order of civilization. No war with a foreign country has produced such results in so short a time, and no troops acquitted themselves with more honor and made greater sacrifices during that period of their services.

The immense wealth of the Mexican Cession of 1848 remained an integral part of the pension debate in Congress.[27]

Speeches extolling the riches won through the Treaty of Guadalupe Hidalgo became popular at reunions. In an oration he gave before the Louisiana Associated Veterans of the Mexican War in 1876, the former president of the Confederate States of America Jefferson Davis declared that the results of the conflict included "the acquisition by purchase of that great land of California, a land of promise and of golden fulfillment. Not only has the gold of California been poured into your treasury as a material result of this war, but exploration and development of the whole territory lying between the Mississippi Valley and the Pacific Coast is a consequence of that acquisition. It has thus made us one of the greatest contributors in the world in adding to its specie." Davis further decried the nation's lack of appreciation for the veterans and claimed "there was a time when to be a soldier in the war with Mexico was a passport throughout the length and breadth of the land. Why is it then that these veterans are without the poor reward of a pension?"[28]

In March 1878 Denver and Kenaday used this same argument when they submitted a petition to Congress supporting the Mexican Pension Bill. In the document, they rhetorically asked, "What did we gain by the war?" They then cited numerous statistics regarding territory, population, and mineral wealth of the Mexican cession. Finally they placed a numerical value on the territory at $1.5 billion. The men argued that the United States could afford modest pensions for the warriors who secured such a fortune for the nation.[29]

Supporters of the bill had to convince Congress that the report of the Bureau of Pensions from 1874 stating that there were thirty-nine thousand survivors was a gross overestimation. After three years of collecting its own data the national association countered with statistics claiming that there were only nine thousand living veterans. The organization further used language that stressed the advanced age of the survivors. In a report submitted to Congress the association declared that a Mexican War pension would be a short-lived burden, as it would be paid only to elderly veterans "during the brief remainder of their natural lives." A favorable response from the Committee on Invalid Pensions echoed this sentiment by maintaining that "there are eight or ten thousand old soldiers, far advanced beyond the meridian of life, now in penury and want."[30]

Llewellyn Powers, a Republican representative from Maine, expressed the feelings of many congressional opponents of the Mexican Pension Bill. He scoffed at the notion that the veterans were a handful of dying paupers and asserted that the pension was too expensive to implement so close to the end of the war when survivors were yet in "the prime of life." He recommended that a pension would be more appropriately granted in 1905, when the men would truly be old. This prompted John Luttrell, a Democrat from California, to ask if they should "wait until all of these survivors die before we make any provision for them?" The absurdity of the charge elicited laughter from the legislators.[31]

Pension data collected after 1887 suggests that both sides exaggerated the statistics during the debate. The actual number of veterans alive at this time was most likely midway between the extreme estimates. In 1887–1902 the Bureau of Pensions awarded 20,533 pensions to Mexican War veterans. As for the ages of the former soldiers, when the legislation was introduced in 1874 the youngest veterans would have been in their early forties, with a projected average life expectancy in their midsixties. More senior soldiers would have been considerably older and, had they reached their sixties by 1875, could expect to live another decade. These facts had little bearing on congressional polemics, however, and both sides stood fast to their disparate statistics.[32]

The veterans themselves helped foster the image of their advancing age. At the Convention of the National Association of Veterans of the Mexican War in 1883 the delegates discussed where to convene their next meeting. Most of the previous reunions had taken place in Washington. One delegate worried that by holding the meetings in the nation's capital "congressmen only see here the youngest and most vigorous of the veterans, which was calculated to prejudice the object we have in view." Another seconded the observation, exclaiming that "intelligent representatives in Congress would be influenced against the cause of the veterans, by the appearance of the men." After giving the idea of holding the convention elsewhere some consideration Kenaday opted to keep the organization meeting in Washington.[33]

The controversy over the venue for the convention revealed one of the national association's greatest challenges, namely, that healthy middle-aged and elderly men with the leisure and means to travel hardly inspired the sympathy of Congress. The veterans therefore had to control their image by shifting the public focus to their declining fortunes and old age. One way they accomplished this was by combining their bill with pension legislation for veterans of the Seminole and Black Hawk Wars of the 1830s. By associating with soldiers of the previous generation the Mexican War veterans claimed that they too were in decline and in need. Linking themselves to a more distant past also helped them escape the perception that they had widely supported the Confederacy during the Civil War.[34]

Sectional and partisan differences nevertheless moved to the forefront of the debate. Northern Republicans projected that two-thirds of the pension recipients would be southerners, and they found the prospect of former Confederates drawing annuities from the U.S. government to be particularly galling. Opponents of the legislation thus repeatedly accused the veterans of the Mexican conflict of disloyalty during the Civil War.[35]

The Republican representative Charles Joyce, a Union veteran from Vermont, was typical of opponents when he charged, "It is proposed by this bill, to pension all these men who fought to destroy it [the Union] whether invalids or not . . . granting privileges to the Confederate which we deny to and withhold from the Union soldier." He further exclaimed that pensioning Mexican War veterans "is only the entering wedge to pry open the vaults of the Treasury for the payment of all sorts of southern claims." He compared the disloyal veterans to Benedict Arnold and asked if Congress should have given the Revolutionary War traitor a pension as well. The partisanship exasperated the Democrat John Goode, a former Confederate colonel from Virginia, who stood and asked, "Will this cruel war never be over?"[36]

Particularly troubling to Republican critics of the legislation was that Jefferson Davis might be eligible for a service pension. While several high-profile Union and Confederate officers and officials had fought with distinction in Mexico, there was no greater surviving hero than Davis. During the second day at Buena Vista, Davis and his 1st Mississippi Rifle Regiment repelled a Mexican lancer charge that shifted the momentum of the battle. Davis suffered a serious wound in the fight and returned home one of the nation's most celebrated warriors. Antebellum accounts of the battle liberally praised the "gallant Colonel Davis" for his clever strategizing and bravery under fire.[37]

After his imprisonment for treason in 1865 Davis disappeared from many of the written accounts of the battle. In 1866 Jacob K. Neff wrote his expansive military history *The Army and Navy of America,* in which, although he dedicated four pages to the Battle of Buena Vista, he only briefly mentioned the 1st Mississippi Rifle Regiment and ignored their commander altogether. Horatio O. Ladd's *Fighting in Mexico* detailed the Battle of Buena Vista in fourteen pages but covered the action of the Mississippi volunteers in two sentences that made no mention of Davis. In 1882 John J. Grindall wrote an epic poem entitled "The Battle of Buena Vista" in which Davis merited only passing mention while the exploits of lesser officers were generously celebrated.[38]

Popular authors may have neglected Davis's war record, but Republican opponents of the Mexican Pension Bill flaunted it on the floors of Congress. When Davis heard that his name had been invoked to deny his Mexican War comrades their pensions, he sent a petition to his representative in Congress, the Democrat Otho Robards Singleton. Singleton read Davis's letter to the House of Representatives: "I am quite unwilling that personal objections to me by members of Congress should defeat the proposed measure to grant pensions to the veterans of the war against Mexico." Davis then renounced his claim to the payments, noting that he was formerly eligible for a disability pension after the war but had refused it because of his comfortable income. While Congress largely dropped Davis from the conversation about the bill, the perception of the disloyal Mexican War veteran remained.[39]

One member of Congress was in a strong position to combat this seditious image. Sen. James Shields of Missouri had served as a general in the U.S.–Mexican War and was wounded at the battles of Cerro Gordo and Chapultepec. Contrary to the Republican stereotype of Mexican War veterans who joined the Confederacy, Shields remained steadfast to the Union and served as a general during the Civil War. Although a Democrat, Shields maintained an impeccable record as a loyal soldier and civil servant of the United States.[40]

On February 20, 1879, General Shields stood before the Senate and discussed the men he had commanded in two wars. He reminded his colleagues that "the soldiers of the last war have been treated by Congress with justice, and, in my opinion, with very commendable liberality. The soldiers of the Mexican War have not been so treated. Those soldiers served their country, and have received nothing in the way of generosity at the hands of the Congress of the United States. I wonder not at seeing the services of young soldiers handsomely rewarded; but the wonder is at seeing the services of old soldiers almost forgotten." Shields then reproved the report of the Bureau of Pensions, stating that its inflated statistics represented "a larger army of Mexican veterans alive today, than ever stood on Mexican soil with arms in their hands." Playing to the aged image of the veterans, the sixty-eight-year-old legislator recited the names of the senior officers who had fought in the war and reminded the Senate that he alone remained alive.[41]

Shields praised his old comrades, boasting that "no government ever sent an army into a foreign country better, braver, nobler than the army America sent to Mexico." In addition to describing the tremendous wealth these warriors brought the nation, he characterized the "simple, honest, brave, manly, generous, and humane" soldiers as having uncommon integrity. In an obvious exaggeration, he declared, "I do not think in all America you will find one of them in the penitentiary. They would die before they would commit a crime. Some of them may die in the poor house, but you may take my word for it no soldier of this nation who fought in the battles of Mexico will ever die the inmate of an American penitentiary." He further stated that "no army ever invaded a foreign country that committed so few offenses as the army that operated in Mexico."[42]

Although American writers in the antebellum period were mixed in their praise of Mexican soldiers, Shields heaped liberal honors upon his former foes: "Some men will say: 'You had only Mexicans to fight?' Yes, very true, we had only Mexicans to fight, and we had plenty of them to fight. But ask the soldiers of France, and they are as brave soldiers as can be found in Europe; ask them their experience of these despised Mexicans, and they will tell you frankly that in all Europe there is no peasantry that are less afraid of death than these very Mexicans." Mexico's victory over the French in 1867 had continued to boost the prestige of the Mexican fighting man in North American eyes. This shifting attitude was also visible in the popular writings of the time, as authors found it difficult to disparage the troops that had defeated the army of Napoleon III. Mexican War veterans found that this trend bolstered their claims of military prowess and exceptionalism while highlighting the tragedy of their victimization.[43]

Shields concluded his remarks with an appeal meant to reinforce the idea that these men were venerable patriarchs nearing death's door. "The remnant of that army," he declaimed in turgid prose, "the army which did so much for this country, speak as it were through me today, hold up their hands in supplication to this body and this Congress and say, 'Give us a little of that we helped to secure for our country; give us a small pittance before we leave the world; give us a pittance to help us on the downward path of life in our old age; give us something to assist us in our last days when we are marching to that field from which no warrior has ever yet returned victorious, and never will.' " The senator skillfully painted a graphic portrait of the honorable veteran suffering in obscurity while the nation enjoyed the fruits of his sacrifice. He appealed to the lawmakers' sense of justice by portraying the veterans as unfortunate victims of age and circumstance. The message was clear: dishonor would never dim the glory of these deserving men; only the inaction of an ungrateful nation could accomplish that.[44]

Shields's speech had its desired effect on Congress, and the bill at long last garnered enough support for a majority vote. Facing defeat, however, the Republican leadership rallied and called a caucus. After a fierce inner-party debate, enough Republican supporters withdrew their votes, once again killing the bill for that legislative session.[45]

Kenaday was furious with the Republicans and vowed to continue the fight. Turning to his training as a newspaper publisher, he founded *The Vedette,* the official organ of the National Association of Veterans of the Mexican War. The first issue had an estimated readership of ten thousand and began with a poem that set the tone for the newspaper:

> Come then, brave "Veterans" of 'Forty-six,
> Shoulder your arms, and fight your battles o'er,
> In the fresh combat now your colors fix,
> Above stale politicians' empty roar,
> Ne'er to descend until your nation's hand,
> Shall own and recompense your noble band!

Kenaday's message was unmistakable: the veterans deserved compensation for their service regardless of how the "stale" Republicans voted.[46]

Kenaday recognized that sectional rivalries had doomed the Mexican Pension Bill to failure, and his first order of business was to heal any lingering divisions within his own ranks. The premiere issue of *The Vedette* contained a poem entitled "The Blue and the Gray," by F. M. Finch, which compared the grave of a Union soldier with that of a Confederate soldier and stressed the equality of both men in death. The last stanza read,

> No more shall the war cry sever,
> Or the winding rivers be red;
> They banish our anger forever,
> When they laurel the graves of our dead!
> Under the sod and the dew,
> Waiting for the judgment-day –
> Love and tears for the Blue;
> Tears and love for the Gray![47]

As the former soldiers sought to overcome sectionalism in order to benefit their plans, they additionally argued that granting a pension "would bring about a reconciliation between the two sections of our country more happily than any other act upon the part of the Government."[48]

In addressing the Second Annual Reunion of the National Association of Veterans of the Mexican War, Col. W. L. Tidball focused on the contributions of his comrades in the Civil War: "The survivors of the Mexican War on both sides of the Mason-Dixon's Line . . . were the first to rush into the conflict and the last to lay down their arms; and it is estimated, by the help of what are supposed to be well authenticated facts, that the loss by death among them, in both the contending armies, was very much greater in proportion to the number engaged than of any other class of contestants." His assertion was meant to imply that Congress had incorrect statistics on the number of surviving pension candidates, but in addition it addressed the veterans' desire to be recognized as legitimate war heroes in the North as well as the South.[49]

The national association's appeal to sectional unity was in keeping with a grass-roots trend toward reconciliation among Civil War veterans. Beginning in the 1880s Civil War reunions often included the former soldiers of both armies. According to the historian David W. Blight, these so-called Blue–Gray reunions "buttressed the nonideological memory of the war." For white Americans this reconciliation came at the expense of African Americans, who suffered under the growing burden of Jim Crow in the 1880s. Regardless of how they felt about evolving race relations, veterans of the U.S.–Mexican War mainly promoted the nonideological memory of the Civil War in the seventies and eighties to achieve congressional support of the pension bill.[50]

Belying his rhetoric of reconciliation, Kenaday turned *The Vedette* into a weapon to attack the Republican Party. During the presidential election of 1880 the newspaper supported the Democrat Winfield Scott Hancock in what turned out to be his losing campaign against the Republican James

Garfield. In 1884 Kenaday alleged that the Republican candidate, James G. Blaine, "evinced considerable antipathy to the Mexican veterans" and attacked his candidacy. In addition to his political campaigning, the old journalist was known for printing cruel personal invectives against anyone he perceived as hostile to his cause. Not all former soldiers agreed with Kenaday's politics, and he made enemies among some northern veterans. Still, he enjoyed the continued support of the national association.[51]

Throughout the early 1880s the Senate debate over the Mexican Pension Bill remained highly partisan as Republican-led majorities continued to reject the legislation whenever it came up for a vote. During this period the measure had no greater foe in Congress than Sen. George Frisbee Hoar, a Republican from Massachusetts and a strong-willed legislator who served in Congress for thirty-five years. Like many of his Republican colleagues he suspected the legislation to be a Confederate plot and rejected outright the idea that the majority of veterans were elderly paupers needing help from Congress.[52]

When Sen. Daniel Voorhees, a Democrat from Indiana, made the oft-repeated appeal to his colleagues that these veterans with "grey locks on their honored heads" desired a mere "pittance" to sustain them in their poverty, Hoar went on the offensive. He countered that his neighbor in Massachusetts, a forty-eight-year-old veteran of the Mexican War, was "a giant in strength, of vigorous health, with I have no doubt a stronger constitution and greater prospect of life and health in the future than any member of this body. He was a man in affluent circumstances. . . . He joined with me in emphatic disapprobation of the careless and reckless legislation which would put a man like him on the pension roll of the government." Hoar then described a Civil War veteran whose height had diminished to four feet because of the deprivations of his service and suggested that pensions were better suited for Union soldiers. Weeks later he accused the Democrats of trying to put wealthy veterans on the pension rolls.[53]

Hoar's allegations infuriated the Democrats and especially inflamed the indignation of John Stuart Williams of Kentucky. Williams had served as a colonel in the U.S.–Mexican War, where his heroism fighting along the National Road earned him the nickname "Cerro Gordo Williams." His former glory held little sway with the Republicans, who recalled more acutely his service as a Confederate general. Nonetheless, Williams took the lead in attacking the senator from Massachusetts.[54]

Williams began his comments by sadly noting that Mexican War veterans had been eclipsed by those of the Civil War. He then went on to declare that the average age of survivors was sixty-five and claimed that "after sixty-five years, there cannot be much marrow left in an old soldier's bones." He alleged that Hoar had exaggerated the youthfulness of his neighbor who had fought in the war. He exclaimed, "I do not know how it is in warlike Massachusetts, but down in Kentucky we keep our small boys at home to wait on their mothers and send grown men only to the wars." He scoffed at the notion of wealthy survivors, stating that "a few of the veterans are independent of the nation's bounty, but the great majority of them are extremely poor men."[55]

Echoing Senator Shields's speech, Williams reminded his fellow lawmakers that Taylor and Scott "contested every inch of ground with a race inured to hardships and familiar with war, commanded by Santa Anna, the most famous captain of the age, who was sustained by subalterns educated in the highest schools of modern military science." In a bit of embellishment, now common to the debate, he declared,

> This war was not more marked for the splendor of its achievement than for the humanity of its conduct. War and not barbarianism bore our victorious banner through Mexico. We made war upon the organized forces of the enemy and not upon the people and property of the country. Private property and church property were everywhere respected by our victorious soldiers. Our camps were safe and attractive markets to the people for all they had to sell. Nothing was taken without a full equivalent being paid for it. I doubt if any friendly army ever marched through its own country with so little damage to the people as ours did through Mexico.

According to Williams, only eight thousand veterans were still alive. The passage of the Mexican Pension Bill was merely a "long-delayed justice" to keep these extraordinary men from the poorhouse "now that they are old and infirm."[56]

How old and infirm the veterans actually were remained a much-debated and difficult to answer question. As much as Williams berated Senator Hoar and the people of Massachusetts for sending boys to war, he often stressed his own youth at the time of his enlistment. After a heated debate in 1882 Williams stood and declared that "all those soldiers are sixty years of age and older. I am over that myself, and I was one of the youngest boys who went to war." In reality Williams was nearly twenty-eight at the outbreak of hostilities, and men much younger than he filled the ranks of American forces and the surviving veterans. Still, to prove his point that all veterans were in their sixties, Williams was fond of discussing his "boyhood" in Mexico.[57]

Once young and brave in their nation's service, the veterans now claimed they were in poor health and circumstances. Veterans' advocates inferred cause and effect—the war in Mexico had taken its toll on these men and made the circumstances of a nation's ingratitude and unfortunate conditions of their old age more difficult to bear. Sen. John Tyler Morgan, a Democrat from Alabama, declared, "They had hard service in every particular, hard marches, and a hard climate. They were young and unseasoned, and it is no wonder that so few of them came back or that those who did come back have become prematurely old." As victims, the veterans were worthy of public support. The pension was not charity but a means to compensate the old men fairly for their sacrifices.[58]

During the early 1880s Republican opponents of the legislation changed their strategy by claiming that Civil War veterans were more worthy of service pensions than Mexican War veterans. Senator Hoar expressed the Republican position best when he stated, "If you open this door to the soldier of the Mexican War you cannot shut it in the face of the soldiers of the war for the Union." Adding an estimated one million Civil War veterans to the pension rolls was a fiscal impossibility, however, and Democrats recognized that this was a tactic to undermine all pension legislation. Nonetheless, the issue touched off a partisan debate about which group of soldiers had contributed most to the United States.[59]

After hearing yet again of the singular exploits of the Mexican veterans, Sen. Charles Van Wyck, a Republican from Nebraska and former Union general, became defensive. Praising his own soldiers, he argued, "They added not one more stripe nor one more star to the flag, but they rescued the whole flag from the destruction by which it was imperiled. The soldier of the Mexican War added a part; the Union soldier gathered in and saved the whole." Such rhetoric did little more than fuel persistent sectionalism and stall the legislation in endless debate.[60]

Ironically, it was the Civil War veterans who eventually turned the political tide in the favor of the Mexican Pension Bill. In 1883 individual posts of the Grand Army of the Republic (GAR)—the Union veterans' organization—began to support the cause of their Mexican War comrades. While several state legislatures had sent petitions to their congressmen asking for their support of the bill, it took the endorsement of the Civil War veterans to break down resistance. From the perspective of the members of the GAR, the passage of the measure would firmly establish a precedent that would benefit them in their eventual quest for a pension. The Forty-Seventh and Forty-Eighth Congresses witnessed an outpouring of support for Civil War veterans, prompting one representative to declare, "There have been more petitions for the passage of this bill" than any other legislation he had seen.[61]

By the mid-1880s the preponderance of public support made the passage of the Mexican Pension Bill a foregone conclusion. All that was left was for lawmakers to reach consensus on the final form of the legislation—a process that would continue through additional congressional sessions. Not all Republicans accepted their inevitable loss with graciousness. Rep. Thomas

Browne, from Indiana, a former Union general, lashed out angrily at the Democrats: "It is because you cannot get your rebel soldiery on any other pension roll. That is the reason of it, and you know it and I know it." Sen. John Ingalls of Kansas complained in words that would be echoed in Grant's *Personal Memoirs:* "I think that a more indefensible war of spoliation and robbery and conquest was never waged by a great people against a defenseless and powerless neighbor. It was a party war waged by one of the political organizations of this country in defense of and for the purpose of extending the limits and aggrandizing the system of human slavery."[62]

By the end, however, such outbursts were rare. The Mexican Pension Bill seemed to be less an issue of division than a step toward healing the nation's Civil War wounds. In one of the last debates over the legislation, the Democratic representative Frank Lane Wolford, a Mexican War veteran and Union colonel, asked his comrades to lay down their sectional animosities forever: "These old men, for most of them are now old, served their country in a foreign land. They endured hardships and privations. They endured them as one people, coming from the North and the South, from the East and the West, with one object in their hearts—to obey their country's call, to vindicate their country's honor, and protect the rights of their fellow citizens. . . . I wish to ask my Union friends, why should you, after a cooling time of more than twenty years, still show your hatred toward your Southern brother?" Wolford's request addressed a growing trend toward national reconciliation. The partisan fight over the memory of Mexican War veterans had finally ceased.[63]

With victory in their grasp, many veterans nonetheless felt betrayed by Congress. A large reunion of Mexican War soldiers at Monterey, California, during the summer of 1886 gave some indication as to their temperament. While Californians celebrated the fortieth anniversary of the occupation of their state by the United States, Edwin A. Sherman, the president of the Associated Veterans of the Mexican War, publicly attacked congressional treatment of the old warriors. He lamented that "their services are forgotten, and ingrate demagogues in power regret that we still live." He then singled out the "degenerate son of Massachusetts" Senator Hoar as the target of his scorn. After recounting the recent death of one of his comrades in a San Francisco almshouse, he declared that Hoar intended "to strike down every tottering war-worn veteran of the Mexican War in his old age, and consign him to a pauper's refuge in a pauper's grave." He concluded with an appeal to memory, stating that "when a nation commences to forget its heroes its decay has already begun."[64]

In spite of lingering resentments, the legislation moved through Congress. In 1887, after twenty-one years of fighting for his fellow veterans,

Kenaday witnessed the passage of the service pension. The Democratic president Grover Cleveland, whose candidacy *The Vedette* had supported, signed the Mexican War Survivors Act, formally making the pension bill a law. For Kenaday the triumph was bittersweet. The new law excluded younger men from receiving benefits but allowed former soldiers over the age of sixty-two, surviving widows, and disabled veterans of any age to receive a monthly allotment of eight dollars. Kenaday immediately began filing applications for potential pensioners. Within months of the passage of the law, he had filed some twenty-five hundred applications at a fee of ten dollars each. At the height of disbursements in 1890 the federal government made over seventeen thousand monthly pension payments to Mexican War veterans.[65]

After the passage of the Mexican War Survivors Act, the National Association of Veterans of the Mexican War continued as a social organization, but the ranks of the group thinned as old soldiers died. By the early twentieth century the association began to hold joint reunions with the GAR, which ultimately had helped them receive their pensions. After years of activism, the elderly veterans were happy to set politicking aside and spend their final years visiting with old comrades and rehashing exciting tales of their youths.[66]

While the national association spent decades fighting for the economic benefit of its members, the Aztec Club of 1847, an exclusive organization of General Scott's original officers in Mexico City, remained aloof from the wrangling in Washington. Its members had little need for pensions themselves and chose to eschew politics in favor of annual social gatherings. Its original constitution and bylaws called only for the members to promote "harmony and comfort" during their occupation of Mexico City. As the group reorganized in the United States after the Civil War, it maintained its social character.[67]

In 1867 the members of the club reunited at the Astor House in New York City, their first meeting in twelve years. There is little sense of sectional conflict in the few records available from that reunion. The men busied themselves with the mundane tasks of electing officers, planning their next reunion, and commissioning a membership medal. A roll call of the original 160 members revealed that 65 had died since the war with Mexico. In spite of its dwindling numbers, the Aztec Club of 1847 continued to hold annual banquets and reunions. To boost membership in 1871, the club's leaders eased former restrictions and allowed all officers who had served in the war to join their ranks. Still, the club did not grow significantly, and the leadership began to entertain other ways to keep the group alive. In 1874 the organization dined at the White House with fellow member President Grant. During that meeting the club considered ways in which to perpetuate its existence beyond its aging ranks. The solution was to add a resolution to the bylaws stating, "On the death of a member, his eldest son, or, in the case he has no son, some person of his own blood nominated by him, shall become a member in his place." In 1875 the first group of eleven descendants was welcomed, and the Aztec Club of 1847 officially became a hereditary society. Eight years later the club extended membership to the nearest blood relatives of officers killed in the war.[68]

The Aztec Club of 1847 and the National Association of Veterans of the Mexican War were not the only organizations representing former soldiers. Such groups as the Michigan State Association of Mexican Veterans, Associated Veterans of the Mexican War, Association of the Soldiers of the Mexican War of the State of Texas, Virginia Association of Mexican Veterans, and the Eureka Association of Mexican War Veterans appeared around the country. After the national association organized in 1874, however, it absorbed many of these smaller independent groups. Very little information exists about the form and function of these scattered organizations. Certainly their political activities were limited, as none of the groups had the numbers to wield anything but local influence.[69]

Toward the end of the century two additional veterans' groups organized in Texas. Contemporary newspaper accounts gave some clue as to why they formed so many years after the conflict. In 1892 the United American Veterans enrolled both Mexican War and Civil War veterans to "cherish and maintain the institutions of American freedom, and to foster true patriotism and love of country that the union cemented by the blood of their fallen comrades may endure forever." Three years later William C. Howell organized the Association of Veterans of the War with Mexico, claiming that "Every southern and northern Mexican War veteran can afford to feel proud and jubilant when he reflects that such heroes as Generals R. E. Lee, Stonewall Jackson, Joe Johnston, Beauregard, Albert S. Johnston, Jeff Davis and many others of less prominence on the Confederate side, and Grant, Sherman and others on the Union side, were soldiers in the Mexican War."[70]

These Civil War references document changing agendas among the late nineteenth-century veterans' organizations. Like earlier groups, both associations pledged to aid their impoverished comrades. Still, with pensions no longer an issue, they focused primarily on promoting patriotism and national reconciliation. Sectional unity had proven an important goal for the national association because it supported its political strategy prior to 1887. The persistence of this objective beyond the passage of the Mexican Pension Bill suggests that reunification had evolved into a larger social issue. The role played by the memory of the U.S.–Mexican War would likewise evolve at the turn of the twentieth century, addressing and satisfying diverse needs in American society.

In April 1893 a frail Kenaday decided it was time to close the doors of *The Vedette*. In his final editorial the old soldier wrote that he had "labored like a Trojan to place the veterans of Mexico on an equality with the soldiers of the late war at least from a *financial* point of view." Even though the nation by now had largely forgotten the contributions of the Mexican War veterans, the aged warriors at least earned an equitable pension. Emboldened by his legislative victory Kenaday had continued to fight for additional benefits. In January 1893 Congress passed a law increasing the Mexican War pension to twelve dollars a month for disabled and impoverished veterans. Shortly thereafter Kenaday contracted pneumonia and nearly died. Decades of political activism on behalf of his comrades had depleted him, and he finally lay down for some much-needed rest.[71]

Once the pension fight was over, public awareness of the veterans declined dramatically. In 1892 Cadmus M. Wilcox documented the waning interest in his *History of the Mexican War*. In the opening paragraph Wilcox lamented that "nearly half a century has elapsed since the war between the United States and Mexico. Other and more absorbing intervening events have almost obliterated it from attention; most of the participants in it have gone from our midst; the names and memories of many of them have been forgotten; no record of their gallant deeds made; no memorial kept of services which, though heroic and patriotic, were poorly rewarded and never fully acknowledged." Wilcox's assessment of public memory at the end of the century reflected the struggles of American veterans of the U.S.–Mexican War throughout this era. Although the National Association of Veterans of the Mexican War achieved a pension, it failed in its goals of publishing a history of the war, erecting a national monument, and securing additional battlefield cemeteries for American casualties. As a new century dawned, the veterans began fading into the night. It would be left to future generations to discover new meanings in the memory of these rapidly aging men.[72]

4 Creating Heroes

MEXICO, 1867–1920

❖

ON AN AUGUST evening in 1871 nine men gathered at the famous Concordia restaurant in Mexico City. As officers in Mexico's army, some of these gentlemen had helped free their nation from French occupation in 1867. More important, these veteran soldiers were distinguished alumni of the Military College and, twenty-four years earlier, had defended their school at Chapultepec Castle against a North American assault. Defying an evacuation order, approximately fifty cadets fought a desperate battle on the heights above the Mexican capital that left a handful of their comrades dead. Now some of the survivors proposed they form the Asociación del Colegio Militar to reunite fellow students who had served during the war with the United States. Like North American veterans, they pledged to support charitable activities and also committed to organizing a commemoration of their doomed defense at the Battles of Molino del Rey and Chapultepec. Finally, they drafted a petition to President Benito Juárez asking him to make the anniversaries of the two battles national holidays.[1]

Early attempts to remember Mexico's loss in the War of North American Intervention had intermittent support from the government and an ambiguous reception from the public. Continued political instability during the 1850s, coupled with a humiliating French occupation the following decade, forced the war further into the recesses of Mexico's collective memory. In 1867, however, Mexican republicans overthrew Emperor Maximilian and drove his French regime from the country. A new wave of nationalism swept the country as citizens once again enjoyed a period of reform and progress. Mexicans were ready to revisit their war with the United States and find new meaning and symbolism in their heroic defeat. After considering the association's proposal to declare the two patriotic holidays, President Juárez compromised and made September 13, the anniversary of the Battle of Chapultepec, an official day of mourning in the republic. While not creating a second holiday to commemorate the Battle of Molino del Rey, Juárez nonetheless promised to support personally any ceremony the association would hold on that date.[2]

The five decades following the French Intervention witnessed a profound change in how Mexicans remembered their war with the United States. After years of suppression and neglect, veterans revived the memory of the conflict by staging commemorations honoring battle anniversaries. Politicians took note of the renewed public interest in the war and adopted these military ceremonies to promote the civic virtues of obedience and self-sacrifice. They also blended the religious and secular fervor of the people to create civic rites which challenged the power of the Catholic Church. During the years between 1867 and 1920 Mexico's rulers enlisted memory in the service of building their modern nation-state.[3]

In spite of Mexico's profound anguish over losing the war, memory found some early expressions. Immediately after the North American occupation of Mexico City in 1847 local authorities declared August 20 a day of remembrance for the Battle of Churubusco. The annual tribute to the fallen members of the National Guard at the convent was so threatening to Antonio López de Santa Anna that he outlawed it upon his return to power in 1853. Mexicans revived the tradition in 1856, although its status during the French Intervention remains unclear. With the restoration of the republic in 1867 Mexicans were again eager to remember the martyrs of the battle. While the early commemorations of Churubusco had been a battleground between radical and moderate factions in the postwar government, subsequent celebrations promoted a nonideological nationalism built on love of country and obedience to authority.[4]

The ceremonies at Churubusco also reflected the growing secularization of Mexican society. Before being utilized by the military as a fortress, Churubusco had been a colonial-era convent. The annual commemorations, however, transformed the religious complex into a civic shrine where the martyrs of the war replaced the revered saints of the church. When the government secularized many Roman Catholic holdings during the reform movement of the 1850s and 1860s, land speculators made two attempts to confiscate properties belonging to the convent. In both cases Presidents Juárez and Sebastián Lerdo de Tejada exempted the building in order to preserve this important relic of Mexican history. Churubusco thus superseded the spiritual world and become a monument of civic devotion. The appropriation of ritual authority challenged the power of the Catholic clergy and helped Mexico's rulers build a secular state in which they, not the church, controlled the nation's destiny.[5]

In 1871 the Mexican politician Genaro Raygosa addressed this transformation at the twenty-fourth anniversary of the battle. He praised the dead of Churubusco, claiming, "The grateful nation annually commemorates their memory, giving them homage, veneration, and respect. Their illustrious names, indelibly engraved on the hearts of all Mexicans, memorializing for posterity this humble monument, lifted up to the people before the theater of their glory." As a theater of civic glory, Churubusco had evolved beyond a Catholic convent, becoming a secular sacred place that emphasized the virtues of self-sacrifice and love of country.[6]

Commenting on the anniversary of the Battle of Churubusco in 1874, the newspaper editor Hilarión Frías y Soto reminded his readers of the value of such civic rituals while attacking the influence of the Catholic Church in Mexico. He declared, "This memory is a harsh lesson that history has given us. It teaches us that a generation educated in fanaticism gives us men without love of country and women who crown the mutinous clergy with roses while they look disdainfully upon the martyrs of our nation. Let us avail ourselves of this bloody lesson and educate citizens on how to die for liberty and the fatherland." Frías y Soto believed that clerics had elevated their interests above those of the nation. Mexico's secular martyrs could, however, supplant those of the church and help Mexico to cast off the influence of the clergy. Indeed, their "bloody lesson" of self-sacrifice was a model for the modern citizen.[7]

Mexico's liberal reformers hoped to appropriate the sacred symbols of the church, including its martyrs and shrines. The Churubusco anniversary celebrations literally secularized the convent and reinvented it as a space of patriotic pilgrimage. The creation of civic shrines to commemorate a glorious defeat is not unique to Mexico. In the United States, the Alamo, popularly known as the Shrine of Texas Liberty, is perhaps the most famous religious building converted into secular holy ground, and to this day it maintains a quasi-religious atmosphere. On entering the renovated chapel, men are required to doff their hats in reverence not to a deity but to the slain Texan revolutionaries. In 1896 former Confederates turned the so-called White House of the Confederacy in Richmond, Virginia, into a place of pilgrimage for veterans of the Lost Cause. The dedicatory prayer of the renovated building specifically set it apart as a Confederate shrine. Like other civic shrines commemorating defeat, Churubusco restored dignity to the vanquished and promised that subsequent generations would honor and defend their legacy.[8]

The symbolic power of Churubusco became apparent after an ailing Santa Anna returned from exile in 1874. Given his controversial reputation and past suppression of the commemoration, Mexican authorities understandably refused to invite him to participate in the ceremonies of August 20. Aware that his exclusion from Churubusco challenged his reputation and memory, the old dictator wrote angry letters to newspapers in the capital protesting the slight.[9]

Public ceremonies have long been important components of memory making in Mexico, as elsewhere. As the nation's rulers sought to extend their hegemony over social, religious, and political institutions, they often appropriated previous rituals, including celebrations and commemorations from the nation's indigenous and colonial past. Porfirio Díaz realized the power of memory in establishing his authority after he seized power in the Revolution of Tuxtepec in 1876. During his years of rule, called the Porfiriato, Díaz began a program of erecting patriotic memorials in the capital that nurtured nationalistic myths stressing obedience and sacrifice. He also adopted existing military commemorations of the War of North American Intervention and transformed the conflict into a potent symbol of Mexican nationalism. His support of such rituals allowed him to solidify alliances with the officer corps of the Mexican army. Díaz also understood the value of allying himself with the nation's veterans, whose organizations owed their existence to his generous political and financial sponsorship. The old soldiers returned the favor by explicitly supporting his military programs and promoting allegiance to the government. Díaz, more than any other Mexican leader, wielded the memory of the war as a powerful state-building weapon.[10]

As Díaz put his plans for building a modern Mexico into action, he needed a strong, centralized military to sustain him. The persistence of National Guard units throughout the nation was a threat to his plans. These irregular troops played a critical role in defeating the French, but their steady growth and erratic loyalties concerned the Mexican president. In his quest for power Díaz had to rein in these local militias while boosting the reputation and power of the standing army. As his first step, Díaz demobilized the National Guard units and forced their officers into retirement. Next, he moved to overhaul the Military College, whose students lacked the respect and prestige necessary to fulfill his military agenda.[11]

In order to elevate the status of the cadets, Díaz tapped into an existing interest in the students who died defending the Military College in 1847. As early as 1867 *El Correo de México*, a newspaper in Mexico City, published a poem written by José Tomás de Cuéllar, a former cadet of the Military College, imploring the nation to remember the student soldiers who had fought against the United States. Three years later, another newspaper, *El Siglo XIX*, petitioned the government to hold a commemoration at Chapultepec Castle similar to the one held annually at Churubusco. In 1871 the periodical *La Revista Universal* added its endorsement to the idea.[12]

Inspired by this growing interest in the Battle of Chapultepec, the former cadets met in Mexico City to organize the Association of the Military College. The veterans additionally planned to hold an annual celebration in the forest and park surrounding the castle on the eighth of September. The event would be staged adjacent to a pre-Columbian monument to Moctezuma I and his brother Tlacaélel. In the mid-1400s the Aztec emperor commissioned the relief sculpture at the base of Chapultepec "in perpetual memory, as reward for our work, so that, on seeing the faces, our sons and grandsons may remember our deeds and strive to imitate them." Centuries later, the former cadets clearly hoped for the same remembrance.[13]

The association held its first public meeting late in 1871. Beneath the monumental cypress trees of the ancient Chapultepec forest, the former cadets claimed to have "made the American Army bite the dust" at nearby Molino del Rey. More important, they honored comrades who had fallen defending the Military College. President Juárez, his cabinet, and various military dignitaries attended as guests of honor. Unlike the commemorations of 1848, those of 1871 honored both the Mexican army and the National Guard units that fought to defend the capital. The tacit approval of the president lent credibility to the group and their activities.[14]

As word spread to other survivors of the Military College, more former cadets joined the association. After Juárez's death, his successor, Lerdo de Tejada, kept up the tradition of presidential attendance at the commemoration, and within a few years the association had become a vibrant and much-celebrated organization in Mexico. As young men and boys they had offered their lives in the defense of their fatherland, and now, as adults, they returned to serve the nation as examples of public virtue. Their annual memorials became civic pageants that hailed Mexican strength, unity, and devotion to country.[15]

After his rise to power Díaz, understanding that the association could help him boost the reputation of the Military College, soon became the group's staunchest supporter. Unlike North American veterans, who consistently battled with Congress, Mexican veterans counted their supreme leader as their greatest patron. President Díaz proudly participated in the annual commemorations at Chapultepec Park. Even when he temporarily stepped down from power between 1880 and 1884 he remained a fixture of association events.[16]

In 1881 the group unveiled a large marble cenotaph known as the *Obelisco a los Niños Héroes y al Honor Militar* (Obelisk to the Boy Heroes and to Military Honor). Ramón Rodríguez Arangoity, one of the cadets captured during the Battle of Chapultepec, designed the monument, which bore the names of the six cadets reportedly killed in the battle as well as those of the forty who survived (see fig. 9). With much pomp and ceremony Díaz personally dedicated the obelisk before a large audience of military and political dignitaries. The monument, situated at the base of Chapultepec Castle, became the meeting place of the annual reunion of the association from that time forward. When he returned to power, Díaz made the castle his presidential palace. The Chapultepec commemorations, now held quite literally at Díaz's feet, reflected their glory on the Mexican president.[17]

Many observers questioned why the association chose September 8 to recognize an event that had actually occurred on September 13. The group claimed at its first commemoration that it celebrated Mexico's near victory at the Battle of Molino del Rey. The Mexican historian Enrique Plasencia de la Parra has suggested that the practice was tied to the Catholic feast day of Our Lady of Covadonga. The Battle of Covadonga in 722 marked Spain's first victory over the Moors and initiated the centuries-long Reconquista of the Iberian Peninsula. Further analysis of that date supports Plasencia de la Parra's claim. Under the Díaz regime, September 8 through September 16 became a patriotic festival that began with the service at Chapultepec Park and ended with celebrations of the War of Independence. After the ceremony at Chapultepec, Díaz spent the evening officiating at the quasi-religious Feast of Our Lady of Covadonga. Díaz was not openly hostile toward the Catholic Church, but his practice of conflating the sacred and the civic to support his power was a hallmark of his rule. His supplanting of ecclesiastical authority kept Mexico on the path of secularization and sustained Díaz's state-building programs.[18]

One of the association's most sacred charges was to preserve the history of its comrades who died at Chapultepec. While the tale of the Boy Heroes would be enshrined in Mexico's public memory during the twentieth century, it took decades for the story to develop a cohesive narrative. The Military College was housed in Chapultepec Castle and had endured a two-day artillery barrage and infantry assault that left the building in shambles. In the chaos following the defeat, authorities were unsure who exactly had died in the siege. A handful of records indicated that on the morning of September 13, 1847, approximately fifty cadets had refused an order to retreat, choosing instead to defend their school. A small number of cadets died during the battle, while approximately forty were wounded or captured. Various documents listed the names of the young soldiers, but apparently these contradicted each other in some details. Authorities furthermore struggled to determine which of the young men were actually enrolled at the college on the day of the battle. The ambiguity of the historical record allowed Mexicans to ascribe their own details and meanings to the tragic

deaths of the cadets. Accordingly, the list of students who died or were captured continued to evolve throughout the 1850s.[19]

The Association of the Military College and its subsequent memorials at
Chapultepec put pressure on Mexican authorities to authenticate the list of
martyred students. At the first commemoration, officials named five cadets:
Juan Escutia, Francisco Márquez, Agustín Melgar, Fernando Montes de
Oca, and Vicente Suárez. Juan de la Barrera, a recently graduated lieutenant
of the army engineers, was later added to the list. Inconsistencies and discrepancies plagued the written record, but members of the association did
their best to piece together a unified account. As a result, much of the early
mythologizing of the cadets occurred during their patriotic celebrations.[20]

At the commemoration at Chapultepec in 1878, for example, a member
of the association declared that Melgar took the Mexican flag that flew over
the castle and wrapped it around his body to keep it from being captured.
This tale closely resembled a well-documented event that occurred earlier
during the battle when Lt. Col. Felipe Santiago Xicoténcatl, though mortally wounded, wrapped his unit's flag around his body to keep it from falling into the hands of the enemy. Apparently the orator attributed Xicoténcatl's story to the youthful Melgar to accentuate the bravery of the cadet.[21]

In 1890 Emilio de Castillo Negrete's four-volume history of the war revised the Melgar flag story. In the prologue, written by Francisco Javier Gaxiola, an unnamed cadet made the ultimate act of sacrifice to keep the Mexican
colors from falling into North American hands. According to Gaxiola, "The
old god of war, Huitzilopochtli, inspired our youth to valor. One of them
wrapped the tricolored flag around himself and, pierced by enemy bullets,
hurled himself from a peak." Two years later the newspaper *El Nacional*
printed a poem in which an unnamed cadet jumped to his death rather than
surrender, wrapped figuratively "in the honor of his flag." A government report of 1894 identified the self-sacrificing cadet not as Melgar but Escutia.
According to the new account Escutia snatched the national colors from the
tower before North American troops could capture the coveted trophy and
then leaped out a window to his death. Three days later his body was recovered at the base of the hill along with the tattered remains of the flag.[22]

What objectives might this story have served? Was it possible for Escutia
to have made his celebrated leap from the heights of Chapultepec? North
American battle accounts, supported by contemporary artwork, portrayed
the Mexican flag flying over the main entrance, the castle tower, or both
during the assault. U.S. troops paid particular attention to this flag because
it played an important role in the fate of the traitorous Saint Patrick's Battalion, whose members were executed as it was lowered. For Escutia to have

rescued the flag from the entrance and jumped over the precipice, he would have had to enter and exit two buildings, scale numerous stairs, run over one hundred meters across the complex, and then, in spite of his serious wounds, vault several meters over the eastern wall. Accounts of him leaping from the castle tower are impossible, as the structure stands approximately forty meters from the cliff. The fact that there are no contemporary military documents mentioning this feat adds to its implausibility.[23]

If Escutia's suicide was indeed a myth, what purpose did the story serve? Both North American and Mexican accounts documented instances of Mexican soldiers jumping to their deaths during the closing moments of the Battle of Chapultepec. A Mexican publication from 1848 considered the troops' suicides to be embarrassing, cowardly deeds. The Escutia story restored honor to these soldiers by turning their acts of desperation into feats of bravery and patriotism. No longer a symbol of a shameful defeat, Escutia's suicide evolved into a selfless act of sacrifice for the fatherland. It also served Díaz's state building by lionizing those citizens willing to die for their country. Juan Escutia therefore became the ultimate example of duty and love of country to future generations of Mexicans.[24]

Escutia's alleged jump was not the only controversy surrounding the Boy Heroes. In spite of being referred to as children, genealogical records show their ages to be quite varied: Escutia was twenty; Márquez, thirteen; Melgar and Montes de Oca, eighteen; Suárez, fourteen; and Barrera, nineteen. What was gained by converting the four young adults into children? During a speech at the commemoration of 1874, for example, Frías y Soto pitted a small student against a monstrous North American soldier: "The boy with smiling lips, of frame not yet developed, with fair hair just caressed by the trembling hand of his mother, crossing swords with the brutal and gigantic soldier of the north, stuffed with meat and wine, drunk with the vapors of the blood of combat." Like authors in the United States who evoked the brutish Mexican as a foil for their valiant Anglo-Saxon warriors, Frias y Soto contrasted the cruel Yankee with the innocent young hero. He further discussed the martyrdom of these boys in distinctly religious terms, noting that "each drop of blood spilled on the ground where we stand was enough to redeem the Republic."[25]

At the commemoration the next year Gustavo Baz read a poem that referred to the cadets as "boys who had not tasted the first kiss of love." Four days later the poet Guillermo Prieto published a short story in the newspaper *La Revista Universal* which stressed the diminutive nature of the cadets as they faced the charging North Americans, referring to them collectively as "those snot-nosed kids." Individually he created childlike nicknames for them, including "pug-nose," "grasshopper," and "the elf." By portraying the

Boy Heroes as innocent and small in stature, these orators could inspire much greater sympathy for them than if they had been portrayed as adults. Further imbued with virginal purity, the boys became a worthy sacrifice upon the altar of the fatherland.[26]

Under President Díaz the Mexican military was well versed in the legend of the Boy Heroes. The story helped boost the reputation of the Military College at a time when the president sought to raise the prestige of the institution. Mexico's growing thirst for information about the young men encouraged the mythologizing of the cadets. Even before Escutia's legend had emerged, the other heroes of Chapultepec began to acquire their own dramatic death stories.

At the memorial of 1884, for example, the former cadet José Tomás de Cuéllar claimed to have known personally the six Boy Heroes. Nearly forty years after the invasion by North Americans he recalled details about each of his old friends and comrades, declaring, for example, that Suárez, "with his little musket in his hand," had knocked back the first U.S. soldier who scaled the castle walls. Cuéllar then turned to the current students of the Military College assembled around him and challenged them to follow the example of his fallen comrades. He implored the young men to develop morals and discipline so that they could prevent Mexico from ever falling to a foreign foe again.[27]

The commemoration of 1906 was particularly significant because it was the last time a surviving cadet spoke publicly about the battle. Ignacio Molino, one of the original founders of the Association of the Military College, stood before a large crowd that included President Díaz. Nearly eighty years old, he apologized for his inability to remember some details, although many of the events of that dramatic day apparently remained etched in his memory. Molino spoke at length about each of the six martyred cadets. The North Americans shot Montes de Oca as he tried to escape through a window of a building. Troops entering the dormitory bayoneted Melgar, who died from his agonizing wounds the next day. The diminutive Suárez also died at the point of a Yankee bayonet while trying to keep the invaders from scaling the castle wall. De la Barrera died at his post in the castle commanding a unit of combat engineers. Molino was ambiguous about the fates of Márquez and Escutia, stating that he was told that their bodies were found on the east side of the hill. Five months after his address Molino joined his beloved comrades in death.[28]

Later critics pointed out that the dying veteran may have embellished his story to compensate for a failing memory. They also suggested that younger members of the association pressured the old man to recount details of the story which he could not have possibly known. Regardless, the association clearly felt an urgency to secure a public declaration of the story while there was still a survivor left to tell the tale.[29]

With the emergence of the Boy Heroes, Mexico had found one of its most potent national symbols. The story of innocent children bravely sacrificing their lives to defend their fatherland had a Homeric quality that continues to resonate in the hearts of the Mexican people. The renowned poet José Juan Tablada was a young cadet at the Military College in the 1880s. As an elderly man he reminisced about the impact the Boy Heroes had on his youth: "The paintings of the heroic cadets had the effect of exhorting me with their peaceful but energetically spiritual gazes to fulfill my duty until sacrificed, according to their noble example. . . . In the midst of the frivolity of adolescence I had the fortune to feel deeply and completely that principle of radiating glory and purity of selflessness that haloed the sacrificed cadets. . . . I felt proud to be what they were, a cadet of the Military College, guest of that same Acropolis that they sanctified with their blood." Díaz quickly recognized the power of the story and used it to his advantage. The doomed cadets of Chapultepec came to exemplify obedience, nationalism, and militarism at a time when he was solidifying his power. The military cult that evolved from the heroic myth corresponded with Díaz's ambitions to centralize the army and restore the prestige of the Military College. The memory of the Boy Heroes gave Mexicans a sense of national pride, but it also supported Díaz's autocratic regime. While the myth and meaning of the cadets evolved over time, they continued to serve the needs of Mexico's rulers.[30]

Commemorating the Boy Heroes also gave North Americans who were living in Mexico an opportunity to improve relations with their new neighbors. In the spring of 1897 Powell Clayton, the U.S. minister to Mexico, asked his host government for permission to pay tribute to fallen Mexican soldiers on Memorial Day. After receiving the blessing of President Díaz, Clayton, along with members of the American legation and the Grand Army of the Republic, traveled to the obelisk honoring the Boy Heroes in Chapultepec Park to lay floral tributes at Mexico's most important memorial to the War of North American Intervention. Representatives of the Mexican army and Military College then reciprocated with their own wreath-laying ceremony at the Mexico City National Cemetery. Such acts of transnational goodwill became the hallmark of future commemorations.[31]

Why would North Americans, who would prove reluctant to celebrate the fiftieth anniversary of the conflict in their own country, be willing to make such a gesture in Mexico? In the midst of the War of Independence in Cuba, the proliferation of yellow journalism, and a growing belligerence toward Spain, the State Department was very interested in keeping President Díaz neutral should war break out in the Caribbean. Minister Clayton's primary goal was to forge strong relations with Mexico even as those with Spain deteriorated. Standing among the graves of the invaders of 1847, Clayton expressed his hope that "what had been done in honor of the dead would bind more closely the ties of friendship between the two countries." Indeed, during the Spanish–American War, Díaz remained largely cooperative with the United States. After the conflict both Mexico and the United States upgraded their legations to embassies, marking an important evolution in relations between the two nations. Yankee flowers laid at the obelisk to the Boy Heroes soothed old wounds and solidified political ties between the United States and President Díaz and his officer corps.[32]

The Association of the Military College was the most visible of the Mexican veterans' groups, but it was not the only one. In that its membership was limited to former cadets, the association was an elite organization, one that excluded the majority of former soldiers. During the 1880s, however, a retired artillery colonel, C. Manuel Mangino, proposed forming a veterans' association uniting soldiers who had fought in the Texas campaigns and the War of North American Intervention. In 1886 Col. Vicente E. Manero and Col. Francisco Vargas joined with Mangino to form the Asociación de Defensores de la República Mexicana de 1836 a 1848 (Association of the Defenders of the Mexican Republic from 1836 to 1848). The primary purpose of his group was to "honor the nation," and the secondary goal was to provide "an example of patriotism to the children of today and the future." Both of these ambitions supported the building of the Mexican state. To demonstrate its support for the regime, the association made Díaz its honorary president. Díaz, in turn, not only gave the group his blessing and the financial backing of the federal government, but also proposed granting land for the veterans to construct a building in the capital.[33]

The association initially gathered at the National College of Mines in Mexico City. At the group's first meeting Gen. C. José Velázquez de la Cadena declared that its mission was to "imbue the hearts of their children and fellow citizens with love of the fatherland so they will defend it from their enemies, and will never allow the country to be broken up under any pretext." In spite of their love of country, the veterans had been powerless to stop its dismemberment. Their failure was therefore a warning to future generations to remain vigilant against foreign threats or invasion.[34]

Perhaps most important, the veterans embraced Díaz's political agenda. Velázquez de la Cadena's speech challenged the former soldiers to unify behind the regime so they could find "true peace and forever see a prosperous and happy nation." He then recounted Díaz's service in the war with the United States. In a largely symbolic gesture, the general offered the services of the graying men in the defense of Mexico. He asserted that they "could still feel in their hearts the warlike fervor to take up arms in defense of their fatherland and to fight and bleed their last drop of blood; and if they die in the fight, it will be glory enough for them to say with their last breath, 'Viva México! Long live her independence!" After the general's remarks, 328 veterans stepped forward and signed the group's charter. Díaz embraced his influential army of supporters.[35]

During his postwar travels, Ulysses S. Grant witnessed one of the commemorations at Chapultepec Park. He admired the devotion of his former enemies, stating that "the Mexicans have shown a patriotism which it would be well if we would imitate in part, but with more regard to truth. They celebrate the anniversaries of Chapultepec and Molino del Rey as of very great victories." Perhaps oblivious to the manipulation of memory in his own country, Grant marveled at how Mexico had turned its losses into triumphs. As a member of the Aztec Club of 1847 and the National Association of Veterans of the Mexican War, Grant should have recognized the value of historical pageantry in supporting the contemporary needs of a people. Díaz's unfailing support of such spectacles attests to the idea that the Mexican president suffered no such confusion.[36]

Mexico's memory of the War of North American Intervention did more than just support the Díaz regime at the end of the century. In the wake of the country's economic growth and entrance into the world market, memory helped ease anxieties about U.S. domination of the continent. During the last quarter of the nineteenth century economic cooperation between the former enemies increased. With Díaz's support, U.S. dollars poured into Mexican railroads and industry. In spite of the stability created by international commerce, many Mexicans feared that the North American trade and capital investments might lead to a "peaceful conquest" of their country. The belligerent and defiant rhetoric of veterans' groups and memorials constituted a safe outlet for popular anxiety without interfering with Díaz's economic agenda.[37]

Other forms of memory also found expression during the latter part of the nineteenth century. Books about the War of North American Intervention again became popular during the 1870s. Ironically, the most famous author to take advantage of the freedoms instituted after the French Intervention was the octogenarian Santa Anna. From his home in the Bahamas the exiled dictator wrote his final memoir in 1874. In a life filled with fortune and poverty, adoration and loathing, the past president of Mexico sought to turn one final reversal in his favor. Having outlived most of his political enemies, he believed he might yet shape the Mexican people's memory of his controversial life. In his opening statement he grieved, "Happy, a thousand times happy, is he who lives his life unknown and dies tranquilly in his peaceful bed! How I have envied this unknown man throughout my life and how I envy him at this moment!" Given Santa Anna's personality, his desire to be forgotten appears disingenuous. Perhaps more accurately, he did not want to be remembered as the leader who allowed the northern half of his nation to fall into the hands of the United States.[38]

To achieve his goal Santa Anna predictably filled his autobiography with fanciful revisions, angry accusations, and excuses for his losses. The final pages of the memoir addressed his hope that he might someday achieve the respect he missed in life: "The future will provide us with Mexican historians who will clear up many deeds and place the truth in its correct light. . . . Being constantly reproached by treacherous slanders from my insatiable enemies, I resolved to write and publish the true history of my public life. . . . I am confident that I will be worthy of my country's gratitude, and I have even greater confidence that posterity will do me full justice." In spite of Santa Anna's desire that his last words reach a broader audience, the manuscript languished in obscurity until published in a limited Spanish edition in 1906.[39]

Other authors found a more immediate audience. Writings about the War of North American Intervention blossomed during the Porfiriato. Important works of his era included José María Roa Bárcena's *Memories of the North American Invasion, 1846–1848* (1883), Manuel Balbontín's *The American Invasion, 1846 to 1848* (1883), Eduardo Paz's *The North American Invasion in 1846* (1889), Emilio de Castillo Negrete's four-volume *Invasion of the North Americans in Mexico* (1890), and Rafael Echenique's *Alphabetical and Chronological Catalogue of the Feats of Arms that Have Taken Place in the Mexican Republic from Independence to the Present Time* (1894). These works frequently pandered to political and military authority. Balbontín, for example, obsequiously dedicated his work "to the Gentleman, Major General, Sir Porfirio Díaz." Likewise, Echenique's history proudly displayed Díaz's personal endorsement in its opening pages. Paz dedicated his book to the Association of the Military College and "to the undying memory of the students who died for the nation."[40]

These books supported Díaz's state building by using the memory of Mexico's defeat to stir patriotism in the younger generation. Balbontín spoke directly to the boys of the nation, declaring, "It behooves the youth who will pursue a glorious career in the armed forces to make a careful study of the mistakes committed in this unfortunate war in order to learn how to avoid their repetition. . . . We should benefit from the experiences that those sad days of the American invasion have given us, in order to prepare ourselves to live vigilant and ready, so we may rebuff those who intend to violate our national territory in the future." Roa Bárcena hoped his work would "be of benefit to the Mexico of today" and cautioned readers that their decision to remember or forget the war would profoundly impact the country's future.[41]

One continuing theme in this nationalistic literature was culpability for the war. With the exception of Santa Anna's unpublished manuscript, the era of military officers laying blame and seeking vindication had largely ended. Instead, most authors focused on the conflict of nations, with the responsibility for the war falling squarely on the United States. Still, the pervasive blaming of the United States did not preclude Mexican authors from exploring the larger domestic issues that led to defeat. Writers decried the corruption and self-interest that had weakened the government and left the nation open to invasion. They charged that dishonest and incompetent bureaucrats sought personal wealth by aiding the invaders while valiant soldiers "who are poorly paid and far from home, suffered in silence." Other authors asserted, in words that echoed the attitude of many antebellum North American writers, that Mexico's "lack of industry" and "death of the spirit of progress" had doomed the nation.[42]

Such charges were not, however, aimed at the current president. Criticism of the past instead supported Díaz's policy of democratizing the officer corps and modernizing the nation's industry. Now that Mexico's army enjoyed the technological advantages of the modern world, the disasters of 1846–47 could be avoided. Mexican writers argued that their loss was owing in part to inferior training and technology, not inferior soldiers. In this context Díaz's plans to overhaul the country inspired confidence in a renewed Mexico that could withstand any future threats to its sovereignty. Díaz had lifted the nation up from its fallen state. By assuring Mexicans that the past would not repeat itself, he inspired the loyalty and fidelity of the people.

Mexican literature of this era placed more emphasis on those who died in the war than on those who survived. Domingo Ibarra's *Memorial in Remembrance of the Mexicans that Died in the War against the North Americans in the Years of 1836 to 1848* is typical in listing the high-ranking officers killed in each battle rather than commemorating living heroes. Ibarra described the deceased as "illustrious valiants" who in death were capable of passing "the sacred flame of love of country to their children." Such cults of the martyred war dead are characteristic of the memory of defeat. As the victors, North Americans could honor both the living and the dead as heroes. Mexico's veterans, although respected, held less status than their martyred comrades. A veteran's survival became tacit evidence of his failure to halt the North American invasion, but the slain were beyond reproach, as they had sacrificed everything for the fatherland.[43]

As in the United States, the number of surviving veterans dropped dramatically in the 1900s. Yet their deaths did nothing to dim the pageantry of the commemorations. This was especially true as Mexico approached the chaos of the Revolution. The year 1910 was a critical juncture in Mexican history, as it marked both the one hundredth anniversary of the nation's War of Independence and rising threats to the Díaz regime. As the aging dictator clung to the last vestiges of power, he chose to shore up his authority with a yearlong centennial celebration focused on the greatness of the Mexican nation.[44]

Throughout the month of September, Díaz hosted an international pageant. His goal, in the words of one contemporary observer, was to demonstrate that Mexico had become "a progressive and advancing nation, entitled to the respect and admiration of the sister nations of the world." The president ordered schools closed for the month so that the nation's young people could witness and learn from the patriotic spectacle. Public buildings and train depots were decorated in the colors of the national flag, red, white, and green, and electric lights in the national colors illuminated the city's formerly darkened streets. Daily parades and concerts kept the plazas and squares resonating with martial music and displays. Thousands of visitors from around Mexico and the world poured into the capital to witness the nation's triumphant entry into the modern era.[45]

Understanding the power of memory, Díaz balanced his forward-thinking exposition with a generous nod to the past. He also continued to blur the line between the sacred and the civic. For example, he brought to the capital the font where Miguel Hidalgo y Costilla, the father of Mexican Independence, was baptized. The relic was paraded in a solemn procession escorted by young women dressed in white. The float on which the font rested, however, was festooned not with religious icons but with the secular symbols of a liberty cap and a rising sun. Twenty thousand children marched solemnly behind it.[46]

To honor the anniversary the secretary of war published a commemorative book entitled *The Military College: To the Eternal Memory of Your Heroes*. The work included numerous tributes written by citizens of Mexico about the Boy Heroes. A woman named Concepción Echeverría wrote a quasi-religious essay entitled "My Violets for the Cadets of Chapultepec" in which she rhetorically asked her readers if the cadets were martyrs. "No," she answered, "martyrs kneel down to receive death, they fought to the death and were victorious over it." She preferred to call them angels. Echeverría summed up her tribute with a benediction: "Blessed are the heroic boys! Example of the Mexican Army that knows to fight to the death rather than surrender to the invader." The cadets now existed in a middle ground between the spiritual and the secular in Mexico's public memory.[47]

On September 8 Díaz and his cabinet attended the commemoration at Chapultepec. The president, dressed in his medal-bedecked major general's uniform, extolled the bravery of the Boy Heroes. The wise statesman fully understood the educational value of the cadets and addressed some of his remarks to Mexico's children. He described the secular martyrs as "shining examples for emulation by the youth of the country" and laid a floral tribute at the obelisk. Perhaps for the first time, an official representative of the United States, Gen. Harrison Gray Otis, attended. The general, a member of the diplomatic delegation, spoke briefly: "Although I am an American, I am a soldier before all else, and thus I pay homage to the brave boys of Chapultepec." He then added his nation's wreath to the others surrounding the monument.[48]

In spite of such overt displays of pageantry, power, and authority, many Mexicans had grown tired of the Porfiriato. Within two months of the patriotic September exposition, popular uprisings spread across the nation in response to Díaz's imprisonment of one of his political opponents, Francisco I. Madero. From his jail cell Madero rallied citizens to revolt, thereby instigating the Mexican Revolution and hurling the nation into a decade of violence. In the spring of 1911 Díaz fled Mexico for exile in France. The turmoil notwithstanding, the commemorations at Churubusco and Chapultepec continued. Their survival during the Revolution testified to their importance to memory and state building in Mexico.[49]

The first revolutionary era memorial at Chapultepec Park took place on September 8, 1911. Francisco León de la Barra, the interim president, officiated, as Díaz had the year before. Although a personal honor guard protected the new president, the ceremony had a less militaristic tone than that of the previous year. Unlike many of the presidents before him, León de la Barra was not a war veteran and did not wear a uniform. In addition to the usual contingent of cadets, army units, and civic leaders, his commemoration included the more benign participation of local public school children who performed musical numbers and recited tributes. Gen. Samuel García Cuéllar gave a speech reflective of the time. Addressing his changed loyalties, he stated that the army "must always be on the side of the law, it is not important who represents this law, nor who is its agent." The occasion also allowed for the symbolic alliance between the president and the military when officials awarded León de la Barra a diploma declaring him "Honorary President of the Military College."[50]

When the commemoration of 1912 arrived, Madero was the self-appointed president of Mexico. The season marked a brief respite in the internal fighting that had wracked the country, although Madero was not without concerns. Alarmed by violence along the border, the U.S. president, William Howard Taft, threatened Mexico's revolutionary government. During the celebration, Mexican newspapers warned of another North American intervention. Disregarding the international tensions, Madero and his vice president, José María Pino Suárez, attended. The ceremonies included the usual speeches and tributes, but, judging by the newspapers, no hostile rhetoric toward the United States. Whatever the symbolic value of the event, the conciliatory Madero was not interested in provoking an international incident with his neighbor.[51]

The annual memorial at nearby Churubusco also continued into the twentieth century, but it did so with declining support of the presidents. Díaz made his last known appearance at the battle anniversary in 1899. In 1900 the army stopped sponsoring the event, and the responsibility for staging the commemoration passed to a private organization known as the Group of Patriotic Gratitude. The anniversary still had official sanction, although it appeared to fall from Díaz's itinerary. This change most likely reflected Churubusco's continued celebration of the heroes of Mexico's National Guard, an organization Díaz fought to dismantle. While never hostile to his authority, the services were not as valuable to the president as those at Chapultepec. Díaz's successors adopted the same attitude, and while the Churubusco memorial continues today, it does so without Mexico's president in attendance. During the ceremony of 1912 the most distinguished visitor to participate was the cousin of Hidalgo y Costilla.[52]

The Group of Patriotic Gratitude had a surprise visitor at its Churubusco commemoration of 1913. An elderly gentleman named José Reynosa stepped forward to identify himself as a survivor of the battle. The excited crowd ushered him to the stage, where he spoke a few words about the fight. Although Reynosa recalled that his brother had died at the convent that dreadful day in 1847, his memory was fading. The eighty-eight-year-old veteran wept openly as the crowd cheered him as a returning hero. Like a sacred statue in the convent, the venerable Reynosa was adorned with paper flowers and presented with a generous cash offering collected from the congregation. The physical presence of one of Churubusco's last remaining links to the past added a sense of historic authenticity to an otherwise simple ceremony.[53]

Predictably, the celebration at Chapultepec in 1913 eclipsed that of Churubusco. It also bore witness to the dangerous political climate of the time. Five months after the previous year's commemoration, Gen. José Victoriano Huerta overthrew Madero's government and executed the president and vice president. Huerta's brutality shocked the world. Woodrow Wilson, the U.S. president, considered Huerta's actions illegal and sought to thwart his growing power. In this context, the ceremony reflected Huerta's resolve to meet opposition from the United States. One of the speakers, Gen. Miguel Ruelas, predicted that Mexicans "in the future, perhaps not too far, will imitate the attitude of those heroic boys who knew how to defend the

dignity of the fatherland from the immense threat of the men of the north."
His words proved to be prophetic.[54]

On April 21, 1914, fifty-three ships of the United States Navy steamed
into the Port of Veracruz. Tensions between the United States and Mexico
had continued to escalate since the ceremony at Chapultepec in September.
The arrest of U.S. sailors in the Mexican Port of Tampico exacerbated an
already volatile situation. When word of German arms shipments destined
for Huerta's forces in Veracruz reached President Wilson, he brazenly ordered the navy to occupy the city. After an amphibious landing reminiscent
of Gen. Winfield Scott's assault sixty-seven years earlier, the bulk of Huerta's army fled the city. Expecting no large-scale resistance, Rear Adm. Frank
F. Fletcher sent in navy and U.S. Marine forces to secure the port.[55]

Whereas the Mexican army abandoned Veracruz, a group of cadets from
the Naval Military School vowed to fight to the death. Joined by armed civilians, the students kept the U.S. forces under constant fire. As the North
Americans pushed toward the Naval Military School itself, several cadets
manned machine gun and artillery emplacements and for a time successfully
repelled the invaders. Two of the young men, Virgilio Uribe and José Azueta,
fell during the action, Uribe dying at the scene while the seriously wounded
Azueta was carried to his home by fellow cadets. Admiral Fletcher heard of
the brave last stand at the Naval Military School and sent a surgeon to care
for Azueta. When the wounded cadet awoke to find a North American doc-
tor treating his wounds, he ordered the man out of his house, claiming he
would rather die than be cared for by an enemy of Mexico. The stalwart
young man succumbed to his wounds three weeks later, joining the pantheon
of Mexico's most revered heroes.[56]

The deaths of the cadets Uribe and Azueta in 1914 are evocative of the
martyrdom of the Boy Heroes in 1847. Each of these young men had stood
steadfast against the foreign invaders while the army retreated around
them and had chosen death over surrender. It is impossible to know the
influence that the War of North American Intervention had upon Uribe,
Azueta, and the other cadets of the Naval Military School. There is no
doubt, however, that the young men had learned about the valor and self-
sacrifice of their predecessors at Chapultepec. The fact that these young
men chose to defend Veracruz and the Naval Military School speaks both
to their personal courage and to the power of memory in educating and inspiring a devoted, loyal citizenry.

In 1847 Veracruz had come under intense scrutiny for its failure to withstand the United States Navy siege under General Scott. Decades after the
war Veracruzanos still felt the need to defend their honor to the rest of the
nation. In 1875 two of the city's residents wrote an impassioned editorial in

El Siglo XIX, a newspaper published in Mexico City, explaining that Veracruz surrendered only after expending all of its ammunition. While the port fell under similar humiliating circumstances in 1914, the city now had its own Boy Heroes to redeem its honor and reputation.[57]

The similarities between the two groups of Boy Heroes were not wasted on Mexico's ruling class. In 1915 the newspaper *El Mexicano* commented on the commemoration at Chapultepec that year by drawing comparisons between them: "Henceforth the names of Chapultepec and Molino del Rey cannot be pronounced without recalling the name of that historic strip of our territory called Veracruz. We cannot glorify Suárez, Melgar, Escutia, Montes de Oca, and Barrera, cadets who fell in September 1847, at Chapultepec without associating them with those of Azueta, Montes, Martinez, Uribe, and other cadets who fell at Vera Cruz in April, 1914. The events took place at different places and at different times, but were provoked by a similar attack against our sovereignty and served to demonstrate the love of country inspiring our youth." The civic myth of the Boy Heroes had taken root in the Mexican military and inspired a rising generation of patriots.[58]

Under assault from rebels within Mexico and unrelenting pressure from the United States, General Huerta's regime collapsed. After the unpopular leader fled the country, Venustiano Carranza presided over the nation. Carranza was the fifth Mexican ruler to officiate at Chapultepec in five years, underscoring the precarious nature of his position. The new president enjoyed attending such military celebrations and staged elaborate photographs of himself and his cabinet at the obelisk, but nevertheless he preferred to use the event to encourage loyalty rather than inspire hatred of the United States. The *New York Times* noted that in spite of the honors paid to Veracruz at Chapultepec, "editorials in the press do not contain bitter references to Americans or the United States." Carranza was anxious to win President Wilson's recognition of his government and could not afford to squander any goodwill.[59]

While that coveted status came four weeks later, tensions between Carranza and Wilson escalated over the next eighteen months. In response to a raid on Columbus, New Mexico, by the rebel Gen. Francisco "Pancho" Villa, Wilson sent the army on a punitive expedition against northern Mexico in March of 1916. While the goal of the maneuver was to kill Carranza's enemy, the presence of North American troops on national soil alarmed the Mexican president. One year later diplomats leaked the Zimmermann telegram to the North American press. This intercepted German communiqué offered to return much of the American Southwest to Mexico in exchange for military support should the United States and Germany go to war. Carranza smoothed over the crisis with assurances of Mexican loyalty and treated the newly appointed U.S. ambassador to a formal military ceremony in his honor.[60]

During the Mexican Revolution the future of the nation's military education system remained in doubt. Unable to insulate itself from the chaos, the Military College suffered throughout the 1910s. Carranza went so far as to close down the school after he took the capital in 1914. The Association of the Military College likewise suffered internal conflict and dissention. The organization was obliged to elect a new president annually—a charge it failed to carry out between 1914 and 1920. Shifting political and military alliances wracked the army and no doubt fractured the unity of the group. The association would reunite following the reopening of the college in 1920, although political intrigue plagued its ranks for another decade. In 1921 the federal government moved the Chapultepec commemoration to September 13, a precursor to its complete co-opting of the event from the association.[61]

Throughout Carranza's tumultuous six-year presidency, radical revolutionaries like Pancho Villa and Emiliano Zapata rebelled and threatened his power. In April 1919 assassins working on behalf of Carranza killed the defiant Zapata. Ironically, the murder of the popular leader sealed the president's fate, for one year later rebel troops ambushed and killed Carranza as he was fleeing uprisings in the capital. His death ended the military phase of the Revolution and ushered in a twenty-year period of reconstruction of a new Mexican state. This postrevolutionary environment would soon inspire further evolution of Mexico's memory of the War of North American Intervention.[62]

Between 1867 and 1920 Mexico's rulers learned to appropriate grassroots memorials of the war to support national agendas. Under the shrewd leadership of Porfirio Díaz, these modest military celebrations blossomed and ultimately supported his consolidation of power. During the chaos of the Revolution, commemorations continued as they had during the Porfiriato. Each successive leader preserved and perpetuated the rituals as his regime rose and fell. Symbols of past Mexican defiance, particularly the Boy Heroes, took on a certain immediacy that ensured their survival in Mexico's pantheon of illustrious patriots. Perhaps most important, Mexico's celebration of the War of North American Intervention demonstrated that a devastating loss has no bearing on the power of memory. In the right hands, defeat may create even more potent symbols than victory.

Lih. of P.S. Daval. Ph.ª

C. Schuessele del.ᵗ

1. Christian Schuessele's lithograph *The Occupation of the Capital of Mexico by the American Army* (1849), which appeared in John Frost's *Pictorial History of Mexico and the Mexican War.*

2. Carl Nebel's lithograph *Scott's Entrance into Mexico* (1851) in *The War between the United States and Mexico, Illustrated.*

3. Detail of James Walker's painting
The Battle of Chapultepec (1857).
Photograph courtesy of the U.S. Senate
Collection.

4. Gen. Antonio López de Santa
Anna's prosthetic leg at the Illinois
State Military Museum. Photograph
courtesy of the Illinois State Military
Museum. Department of Military
Affairs, Springfield.

5. Nathaniel Currier's *View of Chapultepec and Molino del Rey* after an original lithograph by the Mexican artist H. Mendez (ca. 1848). Print courtesy of the Library of Congress.

6. An ex-voto painting of the Mexican lancer Antonio Pliego giving thanks to the Black Christ of Esquipulas for his escape from North American troops (ca. 1847). Mexico, oil on canvas, 50 cm x 38 cm. FA.1971.71.4. International Folk Art Foundation Collection, Museum of International Folk Art. Photograph by Paul Smutko.

7. The monument next to the convent at Churubusco constructed by the Tangassi Brothers in 1856. From D. Enrique Olavarría y Ferrari's *México: A través de los siglos* (1880).

8. The membership medal of the National Association of Veterans of the Mexican War (1875). Photograph courtesy of Troy Thoreson.

9. Ramón Rodríguez Arangoity's *Obelisco a los Niños Héroes y al Honor Militar* (1881) at Chapultepec.

10. The Sloat Memorial (1910) at Monterey, California.

OBEDIENCE TO LAW IS LIBERTY

11. The Alexander Doniphan Monument (1918) at the Clay County Courthouse in Richmond, Missouri.

12. The Mormon Battalion Monument (1927) on the grounds of the Utah State Capitol in Salt Lake City. Photograph courtesy of Robert Cutts.

13. A typical cartouche arrangement of the Boy Heroes found in D. Enrique Olavarría y Ferrari's *México: A través de los siglos* (1880).

14. Juan Fernando Olaguíbel's monument to Gen. Pedro María de Anaya (1942).

15. Bronze statues of the Boy Heroes overlook Mexico City from the heights of the Museo Nacional de Historia at Chapultepec.

16. Cadets from West Point standing guard over the remains of the Boy Heroes at Mexico City in 1947.

17. The Works Progress Administration Mormon Battalion "petrachrome" mural in San Diego, California (1940). Photograph courtesy of the WPA Art Program.

18. President Harry S. Truman and Ambassador Walter C. Thurston pay tribute to the Boy Heroes at Chapultepec in 1947. Photograph courtesy of the Harry S. Truman Library and Museum.

19. The monument marking the mass grave of U.S. soldiers at the Mexico City National Cemetery.

20. West Point cadets meeting their Mexican counterparts from the Colegio Militar prior to the return of captured Mexican battle flags in 1950.

21. Sons of the Utah Pioneers march through San Bernardino, California, in honor of the Mormon Battalion in 1950. From Mary Lambert Taggart, *Modern Day Trek of the Mormon Battalion* (1955).

22. A giant relief sculpture on the Fort Moore Pioneer Monument (1950) showing the flag raising over Los Angeles in 1847. Photograph courtesy of Vsion.

23. Mexican soldiers and cadets gather at the annual commemoration of the Boy Heroes at Enrique Aragón Echegaray's monument *Altar a la Patria* (Altar to the Fatherland) (1952) at Chapultepec.

EN MEMORIA DE LOS SOLDADOS IRLANDESES
DEL HEROICO BATALLON DE SAN PATRICIO
MARTIRES QUE DIERON SU VIDA POR LA CAU-
SA DE MEXICO DURANTE LA INJUSTA INVA-
SION NORTEAMERICANA DE 1847

CAPITAN JOHN OREILY		ABRAHAM FITZPATRICK
HENRY LOGENHAMER	ANDREW NOLAN	JOHN BENEDICK
HENRY VENATOR	PATRICK DALTON	JOHN ROSE
FRANCIS RHODE	JOHN CUTTLE	LACHIAR MCLACHIEN
JOHN KIAGER	JOHN PRICE	PATRICK CASEY
ALFRED K FOGAL	WILLIAM DATHOUSE	JOHN BROOKE
GEORGE W JACKSON	WILLIAM A WALLACE	ROGER DUHAN
WILLIAM O'CONNOR	ELIZIER S LUSK	JAMES SPEERS
RICHARD HANLY	HERMAN SCHMIDT	MARTIN LYDON
JOHN APPIEBY	THOMAS RILEY	DENNIS CONAHAN
GEORGE DAIWIG	JAMES MILLS	AUGUSTE MORSRTAFT
BERNEY HART	LAWRENCE MACKEY	JAMES MCDOWELL
THOMAS MILLET	FRANCIS O CONNOR	GIBSON MODOWELL
HEZEKIAH AKLES	PETER NEIL	HOGH MCCLELLAND
JOHN BARTELY	KERR DELANEY	JOHN MCDONALD
ALEXANDER MCKEE	PATRICK ANTISON	JOHN CAVANAUGH
F W CARRETSON	HARRISON KENNY	THOMAS CASSIDY
JOHN BOWERS	ROGER HOGAN	JOHN DALY
M T FRANTIUS	JOHN SHEEHAN	MARTIN MILES
HENRY MEWER	JOHN A MYERS	PARIAN FRITZ
HENRY OCTKER	RICHARD PARKER	JAMES KELLY
HENRY WHISTIER	LEMMUEL WHEATON	JOHN MURPHY
WILLIAM H KEECK	SAMUEL H THOMAS	JOHN LITTLE
EDWARD MCHERRON	DAVID MCELROY	LEWIS PREIFER

CON LA GRATITUD DE MEXICO
A LOS 112 AÑOS DE SU SACRIFICIO
SEPTIEMBRE – DE 1959

24. Lorenzo Rafael's monument to the Batallón de San Patrício (1959) in the Plaza San Ángel in Mexico City.

25. Gabriel Flores García's ceiling mural at Chapultepec Castle, *La Gesta Heroica de 1847* (The Heroic Deed of 1847) (1967).

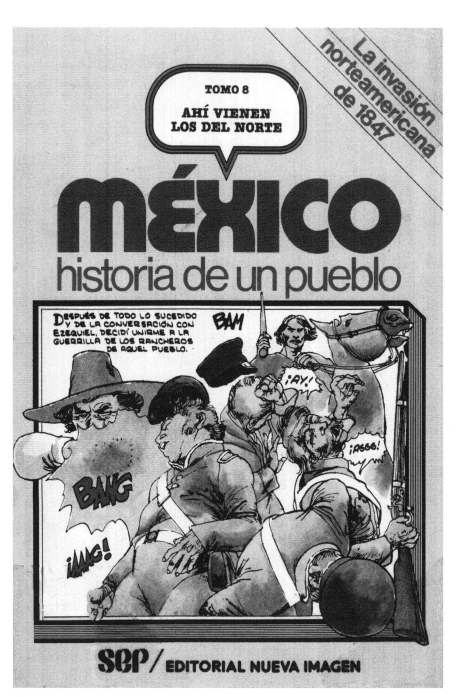

26. Mexican guerillas kill gringo soldiers. The cover of the Ministry of Public Education's scholastic comic book *Here Come the Northerners* (1980).

27. The Brown Berets peacefully occupy Santa Catalina Island during the summer of 1972. Photograph courtesy of David Sanchez.

28. A schoolboy in Mexico City dressed as a Niño Héroe at the commemoration of the 160th anniversary of the Battle of Chapultepec.

29. During the ritual reenactment of their ancestors' trek west, young Latter-day Saint women push hand-carts while their male peers march off to join the Mormon Battalion. Photograph courtesy of Brian Reyman.

30. An artillery crew conducts a living history demonstration at the Palo Alto Battlefield National Historical Park.

5   Empire and Exclusion

THE UNITED STATES, 1896–1929

✤

ON A SPRING afternoon in 1904 the eighty-four-year-old Daniel Gould Burr arrived at the city fairgrounds in Paris, Illinois. Bedecked in the regalia of a U.S.–Mexican War veteran, the frail man took a seat under some nearby trees. At an appointed hour he rose to his feet and read aloud the roster of Company H of the Fourth Regiment of Illinois Volunteers. The Fourth Illinois had fought with distinction under General Scott in Mexico, most notoriously capturing General Santa Anna's prosthetic leg at the Battle of Cerro Gordo. Sergeant Burr, however, was a by-the-book soldier who refused to commandeer even a much-needed blanket from his Mexican foes. His compulsion for abiding by the rules led him to this final duty in 1904. Members of Company H had reunited regularly, and now, nearly sixty years later, Burr was the last survivor. After completing his forlorn roll call, he ate a picnic dinner alone and spent the remainder of the day "in meditation." At nightfall friends took the solitary veteran home. That winter he joined his deceased comrades.[1]

Between 1896 and 1929 the number of Mexican War veterans declined rapidly. As their ranks thinned, interest in the conflict resurged. The Spanish–American War and the Mexican Revolution inspired a new generation of authors to reinterpret the war according to the needs of their time. The growth of the monument-building movement in the 1920s likewise drew attention to U.S.–Mexican War sites in the American Southwest. The rapidly aging veterans, however, had little to do with these new forms of memory. While the men were willing to offer an olive branch to Mexico at the end of their lives, their descendants felt no such obligation. As the last of the old warriors died, control of the memory of the U.S.–Mexican War passed largely into the hands of men and women with very diverse agendas. Devoted to the ideals of American imperialism, nativism, and white supremacy, this younger generation sought to supplant older histories to promote its social, political, and economic prominence in the region. Memory became a means of demarcation and exclusion in the United States.[2]

The year 1896 marked the semicentennial of the U.S.–Mexican War. In a nation enamored of anniversary celebrations, the reaction of Americans to this one was telling. Individual volunteer units like the Palmetto Regiment, Mormon Battalion, and Missouri Mounted Volunteers scheduled reunions to commemorate their founding, but on the national level there was little interest in remembering the conflict. Battles had been fought in New Mexico, Texas, and California, and they seemed more natural places to honor the occasion. What did take place, however, revealed much about the regional dynamics of memory.[3]

Of all the territories annexed by the United States, New Mexico had the largest population. When Stephen Watts Kearny led his army into Santa Fe in August of 1846, the Mexican province had over sixty thousand inhabitants. Kearny's taking of the region was initially bloodless. In January of 1847, however, Hispanos and Native Americans from the Taos Pueblo rose against the authority of the United States in a violent rebellion that cost the lives of hundreds of people. The revolt ended with several prominent New Mexicans being publicly executed in the Taos plaza. The fiftieth anniversary of the conquest of New Mexico and the subsequent Taos revolt drew little attention in the territory.[4]

Another motivation may explain New Mexico's reluctance to celebrate the centennial of the war. In 1896 New Mexicans of all ethnic and racial backgrounds were campaigning for statehood. An important part of that effort was changing popular perceptions that the territory was foreign and unrefined, and reminding the nation of the region's Mexican War origins hindered that goal. New Mexicans instead preferred to identify with the territory's more distant and romantic Spanish, and therefore European, past. Consequently, local newspapers neglected even to mention the anniversary of the war. In a society in which Anglos and Hispanos had learned to accommodate one another, there were no public ceremonies, speeches, or memorials drawing attention to an uncomfortable and inconvenient past.[5]

In February of 1896 a group of Texans proposed holding a semicentennial commemoration to honor the "existence of Texas and acquisition by the United States of all those sister states and territories added to the American union by the Treaty of Guadalupe Hidalgo." The celebration was billed as a commercial venture, and Texas businessmen praised the event for the money it would bring the state. Thirty-five directors incorporated the Texas Semi-Centennial Exposition with a plan to raise money through a variety of public and private sources. In spite of the enthusiastic endorsements of several groups, organizers failed to raise enough funds to make it a reality.

None of the major newspapers in Texas mentioned the anniversary of the war, although the *Dallas Morning News* did run an article noting the fiftieth anniversary of the capture of Mexico City.[6]

While New Mexicans and Texans were unable, or perhaps unwilling, to host commemorations, a number of California-based organizations, including the Society of California Pioneers and the Associated Veterans of the Mexican War, brought three major semicentennial celebrations to their state. In addition to remembering war anniversaries, these civic spectacles honored the California pioneers who came to the West Coast prior to statehood in 1850. The first of the three events honored the Bear Flag Revolt, in which American filibusters in Sonoma rose against the Mexican authorities, declared California an independent republic, and welcomed the United States Army under Capt. John C. Frémont. Thousands of revelers met on June 13, 1896, in the Sonoma Plaza across from the old Mexican barracks building. Before the packed crowd orators extolled the virtues of the revolt and the bravery of its participants. Attempting to obscure California's Native American, Spanish, and Mexican roots, the mayor of Sonoma, Henry Seipp, proclaimed that prior to 1846 California was "an almost virgin soil . . . and the conditions of progress were wanting." He lamented the "dormant energies" of old California and celebrated the fact that "the Indian is a thing of the past."[7]

Taking the podium, the local historian Robert A. Thompson focused on the state's memory of the Bear Flag Revolt. Benjamin Deuell and Henry Beeson, two of the original so-called Bear Flaggers, sat before him as venerated guests. The elderly veterans were mere shadows of the adventurers they were in 1846, but now they served as models of American citizenry for the gathered Californians. From the podium Thompson gestured toward the aging revolutionaries, exclaiming, "May their names be recited, may their deeds be commemorated by successive generations of California for all time to come as we today recite and commemorate them." With gnarled hands the old men then reenacted their raising of the Bear Flag in the plaza to thunderous applause. The ceremony officially transformed the usurpation of the legitimate Mexican government of California into an act of selfless patriotism.[8]

Three weeks later the Associated Veterans, along with several other California organizations, sponsored the semicentennial celebration of the landing of the United States Navy at Monterey. Receiving word of the declaration of war in July 1846, Commodore John Drake Sloat of the United States Navy captured the port cities of Monterey, Yerba Buena (San Francisco), and Los Angeles. Underestimating the Mexicans' will, American troops were caught off guard by native Califorñio resistance. Local ranchers led assaults on American forces at Dominguez Ranch, Natividad, San Pasqual,

Santa Clara, San Gabriel, and La Mesa during late 1846 and early 1847. Although the Califorñios won some short-term victories, they were ultimately unable to stop the American occupation of Upper California.[9]

On July 7, 1896, thousands of spectators watched as members of the Monterey Lodge of the Free and Accepted Masons, dressed in their fraternal regalia, laid the foundation stone of a monument to honor Commodore Sloat's occupation of California. Upon ritually inspecting the foundation, the master mason addressed his hope for the enduring memory of the American invasion of the state: "May the monument which is to rest upon it, remain throughout the ages an eloquent, albeit a silent testimony of the faithful patriot in whose honor it is to be erected, that cannot be forgotten, and that his memory will become more enduring even than such a work of any human hands." Washington Ayer, the president of the Sloat Monument Association and a member of the Society of California Pioneers, stepped forward and hailed the arrival of Anglo-Americans who "gave birth to a new and higher civilization." The final orator, Rabbi Jacob Voorsanger, echoed Ayer's speech, claiming that "two peoples met here in the West, and the Anglo-Saxon stem proved to be the better."[10]

After the cornerstone dedication the participants paraded through the town of Monterey to the old Mexican customhouse on the edge of the bay. The official procession included brightly decorated floats, active duty soldiers and sailors, California pioneers, members of heritage societies, Civil War veterans, firemen, local dignitaries, and young women representing the branches of the armed forces and individual counties of the state. Approximately 150 Mexican War veterans marched while dozens more awaited the procession in grandstands erected at the customhouse.[11]

Although Alexander M. Kenaday's National Association of Veterans of the Mexican War had struggled throughout the 1870s and 1880s to obtain government support for its activities, the Associated Veterans easily secured the participation of the United States Navy and the Marine Corps. The navy, then in the process of modernizing its fleet, was eager to showcase its power and sent the warships *Philadelphia* and *Monadnock* to participate in the festivities. The ships' guns fired throughout the day, thrilling the crowds and punctuating the nation's military prowess.[12]

The navy chaplain A. A. McAllister offered an invocation at the customhouse to open the flag-raising ceremony. Aiding the process of obliterating Native American, Spanish, and Mexican memory, the chaplain's prayer alleged that California had been an austere, unpopulated land before the arrival of the United States. "In Thy wise providence," he intoned, "Thou saw fit to add to the immense area of our territory, the lands of this vast State, when they were yet unexplored and almost uninhabited, that in future generations it might become the home of a progressive and enlightened people. . . . We thank Thee for the memory of the patriots whose chief we have assembled this day to honor. May their example animate us to deeds worthy of their successors." After the prayer, Commodore Sloat's grandson read the proclamation recited to Californios in 1846 informing them that they had become subjects of the United States.[13]

These rituals were a prelude to the reenactment of the flag raising at the customhouse. In 1846 Sloat's aide-de-camp, William P. Toler, had come ashore to raise the colors of the United States at the old adobe building. Now aged and infirm, he returned to reprise his role before the cheering crowd at Monterey. Toler's raising of the first U.S. flag over California symbolized the realization of the nation's manifest destiny. The ritual repetition of this meaningful act therefore assumed the air of a religious rite. After the old veteran hoisted the flag "with a vim and energy of a half century before," he attempted to make a speech but was overcome by emotion.[14]

The reported vigor of Toler and other Mexican War veterans promoted ideals of Anglo strength and virility. One observer of the flag raising at Monterey noted that "it was a touching sight to see the venerable veterans of the Mexican War behave like little boys let loose from school." Such language was typical of press descriptions of the old soldiers at the turn of the century. The perception of these robust warriors contrasted sharply with the enfeebled pension seekers in Washington, D.C., twenty-five years earlier. Secure in their government pensions, the veterans shed their former pitiful image. Americans could then recast their Mexican War veterans as paragons of Anglo-Saxon strength and preeminence.[15]

Two days after the festivities in Monterey, Californians celebrated their third semicentennial anniversary, a final event commemorating the landing of the United States Navy at San Francisco. Attempting to match the festivities at Sonoma and Monterey, the residents of the city held a veterans' parade in which cannon fire, factory whistles, and church bells greeted the old soldiers and their escorts. Once again the warships *Philadelphia* and *Monadnock* sat offshore, the report of their deck guns echoing across San Francisco Bay. The United States Navy and Marine Corps sent troops to reenact the original raising of the Stars and Stripes for the cheering crowd. Rabbi Voorsanger, who spoke at Monterey, reprised his role as orator at San Francisco. He noted that "Spain" was "no pleasant word in the vocabulary of free men" and then chronicled Spain's historical mistreatment of Jews and the blessings of freedom brought by the United States.[16]

After the rabbi's remarks the veterans attended a reception in their honor at a local firehouse. Alcohol flowed as the revelers tried to top one another with accolades and toasts to the Stars and Stripes. In the midst of this jingoistic celebration a descendant of Andrés Pico, the man who led the Mexican resistance in California, stepped forward to offer his tribute. Dressed in the uniform of a major of the United States Army, Pico felt compelled to remind the rambunctious audience that he too was a "true American" and "Native Son" of California. He declared that he would "be proud to go out and fight for that glorious flag if my country needed me."[17]

The California commemorations initiated women's participation in the shaping of the war's memory. In a role secondary to that of the male participants in the semicentennial, women sang songs and recited poetry at the varied events. Alongside the veterans and pioneer groups a select group of schoolgirls served as symbolic ambassadors of the conquest. The planning committee in Monterey requested that each county in California send a young woman to represent it in the grand parade. Specifically it asked for "a daughter or granddaughter of a Veteran of the Mexican War or a Pioneer, and a native daughter of California" to serve as "maids of honor" and representatives of the branches of the armed forces during the parade and subsequent commemorations. The committee believed these girls, "whose fathers had bequeathed to them for that and similar occasions their natural inherent rights," held a privileged position that linked the old veterans and pioneers to the rising generation.[18]

Several young women were honored during the anniversary celebrations, although the greatness of their patriotic ancestors consistently overshadowed their own accomplishments. For example, Alice Stewart, the daughter of the former president of the Associated Veterans of the Mexican War, represented the army in the parade at Monterey. A souvenir program described her as "a perfect little lady, kind and courteous to all, but mostly to be admired for her filial affection and devotion to her honored father." Stewart's dedication to the veteran patriarch ensured she would literally pass his legacy on to her future children. Her burgeoning identity was subsumed in that of her father, making her merely a vessel to carry forward his greatness to future generations of his family.[19]

Even more telling was the inclusion of Special Maid of Honor Dicie May Graves, a dark-haired young woman who stood out among her Anglo peers. As the descendant of Mexican War veterans who fought on both sides of the conflict, she elicited particular interest. The program noted in lofty terms that "in her the streams of the blood of the American and Spanish races are united, and that which once flowed in hot currents of fierce antagonism has found a tranquil and placid reservoir from which new rivers of life will flow on for all time in our Golden State. The olive tint of the mingled Castilian and Mexican blood is crimsoned with that of the sturdy Anglo-Saxon, and produced a marvelous type of beauty particular only to California." Like

United States Army Major Pico, Graves physically represented the co-opting of Mexican California by the North Americans. The description of her also assuaged the fear of miscegenation by assuring that the "sturdy" Anglo-Saxon blood of her grandfather tempered that of her mercurial Mexican grandmother and further reinforced the wartime characterization of the male United States penetrating and subduing the female Mexico.[20]

In the context of the California semicentennial young women played a largely symbolic role. These "maidens," with their implied chastity and virtue, spiritually bridged the past with the present and future. The discussions of bloodlines and the literal inheritance of patriotic traits transformed the girls into worthy vessels of nationalism and the future defenders of their fathers' memory. Their individuality was eclipsed not only by that of their veteran progenitors but also by the "new rivers of life" whose promise they literally carried within themselves. As mere emblems they neither upstaged the aging men nor challenged conservative gender roles in American society.

The elaborate anniversaries in California reveal the regional variations of memory at the end of the nineteenth century. Why did Californians celebrate the U.S.–Mexican War when New Mexicans and Texans did not? Statehood concerns aside, a commemoration in the New Mexico Territory would have found little support in the large, politically powerful Hispano community. Still, if the question was merely about the rivalry between the descendants of the conquerors and the conquered, then Anglo-Texans should have succeeded in hosting their semicentennial exposition relatively unopposed by the Tejano minority. Like Anglo-Texans, the Anglo pioneers of California and their descendants had successfully usurped the position of authority and privilege formerly held by Mexicans. Californios either assimilated and intermarried with ruling Anglos or faced marginalization under the new order. Other factors besides the relationship between old Anglo and Mexican families in California made the celebration of the semicentennial a priority in the state.[21]

In 1896 California was in the midst of rapid change that was transforming the state's social and economic dynamics. Unlike New Mexico and Texas, California experienced heavy domestic and foreign immigration at the turn of the twentieth century. Chinese, Japanese, and Mexicans were worrisome to Anglos on the West Coast. While Californians needed immigrant labor to support the state's remarkable economic growth, the newcomers brought cultures and histories that could potentially overshadow those of the pioneers of 1846–49. To establish Anglo primacy in the state, it was vital for the celebrants to diminish and replace the memories of California's indigenous, Spanish, and Mexican past. The rhetoric of the commemorations therefore deemphasized the state's history prior to 1846 while celebrating the arrival of Anglo soldiers and pioneers as the true genesis of California's greatness. The displacement of earlier memories cleared the way for Anglo pioneer remembrance to establish itself as dominant in the state.[22]

Race, however, was not the only dividing line in California. The historian Richard Hofstadter argued that middle-class Americans experienced a "status revolution" in the decades leading up to and immediately following the beginning of the twentieth century. During this era magnates who became the nouveaux riches displaced men of less abundant means who once commanded authority and respect in American society. As California grew in economic importance, railroad moguls such as Collis P. Huntington, Henry Huntington, and Leland Stanford dominated the state. The German immigrant Henry Miller transformed cattle ranching in the San Joaquin Valley into a massive industry. The discovery of large petroleum deposits in southern California during the 1890s brought Standard Oil, owned by John D. Rockefeller, to the region. At the dawn of the twentieth century plutocrats began to dominate the social, political, and economic life of the Golden State. This power shift was reflected in the diversion of money from California's old communities of San Francisco, Sacramento, and San Diego to the growing metropolis of Los Angeles.[23]

In this context the semicentennials observed in California can be interpreted as an attempt by middle-class pioneers and their descendants to resist the growing power of the newly arrived magnates. Hofstadter believed that the proliferation of heritage societies like those which hosted the events were a consequence of such resistance. Anniversary observances therefore became a defensive measure meant to uphold the privileged position of veterans and pioneer families against newcomers regardless of race or ethnicity. By staging the events exclusively in the Monterey and San Francisco Bay Area and choosing to ignore battles fought in Los Angeles and San Diego, they reinforced the importance of northern California. Through these carefully planned celebrations the pioneers and their descendants aggressively staked their claim in California's landscape of memory. This further allowed them to elevate their group memories to the status of history and attack anyone who threatened their version of events. Ultimately, this form of ancestor veneration instilled a sense of privilege among the descendants of the pioneers.[24]

This hostility became clear as the organizers of the California semicentennials sought to discredit the works of Hubert Howe Bancroft. During a career that spanned the late nineteenth and early twentieth centuries, Bancroft earned a place among the nation's most prolific historians and collectors of historical documents related to the American West. He hired a large team of full-time researchers and writers to help him turn the history of the

Americas into a lucrative publishing business. Libraries and universities throughout the United States, Canada, and Mexico purchased subscriptions to his thirty-nine-volume *The Works of Hubert Howe Bancroft*. Initially, California's growing heritage movement embraced the early volumes of the series. The exclusive Society of California Pioneers, which would later co-sponsor the semicentennial commemorations, granted Bancroft an honorary membership in the organization.[25]

As Bancroft published the individual volumes of his book series, he was eventually obligated to address the U.S.–Mexican War. Influenced by his abolitionist roots, Bancroft attacked the Polk administration in volume 13 of his *Works*. In words that would be echoed by Ulysses S. Grant, Bancroft claimed that the war was "a premeditated and predetermined affair . . . it was the result of a deliberately calculated scheme of robbery on the part of the superior power. There were at Washington enough unprincipled men high in office, senators, congressmen, to say nothing of the president and his cabinet . . . who were willing to lay aside all notions of right and wrong in the matter, and unblushingly to take whatever could be secured solely upon the principle of might." He characterized the supporters of the war as "slave holders, smugglers, Indian-killers, and foul-mouthed tobacco-spurting swearers upon sacred Fourth-of-July principles."[26]

As a result of such charges the National Association of Veterans of the Mexican War denounced Bancroft in 1885. *The Vedette* printed an editorial that asked, "Why does an American historian make such glaring misstatements when the commonest school histories will show them to be false?" It concluded, "It is safe to say that this historian never carried a musket." Other critics, including the outspoken journalist Ambrose Bierce, frequently attacked Bancroft's work as hurried and unprofessional.[27]

The Society of California Pioneers decided to expel Bancroft from its ranks in 1894 because of his critical treatment of Frémont, United States Navy Commodore Robert F. Stockton, the early California pioneer John A. Sutter, and the Bear Flag Revolt. In volume 22 of his *Works* Bancroft referred to the uprising as "a criminal revolt of vagabond settlers," a charge which enraged the society. An investigation by a special committee led the organization to issue several summonses requesting Bancroft to attend a hearing to determine the status of his membership. Bancroft ignored the commands, claiming he never requested to be a member of the organization, and was duly expelled. Maj. Edwin A. Sherman, the organizer of the California semicentennials, later declared the expulsion to be a "seal of infamy" upon Bancroft's legacy. Months later Bancroft's publishing business burned to the ground. He and his "History Company" weathered the setbacks and adversity and continued publishing his otherwise popular books.[28]

During the semicentennial commemorations the National Association of Mexican War Veterans and the Society of California Pioneers strove to reclaim their memory of California's role in the U.S.–Mexican War. They believed that Bancroft had "maligned the memory of many of the men most conspicuous as participants" in the Bear Flag Revolt and the occupation of the West Coast by the United States. They accused one of Bancroft's agents of campaigning against them in Congress to subvert government support of the memorials. From the onset of the anniversary celebrations in California it was obvious that the organizers intended to exact revenge on their high-profile critic.[29]

At Sonoma the orator Merton C. Allen stated that he "resented the unjust criticisms of prejudiced historians" and justified the actions of those who had sought to "relieve California from Mexican dominion." Finally, he pledged to the audience that the Bear Flag would be "assured an honored place in the sacred album of memory." In his tribute to the "noble band of pioneers" that raised the Bear Flag at Sonoma, Robert A. Thompson, the historian of the Society of California Pioneers, likewise defended the Americans against the "calumnies heaped upon them by that self-constituted historian, H. H. Bancroft."[30]

Bancroft was also on the minds of the Freemasons at the dedication of the Sloat Memorial at Monterey. The historian had criticized Commodore Sloat as being "timid and irresolute" during the occupation of California. His attack on the naval commander threatened the very purpose of the gathering. Ayer derided Bancroft at the ceremony, saying, "No cowardly and unscrupulous historian will dare ever again to outrage his memory or attempt to impeach his integrity. The assassination of true history and the malicious libels upon the life and character of Commodore Sloat by a pseudo historian of California should give his voluminous labors a prominent place in obscurity." Once again the society leaped at the chance to protect its group memory from the outsiders' challenges.[31]

Such attacks took a toll on Bancroft's reputation. The historian's unwillingness to defend himself against the allegations of the society and other groups gave the impression that the charges might, in fact, be true. Although not destroying the Bancroft publishing empire, the assaults tarnished his legacy. Bancroft's critics, therefore, gave credence to authors whose works were less critical of the United States and promoted the belief that Mexico was responsible for the conflict.[32]

The Bancroft debate demonstrated that the fight for America's memory of the U.S.–Mexican War remained heated fifty years later. It also illustrated the role that heritage groups played in defending established memories. Bancroft had written histories that criticized the motives of the United

States and disparaged cherished heroes and venerated ancestors. His widely read books had the power to shape collective memory and proved to be a threat to the semicentennial commemorations. California's pioneers aggressively invalidated Bancroft's version of history lest it take root in the state's public memory and threaten their own power and status.[33]

The controversy also showed the role that the soldiers themselves played in defending their own memory. The veterans' movement during this era suffered a setback, however, when the National Association of Veterans of the Mexican War fell dormant after Kenaday's death in 1897. The California-based Associated Veterans of the Mexican War attempted to fill the void for a few years but likewise slipped into oblivion. In 1900 a woman named Mary Moore Murdock, the forty-five-year-old Texas-born daughter of a Mexican War and Confederate Civil War veteran, campaigned to reorganize a national body of veterans. Working with the local Texas Association of Mexican War Veterans, Murdock was able to encourage the old men to reorganize a national society. The group took a variation of its former name around 1901 and reformed as the National Association of Mexican War Veterans. The grateful soldiers elected Murdock secretary of their revitalized association and began holding annual meetings.[34]

In an attempt to boost the profile of the organization, the national association invited President William McKinley to its reunion in 1901. The invitation reminded the president that "these old heroes of 55 years ago are fast passing away." The very day the national association's invitation arrived at the White House, McKinley received requests for his presence at reunions of the Grand Army of the Republic, the State of Ohio Spanish War Veterans, and the National Association of Union Ex-Prisoners of War. Inundated with such queries, the president was forced to decline them all.[35]

McKinley's successor, Theodore Roosevelt, felt more compassion for the aging soldiers and hosted a brief White House reception for the organization in 1906. The last known contact between a U.S. president and the veterans was in 1911, when William Howard Taft visited the National Home for Disabled Volunteer Soldiers in Marion, Indiana. Taft used the visit to the impoverished men to promote his agenda of world peace by declaring that the U.S.–Mexican War should have been settled by an "impartial tribune" rather than fought on the battlefield.[36]

As the veterans aged, their attitudes toward their former enemies continued to evolve. In 1901 Isaac George set off on a pilgrimage that culminated in an unexpected reunion. Traveling with his grandson, George determined to see for one last time the battlefield at Sacramento, Chihuahua, where he had fought as a young man. His first stop was the battlefield at Buena Vista, where he noted human bone fragments in a plowed field in a nearby Mexican rancho. The owner of the rancho escorted the visitors around the grounds and introduced them to a 108-year-old woman who sold relics she had collected from the notorious killing field. At Sacramento, George was thrilled to find that the owner of the battlefield, Leonardo Talavera, had been one of his opponents in 1847. He reminisced that "my old foe and myself had long since buried every feeling of resentment and met as friends." After a lengthy visit George's grandson took a photograph of the former enemies—now united as comrades in the nostalgic memory of their youth.[37]

In 1904 St. Louis hosted the Louisiana Purchase Exposition, a World's Fair that attracted thousands of visitors from around the globe. The reconstituted National Association of Mexican War Veterans planned a reunion in conjunction with the event. In addition to the many spectacles and attractions of the fair, the American veterans looked forward to a meeting with their former enemies on September 16, Mexican Independence Day. Months earlier the group had extended a formal invitation to President Porfirio Díaz and had received assurances that Mexican veterans would attend the exposition. In anticipation, one local newspaper ran the headline, "Díaz Accepts Invitation: Veterans of Mexican War, On Both Sides, to Meet in St. Louis."[38]

Much to the Americans' disappointment the day came and went without the appearance of any Mexican visitors. Shortly after the reunion a courier from the U.S. embassy in Mexico City delivered a communiqué from the Association of Defenders of the Mexican Republic of 1836 to 1848. A translation contained in the letter explained the veterans' absence:

> We could very much desire to comply with your noble and generous request; but it being impossible, by reason of great age and infirmity, to perform so great a journey, we determined to respond to your kind invitation by this method, and to manifest our gratitude; and to express our regrets in not being able to meet a few of the surviving American soldiers whom we met on the field of battle in 1846 and 1847, then adversaries, now no longer enemies but friends and brothers in arms. . . . We have the honor and great pleasure to clasp your valiant hands, spiritually, and to subscribe ourselves your most loyal friends.

The fifty-eight years that had passed since the outbreak of the war were sufficient to heal resentments between the former adversaries. Unfortunately, the veterans had grown too old and infirm to consummate personally this goodwill.[39]

The Louisiana Purchase Exposition, along with George's and Talavera's reunion on the battlefield at Sacramento, represented the willingness of veterans to forget their violent past and embrace their former enemies. This impulse was not unique to soldiers of the U.S.–Mexican War. Civil War veterans also held Blue–Gray reunions in the early twentieth century. Such ecumenical events freed the participants from the ideologies that had inspired warfare and allowed the aging foes to bask in the reminiscence of a shared past. By shifting the focus of memory from the war to the warriors, the old men could celebrate their lives unencumbered by the political baggage of the past.[40]

The graying soldiers may have been willing to forego the use of memory to achieve ideological gains, yet their growing dependence on younger people to facilitate their activities exposed them to outside agendas. The United Confederate Veterans, for example, was deeply involved in planning and hosting reunions for the Texas Association of Mexican War Veterans. The pro-Confederate stance of the Confederate group and its goal of "Anglo-Saxon emancipation" permeated the Texas association's reunions. At their meeting in 1903, the Confederate captain Sam Evans addressed the old men, reminiscing fondly about Jefferson Davis's service in the U.S.–Mexican War before discussing the Civil War at length. He stated that "the causes which brought about that conflict between the States had not yet been removed, and when it was it would be in the interest of the Caucasian race—not the Negro." Such spectacles turned Mexican War reunions into platforms for younger men's social and political goals.[41]

Other individuals and groups were equally brazen in promoting their self-interests at the reunions. Henry C. Gesford, grand president of the Native Sons of the Golden West, represented the descendants of California's privileged pioneers. At the Sonoma semicentennial he boasted, "We honor ourselves in paying homage to the memory of these men." Judge E. B. Muse echoed Gesford's statement during his welcome address to the national association reunion in Dallas in 1905. In a speech that wished the veterans well in the looming hereafter, he vainly assured them that "in honoring you we honor ourselves." While there is no evidence that the veterans resented this co-opting of their gatherings, such events were patently fertile grounds for exploitation.[42]

In the wake of the Civil War, military reunions held throughout the nation afforded financial opportunities for local tourist bureaus, railroads, and hotels. Mexican War veterans' associations now had to compete for resources with countless other veterans' groups from more recent wars. Offers of free travel to reunions vanished in the twentieth century as veterans' meetings became prospects for profit. America's service sector, for example, mailed solicitations to veterans' organizations in an attempt to stimulate business. Infused with patriotic appeals to the "grand old heroes," these self-serving petitions benignly exploited the war's memory for economic gain.[43]

A more sinister attempt to profit from the veterans came from an unlikely source. In 1905 the Texas Association of Mexican War Veterans shipped a

large block of carved granite to be included in the Sloat Memorial in Monterey, California. After the shipment was made, the organization received a
bill demanding an extra one hundred dollars as a "setting fee" for the stone.
An enraged member of the Texas association wrote back accusing the secretary of the Sloat Monument Association, William H. Hilton, of graft. Hilton
had long maintained that he was a Texas Ranger who had fought under both
Generals Taylor and Scott. The Texas veterans, however, did not recognize his
name and quietly pressed for an investigation into Hilton's service record. The
War Department searched its archives on behalf of Rep. John Nance Garner
and found that Hilton was neither a Texas Ranger nor a veteran of the regular army. A further search revealed that Hilton's name was also missing from
federal pension rolls. Before the Texans could expose the pretender, he died.
The Texans halted their investigation, allowing Californians to mourn the
loss of their supposed famous veteran blissfully ignorant of his fraud.[44]

During the first two decades of the twentieth century veteran activity declined significantly. Reunions diminished as entire units withered and succumbed to the onward press of time. The National Association of Mexican
War Veterans held its final meeting in 1909, signaling an official end to the
aging warriors' political activism. The paucity of Mexican War veterans
turned the weathered old men into curiosities. Commemorations and parades
displayed the dwindling remnant as incarnate relics of a distant conflict overshadowed by the Civil War, the Spanish–American War, and the First World
War.[45]

As the Mexican War soldiers slipped quietly down the hierarchy of veterans, they still tried to maintain a public presence. With one original survivor
still on its rolls, the Aztec Club of 1847 secured a place at the dedication of
the Tomb of the Unknown Soldier in Arlington National Cemetery on November 11, 1921. This memorial was built as a place of public mourning
and veneration for American troops lost in the First World War. On the day
before the dedication filial members of the Aztec Club placed a floral tribute
on the bier as it sat in the Capitol Rotunda. Adm. Charles Johnston Badger,
the vice president of the organization, read a public message: "The Aztec
Club of 1847, whose members are descendants of those who served and
those who gave their lives in our war with Mexico, as a token of their appreciation and gratitude for the services and supreme sacrifice in the World
War of those who upheld our cause and of whom he who lies here is representative, do now reverently place this wreath on his coffin." The next day
they took their place in the cortege that escorted the casket to Arlington
National Cemetery.[46]

Another notable development during this time was the direct influence
women had begun to exert on the memory of the Mexican War. The most

important organization to assist the veterans in the twentieth century was the Dames of 1846. Mary Moore Murdock, the woman who had helped revive the National Association of Mexican War Veterans, created this organization. Prompted by the death of her father, the middle-aged widow conceived the idea for a women's heritage group that would "perpetuate the memories of the soldiers of the Mexican War and . . . provide for the material wants of their widows and orphans."[47]

On June 5, 1901, Murdock assembled a group of like-minded women in Fort Worth to draft a constitution for the Dames of 1846. The preamble declared, "As the 'Daughters of the Confederacy,' the women of the South are correcting history, molding opinion, demanding justice, educating youth, and rearing monuments to the men who lived and died for a cause that was invincible. . . . Ah, women of 1846, we have waited too long to crown the victors of that war. In this we memorialize that remnant of that noble army that comprised the flower of our land, of our Southland especially, to permit us under their venerable hand and seal to publicly declare ourselves their heirs and successors." Murdock granted charter status to "mothers, wives and widows," with standard membership opened to all lineal female descendants of Mexican War veterans. Collateral relatives were accepted into fellowship if they were related to officers of "historical renown."[48]

The preamble's praise of the "Daughters of the Confederacy" reflected the sectional nature and bias of the organization. In spite of the constitution's explicit charge "to perpetuate the memory, the sacrifices and indomitable courage and valor of the men who, without regard to section, politics or social condition responded to the call to arms in 1846," the Dames assumed a distinctly southern character. Its membership included female relatives of the notorious Confederates Jefferson Davis, Braxton Bragg, Robert E. Lee, and Thomas "Stonewall" Jackson. Murdock even patterned the Dames on the United Daughters of the Confederacy and began meeting in that group's Robert E. Lee Camp Hall in Fort Worth.[49]

During the organization's nine-year history the number of surviving veterans plummeted from approximately seventy-five hundred to just over two thousand. While it never grew into a large association, the Dames of 1846 took seriously its charge to be the soldier's "heirs and successors." As the veterans grew older and more dependent, the Dames organized their reunions, looked after their material needs, and lobbied Congress on their behalf. Murdock's persistent advocacy for enhanced annuities led to two federal pension increases for the aged men.[50]

Such legislative victories did not come easy for Murdock and her Dames. In ways similar to those of the defunct National Association of Veterans of the Mexican War, the Dames used memory of the conflict primarily to lobby

Congress for financial support of the former soldiers. Nearly twenty years after the passage of the Mexican War Pension Bill, however, the sectional nature of the war's memory continued to impede legislation benefiting the veterans. Rep. James Luther Slayden, a Democrat from Texas, expressed his frustration at raising the service pension in 1905. He lamented, "Most of the veterans live in the South and the Republican Party will not consent to the passage of the measure as it does not affect the people of the North. As long as the Republicans remain in power it will be very hard to pass the bill."[51]

Murdock and her southern-based organization earned the scorn of some northern members of Congress. In 1906 Rep. Henry C. Loudenslager, a Republican from New Jersey and chairman of the House Pension Committee, accused Murdock of profiting from the veterans. In response Murdock wrote an eloquent open letter in which she solemnly declared that her work on their behalf was "a labor of love, pure and undefiled." Such accusations echoed those made against Kenaday of the National Association of Veterans of the Mexican War years earlier.[52]

Although she made enemies in Congress, Murdock could nonetheless count President Theodore Roosevelt among her benefactors. In 1905 Murdock negotiated a place of honor for a handful of veterans to march in his inaugural parade. When it became clear that the men could not make the walk, four were granted seats in the president's reviewing stand. Murdock attended the event and the reception that followed at the White House. Later that year, after Congress denied her request to see the current pension rolls, "in tears she appealed to President Roosevelt," who demanded that she be given the documents. The president's greatest service to the Dames came in 1908, when he signed a bill into law raising widows' monthly pensions from eight to twelve dollars.[53]

Murdock and the Dames of 1846 campaigned for the veterans, but there was another motivation for their charitable work. Murdock founded the Dames in 1901, a critical time in the shifting demographics of the pensioners, as 1901 marked the first year in which the number of war widows surpassed that of the veterans. While the Dames outwardly campaigned for their fathers, many had their mother's well-being in mind too. In 1906, for example, Fanny Pettit wrote to the organization pledging to assist in forming a camp in New Orleans. She complained that Rockefeller's company Standard Oil had destroyed her family's petroleum business, leaving her ailing mother entirely dependent on her Mexican War widow's pension for survival. Pettit hoped her support of the Dames would improve her mother's remaining years.[54]

Still, more than economic need motivated women's participation in memory making. In a society in which gender roles were strictly defined, remembrance of the conflict allowed women to reframe their function as their fathers' caretakers in a larger patriotic context. Mattie Carlton, the unmarried daughter of the recently deceased president of the National Association of Mexican War Veterans, had once been a schoolteacher, but her "happiness and distinction" had been to care for her father in his declining years. In 1905, now in her forties, she struggled to find an identity for herself separate from that of her distinguished progenitor. Carlton found meaning in her sacrifice by embracing the cause of the "dear old veterans." She wrote to Murdock, "I have often wished that I might become a member of the Dames of 1846, but have always been so busy in other work that it has been impossible." She concluded by pledging herself to return to teaching, "now that I have no one depending on me for happiness." Whether she ever taught school again or joined the Dames is not known; nonetheless Carlton recognized that the organization gave deeper meaning to the mundane tasks of caring for the old. The Dames also provided women like Pettit and Carlton a means of reclaiming social standing that was being threatened by the upheaval of the status revolution identified by Hofstadter.[55]

Five years after Murdock formed her organization, the Aztec Club of 1847 established a women's auxiliary named the Guadalupe Club of 1848. This exclusive group of the widows, sisters, and lineal descendants of officers who served in the U.S.–Mexican War accepted members "by invitation only." The express goals of the club were to "discover and preserve family records, otherwise unwritten and unknown relating to the Mexican War, and to teach reverent regard for names, history, character, and deeds of the patriots of that war, and to commemorate events in its history." Lacking the cohesive political agenda of the Dames of 1846, however, the organization failed to grow significantly and by 1913 could boast only of thirty-nine members. To bolster its declining numbers, in 1921 the group made a formal invitation to the women of the Daughters of the American Revolution (DAR) to submit applications should they have the prerequisite lineage. In spite of setbacks, the organization persisted as an elite social club into the 1930s.[56]

Women's desires to serve their country transcended such organizations as the Dames of 1846 and the Guadalupe Club of 1848. Females were barred from joining the nation's armed forces until the Second World War, but remembrance of the U.S.–Mexican War allowed at least one woman the opportunity to imagine a different role for herself. In the summer of 1913 a Mrs. John J. visited the Rock Island Arsenal in Illinois, where cannons captured in the Mexican War were on display. Later, writing to a friend on a picture postcard of the trophy guns, she mused, "I have often told you how the things that have been in some way connected with our country's wars, appeal to me much as if I too had been a soldier." Apparently the sight of the

Mexican cannons was one of many experiences which roused her desire to serve the nation on the battlefield.[57]

Remembrance of the U.S.–Mexican War allowed women at the beginning of the twentieth century entrée into a traditionally masculine world. For the schoolgirls participating in the semicentennial commemorations in California, the ceremonies reinforced their obligation to their fathers. Memory in the hands of more mature women, such as Murdock and her associates, however, proved more liberating. Collective memory enhanced women's patriotic sense of mission in caring for the aging veterans. It also allowed them to fight for the economic well-being of their mothers while outwardly serving and honoring their fathers. Most significantly, memory propelled disenfranchised women into the public sphere, transforming them into congressional lobbyists and political activists. Men continued to dominate many areas of the remembrance of the war, but women were never again denied the opportunity to exercise their influence.[58]

For the veterans and their descendants, memorials were important manifestations of collective memory. In spite of being unable to convince the federal government to erect a national tribute to the U.S.–Mexican War, various veteran and heritage organizations set out to remember the conflict through their own private monuments. The presence of the former soldiers had given these groups tangible symbols of their past greatness. Their decreasing numbers meant that their heirs needed to find a more enduring testament to Anglo power and glory. This proved to be highly imperative in the face of increasing immigration in the United States and the West. Newcomers brought their own histories and memories that could challenge or displace those of the old guard heritage organizations. Monuments became yet another means of demarcating and defending territory in the landscape of memory.

Residents of communities shaped by the war were among the first to mark distinctive sites in the history of the conflict. In the 1890s citizens of Brownsville, Texas, placed a stone tablet on a private ranch to mark the approximate location where the Battle of Palo Alto took place. A few years later soldiers stationed at Fort Sam Houston added a Civil War cannon to the battlefield. In 1907 the Sonoma Valley Woman's Club placed a plaque in the Sonoma Plaza honoring the Bear Flag Revolt. Such modest gestures seemed to have originated not in the coordinated efforts of state or national associations but in a local impulse to commemorate community history.[59]

The first large monument erected during this era was the Sloat Memorial in Monterey, California. As previously mentioned, this massive stone structure paid tribute to the navy commander who conquered the California coast for the United States. Begun during the semicentennial in 1896, the memorial was not completed until 1910. Congressional allies of the memorial were able to secure a small allocation from the federal government, but the majority of funds came from private donors. Thirty-five organizations and individuals (primarily from California) donated the inscribed granite blocks that composed the patchwork monument, and a seven-ton sculpted eagle provided by the United States Navy topped the completed structure. The fourteen-year construction period allowed the Sloat Monument Association to utilize each stone-laying ceremony as a celebration of the greatness of the state's Anglo pioneers and their descendants (see fig. 10).[60]

In 1900 the Military Academy at West Point dedicated Cullum Hall as a memorial to cadets killed in action during America's wars. Set into the walls of the building were over one hundred captured Mexican cannons. Given the Mexican War theme of the edifice, the Aztec Club of 1847 presented a bronze tablet for the hall that honored members of the organization who had died in battle. One year later officials at West Point contacted the Aztec Club and told it to remove the tablet. The exclusive club had run afoul of an even more elite institution which objected to the memorial's inclusion of noncadets. After some negotiation the bronze plaque was removed to the Cadet Chapel.[61]

One of the charter goals of the Dames of 1846 was to "procure the right to protect and make national property, historical spots christened by that war within the limits of the United States [and] to erect monuments to the gallant dead, homes for their widows and orphans, and libraries." While the organization never built a charity home or library, it did attempt to commission memorials. During a reunion in 1905 Murdock called upon the State of Texas to allocate twenty-five thousand dollars for the construction of a triumphal arch honoring the Mexican War to be placed on the grounds of the capital. Murdock and the veterans also lobbied the state legislature to preserve the Palo Alto battlefield and Fort Brown (Fort Texas) as state parks. Ultimately the Texas lawmakers were as unwilling to build memorials to the war as they were to fund a semicentennial exposition. In 1910, however, they did allow the National Society of the Colonial Dames in the State of Texas to place a bronze plaque commemorating Texan casualties in the foyer of the state capitol. It would be left to future generations to continue the fight to preserve the battlefields.[62]

While veterans and hereditary societies struggled to memorialize the U.S.–Mexican War, organizations with no explicit ties to the conflict saw advantage in perpetuating its remembrance. In 1912 the Texas chapters of the DAR announced a "plan to preserve historic places . . . with view of perpetuating patriotic memories." High on its list were sites related to the war with Mexico. Addressing its gendered relationship to memory, the DAR declared, "Woman has awakened to her special service to the country. The sun has shone upon her every effort and her work broadened and expanded until it embraces about every effort that pertains to the advancement and uplift of mankind." The ladies further affirmed themselves to be "vigilant guardians" of American rights.[63]

How did their role as "guardians" relate to their interest in monument building? Throughout this era the DAR was an overtly nativist and racist organization determined to preserve the ethnic and racial status quo of the United States. Facing seemingly unending waves of immigration, it set out to initiate America's neophytes in the ways of Anglo-Saxon patriotism. In addressing the newcomers in 1904 president-general of the DAR, Cornelia Cole Fairbanks, declared that "something must be done to foster patriotism and love for our country and our flag and to make Americans of them" or, she feared, native-born Americans would be "absorbed by the different nationalities among us." In 1919 the DAR helped establish the Americanization School to assist immigrants in assimilating to the nation's institutions. Part of the DAR's civic education involved instilling in immigrants an understanding of the hierarchy of the colonial people of America and a sense of their obligation to honor those at the top of that ladder. Like the Society of California Pioneers, the DAR defended the place of privilege secured by their immigrant ancestors.[64]

In 1901 the Sunshine Chapter of the DAR placed a small stone in the Santa Fe Plaza to honor the place where Gen. Stephen Watts Kearny declared that New Mexico had been annexed to the United States. During the 1920s the DAR identified previously unmarked U.S.–Mexican War sites, including the battlefields at Resaca de la Palma and Fort Brown, which it intended to memorialize with monuments. Following the Texas example, a California chapter of the organization placed the first memorial at the site of the Battle of San Pasqual. The DAR also marked the location where Kearny ended his march to California and where General Taylor camped after he crossed the Nueces River into disputed territory in southern Texas.[65]

The Native Sons of the Golden West and Native Daughters of the Golden West were the most prolific builders of monuments commemorating the U.S.–Mexican War. While technically separate organizations, the native sons and daughters shared a veneration of their pioneer parents and grandparents, who bestowed upon them the privilege of being born on the Pacific Coast. Practicing a racism similar to that of the DAR, the native sons and daughters strove to "hold California for the White Race." In 1924 *Grizzly Bear,* the official magazine of the native sons, reprinted a speech by the California legislator W. B. Shearer which called for military armament, exclusionary immigration, and white supremacy. Shearer's agenda paralleled that of the Ku Klux Klan, which had infiltrated California during the 1920s and boasted a membership of over fifty thousand in the Golden State. His call for "100 percent national policy and 100 percent defense" echoed the Klan's "100 percent Americanism" program.[66]

The racism of the native sons and daughters was complex and nuanced. Like Anglos in New Mexico, they felt an affinity for their region's Spanish history. In spite of an organizational ban against racial minorities, both groups permitted Californios to join. This inclusion reflected the success of what the journalist Carey McWilliams called California's "fantasy heritage," which allowed the more acculturated descendants of the original Californios to portray themselves as pure Spanish and therefore white. This distinction drew a line of race, class, and heritage between the old Californians and the thousands of refugees of the Mexican Revolution who were settling in the state. The native sons classified these recent Mexican immigrants as being below the poorest of Europeans and pressed for their exclusion from the country.[67]

Overseeing monument building, the native sons established a Historical Landmarks Committee presided over by a former U.S. congressman. The native daughters allied with various civic and community groups to form the California Landmarks League. Working alone, together, and in cooperation with other historic associations, the two groups dedicated scores of historical markers to Anglo pioneer greatness in California. Memorials of the U.S.–Mexican War were a small but meaningful part of the organizations' overall work. These monuments included the Monterey Customhouse, Sonoma Plaza, San Pasqual Battlefield, La Mesa Battlefield, and several sites associated with lesser events in the war. The memorial at La Mesa Battlefield, for example, was built upon rough boulders representing "the character of the virgin country" of California. The towering stone and bronze *Raising of the Bear Flag* statue at Sonoma celebrated the "freedom of California from Mexican rule." Like the semicentennial celebrations of the war in 1896, these monuments supplanted earlier memories and helped designate the state as Anglo territory.[68]

The DAR, the Native Sons of the Golden West, and the Native Daughters of the Golden West wielded considerable power during the 1910s and 1920s, allowing them to enshrine their group memories as official history. While none of these organizations had an explicit connection to the U.S.–Mexican War, they realized the value of memorializing the conflict. In California, New Mexico, and Texas they erected monuments at important points of contact between the United States and Mexico. Viewed within these heritage organizations' larger social and racial agendas, the memorials demarcated critical locations where Anglos extended hegemony over the American Southwest. They further functioned as symbolic stone sentinels to guard the landscape of memory against foreign intruders.[69]

Mexican War monuments also became a forum in which to fight old rivalries when descendants of the 1st Missouri Mounted Volunteers and the Mormon Battalion each claimed the distinction of having made the longest marches in military history. Tensions between the groups could be traced back to the Missouri–Mormon War of 1838. At this time political, economic, and religious differences led to acts of violence against members of the Church of Jesus Christ of Latter-day Saints by their neighbors in the state. After continued bloodshed on both sides and threats of extermination by the governor, the Mormons fled to Illinois. Memory of the wrongs committed against them in Missouri remained strong among subsequent generations of Latter-day Saints.[70]

When mobs and militia in Illinois likewise drove the Mormons out of the state in 1846, the church set its sights on northern Mexico. Nervous about thousands of potentially belligerent Mormons joining the Mexicans, the United States Army struck a bargain with the exiled church on the plains of Iowa. In exchange for much-needed money and weapons, the Mormons supplied the army with five hundred volunteers for service in the Mexican War. This aided the Mormons in their westward migration and helped the United States ensure their loyalty. The Mormon Battalion, as it was called, began a march of nearly two thousand miles that would take it from Council Bluffs in the Iowa Territory through Santa Fe, Tucson, and San Diego to a final destination in Los Angeles. Throughout this impressive feat the Mormon Battalion never fired a weapon in aggression.[71]

At the same time, Gen. Alexander Doniphan raised a battalion of mounted infantry in Missouri to join the war effort. After moving overland to Santa Fe, the Missouri Volunteers received orders to secure the Mexican state of Chihuahua and then join Taylor's army in Matamoros—a march of nearly thirty-five hundred miles. The Missourians had little affection for their former neighbors, and although Doniphan had defended the Mormons in 1838, some of his men had taken part in driving them from the state. Tensions were high whenever soldiers from Missouri and Mormon troops marched or camped near one another.[72]

After the war, both the Mormons and the Missourians claimed the distinction of having made the longest infantry march in history. The Missourians took the first step in commemorating Doniphan's Epic March, as it came to be known. In 1918 Clay County, Missouri, unveiled a large monument to honor Doniphan and his soldiers: a bronze likeness of the general standing on a massive block of native red granite. The nineteen-foot-tall structure also included plaques extolling the virtues of Doniphan and "the greatest march in history" (see fig. 11).[73]

Missouri's boast prompted the Mormons, now settled in Utah, to challenge their rival's allegations. A heritage organization known as the Daughters of the Mormon Battalion, under the guidance of the church leader Brigham H. Roberts, set out to counter Missouri's claims and build an even larger monument. Addressing Missouri's assertions in 1919 Roberts stated that their rivals' march officially began at Santa Fe and therefore was only "about thirteen or fourteen hundred miles." By negating the mileage between Missouri and New Mexico, Roberts justified the Mormons' contention that they held the "world's record for a march of infantry."[74]

To formalize their claim and pay permanent tribute to the unit's accomplishments, Roberts and the Daughters of the Mormon Battalion founded the Utah Mormon Battalion Monument Commission. The organization struggled for years to raise the funds necessary to build a sprawling granite and bronze sculpture to be placed on the grounds of the state capitol in Salt Lake City. In the spring of 1927 the ten-thousand-square-foot monument was finally completed and unveiled to a large crowd of Utahns and visiting dignitaries. As the largest monument dedicated exclusively to the U.S.–Mexican War in the United States, the structure included a reflecting pool and towering stone sculpture displaying scenes of the battalion's enlistment and trek through the Southwest and their role in the discovery of gold in California. The monument also included the sculpture of a Native American woman and her baby known as the *Evanishment of Race*. By noting the disappearance of the Native Americans, the Mormons established their primacy and made their memories dominant in the region (see fig. 12).[75]

Interestingly, the dedicatory ceremonies made no mention of the Missouri rivalry. During the commission's ten-year existence Mormon priorities had evolved. Just months prior to the dedication of the monument, church leaders had expunged doctrines and practices that were deemed confrontational toward the government. Keeping in this spirit, Roberts focused his speech on the Latter-day Saints' role in Manifest Destiny. He proudly declared that "the march of that battalion is an incident which connects that band of pioneers with the general movement of the American people." He further stated that the monument would be "a witness to the loyalty of the Mormon people to the United States government." Emerging from decades of persecution and isolation, the Church of Jesus Christ of Latter-day Saints realized that the Mormon Battalion offered an opportunity for inclusion in America's rich cultural tapestry. By promoting the memory of their contributions to the U.S.–Mexican War, Mormons had found common ground with the rest of the nation. In subsequent decades the Latter-day Saints would shower the

Mormon Battalion with tributes and honors unprecedented in the com-memoration of the war.[76]

In addition to monuments, books continued to be another crucial com-ponent of memory during this era. The concerted attack on Bancroft's inter-pretation of the U.S.–Mexican War demonstrated the high stakes involved in controlling the written word. It also coincided with other events to mark a turning point in the field of historic literature about the conflict. Within two years of the semicentennial, the United States had declared war on Spain. This latest campaign devastated the old empire and gave Americans important new lands in the Caribbean and the Pacific. After the war President Roosevelt declared a corollary to the Monroe Doctrine granting the United States the power to intercede in the domestic affairs of Latin American na-tions it deemed to be weak or unstable. Emboldened by a sense of moral and military superiority, the United States launched three decades of foreign interventions unprecedented in the nation's history. War with Spanish-speaking people dredged up old memories of the conflict in which the United States gained an empire in the West. American authors and historians turned to the memory of the U.S.–Mexican War to justify their crusade against Spain and Latin America. For the first time since the antebellum period, American authors perceptibly shifted toward blaming Mexico for instigating the hostilities.[77]

The Mexican Revolution proved an even greater influence on written memory. President Woodrow Wilson's interventionist policies, the shelling and occupation of Veracruz, Pancho Villa's raid on New Mexico, Gen. John Pershing's punitive expedition, and the Zimmerman Affair all pushed the United States and Mexico toward open hostilities. After decades of lagging interest the Yankee intrusion into the Mexican Revolution boosted American awareness of the Mexican War. A new generation, steeped in social Darwin-ism and viewing the conflict through imperialist eyes, worried less about the morality of the war and looked for justification of the conquest in the racial inferiority of the Mexican people.[78]

In 1914 Henry Hutchins Morris wrote *Thrilling Stories of Mexican War-fare* in response to the American occupation of Veracruz. The book com-bined the U.S.–Mexican War with U.S. intervention in the Mexican Revolu-tion and presented them as a seamless narrative. As in other works of the time, Morris's stories saw the conflict between Americans and Mexicans as the predictable source of tensions between the two nations and races. He al-leged that "the Spaniard was far lower than others of the white race . . . a curse to humanity." In addition Morris declared to his fellow Americans that "we must not forget that revolution and savagery in Mexico is only possible when the United States fails to prevent or stamp it out." He concluded his book with a call for the United States to annex Mexico and permanently put an end to the violence.[79]

That same year Reverend Thomas B. Gregory likewise called for Mexican annexation in his book, *Our Mexican Conflicts*. According to Gregory, war between the nations remained inevitable because of "the difference of race, the irrepressible opposition of breed, the uncompromising friction that has always and everywhere existed between the independent, progressive, self-reliant Saxon and the docile, reactionary Latin." He noted that Mexico's high combat casualties were a "very poor compliment to their intelligence. They were brave, oftentimes desperately, foolishly brave, but they did not know how to aim. They lacked the coolness, self-possession and sense of their American opponents." In justifying a modern invasion he reminded his readers that "the Mexicans of the year 1914 are just like the Mexicans of the year 1846."[80]

Countering these imperialistic works was Frederick Starr's *Mexico and the United States*. Starr was a noted anthropologist from the University of Chicago who disagreed with the policy of U. S. intervention. He made reference to history and anthropology to discuss the nations' poor relations with one another since the rule of Santa Anna. While Morris and Gregory invoked the racism inherent in social Darwinism to justify Mexican annexation, Starr used it to promote neutrality: "We have not assimilated Arizona and New Mexico after sixty-five years of ownership. We have not assimilated the millions of Negroes of the South. We have not assimilated the Filipino, nor the Hawaiian, nor the Porto Rican. We have not only not assimilated them, we are nationally today weaker for their presence. To take over all or part of Mexico would be no advantage to its people, would harm us, and would profit only a handful of individuals to whom we owe no great consideration." Espousing sympathy for the Mexican people, Starr believed that the races must remain separated in their respective nations or they would weaken a united one.[81]

As American forces marched into Mexico in search of Pancho Villa in 1916 Robert H. Howe published *How We Robbed Mexico in 1848*. Howe condemned the invasion of Mexico, declaring that "when the causes and results of that war are studied it can be readily understood why the Mexicans hate us and why the rest of the South American republics view us with suspicion." After considering the Treaty of Guadalupe Hidalgo he quipped, "Is it any wonder that the Mexicans hate us and call us 'Pigs?'" Howe then warned that any invasion of Mexico would be "a cleverly planned scheme of financiers" that should be avoided lest the nation enter again into a "additional acts of land piracy." Such negative treatments of the conflict, however, were in the minority during this time.[82]

When Americans returned from the battlefields of Europe at the end of 1918 their strained relations with Mexico remained in the national conscience. The months following the armistice witnessed a spike in interest in books about the U.S.–Mexican War. In 1919 Justin H. Smith, a former professor of history at Dartmouth College, published his two-volume study *The War with Mexico, 1846–1848*. Discounting over seventy years of scholarship, a *New York Times* reviewer declared that the work "told for the first time the complete and detailed story of that conflict." According to Smith, Mexico had no claim to the disputed Nueces Strip of southern Texas and the annexation of the territory "was on legal, moral, and political grounds entirely legitimate." Belligerent and overconfident Mexicans had goaded the long-suffering United States into a fight. Such allegations seemed to reference the current state of affairs between the nations as much as they did the past.[83]

The prevailing prejudices of the era heavily influenced Smith's interpretations of the war. He brazenly proclaimed the Spaniard, Indian, and mestizo to be inferior to the Anglo-American. Although complimentary of Mexicans' courage, Smith categorized it as being "mainly of the impulsive, passionate and therefore transient sort, whereas Anglo-Saxon courage is cool, calculating, resolute and comparatively inexhaustible." Continuing his backhanded compliments, he claimed that Mexican Indians were "naturally among the best soldiers in the world," although he marveled at their perceived "indifference about their miserable lives." Smith's depraved Mexican soldier might demonstrate valor on the battlefield, but it would never compare to that of the pure-blooded American.[84]

Smith broadened his censure to include the Mexican people and their culture, scornfully classifying the average Mexican as having a "brutish disregard for dirt." Drawing upon the stereotypes of the previous century, he assumed that Indian women were "always tricky, obstinate, indolent, peevish and careless yet affectionate and hospitable." "Loving flowers much but a dagger more," the contradictory Mexican woman was a creature to be feared more than trusted. As far as Catholicism was concerned, he believed the faith "gave no help; and the ceremonies of worship benumbed the intellect as much as they fascinated the senses." Throughout his work Smith attacked Mexicans and their institutions, painting a portrait of a degraded people entirely deserving of their fate.[85]

When Columbia University bestowed the prestigious Pulitzer Prize on Smith's *The War with Mexico*, it legitimized this racial interpretation that pitted noble Anglo-Americans against an aggressive "mongrel" nation. After decades of North–South polemics, changing national priorities led Americans to welcome new analyses of the conflict that better fit their evolving attitudes and priorities. Strained relations with Mexico during the 1910s, coupled with an imperialist-charged social Darwinism, inspired American authors to create works that assuaged the nation's guilt for waging a morally ambiguous war. This trend would persist throughout the 1920s.[86]

The rising interest in written histories of the U.S.–Mexican War corresponded with the declining number of the conflict's survivors. As their numbers continued to dwindle into the late 1920s, the fallen warriors of the U.S.–Mexican War occasionally attracted the notice of the nation. The deaths of the last three veterans elicited particular national media attention. The morbid countdown began with the loss of Richard Howard in November of 1928. William F. T. Buckner's death in June of 1929 so moved his fellow Missourians that they designated his home in the town of Paris an official historic landmark. With the passing of Owen Thomas Edgar on September 3, 1929, the nation lost its last living connection to its war with Mexico. The *New York Times* blandly documented his death with no discussion of the war, its controversies, or its accomplishments.[87]

The demise of the veterans signaled the end of an era in the memory of the U.S.–Mexican War. During the second half of the nineteenth century these soldiers had been a notable political force. Wielding control of their own memory, they successfully battled Congress for service pensions. As their vitality waned, other groups learned to manipulate their remembrance in the service of a number of social, racial, and economic goals. Organizations both with and without direct ties to the U.S.–Mexican War deftly wielded the memory of the conflict in a fight for white supremacy, middle-class privilege, and empire building. Using public commemorations and monuments as their weapons, these groups staked out their territory and challenged all who threatened their hegemony. Ultimately, memory became yet another means of demarcating power and position in American society.[88]

6 Rituals of the State

MEXICO, 1921–1952

❖

ON OCTOBER 12, 1921, the president of Mexico, Álvaro Obregón, appointed José Vasconcelos minister of the newly created Secretaría de Educación Pública (SEP). As a young, idealistic attorney and writer who belonged to a group of revolutionaries known as the Ateneo de la Juventud (Athenaeum of Youth), Vasconcelos was a natural choice to head the SEP. His radical ideas intimidated the former president Venustiano Carranza, who had forced him into exile in the United States. The day after Carranza's assassination, however, Vasconcelos returned to Mexico City eager to help his nation. By centralizing the administration of all of Mexico's schools Vasconcelos was able to radically overhaul the nation's education system. He not only spearheaded national literacy programs and built campuses in rural villages and urban slums, but also promoted a romanticized memory of Mexico's past to instill a sense of nationalism and pride in the country's youth. Although his tenure at the SEP was short, Vasconcelos laid the foundation for an educational system that embraced the memory of the War of North American Intervention as a tool to promote an idealized image of Mexican citizenship.[1]

Under Porfirio Díaz, memory of the war with the United States served as a means of solidifying his ties with the military. Elaborate ceremonies at Chapultepec Park celebrated the mythic acts of the heroic cadets who died there and reaffirmed the officer corps' loyalty to the president. During the Mexican Revolution subsequent leaders co-opted these commemorations and likewise used them to enhance their power base. As the bloodshed came to an end in 1920, Mexico faced a shattered economy, struggling democratic institutions, and poor relations with the United States. Confronted with the hard realities of reconstruction, Mexico's rulers forsook many of the idealistic goals of the Revolution. In lieu of radical reform the government gave the people a new nationalistic identity built upon their indigenous heritage and legacy of military heroism. This new nationalism became a hallmark of Mexican identity that was embraced by repressive and progressive leaders alike.[2]

Between 1921 and 1952 Mexican educators, artists, politicians, and military leaders used the memory of the War of North American Intervention to promote patriotism and nationalism. Unlike earlier periods, in this era efforts were aimed mainly at the general population rather than at the nation's military and civilian elites. As Mexico moved again toward democracy, it was vital for leaders to encourage the loyalty and support of the people. The writers of textbooks evoked the memory of the Boy Heroes to inspire a sense of national pride and obedience in young children. Filmmakers enshrined these ideals in popular culture by producing a feature motion picture graphically illustrating the story of the self-sacrificing cadets. Mexican politicians took the reins of the war's commemoration at Chapultepec from the military and built additional monuments around the country. In a bid to regain authority over the memory of the conflict, the Military College and the Mexican army began a quest for the lost remains of the Boy Heroes. Ironically, the increased interest in the war occurred while relations with the United States steadily improved. North Americans, looking for allies in the fight against fascism and communism, made conciliatory gestures toward Mexicans to assuage resentments lingering since 1848. This attitude prompted Mexico's leaders to find ways of celebrating their resistance to the United States without alienating their powerful northern neighbor. Their solution was to focus almost exclusively on the Boy Heroes, nonideological children who might be venerated without offending the United States.

The creation of the SEP in 1921 heralded a massive expansion of the postrevolutionary education system in Mexico. The nation's literacy rates climbed as learned Mexicans answered the call for "cada uno enseña a uno" (each one teach one) and began instructing their fellow citizens how to read. It would take decades for these reforms to touch the far reaches of the republic, yet the SEP brought much-needed progress. Previously, the story of the Boy Heroes had largely served the nation's elite, but increased literacy during the 1920s spread this important myth throughout the country and provided an example for all young Mexicans to follow.

While the United States would always be seen as the aggressor, postrevolutionary textbooks focused on how traitors within Mexico had hastened the nation's defeat. Like writers in the Porfiriato, those of the 1920s criticized the country's technological disadvantages to encourage the nation's industrialization and modernization. The authors also blamed aristocratic officers, scheming clergy, and apathetic citizens for undermining the country's stability. Their publications promoted government efforts to inspire a fiercely loyal citizenry that would put love of country before self. Understanding the need to reach the rising generation, state-supported educators used text-books to extol the virtues of the Boy Heroes and instill patriotism in the nation's youth.

While there was still no unified curriculum program, certain works were popular. For reasons of economic necessity, many postrevolutionary Mexican history textbooks were merely revised editions of works written in earlier eras. Gregorio Torres Quintero, a professor at the Teacher's College of Mexico, originally wrote *The Mexican Fatherland: Elements of National History* during the Díaz's reign. Torres Quintero survived the Revolution to serve in the SEP and in 1922 published the tenth edition of his popular history. In his updated prologue, Torres Quintero declared to the nation's youth that "the love of the fatherland and the things pertaining to it, is one of the most noble sentiments that one could nourish in the human heart. Because of this, from the beginning of the world, the patriot has been praised and the traitor scoffed." He implored the children to "love your Fatherland and prepare to serve it!"[3]

Torres Quintero dedicated several pages to a discussion of the War of North American Intervention. He portrayed a conflict that the United States won not because it had braver or more skilled soldiers but because of its technological advantages. To stress the moral weakness of North Americans he included an account of prisoners of war displaying rosaries to their Mexican captors and pitiably begging for their lives. He likewise showed contempt for the disloyal Mexican clergy and aristocrats who allowed the nation to be invaded. Predictably, he reserved his greatest praise for the Boy Heroes: "Beardless youths, many of them almost boys, felt nonetheless a great love for the Fatherland and hatred for the invader, they fought like men, perishing gloriously with their weapons in their hands. . . . Glory to the cadets of the Military College forever! Noble and heroic youth that offered their blood and life to the Fatherland in its hour of danger!" The six cadets were illustrated in a series of overlapping cartouches ringed in the figurative laurels of victory. This image, or a variation thereof, continued to appear in textbooks for decades (see fig. 13).[4]

In 1926 Alfonso Toro wrote *Compendium of Mexican History,* a textbook whose significance lay in the fact that it was written entirely in the postrevolutionary period. Like Torres Quintero, Toro considered Mexico's defeat in the War of North American Intervention the result of poor equipment and self-interested officers:

> The forces of the invader were physically superior; by their weaponry, by their artillery, precision of their munitions, by the abundance of their rations and money, by their transportation, by their discipline, by their training and re-

cruiting. Our forces were valiant but in terrible condition, without confidence
in their officers and leaders; their weapons were outdated, the old artillery
was of short range and poor condition; the cavalry almost useless and their
maneuvers desperately slow; there were no ambulances, provisions, hospitals,
or proper transport for the army. . . . The misery in which the army lived as a
result of repeated coup d'états is truly disgraceful.

He also claimed that, in addition to Santa Anna's incompetence, a traitor
had betrayed the army at Buena Vista, thereby depriving Mexico of a victory it otherwise would have won.[5]

To describe the Boy Heroes, Toro quoted a supposed eyewitness account
recorded in Edward D. Mansfield's *Life and Services of General Winfield
Scott.* The report discussed the aftermath of the capture of the Military
College: "In it were crowds of prisoners of every rank and color; among
whom were fifty general officers, and about a hundred cadets of the Mexican Military Academy. The latter were pretty little fellows from ten to sixteen years of age. Several of them were killed fighting like demons; and,
indeed, they showed an example of courage worthy of imitation by some
of their superiors in rank." Toro incorrectly claimed that Mansfield had
fought in the battle and was writing as a participant. In reality the author
merely cited a letter written to the *New York Courier and Enquirer.* This
account also portrayed the cadets as being much younger than they were.
Being ten to sixteen years old, they were much closer to the age of the children reading the textbook. There was also a message that these young cadets
were capable of a patriotism that surpassed that of their adult officers. The
example of the brave students helped to inspire a love of country in Mexico's
schoolchildren.[6]

Textbooks were not the only means of promoting the memory of the Boy
Heroes during the 1920s. After a challenging decade, the Association of the
Military College continued to promote its commemorations at Chapultepec
Park. Although the organization began holding annual elections and meetings once again, the varied loyalties of its individual members during the
Revolution sullied the group's public reputation. In 1920 President Obregón
ordered the Military College overhauled and distanced himself from the old
guard of the Revolution. The next year the association attempted to bolster
its ties to a more glorious past by placing tablets at Chapultepec Castle de-
noting the specific locations where the Boy Heroes were reported to have
fallen. Just as historical markers in the United States glorified the groups that
installed them, these memorials served as reminders of the association's
greatness and demarcated its authority in territory disputed with the civil
government.[7]

In spite of the association's markers the group was steadily losing control over the public commemoration at Chapultepec Park. The most meaningful change to the event occurred when the federal government moved the official day of celebration from the eighth of September to the thirteenth. This effectively removed the ceremonies from the control of the Association of the Military College, which had been the sponsor of the event since its beginning. The association attended the public celebration on September 13, but in a show of defiance it continued to hold its own private memorial on the original date, a practice that continues to this day.[8]

In the aftermath of the Revolution, President Obregón was anxious to gain the confidence of the United States. Lest he be perceived as anti–North American, he downplayed the events at Chapultepec until he was officially recognized as president following the Bucareli Accords in 1923. In this agreement Obregón promised to safeguard foreign oil interests in Mexico and participate in a commission to redress North American property losses suffered during the Revolution. Once endowed with international legitimacy Obregón was free to join his predecessors in memorializing the War of North American Intervention. Almost immediately he gave his blessing to the building of a new monument honoring the one hundredth anniversary of the founding of the Military College. Such a gesture, however, concealed his growing contempt for the academy, which languished in neglect during the mid-1920s.[9]

Obregón's successful negotiations with the United States were met with an uprising within the ranks of his own officer corps. In yet another power struggle the former interim president Adolfo de la Huerta led a revolt of disaffected soldiers and politicians against Obregón. After several bloody battles, forces loyal to the president crushed the rebellion. Not satisfied with merely defeating the opposition Obregón had many of his former associates executed by firing squad, a retribution so swift that it stunned even the president's closest allies. Vasconcelos, the architect of the postrevolutionary school system, resigned in disgust. Obregón, however, through intimidation convinced his wayward minister of public education to come back into the fold.[10]

In 1924, six months after crushing the rebellion by de la Huerta, Obregón decided to participate in the celebration at Chapultepec. His increasing disregard for the Military College had provoked discontent in the once-proud institution. Half of Obregón's army had turned against him in the recent revolt, and he had good reason to fear disloyalty. The commemoration therefore allowed Obregón to use Chapultepec to bind him and his handpicked successor, Plutarco Elías Calles, to the nation's rising generation of officers at the college. At the ceremony, however, Obregón could not escape the indignation of those disillusioned by his brutality. The keynote speaker, Vasconcelos's general director of primary education, Francisco

César Morales, obliquely aimed criticism at Obregón's violence, claiming that "crushing rebellions" could not dampen the spirit of the defiant cadets, who "preferred to die than live on their knees." Given his already tenuous relationship to Vasconcelos and the SEP, Obregón overlooked the intentional slight.[11]

His predecessor's growing interest in the Chapultepec commemoration notwithstanding, President Calles was indifferent to the event, although he did order his minister of war, Gen. Joaquín Amaro, to rehabilitate the derelict Military College. Even so, lingering power struggles prevented him from throwing his full support behind the celebrations. In 1927, for example, Calles was scheduled to officiate but canceled after the former director of the college, Gen. José Domingo Ramírez Garrido, was implicated in a plot to murder Obregón. Tensions grew worse the next year, when a religious fanatic named José de León Toral succeeded in killing Obregón shortly after he had been elected for a second, nonconsecutive term as president of Mexico. Toral's subsequent trial and execution overshadowed events at Chapultepec in 1928.[12]

After Obregón's assassination Calles maintained control of the federal government by appointing a succession of three loyal provisional presidents who ruled between 1928 and 1934. In this era the government began to focus more on the heroes and symbols of the Mexican Revolution to instill obedience and patriotism among the people. Calles, a former general in the Constitutional Army, had always favored commemorations of the conflict in which he personally played a role. The celebration of the dead revolutionary *caudillos*—Francisco Madero, Emiliano Zapata, Venustiano Carranza, and Pancho Villa—dominated the landscape of Mexico's memory throughout this era. Although these men had disparate agendas and often fought one another, the government molded their public memories to inspire respect for postrevolutionary institutions and rulers. The emphasis on the masculine nature of these powerful generals temporarily eclipsed the youthful cadets.[13]

During this time of government neglect, the former president of the Association of the Military College Gen. Juan Manuel Torrea moved to reestablish the importance of his organization. In 1931 Torrea published a comprehensive history of the college entitled *The Life of a Glorious Institution*. While the book covered ninety years of the school's history, Torrea highlighted its ties to the War of North American Intervention. The title page included a photograph of the Obelisk of the Boy Heroes decorated for the anniversary of the Battle of Chapultepec. It also contained an illustration of the Greek god Chronos making a burnt offering to the obelisk, ensuring that memory of the cadets would endure through time.[14]

Of the six cadets, Torrea focused principally on Agustín Melgar. The extolling of Melgar was popular in the 1930s, and his story proved to be particularly instructional in the postrevolutionary era. According to Torrea,
Melgar had resigned from the Military College but rushed back to his old
school when he heard that U.S. forces were converging on it. The story of an
errant cadet returning to his duty ensured Mexicans that it was not too late
to rededicate themselves to the nation. Confirming the didactic function of
the story, Torrea declared that Melgar was "the prototype of the patriot and
loyal and valiant Mexican." Although the legend of Juan Escutia's martyrdom while wrapped in the Mexican flag would eventually dominate the
memory of the Boy Heroes, Melgar's story remained prominent throughout
the rest of the decade.[15]

Perhaps inspired by Torrea's book, Interim-President Abelardo L. Rodríguez reversed the trend of presidential neglect and paid a small honor to the
Battle of Chapultepec. During his term as president in 1932–33 he bestowed the Medal of Military Merit on the flag of the Batallón de San Blas.
While awarding an honor usually reserved for soldiers to a unit's colors
might seem odd, this flag held tremendous symbolic value. It was the banner
that Lt. Col. Felipe Santiago Xicoténcatl had wrapped around his bullet-
riddled body to keep it from falling into the hands of the North Americans
at Chapultepec. Generations of cadets at the Military College had pledged
allegiance to this blood-stained reminder of North American aggression.
The medal and its accompanying ribbons were pinned to the upper corner
of the flag.[16]

In 1934 the leftist Lázaro Cárdenas won the presidential election. Under
his Six-Year Plan he returned governance to the original spirit of the Revolution. The new president deftly galvanized the backing of the military,
labor, and intellectual elites to initiate a number of radical reforms. He outlawed capital punishment and redistributed land to the rural poor of the
country. He cut his salary in half and moved the presidential residence from
Chapultepec Castle to the more modest Los Pinos mansion. Cárdenas also
ordered that the former Military College be converted into the National
Museum of History, ensuring that the remembrance of the war would never
be far from the nation's public memory.[17]

Cárdenas further shaped the memory of the war through his Socialist
Education program. Building on Vasconcelos's earlier successes, the president gave new guidelines to the SEP regarding the instruction of Mexico's
youth. This federal program was an extension of educational reforms he
had pioneered as governor of the state of Michoacán. Key to his system was
the philosophy that school should be a place where young Mexicans learned

national solidarity and camaraderie. Bearing exclamatory titles like *Forward!* and *Fatherland!,* the textbooks of the era taught basic lessons in math, reading, and the sciences with a sense of nationalistic fervor.[18]

In 1935 Jorge de Castro Cancio, in cooperation with the Department of Libraries at the SEP, published *History of the Fatherland,* a secondary school textbook that adopted the popular view that southern slave power in the United States had caused the war. Like earlier authors, Castro focused on the technological advantages of the United States. When the United States forced Mexicans to capitulate, the defeated soldiers did so "with all the honors of war." Ultimately, the clergy, aristocracy, and Santa Anna betrayed the nation to the North Americans. Illustrations showed both the typical linked cartouches of the cadets and a photograph of the obelisk. The text explained, "The sacrifice of the Boy Heroes and the many acts of valor and fortitude of our soldiers speak highly of national honor and wash away the torpor and lack of patriotism of Santa Anna and other government officials which stained a painful page in our history." In Mexico's modern secular state the Boy Heroes played the role of Christian redeemers by atoning for the nation's sins with their blood. Perhaps more important, such stories taught Mexican children to place the honor and welfare of the nation before their own lives.[19]

Of all the reforms Cárdenas enacted in his six-year presidency none attracted more international attention than his decision to nationalize Mexico's oil industry. After mediating a year of labor disputes between Mexican unions and foreign oil interests, Cárdenas announced on March 18, 1938, that he was repudiating the Bucareli Accords and enforcing Mexico's subsoil rights as outlined in the nation's constitution. As oil corporations in the United States pressed President Franklin Delano Roosevelt for military intervention, Cárdenas rallied Mexican support with appeals to nationalism.[20]

Among his strategies, Cárdenas turned to the memory of Mexico's greatest symbol of North American resistance, the Boy Heroes, to inspire the public to support his agenda politically and financially. He began attending the September commemorations at Chapultepec. The SEP also increased its presence at the observances, making it clear that the Boy Heroes would continue to be integrated into the nation's education system. Economic defiance of the United States in 1938 was ritually tied to Mexico's military resistance in 1847 and 1914. At the Chapultepec ceremony that year Cárdenas invited survivors of the invasion of Veracruz in 1914 to take part in the celebration. In addition, the names of the two slain cadets of the Naval Military Academy were added to the list of young men honored. Mexicans, rich and poor alike, donated their money, jewelry, grain, and livestock to the national reparation fund to reimburse foreign corporations for their losses. In spite of calls for war, President Roosevelt remained steadfast in his pledge of nonintervention.[21]

Mexican nationalism soared as it became clear that the country's gamble was an undisputed victory. The oil expropriation, with its inherent defiance of the United States, once again inspired interest in the War of North American Intervention. This national exuberance found expression through the new medium of cinema. In 1938 Mexican writers drafted two screenplays about the Boy Heroes: *He Died for the Fatherland: The Boy Heroes of Chapultepec* was an attempt by the historian Alfonso Teja Zabre to bring his recent book, *Chapultepec,* to the silver screen. The script, an overt piece of propaganda filled with nationalistic rhetoric, confirmed the mythic stories of the Boy Heroes that were commonly celebrated at Chapultepec and written about in children's books. Inherent weaknesses in the story doomed the project to failure, however, and Mexican film producers rejected the hagiographic tale.[22]

The veteran screenwriter Íñigo de Martino had more success with his Chapultepec story. He partnered with the first-time author Alfredo de Noriega to write *El Cementerio de las Águilas* (The Cemetery of the Eagles), which presented a fictionalized account of Melgar's final months of life. Jorge Negrete, one of Mexico's most popular movie stars and singers, played the role of Miguel de la Peña, Melgar's friend and mentor. The film chronicled the two young men's romantic pursuit of the aristocratic Nieves de Zúñiga y Miranda sisters as the capital nervously awaited the arrival of the United States Army in 1847. In addition to the lighthearted romance and a musical number by Negrete, the film included dramatic recreations of the battles of Churubusco and Chapultepec.[23]

The widely popular film proved extremely important in solidifying the image of the War of North American Intervention in Mexico's public memory. In spite of government efforts, persistent illiteracy limited the populace's exposure to the written accounts of the war. Older citizens who did not enjoy the fruits of education reform could now visually learn the story for the modest price of theater admission. In spite of a printed disclaimer in the opening credits, many viewers no doubt accepted the dramatized version as historical fact. This allowed the filmmakers to shape the memory of the war for thousands of their fellow Mexicans.[24]

Significantly, the film's first image was a credit thanking "President of the Republic, Major General, Lázaro Cárdenas," a device that harkened back to the turn-of-the-century histories that lavished obsequiousness on Díaz in their opening pages. Such an expression, displayed so prominently in the film, gave the impression that the production was tacitly approved by Cárdenas. At the very least it signaled that the film would celebrate the nationalistic spirit inspired by the president and his policies.

The violent scenes of combat in the final act offset the music and romance of the film's first hour. The filmmakers portrayed the Battle of Churubusco as a near victory that was lost because Santa Anna sent the wrong cartridges to the convent. The audience witnessed a wounded but defiant Gen. Pedro María de Anaya surrender Churubusco only after expending his last bullet. In a scene which boosted Mexico's sense of pride, an impressed Gen. David Twiggs of the United States Army refused to accept the brave commander's sword of surrender.

The film's treatment of the Boy Heroes visually taught Mexicans how their revered martyrs died. One by one the valiant young men succumbed to the North American onslaught. Cadet Escutia seized the Mexican flag that flew over the Military College just as Yankee soldiers breeched its defenses. Without hesitation, he leaped from the castle wall, while a horrified Melgar watched helplessly from his post. As the young cadet tumbled to the foot of the hill shrouded in the nation's colors, a North American officer cradled his head and exclaimed to his men, "He is just a child, but a hero." The invaders paused a moment to salute his lifeless body.

As the slaughter continued, Melgar barricaded himself inside the school and kept up a devastating fire. Finally, two large soldiers pinned him to a door with a bayonet charge. As they moved in for the coup de grâce their commander cried out, "Stop! Brave boy." Melgar survived long enough for Miguel de la Peña to find him in the hospital ward. Perhaps symbolic of his nation's loss, doctors amputated the battered cadet's arm and leg before he died professing his love for Mercedes Nieves de Zúñiga y Miranda. De la Peña then returned to the girl's mansion to break the news of Melgar's death. Devastated by her love's tragic end, Mercedes begged to know where his body was buried. De la Peña stoically replied, "In the cemetery of the eagles." When she asked him where that was, he answered in a swell of melodramatic music, "Any piece of Mexican land covered by those who have given their lives for her." A montage of patriotic Mexican images provided a stirring dénouement.

Like all works of art, *The Cemetery of the Eagles* not only sheds light on the era in which it was created but also reveals important attitudes about the War of North American Intervention. There was a strong appeal to Mexican unity and nationalism. In one of the film's opening scenes Melgar and de la Peña quelled an uprising in the capital by appealing to patriotism and unity in the face of the landing of U.S. forces at Veracruz. As in Torrea's history of Chapultepec, Melgar decided to leave the Military College, but after finding himself shamed before the Nieves de Zúñiga y Miranda family he returned in time to die in its defense.[25]

In its treatment of class and gender the film portrayed women as being virtuous and patriotic. Mercedes boldly crossed class lines by falling in love with the poor Melgar. Her spurned suitor, an aristocratic army officer, proved himself a coward, trembling behind a boulder while the cadets fought to their deaths. The film demonstrated that the upper classes could exhibit both virtue and vice. Nevertheless, it was essential for all Mexicans to work together for the good of the nation.

The cinematic portrayal of the United States revealed the condition of international relations in 1939. President Roosevelt had shown restraint when he refused to interfere with Mexico's nationalization of U.S. oil interests. The North American soldiers in the film therefore exhibited a corresponding honor and chivalry, consistently showing respect and reverence for defeated and fallen Mexican soldiers. From a Mexican perspective it was clear that North Americans esteemed their foes. While not an entirely accurate interpretation of the attitudes of the United States in 1847, the film nevertheless gave the audience a sense of pride in their glorious defeat.

The Cemetery of the Eagles premiered on September 1, 1939. History would not, however, mark this date because of the film. It would remember instead the German tanks, planes, and infantry that blitzed across the Polish frontier that day, igniting the Second World War. The onset of this global crisis had a profound impact on U.S.–Mexican relations. Any lingering anger over the expropriation of oil was forgotten as the need for continental solidarity trumped past resentments. As the United States drew closer to the conflict, it realized that Mexico's natural resources, cheap labor, and deepwater harbors made the nation an indispensable ally should war reach the Americas.[26]

The rising popularity of the Boy Heroes during the Cárdenas administration underscored their unique role in Mexicans' memory. As innocent youths the martyred students rose above partisanship and ideology to represent an ideal of Mexican patriotism and citizenship. Since so little was known about the cadets individually, it was possible to mold their remembrance to fit a number of social and political agendas. Perhaps most important for Mexicans of this era, the Boy Heroes posed no challenge to a healthy diplomatic relationship with the United States. The six cadets no longer engendered feelings of resentment toward North Americans. They instead inspired pride in the indomitable Mexican spirit and forwarded the president's domestic and international goals.

Cárdenas completed his eventful term of office at the end of 1940. In a contentious and violent election his secretary of defense, Manuel Ávila

Camacho, became president. The Federal Bureau of Investigations in the United States, fearing chaos in Mexico, met secretly with Ávila Camacho's brother to offer covert support for his campaign. In an explicit show of Roosevelt's approval, Vice President–Elect Henry A. Wallace attended the inauguration in Mexico City on December 1, 1940. The day after the ceremony Wallace visited the Obelisk to the Boy Heroes and laid a wreath to honor both the cadets and his country's dedication to peace with Mexico. Even though Wallace was not the first North American to make such a tribute, he was the first to do so in an official capacity since General Otis had laid a wreath in the days before the Revolution. Chapultepec had witnessed many similar rituals binding Mexico's rulers to its military. This time, however, it served to bind Mexico to the United States. The importance of the gesture was not wasted on German agents working in Mexico City who hired agitators to harass Wallace at every turn.[27]

As Ávila Camacho assumed leadership of the nation, federal officials commissioned the famed sculptor Juan Fernando Olaguíbel to construct a massive stone and bronze monument honoring Anaya in a prominent square in the Tlalpan district of Mexico City. Although the former general briefly served as Mexico's president during the North American occupation of the capital, the memorial instead commemorated his "glorious defense" of the convent at Churubusco. A popular account of the battle had Gen. Twiggs asking the wounded Anaya where the garrison's munitions were stored. In response the defiant Mexican reportedly quipped, "If I had any ammunition left, you wouldn't be here." Celebrating the unbowed leader, Olaguíbel sculpted relief scenes of the general and his men desperately defending the convent to the last bullet. Sensitive to the growing friendship between Mexico and the United States, however, no portrayal or mention was made of whom Anaya was actually fighting. In spite of its artistic merit, in the 1960s the ambiguous monument was moved to a quiet park adjoining the convent (see fig. 14).[28]

Mexico had remained out of foreign wars since the French Intervention; nonetheless, Mexicans watched world events in 1941 with some anxiety. As violence spread across the globe, Mexican newspapers diligently reported developments from the battlefronts. Ávila Camacho was interested in maintaining friendship with his powerful and supportive northern neighbor and had no desire to dredge up the memory of past aggression. Understandably, he had little use for the commemorations at Chapultepec and chose not to attend the first ceremony held during his presidency on September 13, 1941. The press coverage in *El Universal* reflected the president's attitude. While the newspaper reported on the "brilliant ceremony yesterday in Chapultepec," the single article about the observance never mentioned the United

States by name. The pages were dedicated instead to other events, particularly news of the war.[29]

On December 7, 1941, the Japanese launched a surprise attack on North American forces stationed at Pearl Harbor, Hawaii, thrusting the United States into the war. Attacks by German U-boats on oil tankers in the Gulf of Mexico during the spring of 1942 likewise provoked Mexico to declare war and join the Allies in their fight against the Axis powers. To successfully wage a two-front war, both the United States and Mexico needed to forget their violent shared history and focus on present challenges.[30]

If President Ávila Camacho was to rally support for this unprecedented level of international cooperation he had to counter decades of nationalism built upon resistance to the United States. He therefore continued to distance himself from commemorations of the War of North American Intervention. On September 13, 1942, for example, a party of the recently formed Comisión México–Norteamerica de Defensa Conjunto (Mexican–American Joint Defense Commission) arrived in Mexico City. Paying no attention to the memorials for the Boy Heroes, Ávila Camacho spent the next few days meeting with the U.S. delegation to plan their shared defense strategy. The president's North American guests attended Independence Day celebrations while neglecting those at Chapultepec.[31]

In spite of the military alliance, resentments simmered beneath the facade of pan-American unity. North American oil interests continued to press for the return of their privileged position until Ávila Camacho agreed to a final financial settlement in 1943. Anglo-American racism toward Mexicans, however, further threatened to jeopardize wartime goodwill. The Bracero Agreement of 1942 brought three hundred thousand Mexican laborers to the United States to aid in the war effort. Reported abuses of the guest workers and violence against Mexican Americans in Los Angeles during the Zoot Suit Riots enraged some in Mexico City. In spite of individual acts of racism, the U.S. government augmented the Mexican military through the Lend-Lease Act and loaned millions of dollars to build the nation's underdeveloped infrastructure to facilitate trade and security. While issuing official protests over the mistreatment of his citizens, Ávila Camacho remained focused on the advantages of his political and economic ties to the United States.[32]

As his presidential term continued through the tumultuous war years Ávila Camacho found yet another reason to distance himself from Chapultepec. In the spring of 1944 a graduate of the Military College named José Antonio de la Lama Rojas attempted to assassinate the president. Lama Rojas had published a pamphlet about the Boy Heroes and emulated his cadet idols by wrapping the Mexican flag around his body during the failed attack. In this instance the symbolic defiance of the Boy Heroes backfired against Mexico's rulers. Understandably, Ávila Camacho avoided all remaining commemorations of the cadets.[33]

Even in the face of presidential neglect not everyone was willing to let the memory of the Boy Heroes fade. Mexico was committing troops to the first conflict it had ever fought on foreign soil. Mexican fighter pilots were flying missions in the Pacific Theater of Operations, earning respect and admiration at home and among the allied nations. Thousands of Mexican citizens living north of the border were serving in the U.S. armed forces and bringing further glory to the land of their birth. There was a growing sense of Mexican military prowess, and army officers lobbied for greater recognition of their nation's martial legacy. In his commemoration speech at Chapultepec Park in 1944 Gen. Tomás Sánchez Hernández called upon the government to build a larger monument to the Boy Heroes. Ávila Camacho refused the request.[34]

While the president publicly downplayed the war's memory, the SEP continued using the Boy Heroes to promote nationalism among the youth. The ministry and other educational publishers produced four primary and secondary school textbooks during these years that dealt with the War of North American Intervention. The publications, punctuated with dramatic illustrations and stories of self-sacrificing children, continued to encourage boys and girls to put the well-being of the nation above their own. The fact that these books thrived during his presidency suggested that Ávila Camacho tacitly supported the nationalistic message of the Boy Heroes while at the same time trying to minimize public confrontation with the United States.[35]

Some of this renewed interest in the war was no doubt inspired by the anticipated opening of the Museo Nacional de Historia at Chapultepec Castle. On September 27, 1944, President Ávila Camacho dedicated the museum. In a modest gesture to the Association of the Military College, Ávila Camacho declared that the venerated banner of the San Blas Battalion was to be the official flag of the new institution. The museum exhibited the history of Mexico from the colonial period to the present, but there were still indications that the building had been the location of the most celebrated battle of the War of North American Intervention. The most visible reminders were six larger-than-life bronze statues of the Boy Heroes dramatically mounted on the south-facing patio overlooking the city (see fig. 15).[36]

Compared to the many murals and exhibits in the restored castle, however, the War of North American Intervention was a small part of the overall installation. How Ávila Camacho felt about the details of the museum remains unclear. Lázaro Cárdenas planned the project during his administration, and Ávila Camacho inherited it when he took office. Minor controversies aside, it was an obvious source of pride for the nation and remains an important tourist destination. Even so, this would be the president's last public involvement with the memory of the conflict. A more pressing war continued to unite him with his nation's former enemy, and he worked tirelessly to see it to a successful conclusion.[37]

The coming of peace during the summer of 1945 changed the international landscape. As the victorious Allies competed to control Europe and Asia, their alliance fractured along ideological lines. In the midst of the political realignments of 1946 Miguel Alemán Valdés became president of Mexico. While he sought to maintain strong political, social, and economic ties to the United States, he also brought a new attitude about the War of North American Intervention. Rather than avoid reminders of the conflict, he nurtured and placed them firmly under his control. This was particularly important as he ascended to the presidency during the centennial anniversary. Seeing an opportunity to gain favor with both the United States and the Mexican people, Alemán wisely learned when to embrace the centenary and when to ignore it.[38]

The 1946–48 centennial of the U.S.–Mexican War passed largely unnoticed in the United States (see chapter 7). The opposite was true in Mexico. To facilitate the anniversary commemorations the Mexican government appointed Gen. Aarón Sáenz to head the Comité Nacional Pro-Conmemoración Héroes 1846–1847. While the work of the committee began immediately, the observances focused on the upcoming centennial of the invasion of Mexico City in the summer of 1947. Working with the Alemán government, the national committee oversaw the publication of books related to the war. The president also approved postage stamps depicting the individual Boy Heroes and heroes of the battles of Chapultepec and Molino del Rey. Adding to public awareness of the upcoming events, government and private mints produced a variety of commemorative coins and medallions honoring the Batallón de San Patricio, the Battle of Chapultepec, and the Continental Parade to be held on September 13, 1947.[39]

Outside the authority of the national committee, additional authors contributed to the centennial anniversary excitement. In a flurry of publications, these writers examined a wide variety of topics related to the war. Important general histories written in 1947 included Francisco Castillo Nájera's *North American Invasion,* Vicente Fuentes Díaz's *The North American Intervention in Mexico,* and José C. Valades's *Brief History of the War with the United States.* Two diplomatic histories, Castillo Nájera's *The Treaty of Guadalupe* and Julio Luelmo's *The North American Abolitionists: The Texas Question and the War with Mexico,* along with the Spanish translation of James K. Polk's diary in 1948, revealed a growing academic curiosity about the war during this time.[40]

Demonstrating the revival of interest in the Boy Heroes, the most popular topic during the centennial period was by far the Battle of Chapultepec. Numerous newspaper and magazine articles supplemented several published works dedicated to the event. Government agencies and patriotic presses dominated the publishing of many of these titles, including *The Epic Tragedy of Chapultepec, Chapultepec in the War with the United States, Our Boy Heroes,* and *The Military College and the Defense of Chapultepec in September of 1847.*[41]

As the president's control over the memory surrounding the war grew, the Association of the Military College was pushed further into the background. During the Second World War the association had halted its annual elections once again. After the hostilities ended, the organization attempted to reassert its influence by petitioning President Alemán to build a museum and larger pantheon to the Boy Heroes. Unlike most previous Mexican presidents, Alemán was not an army veteran. As the son of a Revolutionary War general, he had witnessed that generation of officers ruthlessly turn against one another during the 1910s and 1920s. He apparently felt no strong allegiance to the aging soldiers of the association and rejected their proposed monument and museum. When the civilian urban designer Enrique Aragón Echegaray proposed a similar monument in 1947, however, the president gave his support.[42]

In anticipation of the Chapultepec centennial, officers of the Mexican army and the Military College formally requested that President Alemán allow them to conduct an archaeological survey to locate the bodies of the Boy Heroes. The officers pointed out that many visitors to the obelisk were disappointed to find out that it was merely a cenotaph and that the cadets were buried in an unknown location in the forest surrounding the castle. The veneration of the cadets, steeped in Catholic symbolism, required physical relics of the dead to legitimize the cult of the Boy Heroes. The sanitation needs of the capital in the summer of 1847, however, meant that the hundreds of Mexican casualties at Chapultepec were hurriedly buried near where they fell. This deprived those who sought to honor the Boy Heroes of the tangible proof of their martyrdom.[43]

Realizing the symbolic value of such a find, President Alemán gave his consent to a limited excavation. The survey would have to wait a month, however, as President Harry S. Truman was scheduled to visit the capital during the first week of March. Truman was aggressively courting Mexican support in the rapidly escalating Cold War with the Soviet Union, and this would mark the first excursion of a sitting U.S. president to Mexico City. Seizing the opportunity, Alemán proposed discussing a binational solution to combat an outbreak of hoof-and-mouth disease threatening the Mexican cattle industry. Alemán did not want the search for victims of Yankee aggression to tarnish the negotiations.[44]

On March 4, 1947, Truman toured Mexico's capital from the back seat of a bulletproof Lincoln Town Car. After laying a wreath at the Column of Independence, Truman asked to be taken to Chapultepec to see the Obelisk of the Boy Heroes. The unscheduled trip caused an excited commotion as officers and cadets from the Military College quickly formed ranks to welcome the president to their most revered site. Truman, along with Ambassador Walter C. Thurston, exited the motorcade bearing a floral wreath. While journalists jotted notes and took photographs, Truman somberly stepped forward and laid the wreath at the base of the monument. All grew silent as the president stood contemplating the events of 1847 with his head bowed. Foreign Minister Jaime Torres Bodet wept silently, as did some military officials, cadets, and the press corps.[45]

News of Truman's tribute to the beloved Boy Heroes spread quickly throughout the capital. Throngs crowded the route of the presidential motorcade shouting "Viva!" to their newfound North American hero. That evening, as Truman visited a cultural program in the National Stadium, the crowd roared enthusiastically for him. Bands blared martial airs as an honor guard from the Mexican army fired a twenty-one-gun salute. Why did Truman's simple act carry such symbolic power for Mexicans? Many interpreted the gesture as an admission of guilt for the invasion of 1846–47. A taxi driver named Juan Gomez, for example, exclaimed, "I even cry when I hear this. To think that the most powerful man in the world would come and apologize." After a century of nursing wounds to their national honor, Mexicans were eager to accept Truman's act of contrition. The engineer Ramón Garza mused that "one hundred years of misunderstanding and bitterness wiped out by one man in one minute. That is the best neighbor policy."[46]

At an official state dinner that evening Truman dined with President Alemán and other state dignitaries. Finance Minister Ramón Beteta, speaking on behalf of Alemán, addressed Truman, declaring that the president "considers you the new champion of American solidarity and understanding. He feels that this trip of yours to Mexico and your attitude are going to promote a better understanding and friendship between our two countries." Foreign Minister Bodet stood and toasted Truman: "The highest kind of friendship between men and peoples is that which has the courage to base itself upon a feeling for the truth. President Truman, by rendering homage to the immortal glory of the Boy Heroes, in a gesture worthy of a gentleman and a friend, spans an abyss of the past by another bridge into the future."

Truman responded with a toast to the Mexican people in which he praised their show of hospitality "beyond compare."[47]

Not all Mexicans were glowing in their assessment of Truman and his conciliatory gesture. Former president Cárdenas rejected a formal invitation to dine with Truman at the state dinner. That night he recorded his skepticism about "Truman, the war criminal" and his visit to Mexico: "The press in the capital has described this act as 'generous,' 'atoning for,' and 'having healed the wound that Mexico suffered in 1847' . . . but acts of courtesy will not erase the wound unless the government and people of North America correspondingly treat Mexico with a sincere friendship equivalent to the wounds and humiliations that the country suffered." For Cárdenas, the United States needed to do much more than offer symbolic gestures to make amends for Mexico's losses during the war.[48]

The capital's leftist newspaper *El Popular* ran a headline exclaiming, "Truman Renews Our Faith in the Good Neighbor Policy." Like Cárdenas, however, it expressed doubt over the long-term impact of the visit, reminding its readers that North American money would never be enough to make Mexico forget the invasions of 1847 and 1914. It further cautioned its northern neighbor to continue to respect the "liberty and independence" of the Mexican people.[49]

A nationwide surge of interest in the War of North American Intervention marked the five months following Truman's visit. While North Americans congratulated themselves on having put the painful memory of the conflict to rest, Mexicans participated in the greatest period of remembrance in their history. Truman's visit made all Mexicans aware of the centennial. The driving force behind the passion for the anniversary, however, was the search for the remains of the Boy Heroes. With Truman back in the United States, military officials pushed again for an excavation at Chapultepec.

In spite of the implausibility of finding the cadets among the six hundred Mexican soldiers hastily interred after the battle, Torrea claimed to know the exact place where the cadets were buried. According to his account, the skeletons of the Boy Heroes had actually been found and reburied during a construction project in 1896. Officials of the Military College shared the location only with one another until Maj. Gen. Manuel M. Plata showed it to Torrea in 1926. Torrea took photos of the small clearing in the Chapultepec forest to document the sacred site. Twenty-one years later the aging general claimed to still remember the very spot and urged the president to allow the excavation.[50]

On March 20, 1947, army sappers began digging a trench through the alleged burial plot. Five days of searching yielded nothing but animal bones.

After consulting once again with Torrea and an elderly gentleman believed to have originally discovered the remains in 1896, the codirector of the project, Manuel de Jesus Solís, ordered the crew to begin work fifty yards to the northeast. On March 25, three weeks after Truman's homage to the Boy Heroes, soldiers found human bones in the excavation trench. A later investigation alleged that the sappers found numerous skeletons but removed only the smallest from the soil.[51]

As word spread throughout the capital that the bodies of the cadets had been located, military officers and government officials rushed to the scene. Before archaeologists had a chance to examine the bones, Mexicans had already embraced the remains as belonging to their revered Boy Heroes. On the morning of March 26, *La Prensa* ran a front-page banner headline reading, "THE REMAINS OF THE BOY HEROES OF '47 WERE FOUND." The accompanying article stated, "The bodies of the six glorious and heroic cadets of the Military College of Chapultepec, that have for one hundred years offered their youth and ideals on the altars of the Mexican fatherland, have been found in a ditch in the Forest of Chapultepec." The newspaper captured the unquestioning optimism of the nation by proclaiming that the skeletons must be those of the cadets.[52]

In spite of the confidence of the public, the Mexican government convened a board of scientists to confirm the identity of the bones. The archaeologists undoubtedly faced pressure to legitimize the remains. The cadets ranged in age from thirteen to twenty, four of the six being eighteen or older. This would make them difficult to distinguish from many of the other soldiers killed that day. Identification would also be difficult given that the original burial site had been compromised in 1896. As the untrained sappers piled skulls and bones on burlap sacks and removed them from the trench, any hope of preserving the remaining archaeological context was lost.[53]

Notwithstanding the irregularities involved in recovering the skeletons, the government asked the anthropologist Felipe Montemayor García to confirm what was already assumed by the nation. Anxiously awaiting news of the identification, General Solís declared, "I'll be hanged in the Plaza of the Constitution if it isn't them!" After a "laborious and careful classification," Montemayor García's team reported that the skulls belonged to one adult and five adolescents. On the basis of this assessment Secretary of Defense Gilberto R. Limón proclaimed that the remains were without a doubt those of the Boy Heroes. He ordered them placed in gold and crystal urns and laid in state at the Military College. A cadet honor guard remained at their side awaiting their final disposition.[54]

In a nation that had long appropriated the symbols of the Catholic Church, the discovery of the bodies of the Boy Heroes had a deep spiritual resonance for Mexicans. Arturo Sotomayor, a professor involved in the recovery, described General Limón "caressing" one of the skulls, "his fingers moving religiously over the surface of the relic." He alleged that with the exception of the teenaged Aztec emperor Cuauhtémoc "the Boy Heroes are the only figures in our history free of stain. They are the only ones in which opinion is unanimous in regard to respect and veneration. . . . To mention their names is to pronounce a eulogy to purest humanity. . . . They are the paradigm of Mexican heroism." Indeed, the remains took on the role of corporeal relics. According to Roman Catholic doctrine, church altars should be dedicated with the bones of saints or martyrs beneath them, and in keeping with this spirit the government named the proposed tomb of the cadets the Altar a la Patria (Altar to the Fatherland). The Mexican state had conflated once again the sacred and the profane to support its civic cult of patriotic martyrs.[55]

The federal government further trespassed upon the territory of the Catholic Church through the centennial commemoration at the nearby Battle of Churubusco. In 1947 officials added a large plaque to the religious complex that read, "This convent was defended by Mexican troops until they had used their last cartridges against the North Americans on the 20th of August of 1847." Although the government had secularized the building decades earlier, the placement of civic memorials in sacred space once reserved for venerated images symbolically placed the Mexican state above the church.

The co-opting of the buildings, liturgy, and symbolism of the Catholic Church had been a hallmark of the Republic of Mexico since Independence. During the Revolution the rivalry between church and state led to internal warfare and bloodshed. While the violence largely subsided in the postrevolutionary era, Mexico's two great institutions continued to compete for the hearts and minds of the people. As their veneration adopted more of the trappings of Catholicism, the Boy Heroes allowed the Mexican government a unique opportunity to tap into the church's remaining ecclesiastical authority.

With the bones of the Boy Heroes validating and consecrating the anniversary, the centennial commemoration of the Battle of Chapultepec was no small affair. It was, in fact, a three-day spectacle that involved celebrations and ceremonies throughout the capital. On Friday, September 12, the schools of Mexico City devoted the entire day to honoring the Boy Heroes, with thousands of children participating in events. Four thousand students from the Coyoacán district, for example, converged on Churubusco for celebrations hosted at the former convent. Thousands of children paraded through Chapultepec Park bearing banners, while others visited the National Museum of History and marveled at the six bronze statues of the self-sacrificing cadets.[56]

The morning of September 13 witnessed the traditional commemoration hosted by the government at Chapultepec. Thousands of people filled the park to glimpse the dedication of the cornerstone of the new Altar to the Fatherland which honored the Boy Heroes. Repeating the celebrated gesture of President Truman, Ambassador Thurston and Rear Adm. J. Harry Jones laid a wreath at the obelisk. The ceremonies concluded with a parade of the Children's Army in which young students dressed in white uniforms and armed with wooden rifles marched in review. Although Alemán presided over the day's events, he mitigated any outward sign of hostility toward his North American ally by declining to speak.[57]

That afternoon the Mexican Congress held a special session dedicated to the memory of the Boy Heroes. Members solemnly dedicated a gold plaque on the walls of the chamber to the cadets. Deputy Romero took the floor to offer a tribute to the young men. He proclaimed, "Their bloody acts of heroism and martyrdom saved the prestige of Mexico, offering an elevated and brilliant example of civic virtue not only to future generations of our nation, but to all humanity. They could not give the Mexican people a victory, but they taught us how to die for the fatherland with honor." After the congressional commemorations Mexico City hosted the Parada Continental, which included soldiers from the United States, Canada, Mexico, and nineteen Latin American countries. Ironically, the U.S. troops marched peacefully through the same streets that their invading predecessors had trod a century earlier.[58]

The final act of the centennial celebrations was held on September 14 in the historic Plaza of the Constitution. There, the president and his cabinet reviewed a parade of young soldiers from military academies around the world. Cadets from West Point stood as an honor guard over the remains of the Boy Heroes (see fig. 16). After the parade thousands of spectators crowded around a large elevated altar to see the urns containing the bones of the martyred cadets. Strategically centered in the plaza between the National Cathedral and the National Palace, the placement of the urns revealed the Mexican government's continued practice of appropriating the symbols of the Catholic Church.[59]

The newspaper *Excelsior* also conflated ecclesiastical and civic power in its reporting of the commemorations. Attributing messianic qualities to the Boy Heroes, one article asserted that "one century ago today six young cadets earned eternal life by dying for the fatherland." Another described the commemoration as an "act of veneration without precedent" and claimed that Mexico was "the only nation in the world which can glorify itself with heroic children." The boast paralleled the Latin phrase *non fecit taliter omni nationi* (God has not done it for any other nation), which Mexican Catholics commonly used to describe the appearance of Our Lady of Guadalupe to an Aztec man in 1531. In this context the Mexican government could claim a culturally familiar spiritual authority and exceptionalism that emanated not from the Catholic Church but from their secular martyrs.[60]

The appropriation of symbols was not limited to the government, however, and Protestants co-opted the Boy Heroes as a spiritual proselytizing tool in Mexico City. Around the time of the centennial celebrations the Jesus Christ Heals and Saves Church disseminated a religious tract entitled "Mexicans at the Cry of War" which featured an image of the dying cadets on the front cover. Referencing the national anthem, the pamphlet declared that Mexico was under attack by an invader much greater than "any empire or nation of the Earth." Mexico's new battle, as perceived by the Protestant minority, was to cast off the "cruel yoke" of sin. In a clear allusion to the Catholic veneration of intercessory saints and the Virgin Mary, the text specified that Jesus Christ was the "only authentic intermediary for the salvation of your soul." In this instance the Boy Heroes inspired potential converts to join the mortal struggle for the spiritual salvation of Mexico.[61]

The excitement over the Boy Heroes quickly spread beyond the capital. The city of Guadalajara, for example, commissioned Olaguíbel to create a fifty-meter-tall statue to honor the youths. At the base a bronze sculpture displayed the six cadets bearing the Mexican flag forward with weapons at the ready. At their feet was the slogan "Murieron por la Patria" (They Died for the Fatherland) and a list of their names. The top portion of the monument was an allegorical stone sculpture of Mexico as an indigenous woman standing on the wings of an eagle and serpent. The impressive work towers over a public square at the intersection of Avenida Chapultepec and Avenida Niños Héroes. Other monuments would appear in cities and towns throughout the country. Since 1947 Mexicans have named countless streets, schools, and parks in their remembrance.[62]

The centennial of the War of North American Intervention marked the anniversary of an invasion which deprived Mexico of half of its territory. Why, then, did its people so fully embrace its remembrance? For decades the nation's rulers had consciously molded memory to alter the war's meaning. After witnessing the commemorations at Chapultepec, a resident of the capital mused, "It is easy to celebrate victories. It is difficult to remember defeats. . . . They [Boy Heroes] nobly sacrificed themselves to save, not Mexican territory that was lost, but the honor of the nation." The anniversary was therefore a celebration of Mexican honor and nationalism. Defeat had become victory.[63]

Creating triumph from disaster was no easy accomplishment. Such a radical transformation required years of careful planning and manipulation. Nonetheless, the ability of collective memory to alter perception of historical events is perhaps its greatest strength. Mexico's rulers long understood the power of remembrance and jealously guarded their authority to shape and control it. While reaching the apex of its influence during the centennial in 1947, memory of the war continued to evolve to serve the needs of the government for many more years.

Moved by President Truman's enthusiastic reception in Mexico City, North Americans offered other acts of penance to inspire continental goodwill. A grass-roots movement emerged in the United States to return to Mexico the many battle flags captured during the war. Initially North Americans had hoped that Mexico would reciprocate by returning the small number of flags it had captured during the Battle of Buena Vista. The two sets of flags, however, held vastly different symbolism for the nations. As embarrassing evidence of North American imperialism, Mexico's captured colors were stored out of public view at West Point. The banners of the United States displayed by Mexico in its museums, however, represented the nation's tenacious resistance to North American aggression. Mexican lawmakers were willing to accept the return of their lost flags, but they would not surrender their esteemed tokens of bravery to the United States.[64]

On the afternoon of September 13, 1950, an honor guard of West Point cadets assembled in the Plaza of the Constitution. With their colors dipped in salute to their Mexican hosts, the cadets marched sixty-nine captured battle flags into the National Palace. Once inside, Ambassador Thurston read a letter to President Alemán and his cabinet: "The Congress of the United States, in accordance with the wishes of the people of this country, authorizes me to return these flags which have been held in honored custody. They are being brought to you by Gen. Wade H. Haislip and a group of the finest youths of this country, cadets from the United States Military and Naval Academies and from the Air Force. Their delivery is a fitting tribute to the spirit of friendship and peace which marks the present-day relations between our two countries." General Haislip, the United States Army assistant chief of staff, then stepped forward to pay tribute to the Boy Heroes. He declared that the cadets "will never be forgotten; but happily we have forgotten long since the passions and suspicions which gave rise to the struggle in which they perished." He then personally handed the first flag to the Mexican president.[65]

What the North Americans failed to recognize, however, was that the captured colors represented the failure of the Mexican military to stave off invasion. Nineteenth-century Mexicans preferred to honor the war's dead over its survivors, and twentieth-century Mexicans had similar feelings about these surviving flags. The blood-stained banner of the San Blas Battalion went uncaptured thanks to Lieutenant Colonel Xicoténcatl. It therefore held a very public place of honor at the National Museum of History. The sixty-nine flags returned by the United States were, however, tainted by capture and defeat. President Alemán astutely understood the balance between remembering and forgetting the War of North American Intervention. After politely accepting the flags, he consigned them to the storage vaults of the National Museum of History, where they remain out of public view.[66]

President Alemán's administration had one last impact on Mexico's memory of the conflict. On November 27, 1952, cadets from the Military College, clad in black dress uniforms, escorted the remains of the Boy Heroes to their final resting place in Chapultepec. After five years of construction and an expense of six million pesos, laborers and artisans had completed Aragón Echegaray's Altar to the Fatherland. The massive marble memorial stood upon a sixty-meter-wide stone riser. It was composed of an allegorical statue carved by Ernesto Tamariz that portrayed Mother Mexico holding the limp body of one child while another stood sentinel next to her. The sculpture was flanked by a crypt and six towering columns approximately thirty meters high, each topped with a bronze eagle. More than a mere monument, the structure was truly an altar sanctified by the bones of innocent martyrs. In a tribute to the Mexican army, President Alemán ordered the body of Lieutenant Colonel Xicoténcatl reinterred with the cadets. As one of modern Mexico's largest examples of monumental architecture, the Altar to the Fatherland became the focus of Chapultepec Park and remains an important destination for civic pilgrimage.[67]

Despite its symbolic importance to the Mexican people, the dedication of the Altar to the Fatherland was a subdued event compared to the centennial celebrations of the Battle of Chapultepec five years earlier. At the time President Alemán was three days away from leaving office, after a contentious election that had sparked deadly violence and left the political atmosphere in the capital filled with tension. The dedication followed an unusually severe rainy season which deluged one-third of the nation's agricultural lands and threatened thousands of Mexicans with starvation. The modest service featured speeches by Secretary of Public Education Manuel Gual Vidal, President of the National Committee for the Commemoration of the Heroes of 1846–1847 General Sáenz, Director of the Military College General Tomás Sánchez, and cadet Gonzalo Vázquez Colmenares. With little to be gained politically in the final hours of his presidency, Alemán did not address the crowd and departed quickly for other ceremonies and dedications in the capital. It would be left to his successors to discover and utilize more fully this newly consecrated sacred space.[68]

During the Porfiriato and the Revolution, Mexico's rulers used the memory of the War of North American Intervention to solidify their relationship with the military. Commemorations like those held to honor the Boy Heroes ritually united the president with the rising generation of army officers at the Military College. After 1920, however, Mexican leaders became more sophisticated and adept at wielding the memory of the war for their own purposes. The creation of a federal educational system centralized control of the country's memory and helped instill a sense of patriotism and nationalism in Mexico's schoolchildren. Popular cinema and public monuments further supported the democratization of memory and ensured that the Mexican people would remain an integral part of the nation's remembrance of the war.

7   Good Neighbors and Bad Blood

THE UNITED STATES, 1930–1965

❖

ON FEBRUARY 26, 1931, dozens of law enforcement officers surrounded a park in Los Angeles known as La Placita. In a meticulously planned operation they corralled approximately four hundred people who had been enjoying a leisurely afternoon in the sun. Immigration and Naturalization Service (INS) agents lined up the detainees and demanded proof of citizenship or legal immigration status. News of the raid spread rapidly throughout Los Angeles. The Mexican vice consuls Ricardo Hill and Joel Quiñones rushed to the scene to protest the mistreatment of their countrymen. In spite of allegations that large numbers of illegal aliens frequented the park, the INS arrested only one Japanese, five Chinese, and thirty Mexican immigrants. Still, the action sent a wave of fear through the Mexican American community. Many people with deep roots in Mexican California wondered how they had come to be foreigners in their own land.[1]

The 1930s dawned on a rapidly changing United States. The crash of the stock market in October of 1929 heralded the advent of the Great Depression. Economic instability inspired collective dread and fostered a climate of fear in the nation. Mexicans bore the brunt of America's economic anxiety in the Southwest. Once accepted as a source of cheap labor, Mexican immigrants and refugees now competed with Anglo-Americans for scarce jobs and resources. In response to the perceived threat, President Herbert Hoover instigated repatriation programs which eventually forced hundreds of thousands of people to move south across the border. The American attitude toward Mexicans at the beginning of the Great Depression was predictable when viewed in the context of the nation's collective memory of the past eighty years. Anglo-Americans' remembrance of the U.S.–Mexican War had labeled Mexicans as undesirable others years before the Great Depression deemed them expendable.[2]

153

The years between 1930 and 1965 marked a time of transition in the memory of the U.S.–Mexican War. The era began with the United States rejecting Mexican immigrants but ended with the nation giving back land it had illegally occupied a century earlier. The growing need for continental solidarity in the face of both fascism and communism inspired this change of attitude and goodwill. While state and federal governments had previously ignored the conflict with Mexico, they learned to turn to the past to make symbolic gestures of reconciliation. Official remembering—not forgetting— became a means of healing the wounds inflicted by the war. Diplomatic progress changed how the governments related to one another, but would the newfound friendship alter the memory that the United States held of Mexico?

The repatriations of Mexicans in the early 1930s symbolized the difference between official relations among heads of state and the attitudes of their citizens. Even as the mass deportations provoked a popular outcry from Mexicans on both sides of the border, the Mexican government secretly welcomed the social and economic benefits of reintegrating thousands of skilled laborers and their literate, bilingual children back into the workforce. Amicable closed-door dealings between bureaucrats often did not reflect the feelings and attitudes many Americans had about their southern neighbors. For decades North American remembrance of the U.S.–Mexican War had justified empire building in Latin America and promoted an attitude of Anglo supremacy. This pervasive bigotry proved embarrassing at a diplomatic level, however, prompting the U.S. government to attempt to change popular attitudes by exerting control over the memory of the conflict.[3]

The presidency of Franklin Delano Roosevelt marked the beginning of meaningful progress in relations with Mexico. In his inauguration speech of 1933 Roosevelt pledged the United States to a Good Neighbor Policy which repudiated military intervention in Latin America and the Caribbean. True to his word, the president withdrew U.S. forces from Nicaragua and Haiti. Large-scale deportations of Mexicans also came to an end. Lingering memories of past American aggression, however, jeopardized Roosevelt's proposed goodwill. Forgetting about the intervention in 1914, the president selected Josephus Daniels to serve as the new ambassador to Mexico. Daniels had been the secretary of the navy during the occupation of Veracruz, and news of his appointment sparked riots in Mexico. The Mexican government, however, believed that Roosevelt was nevertheless sincere and welcomed the new U.S. ambassador. The Daniels controversy taught Roosevelt that he needed to tread carefully through the landscape of memory if he wanted to maintain positive relations with his southern neighbor.[4]

It was perhaps no surprise that Roosevelt pioneered the federal government's involvement in creating a state-sanctioned public memory. Among the sweeping economic reforms of the New Deal was legislation that ended the monopoly that private organizations had over the nation's memory. On August 21, 1935, Roosevelt signed the Historic Sites Act, a comprehensive plan "to preserve for public use historic sites, buildings, and objects of national significance for the inspiration and benefit of the people of the United States." The legislation allowed the federal government to participate actively in memory making by systematically purchasing lands, erecting memorials, and creating educational programs. The National Park Service focused primarily on preserving battlefields, colonial sites, and national monuments in the East and protecting scenic wilderness in the West. At a time when the federal government was interested in improving relations with Mexico, sites commemorating the U.S.–Mexican War were a low priority.[5]

Looking to capitalize on the growing interest in historic preservation, individual states also became involved in the movement. In controlling their own forms of remembrance, the states often competed with the federal agenda and had divergent goals in regard to preserving memory. California, for example, had a long tradition of private conservation, with groups like the Native Sons and Native Daughters of the Golden West shaping the state's remembrance. When the Great Depression tapped the financial resources of these organizations they turned to public support. In 1931 the state government in Sacramento created a landmarks registry. Working closely with private associations, the Office of Historical Preservation identified and marked hundreds of sites. Because of their close relationship, government agencies often supported the agenda of California's private heritage groups and celebrated their Anglo pioneer legacy. Not surprisingly, the first site the state government marked was the Monterey Customhouse, where Commodore John Drake Sloat claimed California for the United States in 1846. In addition to numerous peaceful sites, California would honor five Mexican War battlefields with bronze markers.[6]

Texas presented a different scenario. The one-hundredth anniversary of Texas independence from Mexico inspired the state to support historic preservation. In 1936 the Texas Centennial Commission marked over eleven hundred historical sites with a distinctive granite monolith. Only five of these—Taylor's Campsite, the Thornton Skirmish, Fort Brown (Fort Texas), the Battle of Palo Alto, and Battle of Resaca de la Palma—honored sites of the U.S.–Mexican War. This meant that the commission overlooked many important civilian and military sites. The neglect of the U.S.–Mexican War in state commemoration was part of a larger phenomenon in which Texans focused their preservation impulse on the short-lived Republic of Texas and mythologized its decade-long history. In this context the U.S.–Mexican War was an uncomfortable reminder that the supposedly independent Texas was completely reliant upon the federal government to defend its disputed southern boundary against Mexican incursions.[7]

During this era New Mexico took yet a third approach to remembering the war. In this racially balanced state the memory of the conflict was an uncomfortable nuisance. Unlike California and Texas, New Mexico did not expend scarce Depression-era funds to support the war's commemoration. In 1940, however, a committee of private citizens working with the Utah Pioneer Trails and Landmarks Association proposed building a large monument to honor the Mormon Battalion in New Mexico. As noted previously, the unit had marched with Kearny's army through the state, and Mormons who lived in the intermountain West were interested in honoring its accomplishments. Since the battalion never participated in combat, the monument benignly paid tribute to its two-thousand-mile march and not its military conquest. The committee built the sandstone structure near a stretch of the Spanish Camino Real (Royal Road) adjacent to the San Felipe Indian Reservation, where it remained largely overlooked.[8]

Remembering the march of the Mormon Battalion prompted the federal government to take its first step toward commemorating the U.S.–Mexican War since installing a statue of Gen. Winfield Scott in the nation's capital in 1874. In the late 1930s the Works Progress Administration accepted a proposal for a memorial to honor the arrival of the battalion at San Diego, California. On the site of Fort Stockton near the city's Old Town district, federally funded artists constructed a multicolored concrete and stone "petrachrome" mural of eight Mormon soldiers to mark the place where the battalion billeted during the war (see fig. 17). In 1940 local dignitaries and leaders of the Church of Jesus Christ of Latter-day Saints attended the unveiling. Like other tributes to the group, the monument and dedication ceremony celebrated the Mormons' difficult trek and their role in settling the American Southwest. The church had a controversial reputation, but nevertheless the monument both celebrated and legitimized the Mormon presence in California. The leader of the church, President Heber J. Grant (the last polygamous president of the church), further staked claim to history and the state by publicly expressing a desire to build an expansive temple in San Diego similar to one already under construction in Los Angeles.[9]

The relative dearth of monuments celebrating the conquest of Mexico certainly helped maintain the appearance of a good neighbor. This was particularly important following the Japanese attack on U.S. forces stationed at Pearl Harbor, Hawaii, on December 7, 1941. In a sign of solidarity with the United States, Mexico ceased diplomatic relations with all Axis powers and their occupied nations. Within weeks Roosevelt and Ávila Camacho had organized the Mexican–American Joint Defense Commission to coordinate continental security. When German U-boats sank two Mexican oil tankers in May of 1942, Ávila Camacho declared war on the Axis powers. For the first time in history the United States and Mexico were formal military allies.[10]

This wartime alliance proved mutually beneficial to both nations. Oil, rubber, lead, and a variety of raw materials from Mexico poured into American factories as 90 percent of Mexico's exports went to the U.S. defense industry. Yankee dollars likewise flowed south to create the infrastructure needed for expanding trade. According to the Bracero Agreement of 1942 American agriculture and industry could contract directly with Mexican guest workers who would labor in the United States for the duration of the war. In a reversal of the trends of the 1930s, over three hundred thousand Mexicans, as noted earlier, traveled north to work during the Second World War. While abuses abounded, the Bracero Program gave the appearance of a harmonious relationship between the neighboring countries.[11]

The strengthening ties between the United States and Mexico prompted an outpouring of Pan-American goodwill. The most unusual gesture of amity dealt with President Santa Anna's prosthetic leg, which was captured by Illinois volunteers at the Battle of Cerro Gordo. After the war, members of the unit brought the trophy back to the United States, where it became part of a traveling exhibit. The veterans eventually donated the leg to the State of Illinois, which displayed it in the statehouse throughout the early twentieth century. Local folklore claimed that a visiting dignitary from Mexico during the 1920s was deeply embarrassed by the artifact during an official visit, prompting its removal from public view.[12]

Santa Anna's disembodied leg was oddly symbolic of Mexico's physical losses, and Americans were fascinated with the story behind it. Removing it from display did little to dampen its legend. Some bawdy doggerel recited in Arkansas during this era confirmed the persistence of the leg in memory:

> The Illinois men went bustin' in to catch old Santa Anna.
> He hopped away but left his leg along with his banana.
> They found his whore behind the door,
> So they took them both as booty,
> To show that they had done performed their military duty.

The poem conflated the story of Santa Anna's capture at San Jacinto in 1836 with the loss of his prosthetic leg in 1847 but demonstrated the odd attraction Americans had for this singular souvenir.[13]

In 1938 the leg again made a public appearance when Gov. Henry Horner of Illinois requested that the Illinois Military and Naval Department exhibit the artifact during the state fair. The prosthetic was a popular draw at the event and garnered nationwide attention. Word of the display reached Texas, where tour guides at the Alamo were bombarded with questions about Santa Anna's leg. Texans, eager to publicly humiliate their old foe, repeatedly asked Illinois to give them the prosthetic. The adjutant general rebuffed all efforts to remove the coveted trophy from the state and placed it in storage once again. He denied every formal request to see or photograph it.[14]

The attention the leg received in the years leading up to the Second World War brought it to the forefront of an international dilemma. Rumors had circulated since the mid-1930s that Illinois intended to return the prosthetic limb to Mexico as a show of support for Roosevelt's Good Neighbor Policy. In 1942 the Illinois State Legislature announced that it was, in fact, considering a bill to repatriate the artifact. The Association of Limb Manufacturers, undoubtedly inspired by its rising wartime business prospects, officially petitioned the secretary of state of Illinois to be a part of the leg-returning ceremonies. Lawmakers eventually passed a nonbinding resolution requesting that the prosthetic be returned to Mexico. Officers in the Illinois National Guard denied the legislature and, concerned that others might attempt to take possession of their hallowed artifact, locked the leg in a vault, where it remained until 1970.[15]

The Illinois National Guard may have been unwilling to surrender Santa Anna's prosthetic leg, but Americans in general appreciated Mexico's assistance during the Second World War. In 1944 the State Department issued a formal proclamation of gratitude to Mexico for its contribution to the war effort. Mexico's participation included sending an air squadron to the Pacific to fight alongside the United States Army Air Force and another proposed unit to fly missions over Europe. Presidents Roosevelt and Ávila Camacho signed a treaty allowing the Selective Service to draft Mexican nationals living in the United States provided they be given citizenship upon return. Over fifteen thousand Mexican citizens served in the United States armed forces and suffered approximately fifteen hundred casualties.[16]

Schoolchildren's understanding of the U.S.–Mexican War shifted in the context of the wartime alliance and the Good Neighbor Policy. Authorities convened the American Council on Education's Committee on the Study of Teaching Materials on Inter-American Subjects to survey textbooks to ensure that students were appropriately instructed about their new *amigos* to the south. During this era American high school students learned about the war in a variety of comprehensive texts. In *The Epic of America* (1936) students discovered that "Mexico had no intention of declaring war. War was necessary, however, for Polk's plans, and would have to be forced." In *A Short History of the United States* (1939), the author alleged that the disputed Nueces Strip of Texas "was uninhabited, and it is probable that time and diplomacy would have given it to us without a struggle. Such a course was not to be followed, for Polk had other ends in mind." Both books placed responsibility for the war firmly on President Polk's territorial ambitions.[17]

Not surprisingly, the committee's report in 1944 concluded that American authors had become critical of their nation's handling of the war. The report asserted, "It is very probable that the student who reads any of these accounts . . . would be led to take a critical view of the American position and to acquire a tolerance, if not complete approval, of Mexican acts." This observation reflected an important shift. Racist and imperialist interpretations common during the 1910s and 1920s had fallen out of favor during Roosevelt's administration. The change was so profound that federal authorities were concerned that the country's youth would question American motives in waging the U.S.–Mexican War.[18]

While the government survey found new sympathy for Mexico in American textbooks, the results for historical monographs of the time were less conclusive. A modern review of twenty-nine histories written during the Roosevelt administration shows a range of interpretations, from those that blamed the United States to those that faulted Mexico to those that took an ambiguous stance. Authors now rarely addressed the old slave power conspiracy claim. The principal debate concerned the legality of Texas annexation and Polk's determination to conquer New Mexico and California. Critics of the United States believed that annexation was a morally questionable act designed to force Mexico into war. Supporters countered that Mexico overreacted to America's sovereign right to add independent Texas to the Union.[19]

Although scholars lacked consensus, there was no doubt that the relations between the United States and Mexico had reached a historic high. This friendship between the nations endured through the end of the Second World War, as Truman took the reins of government following Roosevelt's unexpected death in the spring of 1945 and continued his predecessor's legacy in Mexico. Some observers wondered, however, if the United States would be as good a friend in peace as it had been in war. Mexicans took note of the fact that money once channeled to their nation for trade and infrastructure was now doled out to rebuild their former enemies. Although there would be no Marshall Plan for Mexico, shifting political alliances in the postwar world still played to the nation's benefit. This sustained goodwill continued to affect how the United States remembered its war with Mexico.[20]

The most immediate impact that the United States–Mexico alliance had on memory was the lack of American interest in the war's centennial. As

Mexico turned the anniversary of defeat into a national pageant, the United States largely ignored it. Having just waged a costly crusade against imperialism, Americans found the memory of the expansionist U.S.–Mexican War to be fraught with contradictions. Other factors influenced the nation's apparent amnesia. If May 8, 1946, marked the one-hundredth anniversary of the beginning of formal hostilities at Palo Alto, it was also the first anniversary of Victory in Europe Day and President Truman's sixty-second birthday. All over the United States, veterans and civilians celebrated the end of the war in Europe, and Truman's birthday was front-page news. Still, the short attention span of some Americans revealed itself in a poll conducted by the *San Francisco Chronicle* that found that only 25 percent of respondents remembered the significance of May 8 just one year after the end of the war in Europe.[21]

The centennial of the declaration of war against Mexico on May 13, 1946, also failed to attract attention. Even major newspapers in the American Southwest overlooked the significance of the day. The only mention was in an article published in the *Washington Post* on May 12 which reminded readers that the war with Mexico marked the beginning of the use of artillery rockets in warfare conducted by the United States. Understating the nature of the conflict, the brief article described the "Mexican fracas" as being a "very small-time" event. The one-hundredth anniversary of the Treaty of Guadalupe Hidalgo on February 2, 1948, likewise passed quietly. The *Dallas Morning News* ran a small article in its "This Day In Texas" column acknowledging the treaty, but the nation was otherwise silent.[22]

Only one anniversary related to the U.S.–Mexican War received any attention. On August 18, 1846, Gen. Stephen Watts Kearny led U.S. forces into Santa Fe, New Mexico. The next day he stood in the plaza and declared that the province was annexed to the United States. Prior to the centennial New Mexicans had largely ignored the commemoration of the war. That summer, however, the Historical Society of New Mexico hosted a Kearny Exhibition at the Palace of Governors which displayed a number of artifacts associated with the general. New Mexicans also successfully petitioned the U.S. Postal Service to issue a commemorative postage stamp marking the anniversary of Kearny's arrival in Santa Fe.[23]

Why did New Mexicans finally decide to commemorate the U.S.–Mexican War, especially at a time when the rest of the nation failed to do so? The anniversary ceremony in Santa Fe offers some clues. On August 19, 1946, approximately two hundred members of the Daughters of the American Revolution (DAR), the Sons of the American Revolution, and Children of the American Revolution marched through Santa Fe to join their fellow townspeople in the city plaza. There, the large crowd listened to speeches and watched heritage groups decorate the diminutive Kearny memorial that the DAR had placed in 1901.[24]

The speakers at the so-called Centennial of Good Will did not praise the military operations of the war or mention the terrible loss of life that took place during the Taos Revolt. Mayor Manuel Lujan proclaimed rather that "for these past 100 years the descendants of the Anglo pioneers and those of the Spanish settlers have lived a tranquil and peaceful life." An editorial in the *Santa Fe New Mexican* declared, "New Mexico has given the United States the contribution of an unfailingly loyal citizenry and the example of how people of differing races and creeds can live together harmoniously. And so we celebrate the Kearny centennial, not as a conquest, but as a joining of hands by men of good will for mutual betterment." The anniversary had little to do with the war itself. Instead, New Mexicans touted it as a celebration of their state's ability to maintain racial harmony.[25]

The mayor's focus on New Mexico's founding Hispano and Anglo families suggests that the Santa Fe celebration actually served the same purpose as the commemorations of the war in California fifty years earlier. The California semicentennials honored the influential founding families of the state at a time when newcomers were threatening their hegemony. In 1940 half of the population of New Mexico had Spanish surnames. That number dropped to around one-third in 1950 as the Second World War and the development of the atomic bomb at Los Alamos accelerated the influx of immigrants to the once-isolated state. The old residents of Santa Fe, regardless of race or ethnicity, saw their way of life rapidly changing. In this context, the Kearny celebration was a means for the old elite in New Mexico to reclaim their place in the state's memory.[26]

Ultimately, the Second World War overshadowed the remembrance of the U.S.–Mexican War just as the Civil War had decades earlier. The historians Seymour V. Conner and Odie B. Faulk would write of the forgotten centennial that "no other such notable event in American history has been allowed to pass so unnoticed, so disregarded, so uncelebrated." Other factors besides the proximity to the Second World War also contributed to this historical amnesia. Unlike the popular semicentennial, the one-hundredth anniversary could not trot out surviving veterans of the conflict to draw attention to its commemoration. Perhaps most important, the United States and Mexico were experiencing an unprecedented era of cooperation and peace.[27]

Not all Americans were willing to minimize the centennial of the war. The military historian Alfred H. Bill watched with contempt as the date passed largely unnoticed. In his book *Rehearsal for Conflict: The War with Mexico, 1846–1848* (1947) he decried American hypocrisy and argued that the war was "one of the most misrepresented, misunderstood, and by all but the special student, neglected. . . . [I]t has long been our national habit to deplore the war with Mexico as an act of unprovoked aggression, to belittle the victorious campaigns of Taylor and Scott, and while enjoying the full fruits of conquest, to shed crocodile tears over the means by which they were won." He rejected government pandering too and blamed Mexico for provoking a patient and restrained United States.[28]

Disregarding such criticism, the federal government continued its official course of fostering friendship with Mexico. Truman's concern about the spread of communism in the Western Hemisphere gave new impetus to maintaining a healthy relationship. Specifically, the president pushed for the ratification of the Inter-American Treaty of Reciprocal Assistance and the chartering of the Organization of American States so he could galvanize hemispheric military cooperation. He understood that Mexico's support was critical to achieving this goal.[29]

As part of his diplomatic agenda, Truman made an official visit to Mexico City in March of 1947. After laying a wreath at the Column of Independence, Truman asked to be taken to Chapultepec to visit the Obelisk of the Boy Heroes, where he laid a wreath at the monument to honor the cadets. As previously mentioned, the gesture had a profound effect on Mexicans. Part of what made Truman's act so endearing was its spontaneity and lack of pretension. When interviewed about his decision to deviate from the scheduled itinerary and visit Chapultepec, the president replied that he had known the story of the cadets his entire life and "thought they ought to have the wreath." He further declared, "Brave men don't belong to any one race or country. I respect bravery wherever I see it." Truman was a history enthusiast, and writings in his personal journal demonstrated a knowledge of Winfield Scott and his Mexico campaign. Given that Truman was born in 1884, however, it was highly unlikely that he knew the story of the Boy Heroes from childhood since the legend had barely taken root in the military culture of Mexico.[30]

In reality the wreath laying at Chapultepec was a carefully orchestrated event meant to have the maximum emotional impact on Mexico. The new U.S. ambassador, Walter C. Thurston, was a clever diplomat who understood the importance of the memory of the U.S.–Mexican War to international relations. For weeks prior to Truman's visit he had searched for symbolic gestures that the president could make to strengthen relations between the two nations. Thurston had friends at the Military College and undoubtedly knew about the excavation of the remains of the Boy Heroes that had been postponed to accommodate the president's visit. According to an early account published by the *New York Times,* the ambassador's contacts at the school suggested that a tribute at Chapultepec "would do a great deal to obliterate any lingering traces of bitterness over the war." Thurston had no guarantees that Truman would agree to the visit, although he was optimistic enough to bring a wreath and have Mexican officers and cadets on alert near the monument. Truman silently recognized Thurston's role by posing alongside him for the photographers at Chapultepec (see fig. 18).[31]

The fact that Thurston had prearranged Truman's visit to Chapultepec did not diminish its impact on Mexico. While some Mexicans were unimpressed with Truman's homage to the Boy Heroes, President Alemán declared him the "new champion of hemispheric solidarity." There is no doubt about the U.S. president's sincere reaction to the outpouring of magnanimity at Chapultepec. Caught off guard by the spontaneous display of emotion, Truman confessed in his private journal that he struggled to hold back his tears. The president remained overwhelmed by the excitement and warmth of the Mexican people. He ended his journal entry by declaring emphatically, "What a time!"[32]

On July 16, 1947, Truman made a decision which would further affect how Mexico remembered its war with the United States. In Executive Order 9873 the president transferred jurisdiction of the Mexico City National Cemetery from the War Department to the American Battle Monuments Commission. Reflecting the change over to a civilian bureaucracy, the commission ordered new text for the monolith marking the mass grave of North American soldiers killed in the U.S.–Mexican War. The first line of the original marker read, "To the Memory of the American Soldiers Who Perished in this Valley in 1847." The monument now read, "To the Honored Memory of 750 Americans, Known but to God." The new legend removed references to soldiers and the war of 1847, obscuring the reason so many Americans lay dead in Mexico City. Mexicans who visited the gardenlike cemetery would no longer have to confront unpleasant reminders of the past (see fig. 19).[33]

Truman's visit to Mexico City in 1947 inspired other acts of contrition. In 1929 Capt. Emilio Carranza, the "Lindbergh of Mexico," had died while completing a goodwill flight between New York City and Mexico City. Members of the Mount Holly Post of the American Legion trekked twenty-five miles into the New Jersey forest to retrieve his body, an act which inspired an enduring friendship between their organization and the people of Mexico. Ever since that time the post has sponsored an annual memorial at the crash site. To honor their camaraderie with Mexico, the post proposed to the National Convention of the American Legion in 1949 that it press Congress to return flags captured by U.S. forces in Mexico. Although these spoils of war had been dispersed around the country, the army had given sixty-nine colors to the Military Academy at West Point.[34]

On September 29, 1949, Sen. Tom Connally of Texas and Rep. Charles Howell of New Jersey introduced Joint Resolution 133 to their respective houses of Congress. The resolution read as follows: "The President is authorized to cause to be delivered to the Government of the Republic of Mexico, with such escort and such appropriate ceremony as he shall deem proper, the flags, standards, colors, and emblems of that country which were captured by the military forces of the United States in the Mexican War of 1846–1848 and are now in the custody of the National Military Establishment." The following summer Congress unanimously passed the resolution. The House of Representatives declared, "The long era of cordial and friendly relations between these neighboring Republics could be suitably emphasized at this juncture by ceremonies appropriately celebrating the return to Mexico of the colors under which its sons fought so gallantly long ago." The Senate echoed that sentiment, stating that such a gesture would "strengthen the spirit of friendship which already exists between our country and theirs."[35]

The Department of Defense, representing the interests of West Point, did not agree with the plan to strip the academy of its valuable trophies. In a report dated March 3, 1950, it submitted an unfavorable recommendation. When it became clear the resolution would pass, however, Secretary of the Army Frank Pace Jr. revised the position of the military. Even as he maintained that the return of the flags represented a "departure from the traditional practices of all sovereign states," he declared that the "Department of Defense does not recommend a veto." He further stated his belief that the "international import" of the exchange warranted the exception.[36]

The timing of the resolution was significant for Truman. As the Cold War escalated, Mexico had refused to sever its ties to the Soviet Union. This proved especially troubling to Truman when the Soviet Union ended the monopoly of the United States on atomic weapons by successfully detonating its own bomb on August 19, 1949. The fall of China to a communist insurgency and a number of high-profile espionage cases had rounded out a difficult year for the American president. Truman no doubt hoped another public show of contrition might earn him more support from Mexico and Latin America.[37]

Before he approved the flag-returning proposal Truman studied ways to gain the maximum benefit from the transaction without causing embarrassment to either side. He spoke with President Alemán about the possibility of trading the Mexican colors for American flags captured in the Battle of Buena Vista. Residents of Brownsville had suggested that the presidents of both nations make the exchange at their international bridge. President Truman liked the idea but was concerned that the disparity in numbers of captured flags might be a reminder of the overwhelming victory of the United States. He instead proposed that they exchange a single flag on the international bridge and then discreetly return the other colors at a later date. When the Mexican Congress refused to authorize a return of the captured North American banners, Truman suggested a less formal ceremony that would not include his personal participation.[38]

Truman's official approval of the resolution came on August 5, 1950. He proposed to send the flags to Mexico City for the commemoration of the Boy Heroes on September 13. Earlier that summer, communist North Korean soldiers had invaded South Korea, prompting Truman to commit troops to the campaign. Since that time, American forces had suffered blistering defeats. Because of the escalating troubles in Korea, Truman opted not to attend the ceremony himself. Instead, the president sent an escort of twenty-four West Point cadets along with Army Assistant Chief of Staff Gen. Wade H. Haislip (see fig. 20).[39]

The return of the captured flags on September 13, 1950, did not attract the attention that Truman's wreath-laying at Chapultepec had. U.S. troops were losing a desperate battle for the Korean Peninsula, and larger events were about to eclipse the presentation in Mexico City. Driven into a small pocket around the city of Pusan, South Korea, Gen. Douglas MacArthur was preparing for a major amphibious landing at Inchon on September 15. American representatives of the joint defense commission were about to meet with their Mexican counterparts to discuss their participation in the conflict. A columnist for the *Dallas Morning News* hoped that the return of the colors would counter the perceived threat at home, claiming that the national chairman of the U.S. Communist Party "fairly foams at the mouth about the return of those flags." Mexico's involvement in another foreign war would not be so cheaply bought, however, and in spite of the flag repatriations Mexico refused to send troops to Korea.[40]

While Truman used the U.S.–Mexican War to garner support for his containment of communism, members of the Church of Jesus Christ of Latter-day Saints continued to leverage the memory of the Mormon Battalion in their bid for wider public acceptance. In 1945 Heber J. Grant, the president of the church, died. His replacement by George Albert Smith signaled a new era in the modernization of the public image of the Mormons. Smith continued to foster the perception that the church was an important American institution with deep roots in mainstream Western history. To illustrate his point he joined the Sons of the American Revolution and rose to national prominence within that organization. He also founded the Utah Pioneer Trails and Landmarks Association, which oversaw the placement of more than one hundred historic monuments in the West. As the leader of the church he traveled widely to end the isolation of the Mormons and win friends for the fast-growing religious movement.[41]

In 1950 Smith and the Sons of the Utah Pioneers (SUP) planned to help celebrate the centennial of California's statehood by retracing the route of the Mormon Battalion through the Southwest. The so-called Pioneers Trek eventually included over three hundred participants who rode in chartered buses along the roads blazed by their Mormon Battalion ancestors. To celebrate the role Mormons played in the settlement of Arizona and California, the organizers of the trek scheduled parades in Mesa, San Diego, Los Angeles, and San Bernardino. The SUP also took part in various flag raisings and historical commemorations during their one-week journey.[42]

The trek proved a tremendous success in boosting the image of the Church of Jesus Christ of Latter-day Saints. Mormon Day in San Bernardino drew over thirty thousand participants. In Los Angeles ten thousand people turned out to witness the Mormon Battalion parade. From the steps of city hall the famous Mormon sculptor Avard Fairbanks gave Gov. Earl Warren a bronze statuette. Fairbanks boasted that the discovery of gold by the battalion at Sutter's Mill had bankrolled the Civil War, thereby saving the Union and ending slavery. Warren then accepted a golden spike from the delegation as a symbol of the ties between California and Utah. President Smith concluded the proceedings by reciting his family ties to Mayflower Pilgrims, Revolutionary War veterans, and the founder of Mormonism, Joseph Smith.[43]

Throughout the events the SUP carefully controlled the group's memory of the war. The Mormon Battalion, ill-equipped and lacking financial resources, often marched barefoot and wore tattered civilian clothing and animal skins as uniforms. Historical accuracy was secondary, however, to the more prosperous impression that the modern-day Mormons sought to create. According to the guidelines of the SUP, those marching in the parades were to wear Federal Civil War–era costumes (see fig. 21), a decision that was significant for two reasons: In their conservative navy blue Civil War uniforms, the parading members of the SUP would look much more impressive than their ragged ancestors; in addition, by wearing the distinctive dress of the Civil War the Mormons would be associated not with the controversial U.S.–Mexican War but with a more celebrated conflict.[44]

Smith's speech in Los Angeles also reframed the memory of the war to create greater connections between California and Utah. He proclaimed, "I am happy to be one of those here today honoring the Utah men who left home and family and marched here to fight for the United States." While technically true, his statement overlooked basic details of the battalion's history. None of the men who marched to California had ever been to Utah. Although most would resettle there after the war, they did not leave Utah to

GOOD NEIGHBORS AND BAD BLOOD   167

defend California. The claim that they "marched here to fight for the United States" also obscured the fact that they had attempted to immigrate to Mexico to escape religious persecution in the United States. Although it marched through hostile territory, the unit prided itself on never having had to fight the Mexicans. For the modern Church of Jesus Christ of Latter-day Saints, however, the memory of the Mormon Battalion continued to be a means both to claim a place in the history of the American West and to gain wider acceptance in the nation.[45]

The advances of the Roosevelt and Truman administrations in U.S.–Mexican relations were fundamental, but the 1950s brought new challenges. When Truman left office in 1953, Latin Americans wondered if his Republican successor, Gen. Dwight D. Eisenhower, would continue the policy of nonintervention. All hopes were dashed when the new president orchestrated a coup to oust the leftist president of Guatemala, Jacobo Arbenz, in 1954. That same year Eisenhower began Operation Wetback, a massive deportation program aimed at ridding the American Southwest of illegal aliens. INS agents, working in tandem with local law enforcement, raided businesses in California, Arizona, New Mexico, and Texas looking for undocumented workers. Within a year the INS claimed that 1.3 million illegal immigrants had been deported or left the United States voluntarily. Eisenhower made it clear he would not seek the same level of cooperation with Mexico as his predecessors.[46]

During the 1950s the American people showed a corresponding coolness toward their southern neighbors. Perhaps sensing the changing political attitude toward Mexico, American popular culture in the fifties and sixties began once again to vilify Mexicans. It was not the memory of the U.S.–Mexican War of 1846–48 that inspired this movement but the remembrance of the Texas War of Independence of 1835–36. "Remember the Alamo," the battle cry of Texans at the Battle of San Jacinto, became the slogan of publishers, television producers, motion picture executives, and Madison Avenue advertisers during the 1950s.

The phenomenon began in December of 1954, when the network television show *The Wonderful World of Disney* broadcast the first of three episodes of its series *Davy Crockett, King of the Wild Frontier*. By the time Fess Parker reenacted the beloved frontiersman's last breath at the hands of Mexicans at the Alamo, "Crockettmania" had spread nationwide. American youth bought over $100 million worth of coonskin caps. Three singers crooned their versions of "The Ballad of Davy Crockett," selling millions of copies of the single and sending the song to the top of the radio charts during the decade. Most important, Santa Anna's decrepit Mexico became the foil to American expansion and greatness.[47]

The growing racial tension between Anglo-Americans and Mexicans occurred as African Americans stepped up their campaign for equality in the United States. In the context of the civil rights movement Crockett assumed the mythic role of the protector of the white race. His doomed defense of the Alamo became a metaphor for white America's last-ditch struggle to maintain its supremacy. The Chicano generation had yet to enter the fray, but the astute observer had little doubt that Anglos and Mexicans would soon battle over more than the Alamo.

The excitement over Crockett and the Battle of the Alamo not only overshadowed the U.S.–Mexican War but also inspired a conflation of the two events. For many in the baby boom generation born in the years after the Second World War, the two conflicts with Mexico blended into a single action which pitted an evil Santa Anna against the brave men of the United States. The expansionist-driven U.S.–Mexican War merged with the Texas War of Independence to become the quintessential American struggle for freedom.

Popular culture played an important role in fixing this confusion in the minds of America's baby boomers and their parents. In Texas, for example, schoolchildren learned their state history through a comic book called the *Texas History Movies: 400 Years of Texas History and Industrial Development Portrayed by Action Cartoons.* Sponsored by the Mobil Oil Company, these free textbooks were distributed by the state education system to all Texas schools beginning in the 1930s. While nominally covering four centuries, the comic focused primarily on the glory of the Texas Republic period. Discussion of the Texas War of Independence filled eighteen pages and was supplemented with over one hundred corresponding illustrations. The U.S.–Mexican War, on the other hand, warranted three sentences of explanation along with five illustrations. The conflict of 1846–48 had become merely a postscript to the earlier Texas war with Mexico. An updated and revised version of this original textbook continued to be used in the state into the twenty-first century.[48]

Popular educational comic book serials also contributed to the blending of the Texas War of Independence and the U.S.–Mexican War. In 1958 the series *Classics Illustrated* released a special issue entitled *Blazing the Trails West.* The authors bridged the final two chapters of the comic, "Texas and the Alamo" and "The Mexican War," with the simple explanation that "Mexico did not want to lose Texas so easily." It showed General Santa Anna fuming over annexation even though he was neither the president nor a resident of Mexico at the onset of the war.[49]

The next year, the series *The World Around Us* published *The Illustrated Story of the Marines,* an educational comic that promoted a similar blending of the two conflicts. The chapter entitled "The Halls of Montezuma" began by showing Santa Anna storming the Alamo. The first caption read, "Long after the Alamo fell in 1836, there was bitter feeling toward the Mexican General Antonio Lopez de Santa Anna, who conquered it." Texan animosity toward Santa Anna appeared to be the origin of the U.S.–Mexican War, further conflating the two events in the minds of young readers. The publishers of these educational comics obviously played upon the popularity of the Alamo to sell books, but they also contributed to a widespread and misleading interpretation that Santa Anna provoked the U.S.–Mexican War as a mere second act to his war against Texas.[50]

The dearth of films about the U.S.–Mexican War contributed to the confusion about the two conflicts. While numerous motion pictures and television programs portrayed the Texas War of Independence, there were no movies about the U.S. war with Mexico. The closest Hollywood dared to tread was *The Robin Hood of El Dorado*. Although this film, made in 1936, addressed racial violence during California's gold rush, it was set in the period immediately after the war and was not a film about the conflict itself. A generation increasingly educated by motion pictures could not draw on Hollywood images about the Mexican War except through the lens of the Texas Revolution.[51]

In the midst of Crockettmania, two California cities commemorated the U.S.–Mexican War with vastly different monuments. In 1958 city officials in Los Angeles unveiled the Fort Moore Pioneer Monument. Spread across Hill Street near Chinatown, the memorial included an eighty-foot brick waterfall and a sixty-eight-foot-tall concrete pylon. An eighty-foot terra-cotta relief presented images of the coming of Anglo civilization as represented by ranching, agriculture, modern transportation, and an electric power plant. The centerpiece of the relief showed members of the Mormon Battalion, United States Dragoons, and New York Volunteers raising a flag over the city on July 4, 1847 (see fig. 22). A more modest panel positioned to the side of the main sculpture showed scenes from the march of the Mormon Battalion.[52]

Like the semicentennial celebrations in northern California in 1896, the Fort Moore Pioneer Monument effaced the state's Native American and Mexican roots. The dominant image of U.S. soldiers raising the flag represented the genesis of the city. The other symbols of "progress" emerged as appendages from this founding moment. Ignoring its rapidly diversifying population, Los Angeles portrayed itself as an Anglo city born on the Fourth of July and neglected its indigenous, Spanish, and Mexican pasts. The fact that the Mormon Battalion earned a place on the monument spoke to the success of the campaign conducted by the Church of Jesus Christ of Latter-day Saints to include the unit in the history of the region. An aggressive fundraising campaign in Utah may have facilitated this inclusion.[53]

As Los Angeles celebrated its Anglo roots one racially mixed community on the central coast of California revived the binational spirit of reconciliation experienced during the 1940s. Near the town of Salinas, Californio lancers intercepted U.S. troops at Rancho Natividad, on November 16, 1846. The Americans were driving a large herd of horses south to resupply the army in Los Angeles when the Mexicans attacked. The resulting skirmish was largely inconclusive, the Californios being unable to capture the horses but sustaining fewer casualties than their foes. The battle had remained a part of local memory since the end of the war.[54]

In 1958 the California State Landmark Commission, working with the Monterey County Historical Society, erected a monument near the site of the battle. The bronze plaque, attached to a five-ton block of dolomite, was unremarkable. However, the dedication ceremony, held on the 112th anniversary of the battle, demonstrated the unique attitude of the community. A United States Army colonel and a representative of the Mexican consul shared the unveiling of the historical marker. A press release at the time claimed that the "commemorative program is intended as a tribute to both sides . . . the Californians and the Americans. United States and Mexican flags will share equal honors in the plaque unveiling." As promised, young American and Mexican boys holding their respective national flags flanked the stone during the ceremony. Unlike Los Angeles, Salinas was an agricultural town in which Anglos and Mexicans relied on one another for their economic survival. The conciliatory nature of the dedicatory service reinforced the ethnic interdependency and cooperation that had long been a hallmark of the community.[55]

As the 1950s ended, a different commemoration captured the popular imagination in the United States. Since 1957 the federal government had been planning the centennial observance of the Civil War. Although the four-year celebration eventually became mired in the social and political turmoil of the time, it nonetheless sparked national interest in war. To help prepare for the anniversary, the National Park Service expanded existing battlefields and purchased new lands of Civil War significance. The vast majority of these historic sites were in the eastern United States, leaving some people in the West feeling excluded from the festivities. This neglect inspired westerners to take an interest in sites of military importance in their own states and lobby for their preservation. These activities led to the nation's first coordinated effort to identify and conserve battlefields of the U.S.–Mexican War.[56]

On December 19, 1960, Secretary of the Interior Fred A. Seaton announced that seven new national historic landmarks would be established in Texas. Although the Alamo predictably topped the list, Seaton added the battlefields of Fort Brown, Palo Alto, and Resaca de la Palma to the registry. In spite of the intended honor, the National Park Service refused to allocate money for acquiring or preserving the sites. The California State Park Commission also designated the battlefields at San Pasqual and Santa Clara as state historical sites in 1962 but likewise let the lands lie fallow. Because scarce resources were going to Civil War preservation, these forgotten battlefields were yet to become state or federal parks, but the groundwork had been laid for their eventual inclusion into America's booming heritage tourism industry.[57]

In 1961 President John F. Kennedy took the helm of the nation intent on restoring the status of the United States in Latin America. Kennedy, however, adopted an aggressive attitude toward the nascent communist government in Cuba. Within months of taking office he authorized an invasion of the island that was supported by the Central Intelligence Agency. The subsequent debacle at the Bay of Pigs on the southern coast of Cuba tarnished Kennedy's reputation at home and throughout Latin America. In a clear show of defiance to Kennedy's policies, Mexico rejected his call for sanctions against Cuba and refused to support the expulsion of the nation from the Organization of American States.[58]

In the midst of struggles with Latin America, the memory of the U.S.–Mexican War haunted the Kennedy administration in an unexpected way. In 1962 the president's brother, Attorney General Robert F. Kennedy, flew to Indonesia for an official visit. During a contentious news conference in Jakarta, Robert Kennedy addressed the threatened war between Indonesia and the Netherlands over control of New Guinea. When he touted the value of diplomacy in settling international disputes, a university student asked him about the U.S.–Mexican War. The attorney general reportedly responded, "I would say we were unjustified. I don't think this is a bright page in American history."[59]

The outrage against Robert Kennedy in Texas was immediate. His statement, uttered just fifteen months after the release of the Academy Award–winning film *The Alamo*, directed by and starring John Wayne, demonstrated how completely the U.S.–Mexican War and the Texas War of Independence had coalesced in American memory. Ironically, the criticism of Kennedy dealt with his supposed ignorance about the Battle of the Alamo, not of the U.S.–Mexican War. Goaded by inflammatory press reports, individuals and groups sent Texas history textbooks to the attorney general. Gov. Price Daniel, a Democrat and John F. Kennedy supporter, assailed the president's brother, declaring, "He is completely misinformed and unfamiliar with the facts." The Democratic gubernatorial hopeful Marshall Formby called his remarks "unnecessary and stupid." In an odd partisan reversal

Republicans jumped to defend America's actions during the war to make political inroads in the Democrat-dominated state. The Republican National Committee declared that Kennedy "doesn't remember the Alamo." The Republican senator John G. Tower accused the attorney general of "glaring ignorance."[60]

Some Texans, realizing that the attacks on Kennedy were misplaced, attempted to clarify his position. In an open letter to the *Dallas Morning News* William Cope expressed disbelief in the angry letters: "Most of the writers are indignant because they feel that the heroes of the Alamo and San Jacinto have been slurred. Many of these writers advocate sending Texas History books to Bob Kennedy to teach him of the heroism of Travis, Crockett and Houston. . . . I suggest that they invest the money in texts on American History for themselves." Throughout the next month editorials in Texas newspapers attempted to clear Kennedy's record by explaining that the Battle of the Alamo had not been a part of the U.S.–Mexican War. The confusion about the two wars would continue into the twenty-first century.[61]

When Kennedy was assassinated on November 22, 1963, his Texas-born vice president, Lyndon B. Johnson, assumed the reins of power. Ten months later, on September 25, 1964, Johnson's motorcade wound through the streets of El Paso. Some 250,000 people from both sides of the border flocked to greet him. Stopping briefly in a Mexican American *barrio,* Johnson emerged from his limousine and shouted, "Buenos días, mis amigos!" He then proceeded to the international bridge. There, waiting midway across the span, was President Adolfo López Mateos of Mexico. The two men embraced like old friends, then sat down to end a dispute which had plagued their nations for a century.[62]

The Treaty of Guadalupe Hidalgo of 1848 had stipulated that the international border between the United States and Mexico ran in part through the center of the Rio Grande. A flood in El Paso in 1864 had radically altered the flow of the river, however, giving the United States an extra six hundred acres. Although Americans quickly occupied the barren strip, known as El Chamizal, the land remained contested by Mexico. President Woodrow Wilson's refusal to honor an arbitration agreement which gave the territory back to Mexico made the area an enduring blight on U.S.–Mexican relations. Now, after years of negotiations, Johnson signed a treaty giving back to Mexico land the United States had illegally claimed in 1864.[63]

Republicans and Democrats alike supported the return of Mexico's coveted soil. Walter B. Moore of the *Dallas Morning News* declared, "Losing a slice of Texas' sacred soil doesn't seem to bother twentieth-century Texans nearly as much as it bothered their ancestors." Moore, like many Americans, believed that the return of El Chamizal would "advance the international image of the United States as a nation that upholds the value of arbitrating disputes . . . and it should help to win greater support for the United States in its program of uniting with Latin-American countries in meeting social and economic problems and the challenge of international communism." While Americans congratulated themselves for their fair play, the looming specter of communism in Latin America ultimately lay at the heart of the resolution.[64]

Fear of foreign totalitarianism had inspired American goodwill toward Mexico between 1930 and 1965. Although there were sincere moments of international benevolence, the American people were not yet ready to surrender their belief in racial and cultural supremacy. To alter the nation's bigoted views, American leaders used their authority to attempt to exercise control over public memory. Individuals and groups, accustomed to exerting their influence over remembrance, ultimately undermined governmental efforts to create real change. While politicians maintained peaceful relations with Mexico, popular culture portrayed its people as the enemy of American liberty. This contrasted with the experience of Mexico's government, which had controlled the nation's recollection of the conflict for decades. By ignoring the war the U.S. government allowed opposing memories to take root in the popular consciousness that would be difficult to extricate. While future leaders continued to try to shape America's public memory, groups and individuals would continue to contest their authority.

In reaction to Truman's visit to Chapultepec the former Mexican president Lázaro Cárdenas warned that "acts of courtesy" alone would not be sufficient to foster long-term improvements in international relations. Subsequent American presidents continued official gestures of reconciliation but did not create meaningful policy change. In the quest to control and contain world communism, the United States would once again engage in military intervention and strain its relationship with Mexico.[65]

8 Resisting the Gringos

MEXICO, 1953–1989

✤

ON SEPTEMBER 13, 1953, President Adolfo Ruiz Cortines of Mexico officiated at the commemoration of the Boy Heroes held at the newly dedicated
Altar to the Fatherland in Chapultepec Park. Curious visitors crowded around
the towering stone pillars and marveled at the crypt that enshrined the bones
of the beloved cadets. This was Ruiz's first ceremony as president, and he
carefully choreographed the event to usher in a new era in the memory of the
War of North American Intervention. The observance deviated from those
formerly held at the nearby obelisk in several key ways. Ruiz, along with the
presidents of the Supreme Court, the Senate, and the House of Deputies,
stood on a large dais and was the central focus of the ceremony. Ruiz also
shortened the service by reducing the number of participants. Only two men,
a government representative and a cadet, stepped to the podium to offer
brief orations extolling the virtue of the Boy Heroes and the greatness of the
Mexican state. While the hundreds of cadets in attendance evinced the anniversary's military roots, the commemorations had evolved into a civic affair
that celebrated the federal government (see fig. 23).[1]

In the postrevolutionary era Mexico's leaders used the memory of the
War of North American Intervention to instill a renewed sense of patriotism
and unity in a nation devastated by a terrible civil war. Over time the federal
government wrested control of the Chapultepec commemorations away
from its military founders. Drawing upon the authority of Catholic liturgy,
the state made secular martyrs of the Boy Heroes and built the Altar to the
Fatherland to house their sacred relics. With all the components of the civic
cult firmly in place, the Mexican government persisted in promoting the
memory of the slain cadets to encourage obedience to the state.

Between 1953 and 1989 the Mexican government continued to use the
Boy Heroes to indoctrinate the nation's children. The Secretaría de Educación Pública (SEP) strengthened its control of Mexico's curriculum by es-

174

tablishing a centralized textbook program entirely under its authority, allow-
ing the government to dictate how public memory was presented to students.
The resulting materials superseded mere lessons in patriotism and explicitly
taught schoolchildren that they should be willing to sacrifice their lives for
Mexico. This strategy backfired during the student movement of 1968, when
Mexico's youth rejected the tired symbols of the past in their struggle to
achieve social and political change. Memory of the War of North American
Intervention also found new and different expressions as Irish immigrants
rediscovered the story of the Batallón de San Patricio. Social and economic
changes further forced an evolution of the memory of the conflict to meet the
challenges of a new era. As Mexicans became more resentful of the perceived
continental hegemony of the United States, they evoked the memory of the
war to defy their powerful neighbor.

Despite later challenges, this period began with a marked optimism in
Mexico. Spurred by exports to the United States during the Second World
War, Mexico experienced three decades of economic growth. A high demand
for petroleum and the nation's promotion of domestic manufacturing through
the Import Substitution Industrialization program sustained this Mexican
miracle and boosted the country's confidence in its power. As a result of
rising hopes and fortunes, Mexicans looked more to the future than the
past.[2]

In the midst of this prosperity President Ruiz proved a master at using the
memory of Mexico's history to promote respect for his authority. While he
supported the commemorations at Chapultepec Park, his primary interest
was in the War of Independence and the Revolution. Beginning with his presidency, the remembrance of Mexico's heroes was promoted generationally, the
martyred cadets being specifically presented as role models to primary school
children. The new monument at Chapultepec reinforced this goal and provided yet another means to celebrate Mexico, its institutions, and its rulers.[3]

The commemoration of the Boy Heroes evolved slightly over the next
decade, but it nonetheless continued to preserve the central role of the
Mexican president. After Adolfo López Mateos took office in 1958, a new
tradition began at Chapultepec, one that ritually reaffirmed the president's
position as Mexico's supreme commander of the military. Cadets of the
Military College receiving their officer's commissions paraded before the
chief executive, who handed each a ceremonial dress dagger. The dispensing
of the symbolic emblem of authority from the president rather than from a
military official accentuated the civilian nature of Mexico's modern government and confirmed the president's power over the armed forces.[4]

As the Chapultepec commemoration assumed its final form, Mexico's
memory of the War of North American Intervention took an unexpected

path. During Gen. Zachary Taylor's campaign along the Rio Grande, dozens of North American soldiers deserted the United States Army and fled to Mexico. Attempting to supplement their forces, Mexican military authorities offered a number of incentives to any North American soldier who joined their ranks. The result was the Batallón de San Patricio, so named because of the many Irish-born soldiers who filled its ranks. Augmented by additional deserters, the unit fought with distinction at the Battles of Monterrey, Angostura (Buena Vista), and Cerro Gordo before withdrawing to Mexico City for the final defense. At the Battle of Churubusco the San Patricios fought desperately, reportedly tearing down the Mexican flag of surrender three times before running out of ammunition. At the end of the battle U.S. troops captured approximately eighty-five wounded and beleaguered survivors. After a series of courts-martial fifty members of the battalion were condemned to die for desertion. In one dramatic spectacle North Americans hanged thirty San Patricios simultaneously on massive gallows facing the battle raging at Chapultepec. The executioners told the condemned that the signal for their death would be the raising of the American flag over the castle so that their last sight would be of the fall of Mexico to the United States.[5]

In the mid-1950s an Irish immigrant named Patricia Cox organized an annual gathering of her compatriots living in Mexico City. Cox was an amateur historian who had published a book entitled *El Batallón de San Patricio*. Anxious to promote an understanding of Ireland's contributions to Mexican history, Cox's group began honoring the anniversary on September 10 of the mass hanging of sixteen San Patricios in the Plaza San Jacinto in the San Ángel borough of the capital. In 1959 Cox's son, Lorenzo Rafael, sculpted a large marble plaque as a tribute to the unit. Under the insignia of the Mexican eagle gripping a Celtic cross were seventy-one names with the legend, "In Memory of the Irish Soldiers of the Heroic Saint Patrick's Battalion, Martyrs Who Gave Their Lives for the Cause of Mexico during the Unjust North American Invasion of 1847—With the Gratitude of Mexico 112 Years after Their Sacrifice." On September 10 of that year a group of Irish and Mexicans gathered in the Plaza San Jacinto to dedicate the unique memorial (see fig. 24).[6]

Ever since then, Irish expatriates in Mexico have congregated at the monument on September 12 to honor the legacy of the San Patricios. During the 1960s an Irish immigrant named Martin Foley assumed leadership of the commemoration and expanded the celebrations to include Saint Patrick's Day. The services began with a mass held at a Catholic Church, followed by speeches and musical tributes to the battalion in the Plaza San Jacinto. Not accustomed to being excluded from memorials to the War of North American Intervention, the federal government made itself part of the commemoration. Soon, September 12 became an official event attended by representatives of the Mexican government and the Irish legation. Under government authority, the ceremony incorporated elements of the Chapulte-pec celebrations. Similar to the veneration of the Boy Heroes, the audience cried out "Murió por la patria!" (He died for the fatherland!) as each name on the plaque was read.[7]

While these annual gatherings proved popular, they were steeped in myth and misinformation. Although Ireland provided the greatest number of sol-diers, the majority of battalion members came from the United States, Germany, and other European nations. Robert Ryal Miller, the foremost scholar of the San Patricios, discovered that of the seventy-one supposed Irish martyrs listed on the plaque in the Plaza San Jacinto, less than half were from Ireland and one-third did not die in the war. Furthermore, one of the men never actually served in the battalion and perished fighting for the United States at the Battle of Molino del Rey. Miller believed that the myth had been augmented in 1960, when the federal mint in Mexico City issued silver medals honoring the battalion. The demand for the medals was large enough that a private manufacturer minted replicas in gold, silver, and bronze for public purchase. An informational pamphlet included with the medals befuddled the unit's history even more by claiming they were all Irish settlers from San Patricio, Texas, whom Stephen Austin forced to fight against Mexico. The fact that Austin died a decade before the war was the least of the account's historical inaccuracies.[8]

The veneration of the Batallón San Patricio in Mexico is an interesting study in the creation of memory. While its remembrance had faded during the early twentieth century, Irish expatriates looking to boost their status in their adopted Mexican homeland celebrated an exaggerated and mytholo-gized version of the battalion. Declaring themselves the "Mexicans of Europe," the Irish sought common ground with their new neighbors. They found this connection in the honoring of their countrymen who had fought and died for Mexico during the North American invasion. As the govern-ments of Mexico and Ireland worked toward establishing formal diplo-matic relations during the 1970s, the memory of the Batallón San Patricio gave the nations groundwork to build upon. Their shared Catholic culture also provided a religious tie between the two peoples. The Irish inclusion of the Catholic mass during the memorial bypassed Mexico's secularization and allowed the church a small role in an otherwise civic celebration. In-deed, the commemoration of the battalion has become the major diplomatic bridge linking the two countries.[9]

While remembrance of the War of North American Intervention helped Irish Mexicans to find acceptance in their new homeland, it also continued to assist federal authorities in their indoctrination of the nation's youth. On February 12, 1959, President López Mateos and the SEP convened a committee of educators to discuss an ambitious strategy to overhaul the curriculum of the nation's schools. Central to his success was a plan to control and standardize the nation's textbooks. From this came the Comisión Nacional de los Libros de Texto Gratuitos (National Commission of Free Textbooks), which published government-approved educational materials that were distributed at no cost. By making the system both free and compulsory, the federal government garnered popular support while gaining complete control over the instruction of Mexico's children. Jaime Torres Bodet, the former foreign secretary who had escorted Truman during his famous visit to Chapultepec in 1947, headed the commission. Among its goals, the SEP hoped that its free textbooks would "instill a love of the fatherland" in Mexico's youth.[10]

Unashamedly flaunting its agenda, the SEP designed the free textbooks with covers that, regardless of the books' subject matter, portrayed patriotic themes. Heroes from the War of Independence, the Reform, and the Revolution were the most popular images, although an allegorical painting of Mother Mexico graced the cover of the *History and Civics* series. With considerable fanfare the SEP distributed the textbooks in time for the 1961–62 school year. Using trucks and donkeys government employees delivered over 350,000 boxes of free books throughout the nation. For the first time in Mexico's history the children of both rich and poor shared the same learning materials.[11]

Predictably, the Boy Heroes and references to North American interventions figured into the lessons. For example, seven-year-olds were taught civic lessons and received *My Second Grade Workbook,* which helped them with basic reading skills. One page in the book was dedicated to teaching the children a portion of the national anthem. Beneath two illustrations students were expected to fill in blank portions of two verses of the beloved hymn. The first showed Mexican soldiers firing an artillery piece and directed the child to fill in the title line "Mexicans at the Cry of War." The second illustration showed U. S. forces landing at Veracruz in 1914. On the beach a mother pointed at the invaders and pushed her diminutive son, armed only with his clenched fist, toward the North Americans. A blank space prompted the student to fill in the last line of the verse:

> But should a foreign enemy
> Dare to profane your soil under his foot
> Know, beloved fatherland, that heaven gave you
> *A soldier in each of your sons.*

The message to these children was that they should be prepared to give their lives in the defense of Mexico regardless of their age.[12]

The textbook for the third grade used the example of the Boy Heroes to introduce the students to their responsibilities as citizens of the nation. The *History and Civics* manual presented them with a lesson about the Mexican flag. A caption beneath an illustration showing a child marching with the national colors stated, "We have all attended more than one military parade. With much pride we have watched our glorious flag pass by blowing in the wind!" The text then advised students, "If it is necessary, we should die for it. We remember the children of Chapultepec and many other heroes who gave their lives defending the beloved tricolor flag." The facing page again quoted the "soldier in each of your sons" stanza from the national anthem.[13]

Fifth-grade students received a much more detailed lesson in their *History and Civics* textbook. Like children's books in the United States, it combined the Texas War of Independence with the War of North American Intervention. The text asserted, "In 1836, they [the United States] favored the independence of Texas from Mexico, to whom it belonged at the time and annexed it; and a little later declared war on our country, which was resolved by their further expansion." This was followed by a brief explanation of the war: "During that conflict, Mexicans defended the national territory with great heroism, as was witnessed by the many military actions, among them the Battles of Angostura, Veracruz, Churubusco, Molino del Rey, and especially Chapultepec, where the Boy Heroes died exalting the flag of our fatherland." The account was accentuated with an illustration of a father and child visiting the Altar to the Fatherland monument in Chapultepec Park.[14]

During this time the SEP also collaborated with comic book publishers to add approved lessons to their popular periodicals. In 1959 the mystery comic *New Tales of the Narrow Street* included an eight-page feature on the Boy Heroes titled "Heroes of Mexico." The segment illustrated the martyrdom of each young man along with text that extolled a distinct virtue (discipline, love of country, valor, etc.) that he embodied in death. Like other creative works addressing the slain cadets, the comic drew more from popular myth than from the historical record. Highlighting this superficial treatment of the past, the text never identified the faceless foreign invaders who were only portrayed in the background of a single image. While this might be interpreted as pandering to the United States, it actually kept the entire focus on the self-sacrificing actions of the Boy Heroes. With the SEP's seal of approval, the comic was intended to be a civics lesson, not a historical discourse.[15]

Students in Mexico not only read about the Boy Heroes in comics and textbooks, but also held commemorations in their schools. In Mexico's education system Monday mornings were set aside for patriotic displays. Individual classes took turns leading the school in flag ceremonies and the pledge of allegiance. Each month had a specific patriotic theme allowing students to honor the nation through a variety of activities. The Primaria Colegio México, a private elementary school in Matamoros, Tamaulipas, focused on the Boy Heroes for the entire month of September. Children recited poems, sang songs, and performed skits about the lives of the cadets. The programs reinforced the idea that the students of the Military College had preserved the nation's honor in spite of its defeat. Teachers specifically taught that Juan Escutia's death was not a suicide, but a duty he was obligated to perform. The impression of many primary school children during this era was that the Boy Heroes were close to their own ages.[16]

Oscar Arriola attended primary school in Mexico City during the 1960s and participated in these Monday morning exercises. At the age of six he could recite a poem about the eldest of the cadets:

> To Juan de la Barrera:
> The name of this hero we carry with honor.
> We sing with pride of his triumph and valor.
> Glorious cadet, I must follow his example.
> Fighting for my fatherland, even if I must die!

His history lessons included field trips to the convent at Churubusco and the Altar to the Fatherland at Chapultepec Park. Such events gave him a sense of civic responsibility and made him "feel more Mexican" at an early age.[17]

The SEP's insistence that children be willing to give their lives for the country had little to do with national defense. In the 1960s Mexico was no longer in danger of foreign invasion, and it was unlikely that the president would ever call upon an army of young people to defend the nation. The lessons of the Boy Heroes instead promoted unquestioning loyalty to the state. Although students would not be required to give their lives for Mexico, they could nonetheless pledge mortal fidelity to the power behind the flag. While the bureaucrats at the SEP no doubt felt confident in the success of their message, schoolchildren of the 1960s would later prove themselves to be independent-thinking adolescents and adults.

As the SEP's free textbooks and centralized curriculum spread throughout the nation individual states exercised their authority by also publishing free textbooks. To avoid trespassing on the territory of the SEP and the federal government, however, these books were limited to local history topics. One such work, commissioned by the State of Veracruz in 1966, exemplified the amnesia occasionally found in local histories. *My Third Grade Text and Workbook: History of Veracruz Free Textbook* failed to mention the role that the state played in the War of North American Intervention. Although it ne-glected the shameful siege of 1847, it did include an account of the invasion of 1914: "The fight was brief but bloody, and many of the patriotic defenders of our soil were killed and wounded. Among the martyrs who fell on the al-tars of the fatherland were Virgilio Uribe, Eduardo Colina, José Azueta, and other heroes." The Boy Heroes of Veracruz, like those of Chapultepec, re-deemed the city and turned the state's military defeat into a moral victory.[18]

Mexico's unprecedented economic growth also helped soothe the mem-ory of past defeats. In spite of such advances, however, it appeared to many Mexicans that the United States was always pulling ahead. This disparity was most obvious to Mexicans living along the border who had to do noth-ing more than look across the Rio Grande to see a higher standard of living. During the mid-1960s the folklorist Américo Paredes collected a humorous tale that captured Mexico's growing resentment over the wealth of its for-mer territory. In the story two Mexican men bitterly discuss their northern neighbors:

> "These Gringos are terrible people," says one. "Cheaters, liars and robbers."
> "Sure, *compadre*," says the other, "Look what they did in '46. They took half our national territory."
> "Yes, *compadre*," says the first, "and the half with all the paved roads."

For these two Mexicans the prosperity enjoyed by the United States was a constant reminder of what might have been theirs if not for the War of North American Intervention.[19]

While many Mexicans enjoyed their continued prosperity, the nation's economic growth came at the expense of human rights. When Gustavo Díaz Ordaz assumed the presidency in 1964 he brought an authoritarian rule that had not been seen in the country for decades. As the youth of Mexico chafed under his regime, Díaz Ordaz turned to the Boy Heroes to encourage obedience to his administration. In 1967 the government commissioned the famous muralist Gabriel Flores García to paint an enormous ceiling mural at Chapultepec Castle entitled *La Gesta Heroica de 1847* (The Heroic Deed of 1847). The painting depicted the cadet Juan Escutia, surrounded by styl-ized United States Dragoons, falling from the heights of Chapultepec with the national colors clasped in his hand. The scene captured his ashen, child-like face transforming into a skull as the spirit of an eagle departed from his doomed body (see fig. 25). The president soon learned that such gestures would fail to inspire many of his young constituents.[20]

Popular discontent with Díaz Ordaz's authoritarianism found an outlet in the nation's universities, culminating in the México 68 student movement in the capital. Protesting the violent suppression of labor disputes and the deployment of paramilitary police, students began a massive strike against the Díaz Ordaz administration. Thousands of reform-minded youth occupied the Universidad Nacional Autónoma de México (UNAM) in July of 1968 and forced it to shut down. The student strikes and closure of UNAM came as Mexico City looked forward to hosting the Summer Olympics in October. As the federal government prepared for the world spectacle, demonstrators took up the chant, "We don't want Olympic Games! We want a revolution!" A deeply enraged and embarrassed President Díaz Ordaz used the memory of the Boy Heroes in a last-ditch attempt to inspire the loyalty of Mexico's youth. The first strategy involved the Olympic Games themselves. The government named six new Olympic sports venues after each of the Boy Heroes, tying the memory of the fallen cadets explicitly to the international competition.[21]

On September 12 the SEP held a massive youth rally at Chapultepec Park. While their older siblings demonstrated at UNAM, approximately ten thousand primary school students from around the Federal District were bused to the Altar to the Fatherland. Under the watchful eyes of senior education officials the students paid tribute to the Boy Heroes. After a short program of musical numbers, youth speakers, and wreath layings, the children dined on a free banquet and spent the balance of the day playing on rides and attractions in the park. The federal government timed this patriotic spectacle to draw attention away from the unrest in the city and reconfirm the citizenry's allegiance to the state. An anonymous editorial in the newspaper *Excelsior* exhorted schoolchildren visiting the capital for the event to obey the words of the president. A large advertisement in the same issue reminded readers that the Boy Heroes represented an "exemplary page" in Mexican history.[22]

September 13 marked the official day of remembrance of the Boy Heroes, and Díaz Ordaz was prepared to turn the commemoration to his advantage. At the Altar to the Fatherland the statue of Mother Mexico holding a fallen cadet was adorned with a huge floral banner reading "Example for Mexico's Youth." Predictably, this was the theme of the day's speeches and celebrations. The president, his cabinet, justices of the Supreme Court, and members of Congress listened to youth speakers reaffirm their undying loyalty to the government. One young orator appealed to his rebellious peers by evoking the memory of the martyrs: "Young compatriots, we are the heirs of their sublime example." Cadet Saúl Hernández Dorantes addressed Díaz Ordaz directly in his speech: "Mr. President, through my conduct, the youth of the Mexican military manifest their complete solidarity to the concepts that spill forth from your last government speech."[23]

The concluding speaker was Alfredo V. Bonfil, the secretary of Acción Agraria de la Confederación Nacional de Campesina (Agrarian Action of the National Confederation of Peasants). This federal bureaucracy was once independent, but it had been firmly under presidential control since the Miguel Alemán administration of the 1940s. Bonfil's tribute to the Boy Heroes quickly degenerated into servile pandering to the president. He attacked the striking students, declaring that they must keep their protests "within the limits of the rights that society establishes." He further asserted that the example of the Boy Heroes "will have to be a guide for the youth of today, who with daily work, study, and silent heroism become the barrier to all invasions looking to disturb the peace of our land. The immediate task is to unify for the greater goal of aggrandizing Mexico." After a thirty-three-gun salute, President Díaz Ordaz presented daggers to the newly commissioned officers of the Military College.[24]

The student-led Consejo Nacional de Huelga (National Strike Committee) upstaged the commemoration of the Boy Heroes by holding a major demonstration at Chapultepec later that same day. Thousands of student protestors gathered to the east of the monument at the National Museum of Anthropology for the famous Manifestación del Silencio. Marching silently, withholding their usual chants, placard-bearing youths walked along the Paseo de la Reforma toward the Plaza de la Constitución. Soldiers and cadets from the Military College protectively set up a barrier along the marchers' Chapultepec route to shield and protect their beloved Altar to the Fatherland.[25]

Although the official press of Mexico City downplayed the Manifestación del Silencio, upwards of fifteen thousand strikers marched while another six hundred thousand people watched from the streets. This number dwarfed the mere dozens reported to have attended the official commemoration of the Boy Heroes. Díaz Ordaz's attempt to use the celebrations of September 13 to shame the rebellious youth into compliance with his policies was a failure. The impact that the Boy Heroes propaganda had on the ten thousand children attending the SEP-sponsored event the day before is uncertain. Perhaps telling, however, was that in the 1970s education authorities would scale back their focus on the Boy Heroes.[26]

As September came to a conclusion, Díaz Ordaz's attempts to rein in the student movement through intimidation and violence continued to fail. On October 2, with the opening ceremonies of the Olympic Games just ten days away, the president unleashed his full fury on the students. That afternoon leaders of the National Strike Committee called a meeting at the Plaza de las Tres Culturas (Square of Three Cultures) in the Tlatelolco neighborhood. Ten thousand demonstrators had filled the plaza when Olympic security forces, soldiers, tanks, and helicopters converged on the scene with guns blazing. History may never record the exact number of civilians killed in what was soon called the Tlatelolco Massacre, but the body count was certainly in the hundreds. In one brutal act the Mexican government lost the confidence of a generation. A surviving student, appropriating the symbols and language of the government, later declared that her murdered friends were the "modern Niños Héroes."[27]

Months later the SEP again attempted to harness the myth of the Boy Heroes to instill patriotism among the rebellious youth. Aiming at a younger demographic, it partnered with the comic book *Epic* to release an entire edition devoted to the cadets. Predictably, the cover portrayed Juan Escutia vaulting over the walls of Chapultepec Castle wrapped in the Mexican flag. The book followed the adventures of a fictional Captain Perales and his son Ismael over the course of one year, from the Battle of Monterrey to the fall of Mexico City. While his father fought valiantly against the North Americans at a number of campaigns, Ismael enrolled in the Military College. The story redeemed Mexican honor as the invaders prevailed only through numerical and technological superiority. After each engagement U.S. officers marveled at the courage of the Mexican soldier.[28]

In addition to commending the prowess of the military, the comic sought to promote political unity among Mexico's discontented youth. Captain Perales was depicted as a supporter of the rebellious "Polko" faction that rose against General Santa Anna in 1847, a political stance that made Ismael a target of hazing and pranks at the Military College. Eventually the cadets realized that their political differences paled in comparison to their external enemies. As the Yankees surrounded Chapultepec one of the Boy Heroes embraced Ismael, exclaiming, "There are no more parties except the fatherland!" The young Perales then fought alongside the Boy Heroes as they died bravely at their posts. This thinly veiled parable of the contemporary divisions within Mexico did little to stem youth unrest, as it spread throughout the Republic during the coming years.[29]

Adolfo García Zamora was a high school student at the Preparatoria Número Uno in Monterrey, Nuevo León, when the strikes spread north in the early 1970s. Like many Mexican youths, he had learned to revere the Boy Heroes through the free textbooks and patriotic programs held in primary school. By his turbulent adolescent years, he and many of his peers recognized the story of the cadets for the propaganda it was. They rejected the young men as foolish for giving their lives so cheaply. To García Zamora the democratic struggle at hand was far more important than the myths of the past. He and thousands of his fellow students fought in an attempt to bring their city to a standstill.[30]

Thelma González was also a part of the student movement in Monterrey. As an incoming freshman at the Universidad de Nuevo León, she worried about the permanent posting of troops near the campus. Students also charged the institution with corruption, citing the long line of university presidents who had become state governors. Local politics were not the only issue worrying the youth on Mexico's northern frontier. As the Vietnam War escalated, many radical students vented their anger at U. S. imperialism. In a series of strikes and sit-ins that closed the campus, protesters assailed both their local leaders and the United States. Speeches included frequent comparisons between the Vietnam conflict and the War of North American Intervention.[31]

The killing of unarmed college students at Kent State University and the spread of U.S. military operations into Cambodia and Laos provoked more outrage against the United States. The country's escalating involvement in Asia prompted Manuel Medina Castro to write *The Great Plunder: Texas, New Mexico, and California* in 1971. Criticizing the covert operations of the Central Intelligence Agency throughout the world, Castro Medina compared the nineteenth-century intervention by the United States to the present-day "criminal war in Vietnam." Medina's work focused on atrocities committed by North American forces, declaring that "the invaders conducted the war with inexcusable sadism." He described the bombing of civilians in Veracruz and alleged that the North American army allowed prisoners of war to be burned alive. In short, he declared the conflict with Mexico to be genocide. Ultimately, *The Great Plunder* drew upon the memory of the past to condemn the United States in the present.[32]

The youth rebellions of the late 1960s revealed that the Boy Heroes' hold on the imagination of Mexico's children had become tenuous at best. In this changing environment of memory, the government sought ways to revitalize and legitimize the story of the cadets. In the past, visitors to Chapultepec Castle had examined the stone walls of the former school looking for tangible evidence of the violence that took place there. During the French Intervention, however, Emperor Maximilian had repaired and remodeled the castle, leaving no signs of the death and destruction that had occurred there. To acknowledge the past, in 1970 the Museum of National History added six brass plaques around the castle, each displaying an image of a cadet and marking the location where he had fallen. Given the scant reliable information about their deaths, the markers were fanciful creations. To the civic pilgrim the plaques drew from the authority of the Catholic Church in that they were reminiscent of the Stations of the Cross found in every chapel, which allowed the devoted to ritually follow the last steps of Jesus Christ. Perhaps most important the markers offered concrete evidence that the cadets were not mythological but had indeed lived and died at Chapultepec.

In another attempt to revitalize the Boy Heroes, educators in Mexico City published a textbook in 1971 entitled *Synthesis of the History of Mexico*.

The work boldly appealed to the nation's youth to embrace again the patriotic paradigm of the Boy Heroes. In describing the Battle of Chapultepec it stated, "In this unequal duel the Mexican cadets, all adolescents, gave the marvelous example for future generations to die for the nation when its soil is trampled by foreign soles." The text offered suggestions to teachers to help their students internalize the story by visiting Chapultepec, reading the boys' biographies, and enacting patriotic plays.[33]

In spite of such endorsements the Mexican youth movement made the government cautious about celebrating the Boy Heroes. Although the presidents of the country maintained a presence at Chapultepec throughout the 1970s, the SEP focused more on the heroes of Independence and the Revolution than it did on the cadets. Sylvia Casares attended the Primaria Franklin D. Roosevelt in Matamoros in the 1970s. During her time at the school, teachers limited their lessons about the Boy Heroes to an illustrated textbook in the third grade. The school complied with the national mandate to hold weekly flag ceremonies, but it failed to host the once-ubiquitous pageants to the Boy Heroes seen in the city a generation earlier. The focus on the youthful martyrs in primary school continued to decline into the 1980s.[34]

The 1970s brought additional challenges to Mexico besides youth unrest. President Luis Echeverría ended the protectionist economic policies that had previously boosted Mexican industrialization. He also required foreign investors to establish factories in underdeveloped and thus less profitable areas of the country. Rather than promoting manufacturing, the president's policies led North American entrepreneurs to abandon Mexico for more lucrative climes. Echeverría further alienated the United States by establishing trade treaties with the Soviet Union, China, and Eastern Bloc nations. Thanks to Mexico's "economic nationalism" the industrial miracle of the previous thirty years sputtered and stalled.[35]

In contrast to Mexico, the American Southwest appeared to thrive during this time. Mexicans could not help but wonder how their nation's economy would be different if they still owned the lands lost in 1848. The growing awareness of the territory and people severed from Mexico by the Treaty of Guadalupe Hidalgo inspired Mexican writers to look to the north. This rekindled interest in the war that had transformed their compatriots in Texas, California, and New Mexico into foreigners, a particularly important development since past writings about the war rarely explored the fate of these lost Mexicans. The Chicano civil rights movement of the 1970s demonstrated to Mexicans that their northern brothers and sisters still shared in their struggle. Two books published in Mexico in 1976 addressed the forgotten resistance of Mexican Americans. Ángela Moyano Pahissa's *The Santa Fe Trade and the War of '47'* challenged the myth of New Mexico's putatively bloodless conquest by reminding its readers that many patriots fought against the North American invaders. She cited the Chicano movement as having effectively challenged the Anglo-American desire to feel superior to Mexicans.[36]

Gilberto López y Rivas likewise chose to remember Mexican Americans in *The War of '47 and the Popular Resistance to the Occupation*. Propounding themes similar to those of Moyano Pahissa, he attacked the notion that Mexicans living north of the new border passively accepted occupation by the United States. He portrayed his besieged brethren as continuing their struggle for cultural and political autonomy long after North Americans claimed sovereignty over them. He also attacked the capitalist system that the United States brought to the occupied territory by claiming that it forced Native Americans and Mexicans to the bottom of the economic ladder, where Anglo-Americans could exploit their labor and resources. Such works demonstrated Mexico's awareness of their former compatriots in the north as well as the growing cultural connection between Mexicans on both sides of the border during the 1970s.[37]

This northern focus played a critical role in developing attitudes about the War of North American Intervention during the 1980s. Mexico's economy had largely plateaued during the previous decade, prompting an increase in the flow of undocumented workers across the international border. Many Mexicans watched resentfully as the United States consumed these economic refugees amidst reports of their abuse. In a clear demonstration of diplomatic autonomy, Mexico ignored North American foreign policy and established friendly relations with insurgent revolutionaries in Nicaragua and El Salvador. To add insult to injury, Mexico solidified economic ties with Cuba and promised the communist nation assistance in the development of its oil industry.[38]

To accentuate these new political alliances and to deflect concern over economic stagnation, the Mexican government harnessed the memory of the War of North American Intervention to vilify the United States. This marked a significant change of policy given that Mexico's leaders had long avoided the explicit condemnation of their powerful northern neighbor. Such official munificence had been more a reflection of Mexico's economic and political reliance on the United States than an expression of popular sentiment. Seething resentment had always been apparent in popular Mexican literature, but now it spread to government publications.

In 1980 the SEP published the eighth volume of its series *Mexico: History of a People.*" Entitled *Here Come the Northerners,* the high school history text, richly illustrated with colorful artwork, was more comic book than textbook (see fig. 26). The volume related the fictional story of an outlander named Irish who wandered the Mexican countryside in the aftermath of the War of North American Intervention. Addressing the reader directly, Irish recounted the history of Manifest Destiny and his disillusionment with his service in the United States Army. After Irish saw the atrocities committed by the North Americans along the Rio Grande, he deserted and joined the Batallón de San Patricio. In its portrayal of valiant guerillas and their Navajo allies slashing and disemboweling the invading North Americans the book is more fantasy than fact. Significantly, it referred to the heartless Anglo-Americans as *gringos* as opposed to the less pejorative *Yanquis* of earlier literature. The book ended with the Battles of Churubusco and Chapultepec and the execution of the San Patricios. Irish escaped and fled to New Mexico to live among the Navajos and continue his fight for freedom. Rather than extol the example of the Boy Heroes, this SEP publication celebrated the popular San Patricios and created a fictitious alliance between Mexico and the indigenous people of the Southwest. The tale gave historical continuity to the Chicano movement by rooting its struggle in the resistance of Native Americans and Mexicans living north of the new border.[39]

Mexico's growing fascination with the Batallón San Patricio revived interest in its final battle at Churubusco. During the 1970s the Instituto Nacional de Antropología e Historia (INAH) developed an interest in creating permanent exhibits dealing with the War of North American Intervention. First, it opened a small museum in the border city of Matamoros. Fort Casa Mata housed troops and supplies used in the Siege of Fort Texas during the opening days of the conflict. INAH restored the small brick fortress and converted it into a museum displaying artifacts of the Rio Grande campaign. The organization then proposed expanding an existing facility at Churubusco to create a national institution devoted to the military history of Mexico.[40]

On September 13, 1981, the Museo Nacional de las Intervenciones opened its doors at Churubusco. Using the large rooms and hallways of the former convent, the museum presented a variety of installations highlighting Mexico's wars with Spain, France, and the United States. The building's ties to the war made it a natural place to feature the invasion by the United States and the loss of half of Mexico's territory. The portion of the museum dedicated to the war filled a large space in two adjoining halls. It included exhibits about both the Texas Revolution and the War of North American Intervention. Carl Nebel's famous color lithographs from 1850 illustrated individual battles. Major campaigns like the Siege of Veracruz merited their own displays of artifacts, flags, and weapons.[41]

The installation of the War of North American Intervention revealed the official government outrage at the United States. Large maps illustrated the gradual expansion of the United States throughout the first half of the nineteenth century. The final map was titled "The Mutilation of the Territory: The Treaty of Guadalupe Hidalgo, 1848." While maps of the treaty drawn by North American cartographers almost always showed the annexation of Texas as being separate from the cession of New Mexico and California, this map combined the three Mexican provinces into one mass to demonstrate graphically how the nation was literally bisected. Lest there remain any confusion as to what the display represented, a plaque with the title "What We Lost" explained in detail the statistics of the land seized by the United States. Another plaque suggested that President Franklin Pierce coerced President Antonio López de Santa Anna into selling the La Mesilla tract in modern-day Arizona.

As the Mexican government prepared to open the National Museum of Interventions, increasing interest rates and a rapid decline in global crude oil prices dashed all hopes of a quick economic recovery. By early 1982 the value of the Mexican peso plummeted as inflation skyrocketed. Investors in the United States rushed to remove their money from Mexico. As the economy worsened, the national Banco de México added the image of the Boy Heroes to the obverse of its new five-thousand-peso bill. While the likeness of the cadets symbolized Mexico's defiance of the United States, the high face value of the new currency underscored the inflation that was destroying the country. Mexicans named this financial crisis the Década Perdida (Lost Decade). The flow of desperate Mexicans crossing into the United States turned into a flood. Although North Americans faced their own financial crisis at this time, Mexico's economic desperation increased the nation's bitterness toward the United States.[42]

The resentment was manifest in a government publication of the time. In 1983 the Secretaría de la Defensa Nacional republished Heriberto Frías's volume *Episodes of the Mexican Military* (1901), a detailed and at times fanciful accounting of the War of North American Intervention. The following year a different press published yet another edition of the book under the more provocative title *The War Against the Gringos*. The sudden resurgence of interest in this nationalistic work revealed the growing animosity Mexicans felt toward the United States.[43]

Frías portrayed an impoverished Mexico as an innocent victim of unbridled North American ambition. Mexican troops at the Battle of Palo Alto fought "almost nude" with "antique artillery." This same army, however, made a glorious return at the Battle of La Angostura (Buena Vista). The author relished the carnage of the day: "The resistance of the U.S. columns did not last long as the Mexican soldiers charged over them with bayonets and a courage worthy of the cause they defended. The fury of our troops knew no bounds: they struck without mercy, piercing the bellies and breasts of the enemy invaders, some of whom vainly displayed their rosaries after tossing away their arms, shouting that they were Catholics, or dropping to their knees before our officers pleading for their lives! It was a moment of retaliation and vengeance! A beautiful moment!" He claimed the battle was a Mexican triumph, although Santa Anna's treachery ultimately deprived the troops of their victory.[44]

The wanton violence against North Americans portrayed in books like *Here Come the Northerners* and *The War Against the Gringos* illustrated Mexico's simmering animosity toward the United States during the 1980s. The official celebration of the conflict through government-sponsored memorial rites, textbooks, bank notes, and museums shaped the memory of the war for a generation of Mexicans who watched as family and friends fled north to escape economic disaster at home. In reality, most Mexicans did not wish physical harm on North Americans. The remembrance of the intervention was instead a cathartic expression of Mexico's fierce spirit of independence during a decade of insecurity and struggle. Perhaps most important, it enabled the Mexican government to deflect public discontent away from its struggling institutions and onto a gringo scapegoat.[45]

On October 3, 1989, President Carlos Salinas de Gortari visited President George H. W. Bush, in Washington. Salinas de Gortari, a Harvard-educated economist, had served as chief executive for a tumultuous ten months. His election was marred by suspicious irregularities, and many Mexicans believed he had fraudulently usurped his office. Yet, putting his difficult start behind him, Salinas de Gortari proved himself to be a shrewd diplomat. Ignoring popular calls to repudiate Mexico's debt to the United States, he eased international fears by renegotiating repayment terms with the nation's creditors. Now, as an honored guest at the White House, the Mexican president signed an agreement expanding North American trade with his nation. This small token was a precursor to more ambitious plans for continental free trade. To promote his economic agenda, he needed to change Mexican attitudes toward the United States. Like Mexico's rulers before him, control of the memory of the War of North American Intervention would prove important to shaping the nation's opinion of the United States.[46]

The years between 1953 and 1989 exposed long-term challenges to the maintenance of official public memory of the War of North American Intervention. After decades of deliberately manipulating remembrance to their advantage, the leaders of Mexico found that control was more tenuous than they had believed. The student movement of the sixties and seventies largely eschewed government appeals to follow the example of the Boy Heroes, a rejection that foreshadowed the struggles that lay ahead for official memory makers in Mexico. In particular, Mexicans had internalized certain elements of the War of North American Intervention and defined their national identity in terms of resistance to the United States. Sensing that such hostility could impede diplomacy with the North, Mexico's leaders attempted to disassemble the public memory that their predecessors had so carefully crafted. They discovered, however, that memory, like a conflagration, could quickly burn out of control and endanger the very power structures that gave it life.

9   Contesting American Pasts

THE UNITED STATES, 1966–1989

✣

ON APRIL 1, 1967, a dragline construction crew in Brownsville busily excavated a new home site along the scenic Resaca de la Palma. As a large load of soil dropped from the steel bucket, a worker noticed human bones spilling out onto the ground. While modern residents of the city enjoyed the natural beauty of the oxbow lake, in 1846 its meandering banks provided the forces of the Mexican general Mariano Arista with a natural defensive line against U.S. troops. The Battle of Resaca de la Palma was a rout, and the Mexican army retreated in chaos across the Rio Grande. Gen. Zachary Taylor ordered burial parties to inter the approximately 150 Mexican casualties in mass, unmarked graves. The construction workers had unwittingly uncovered one of these forgotten burial sites. Word quickly spread and souvenir collectors pilfered skulls and other relics before archeologists from the University of Texas cordoned off the site.[1]

As a border town, Brownsville depended on good relations between the United States and Mexico for its economic survival. The workmen had disturbed more than the dead that day. For the living, these thirty skeletons were a painful reminder that the twin cities of Brownsville and Matamoros were born of warfare between the United States and Mexico. No groups attempted to claim the bones; nor were any efforts made to organize a memorial. Aside from some minor coverage in the back pages of the local newspaper little was made of the morbid discovery, and people on both sides of the Rio Grande largely ignored it. The contractor was rumored to have encountered additional burials and to have built houses over them without reporting his findings to the state. Texas authorities offered the excavated skeletons to Mexican officials in Matamoros but found no one who was willing to claim them. Without further ceremony the archeologists boxed up the remains and took them to Austin, where they remained largely forgotten.[2]

192

The skeletons of Brownsville's past were symbolic of an era when many people in the United States wanted to forget about the war with Mexico. This had not always been the case. As we have seen, the desire for a military alliance from the 1930s through the 1960s inspired gestures of goodwill and reconciliation. Remembering and not forgetting became the means of healing old wounds between the nations. America's leaders tapped the power of memory when they paid respect to the Boy Heroes in Chapultepec, returned captured battle flags, and ceded land rightfully belonging to Mexico under the terms of the Treaty of Guadalupe Hidalgo. By the mid-1960s, however, attitudes were once again changing. Memory of the war had again become a point of contention. Mexico was now of less importance to the United States, and the battle for memory that took place between 1966 and 1989 became a domestic affair that had little to do with relations with Mexico.[3]

In the context of the ongoing Vietnam conflict, the war with Mexico was an uncomfortable reminder of American aggression. Academic monographs of the time reflected the anti-imperialistic attitude that was growing prevalent in universities in the United States. Mexican Americans, inspired and emboldened by the victories of African Americans in the 1950s and 1960s, organized the Chicano civil rights movement. The politically charged writings of the activists challenged past assumptions about the war and created a new recollection that aided them in their fight for social justice and ethnic self-determination. White Americans met this challenge to their historical hegemony by attempting to reassert traditional memories of the past. Public parks, historical reenactments, and heritage societies were enlisted to ensure that America's forgotten war would not remain in the shadows.

The evolving memory of the U.S.–Mexican War was first discernible in the late 1960s. The change was neither dramatic nor consistent but revealed a gradual shift in public attitude. In spite of the social and political upheavals of the era Americans could find a large number of books that ascribed culpability to Mexico. Typical was Donald Barr Chidsey's history *The War with Mexico* (1968). Like many writers of American history in the fifties and sixties, Chidsey placed the war in the context of the Texas Revolution. After characterizing that conflict as the "defiance of oppression," he described the legal and justifiable annexation of Texas by the United States in 1845. Mexicans had provoked bloodshed when they crossed the left bank of the Rio Grande to attack Capt. Seth Thornton on "American soil." Chidsey's approach was the same as that taken more than a decade earlier by Ernest R. Dupuy in his *The Compact History of the United States Army.* Typical of his time, Dupuy wrote that it was the Mexicans "who started hostilities, crossing the river . . . and ambushing a scouting party."[4]

Central to the shifting attitudes was the Vietnam War. Modern warfare forced Americans to confront their history and revisit past issues of intervention, aggression, and imperialism. Similarities between the two conflicts inspired changing historical perspectives. President Lyndon B. Johnson unwittingly popularized such comparisons during a televised news conference on November 17, 1967. Addressing lagging congressional support for involvement in Vietnam, the president drew parallels to "the Mexican War when the Congress overwhelmingly voted to go in and later passed a resolution that had grave doubts about it." Perhaps taking a cue from the president, columnists, politicians, and activists disparagingly compared the two events. In a partisan display during the closing weeks of the Vietnam War, President Gerald Ford hailed the resistance of Abraham Lincoln to the Democratic-led invasion of Mexico. Obliquely alluding to President Johnson's failed policies in Southeast Asia, Ford quoted Lincoln as describing the U.S.–Mexican War as being "unnecessarily and unconstitutionally begun by the president without congressional consent."[5]

This public dialogue likewise influenced academic writings. In 1970, for example, three important American historians collaborated on a book entitled *Dissent in Three American Wars*. The authors, Samuel Eliot Morrison, Frederick Merk, and Frank Freidel, contrasted the U.S.–Mexican War to the War of 1812 and the conflict in Vietnam. The next year Seymour Martin Lipset wrote *Rebellion in the University,* which also compared activism during the two wars. By rooting political dissent in the distant past, these writers demonstrated that to "decry wars, to refuse to go, is at least as American as apple pie." In 1974, K. Jack Bauer prefaced his book *The Mexican War, 1846–1848* with a comparison of America's military and diplomatic struggles in Mexico and Vietnam. Changing attitudes during the 1970s were palpable as American books that blamed Mexico for initiating the conflict dropped to under 5 percent of the total material published on the subject.[6]

While academics debated the morality of the American involvement in Vietnam, it had particular immediacy to young Mexican Americans living in the Southwest. A study by the Department of Defense later revealed that Hispanic soldiers from California, Arizona, Colorado, New Mexico, and Texas made up an inordinate percentage of the casualties from those states. Consequently, America's call to arms was especially bitter to young men who, having experienced discrimination at home, were now expected to make sacrifices abroad. In 1969 Manuel Gomez wrote a letter to the draft board of Temescal, California, informing the members of his intentions to "refuse induction." Justifying his disobedience, Gomez invoked an earlier intervention: "It is well known that Mexicans were among the first victims of your empire.

The memory of the Mexican–American War is still an open wound in the souls of my people. The Treaty of Guadalupe Hidalgo is a lie. . . . The war did not end. It has continued in the minds and hearts of the people of the Southwest." Gomez's letter underscored the symbolic power of the war for individuals opposed to American involvement in Vietnam. It also demonstrated the ability of Mexican Americans to harness its memory as they fought for social justice and civil rights during the 1960s and 1970s.[7]

To Mexican Americans who sought inclusion in the larger American experience, textbooks that outlined their history, struggles, and social contributions were an important means of bridging racial and ethnic divides. By creating these works themselves, Mexican American authors exercised a degree of ethnic and historical autonomy lacking in earlier educational materials. Although these textbooks blamed unbridled Manifest Destiny for causing the U.S.–Mexican War, they typically moderated their criticism of the United States. This made the material acceptable to a broad audience and ensured its salability in the competitive educational book market.[8]

Among the earliest of such texts was Ramón Eduardo Ruiz's and John Tebbel's high school textbook *South by Southwest: The Mexican-American and His Heritage* (1969). In a chapter contextualizing the creation of the borderlands, the authors presented a well-balanced account of the beginning of the war. Invoking a subtle parallel to the ongoing conflict in Southeast Asia, the authors claimed that the U.S.–Mexican War "was one of the most unpopular wars ever fought by the United States." Like many history books published in Mexico, *South by Southwest* boasted of the skill and bravery of the defeated Mexican troops. The lesson was that Mexicans were honorable people with deep roots in the American West.[9]

That same year Julian Nava, a professor at San Fernando Valley State College, wrote *Mexican Americans: Past, Present, and Future*. In his foreword Nava supported the need for his textbook, declaring that "understanding minority group problems helps to make better citizens for a better society." His approach to the war was similar to that of *South by Southwest*, demonstrating that in defeat "Mexicans fought valiantly for their country." He noted that victories by the United States were attributable to "good planning, better guns, and a united American leadership," as opposed to racial superiority. Nava further broached the subject of war crimes—a topic that previous American authors largely ignored. He asserted, "Both sides committed atrocities, and even American historians say that the American troops behaved very badly toward the Mexican population." Such statements established a moral high ground for the Chicano movement while helping white American schoolchildren develop a greater understanding and empathy for their Mexican American schoolmates.[10]

Historical writings were not the only form of memory in flux during the era. In 1966 the *Encyclopedia Britannica* released an educational documentary film entitled *Texas and the Mexican War*. The producer of the film, John Walton Caughey, a professor of western history at the University of California at Los Angeles, guided the project along a politically left-leaning path. The film characterized the conflict as an inevitable consequence of the racism inherent in Manifest Destiny. It also explored the social and political dynamics of the American conquest of the Southwest. The final scene portrayed a friendly Yankee soldier visiting a young Mexican boy while the narrator stated, "But there was another price to be paid for our gains." At that moment the boy's mother emerged from a building and scolded her son, while the narrator continued: "A heritage of ill feeling must now be counted as part of the cost of our war with Mexico." The film was widely distributed to American schools and alerted children to the cultural implications of the war.[11]

Whereas Mexican American textbook authors sought a broader acceptance in white society, more militant writers gave voice to the radical El Movimiento, or Chicano civil rights movement. Although the struggle for social and economic justice dated to the Treaty of Guadalupe Hidalgo, the political activism and ethnic nationalism of the Chicanos breached America's consciousness during this era. Chicano authors, many of whom were schooled in the black civil rights movement, used the U.S.–Mexican War to nurture a group memory based on the social, economic, and political needs of Mexican American and Mexican immigrant communities. In their early work Chicanos often expressed anger toward the white scholars who had created a collective memory that vilified the Mexican and belittled the resistance of the people of New Mexico and California. Chicano activists called for their people to take control of their history and memory.[12]

Rodolfo Acuña, a professor at California State University at Northridge, led the challenge in 1972. His *Occupied America: The Chicano's Struggle toward Liberation* became the most influential Chicano history book of its generation. In what he would later call his "war with American historians," Acuña portrayed people of Mexican ancestry pitted in a moral struggle against a racist, oppressive U.S. government. Acuña addressed the idea of history as memory by stating that "History can either oppress or liberate a people." He declared that for Chicanos, "Awareness of their history—of their contributions and struggles, of the fact that they were not the 'treacherous enemy' that Anglo-American histories have said they were—can restore pride and a sense of heritage to a people who have been oppressed for so long. In short, awareness can help them to liberate themselves." The control of memory was therefore vital to the success of the movement.[13]

Acuña was not the only writer who called for Chicanos to exert power over memory. In 1972 Armando B. Rendón wrote *Chicano Manifesto,* a politically provocative book that appealed to Chicanos to take back their history from the Anglo-Americans: "The Chicano's sense of history is only that—a sense—not a deep knowledge of his contributions in the past or his role in shaping the present and future of his country. . . . The Chicano must gain the correct perspective on his own history and rewrite the textbooks in which we have never been mentioned except in a role that reassures the Anglo of his supremacy over all peoples." Like Acuña, Rendón promoted historical self-determination as a means of achieving the objectives of El Movimiento.[14]

The following year Octavio Ignacio Romano-V addressed the idea of memory as history in his anthology *Voices: Readings from El Grito.* A professor at the University of California at Berkeley, Romano was nevertheless an outspoken critic of Anglo-American academia who strongly advocated that Chicano historians apply their skills to serving their community. In addressing memory, Romano began with the query, "To whom does a people's history belong?" He responded with a denunciation of the historical profession for ignoring the needs of the people who "made it and experienced it." He ended his appeal with the charge that "the writers of history must be the servants of those about whom they write." Such a statement ran contrary to the practice of the historical profession, yet it expressed a valid Chicano impulse to frame their memory without interference.[15]

A crucial factor in controlling Chicano remembrance was asserting authority over the U.S.–Mexican War. The conflict was more than a collection of historical facts for Chicano writers—it explained their genesis as a people. As such, the war became as much a cosmogonic myth as it was a history. Like many creation stories, Chicano accounts of the war drew upon a combination of historical events, myth, and collective memory to explain the emergence of a people from fire and blood. For Chicanos, the prewar Southwest represented Aztlán, the legendary ancestral homeland of the Aztecs. Native Americans, followed by their mestizo brethren, lived harmoniously in this place of pastoral contentment until 1846. The invasion by the United States represented the end of this edenic life and the separation of the Chicanos from Mother Mexico. Cast into a world of Anglo violence and exploitation, the Chicanos tenaciously resisted the conquest of their identity, culture, and religion. The American Southwest was therefore the legitimate birthright of all descendants of Mexico, and El Movimiento a vehicle to return Chicanos to their destined role as possessors and rulers of the land.[16]

This creation story was aptly expressed by the Chicano poet Alberto "Alurista" Urista. In 1969 Alurista wrote a preamble in verse for the *Plan*

Espiritual de Aztlán, which served as the political platform of the First National Chicano Liberation Youth Conference, held in Denver. In his poem
Alurista alluded to the U.S.–Mexican War and its role in Chicano memory:
"In the spirit of a new people that is conscious not only of its proud heritage
but also of the brutal 'gringo' invasion of our territories, *we,* the Chicano,
inhabitants and civilizers of the northern land of Aztlán from whence came
our forefathers, reclaiming the land of their birth and consecrating the determination of our people of the sun, *declare* that the call of our blood is our
power, our responsibility, and our inevitable destiny." The assertion of the
cruel Anglo-American invasion typified Chicano accounts of their history.[17]

To Acuña and other writers the U.S.–Mexican War was a two-year holocaust that marked the great divide between the peace prior to 1846 and the
turmoil following the Treaty of Guadalupe Hidalgo in 1848. The conflict was
therefore the first act in a long narrative of the many historic wrongs committed by Anglo-Americans. In keeping with this apocalyptic perception of the
war, Acuña stated that the "Anglo-American invasion of Mexico was as vicious as that of Hitler's invasion of Poland and other central European nations, or, for that matter, U.S. involvement in Vietnam." Nephtalí De León's
Chicanos: Our Background and Our Pride likewise stressed the traumatic
nature of the war by renaming it the "Rape of Mexico." De León's book compared the killing of "Mexican patriots" to the genocidal massacres of the
Native Americans by North Americans. Claiming that the war against Mexico was among history's most reprehensible events, he stated that the "in-
trigues, the schemes, the secret plots, the frauds, and the outright lies can find
no equal in the annals of infamy."[18]

Understandably, many Chicano writers of the time discussed the invasion
by the North Americans in catastrophic terms. Under the subtitle *Myth of a
Nonviolent Nation,* Acuña alleged that "Zachary Taylor's artillery leveled
the Mexican city of Matamoros, killing hundreds of innocent civilians with
la bomba (the bomb). Many Mexicans jumped into the Rio Grande, re-
lieved of their pain by a watery grave." Contemporary battle accounts documented that American forces did, in fact, return fire on Matamoros during
the seven-day siege of Fort Texas (Fort Brown). While at least twenty Mexican soldiers and civilians were killed in the artillery duel, American forces
largely halted fire to conserve ordnance for the ground assault expected
from Matamoros. Acuña cited as his source of the alleged massacre Abiel
Livermore's *The War with Mexico Reviewed,* which actually discussed not
the burning of civilians but retreating Mexican soldiers drowning in the Rio
Grande following the Battle of Resaca de la Palma.[19]

Although Acuña was mistaken about the destruction of Matamoros, he
effectively used the contemporary writings of soldiers like Ulysses S. Grant

and Samuel E. Chamberlain to document the murders and outrages committed by unruly American volunteer units in Mexico. Ultimately, Acuña's creation of a massacre directly on the modern border of the United States and Mexico became a symbolic component of the Chicano creation story that presaged the racial hostility and civilian deaths that ravaged the region for nearly a century.[20]

By drawing attention to the atrocities in Mexico's occupied northern territories, Chicano historians challenged the cherished Anglo myth that the American Southwest had been conquered without violence. Superficially, the "bloodless" claim was true, as Mexican authorities had surrendered Santa Fe, Taos, Tucson, San Diego, Los Angeles, Monterey, San Francisco, and other communities without a fight. Most accounts, however, ignored the uprisings that took place after the occupation. Throughout California and New Mexico irregular troops and civilians rose against the Americans and fought several skirmishes and battles, including the relatively small Battle of San Pasqual near San Diego, which marked Mexico's only significant victory in the war. These accounts directly contradicted past Anglo histories that portrayed the docile Mexicans of the Southwest as passively submitting to the invaders.[21]

Chicano writers also appropriated and altered the myths of Mexico to support their agendas. The most enduring legend was that of the Boy Heroes of Chapultepec. Chicano works frequently discussed the slain students but typically deviated from the established Mexican narrative. The textbooks *South by Southwest* and *Mexican Americans: Past, Present, and Future* both referenced the self-sacrifice of the heroic students. *South by Southwest* alleged that "some of the young Mexican cadets committed suicide rather than surrender to Scott's superior force," while *Mexican Americans* gave a more detailed account of the legend: "When the American forces entered Mexico City, they overcame the Castle at Chapultepec, which served as a military academy. When all the soldiers were killed, Mexican boys killed themselves rather than surrender to the invaders. The young cadets wrapped themselves in Mexico's flag and jumped over a cliff in plain view of the *americanos*." Both versions described multiple students taking their lives. This variation of the original Mexican story demonstrated the flexibility of the myth that allowed it to fit different situations and audiences. In this case, the textbooks introduced American schoolchildren to their brave and honorable peers in Mexico.[22]

The most interesting account of the Boy Heroes was recorded in De León's *Chicanos: Our Background and Our Pride*. De León lauded the "young children" for their bravery and claimed that on September 12 Vicente Suárez saved the banner of the San Blas Battalion by jumping from the walls of

Chapultepec. This account gave the wrong date, cadet, and flag. Nonetheless, the power of De León's version lay in his impassioned evoking of the boy's memory: "The love of a country and the hatred of the Americans was heroically given a new meaning and dimension by the incredible act of Mexico's youngest patriot—Vicente Suárez. The name is now a fountain of inspiration across the face of the Americas. Vicente Suárez, *La Raza* [the race] loves you, *La Raza* weeps for you, *La Raza* pays honor and tribute to you." To the youth-driven Chicano movement, the martyrs symbolized complete devotion to the cause of resistance.[23]

Most of the Chicano accounts of the Boy Heroes, in fact, varied from the official version advanced in Mexico. Ultimately, the discrepancies demonstrated that the power of the story lay not in its historical details but in its emotional impact. Prior to being codified by the Mexican government, the legend had evolved significantly. Not having to answer to institutional oversight, Chicanos merely continued an already dynamic process and gave the Mexican myth new life and fresh meaning in the United States. The memory of the Boy Heroes now inspired a new generation of Chicanos to resist the social and racial status quo of the nation during the 1970s and beyond.[24]

While written memory was an important component of El Movimiento, Chicanos frequently turned to political action, strikes, and protests to fight for the civil and economic rights of their community. Because the U.S.–Mexican War was rooted deeply in the past, however, Chicano activists rarely had the opportunity to utilize the conflict as a point of protest. One important exception was a paramilitary Chicano nationalist organization known as the Brown Berets. Founded by David Sanchez in 1967, the Brown Berets quickly learned to utilize the power of memory in their fight for social justice.[25]

In 1971 Sanchez led dozens of Brown Berets in an expedition through the Southwest known as the Marcha de la Reconquista. The purpose of the trek was to raise public awareness of the "many sufferings and humiliations endured daily by our people." These degradations included poverty, political marginalization, police brutality, and high casualty rates among Chicanos serving in Vietnam. Outfitted in combat boots, bayonets, khaki shirts emblazoned with the Mexican flag, and their signature headgear, the Brown Berets inspired both excitement and anxiety as they journeyed through California, Arizona, New Mexico, Colorado, and Texas.[26]

Sanchez was a well-read young man who looked for opportunities to mold collective memory to the benefit of his organization and people. Throughout their tour of Aztlán, the Brown Berets erected a number of makeshift monuments commemorating individuals and events from Chicano history. While local Anglos destroyed some of these structures, Sanchez understood the symbolic and practical importance of staking a claim in the landscape of memory.

By physically marking historical space he both legitimized and enshrined the forgotten histories of his people. Each dedication also gave him an opportunity to recruit like-minded individuals who shared his vision.[27]

Sanchez counted the invasion of Mexico by the United States as one of his primary inspirations. Indeed, the U.S.–Mexican War was in his thoughts throughout the expedition. When a farmer in California drew a rifle on thirsty Brown Berets, Sanchez remarked, "First they steal our land, and then they deny us water. What next?" In Sacramento the group joined a protest that tore down the U.S. flag on the grounds of the statehouse and burned it. After the protestors attached their beloved eagle and serpent banner to the halyard, Sanchez mused that "for the first time since 1846, the Mexican flag was raised on the State Capital flag pole." Although the actual capital of Alta California was Monterey, the act carried great symbolic meaning to Sanchez and his *soldados*.[28]

As the Brown Berets marched through New Mexico, Sanchez sought out opportunities to confront the memory of Gen. Stephen Watts Kearny and his Army of the West. First, the group attempted to raise the Mexican flag over the Plaza of Santa Fe, where Kearny had declared the annexation of the territory to the United States. Law enforcement officers moved in before they could achieve their goal and arrested several Brown Berets for marching without a permit. After posting bail, the group moved on to the small town of Las Vegas, Kearny's first stop in the conquest of Nuevo México. On the outskirts of the village the Brown Berets raised the Mexican colors on the flagpole of the local high school, and Sanchez then marched to the town plaza along the same road the Yankee general had used 125 years earlier. Some two thousand residents turned out to see the spectacle of Chicano militiamen peacefully occupying the plaza and demonstrating for civil rights.[29]

In the Lower Rio Grande Valley of Texas the Brown Berets traveled along the Old Military Highway, which had originally been used by General Taylor's troops in their Rio Grande campaign. The group rested at the Daughters of the American Revolution monument commemorating the Thornton Skirmish, which had led to President Polk's claim that "American blood had been spilled upon the American soil." Sanchez no doubt took comfort in the nearby memorial he had just dedicated to Juan Cortina, a veteran of the U.S.–Mexican War whose bloody resistance against Anglo Texans continued into the 1860s.[30]

Declaring their Marcha de la Reconquista a success, the Brown Berets returned home. Building from the momentum of the expedition, Sanchez proposed an even more ambitious mission: the peaceful occupation of Santa Catalina Island, twenty-two miles west of Los Angeles. According to his interpretation of the Treaty of Guadalupe Hidalgo, the eight Channel Islands off the coast of southern California were excluded from Mexico's cession. Sanchez considered this an opportunity to raise further awareness of the "true plight of the Chicano, and the problems of people of Mexican descent living in the United States." Standing before his assembled soldiers, he optimistically predicted "this invasion can mean a victory for the people. Ultimately, it can mean the restitution of the land for those who need a place to be free."[31]

On August 30, 1972, twenty-six Brown Berets climbed a ridge overlooking the tourist-filled Avalon Harbor and raised a large Mexican flag. Upon seeing the uniformed activists raising the Mexican tricolor, one woman panicked and ran to the Avalon City Council office crying, "We're being invaded. Mexican soldiers are claiming the island!" In spite of their perceived aggression, the Brown Berets were making a symbolic statement about the U.S.–Mexican War. In a press release prepared before the occupation Sanchez wrote, "We are citizens of the United States and descendants of Mexican citizenship; not by natural choice, but rather by the takeover of the southwest in 1848." The protestors marked the 125th anniversary of Gen. Winfield Scott's capture of Mexico City by flying their banner over American territory. The Brown Berets kept a presence on the island for three weeks and left peacefully when a municipal judge ordered them to vacate their camp. Although Sanchez and the Brown Berets failed to secure possession of Santa Catalina Island, they had discovered a powerful symbol in the unfulfilled promises of the Treaty of Guadalupe Hidalgo (see fig. 27).[32]

For many Chicanos, invoking the peace accord had a potency that surpassed that of the war itself. As early as the 1950s the religious leader and political activist Reies Tijerina had demanded that the United States return private and communal lands in New Mexico that had been seized in violation of the Treaty of Guadalupe Hidalgo. In 1962 he founded La Alianza Federal de Mercedes Libres (Federal Land Grant Alliance) to petition both the U.S. and Mexican governments on behalf of the descendants of the original land grant holders. When diplomatic efforts failed, La Alianza resorted to civil disobedience to raise awareness of treaty violations. In the fall of 1966 the group occupied Kit Carson National Forest. After several members of La Alianza were arrested the following June, Tijerina led an armed assault on a county courthouse in Rio Arriba, leading to the wounding of two police officers. In addition to earning him a prison sentence, Tijerina's efforts yielded modest results when the U.S. Congress briefly entertained the idea of establishing a Special Commission on Guadalupe Hidalgo Land Rights in 1975. Similar proposals, unable to garner the broader support of the American people, died in congressional committees over the next five years.[33]

The Brown Berets and La Alianza were not alone in recognizing the power of the peace treaty. Chicano groups frequently referenced the accord while fighting for civil rights during this era. In his *Chicano Manifesto,* for example, Armando Rendón declared, "The Treaty of Guadalupe Hidalgo is the most important document concerning Mexican Americans that exists. From it stem specific guarantees affecting our civil rights, language, culture, and religion. . . . The United States should be required under law to make restitution for the damages and losses the Chicano people suffered as a result of treaty violations." Notwithstanding the importance of the war to Chicanos, the treaty eventually moved to the forefront of their political dialogue.[34]

Why did activists draw more authority from the treaty than from the conflict itself? To Chicanos the war was the seminal event in their emergence as a distinct people. Their focus on atrocities, resistance to the American occupation, and the Boy Heroes challenged the Anglo-dominated memories of the past. The portrayal of Mexicans as the innocent victims of American aggression also gave the Chicanos the moral high ground necessary for the founding of a strong, viable social movement. Nonetheless, Mexico's defeat was a political and historical reality that could not be altered. The Treaty of Guadalupe Hidalgo, however, whose legal authority reaches into the present, offered the promise of restitution. In spite of—or perhaps because of—its failures, the treaty would be an enduring reminder to Chicanos that they were not foreigners or immigrants, as the Anglos had viewed them, but the original and therefore rightful owners of the American Southwest.[35]

The Chicano civil rights movement proved a threat to the social and racial status quo of the nation. The uneasy balance of power between Anglos and Mexicans was forever changed. Like the struggle of African Americans in the South, the fight for civil rights radically altered the landscape of memory in the American Southwest. Academic writers took notice and bolstered the claims of Chicanos by criticizing the ways in which the United States treated the war in their historical monographs. Anglos, whose beloved memories had come under attack, searched for ways to reassert their historical claims in the region. Key to this effort was recovering control of the remembrance of the U.S.–Mexican War. Having lost authority over the written word, however, they looked for new ways to support their varied agendas.

One consequence of the Chicano–Anglo rivalry is that it created additional opportunities for the Church of Jesus Christ of Latter-day Saints to promote the memory of the Mormon Battalion. Having never fired a weapon at the Mexicans, the Mormons attempted to occupy a nonideological middle ground between the groups in the American Southwest. The bicentennial celebration of the founding of San Diego in 1969 gave the Sons of the Utah Pioneers a chance to honor their ancestors and publicize their religion beliefs. After conducting a national fundraising effort, the organization presented a nine-foot-tall bronze sculpture of a battalion member to the city. Overlooking San Diego Bay from Presidio Park, the heroic image of the Mormon soldier, musket slung over his shoulder, guarded his people's claim to the early history of California.[36]

At this same time the Church of Jesus Christ of Latter-day Saints purchased adjoining land in Old Town San Diego to create the Mormon Battalion Memorial Visitors' Center. This museum was devoted to the accomplishments of the soldier-explorers and other early Mormon settlers in southern California. At the grand opening of the center on November 6, 1972, the church president, Harold B. Lee, gave a dedicatory prayer. The prayer revealed that the Mormon agenda regarding the memory of the war had expanded since the monument building and historic trek of the 1940s and 1950s. Referring to the center, Lee prayed that God would "set it apart as a place of missionary dedication that it may stand here enriched by thy spirit; that all who come within these walls might feel the influence that shall be found here and go from here sobered in their minds to pray, to listen, and to learn, and hopefully to come into thy kingdom and enjoy that which can be had by those who drink deeply from the waters of eternal life." Latter-day Saints of earlier generations had relied upon the memory of the Mormon Battalion to aid the church in its quest for tolerance. Now they hoped that the memory of their forebears would also inspire conversions to their religion.[37]

Missionary work aside, Latter-day Saints understood that tolerance of their religion was not the same as acceptance as mainstream citizens. The visitors' center therefore allowed Mormons to continue to promote themselves as typical Americans. In addition to sharing the history of the church in California, the facility offered exhibits addressing the U.S. Constitution and the Declaration of Independence. English- and Spanish-language pamphlets distributed at the center devoted nearly as much space to documenting these events as they did to the battalion itself. The text noted proudly that "Joseph Smith, first president-prophet of the Church of Jesus Christ of Latter-day Saints (Mormon), called 'The Constitution of the United States . . . a glorious standard.'" As co-inheritors of their nation's greatness, Mormons hoped to find additional common ground with their fellow Americans.[38]

Which Americans were the Latter-day Saints specifically hoping to identify with? The promotional materials offered at the Mormon Battalion Memorial Visitors' Center further revealed an appeal to conservative Anglo-American patriotism. Church-produced radio advertisements declared that the center honored the "intrepid band of 500 who marched from Kansas to San Diego in 1846 and 47, during the Mexican War, to help secure California for the nation." A second advertisement asserted that the facility "commemorates the soldiers who undertook the longest infantry march in U.S. military history to help defend California during the Mexican War." The latter claim was particularly interesting, as it portrayed the American invasion as a defensive fight against Mexico. These conservative appeals to Manifest Destiny were no doubt aimed at those people the church was most interested in indentifying with and converting.[39]

While the Mormon agenda was unique in its immediate goals, Latter-day Saints merely reflected a larger trend toward using the memory of the U.S.–Mexican War to establish ethnic claims to the history of the American Southwest. The politically active Anglo and Chicano communities of southern California ensured that the region remained the epicenter of the battle for memory throughout the 1970s. During that decade the town of Escondido in San Diego County took its first steps toward commemorating the nearby Battle of San Pasqual. The Daughters of the American Revolution, Native Daughters of the Golden West, and the State of California had previously marked the battlefield, but city residents wanted to turn the site into a state park. Such a move was a departure from past expressions of memory because it forced California to take an official stance on the interpretation of the U.S.–Mexican War. Local economic interests initially trumped political concerns, as the battlefield was adjacent to the popular San Diego Wild Animal Park, and local businesses hoped to attract additional visitors to their community. The Escondido Chamber of Commerce actively supported the passage of a municipal bond issue, and in 1980 the State of California committed to provide funding for the park. The bond was merely a first step in a long process to raise sufficient public funds to turn the San Pasqual battlefield into a tourist attraction.[40]

Proponents of the park desperately needed political allies to make their dream a reality, and they found their champion in State Sen. William A. Craven. Craven was a well-respected, powerful politician who was highly outspoken against what he considered the flood of illegal immigration. Later in his career he chaired the controversial Special Committee on Border Issues and pushed for legislation requiring all Hispanic Americans to carry proof of legal residency. In 1983 he was able to secure nearly two million dollars for a survey of the battlefield and the construction of a visitors' center. The following year Craven, alongside a California Indian and a Californño, grasped a symbolic three-handled shovel and broke ground on the new facility.[41]

In November of 1987 the San Pasqual Battlefield State Historic Park opened its doors to the public. The visitors' center included murals, dioramas, and artifacts of the battle along with displays of the early California

Indians who had lived in the San Pasqual Valley. Large windows gave a pan-oramic view of the field where the fight actually took place. California State Parks strove for objectivity in its management of the facility and presented interpretative text in bilingual, politically neutral language. Although the park hosted a mere handful of visitors a day, it was at the time the only facility of its kind in the United States to commemorate the war.[42]

To aid in the management of the park a number of local citizens joined to form the San Pasqual Battlefield Volunteer Association. The duties of the association included giving tours and fundraising for the park. Their vice president was Walter Brooke, the great-grandson of General Kearny, the conqueror of the American Southwest who was wounded during the battle. California State Parks, however, had an uneasy relationship with its various volunteer organizations. While the government bureaucracy needed the additional local labor and fundraising, it often clashed with individuals about how sites were to be interpreted. To help ensure that community docents were sensitive to the Mexican perspective, state officials required them to undergo training before interacting with the public. Unable to control the volunteers, however, California State Parks eventually banned them from working in historical sites entirely.[43]

While Californians struggled to create a state park at San Pasqual, Texans considered a more ambitious project at the battlefield of Palo Alto in Browns-ville. It began simply in 1936, when the State of Texas placed a stone marker near the site at the intersection of two farm roads. Over subsequent decades chaparral reclaimed the little memorial, obscuring it from traffic. The growth of the historic preservation movement in the mid-twentieth century, how-ever, renewed interest in Palo Alto and the U.S.–Mexican War.[44]

Local and federal interests merged in 1956, when the Department of Interior announced its Mission 66 National Park Service ten-year development plan. Among the steps taken by the agency was to conduct a formal survey of sites and buildings to be preserved as part of the new National Historic Landmark Program. In 1960 a committee of scholars submitted a list of 116 sites that represented twenty-one themes in American history and development. The list included 3 U.S.–Mexican War battlefields: Fort Brown, Palo Alto, and Resaca de la Palma; and 3 sites with incidental connections to the conflict: Old Customhouse at Monterey, Sonoma Plaza, and Santa Fe Plaza.[45]

The residents of Brownsville were thrilled to have three historic landmarks in their city. Still, the battlefields remained in private hands and thus were easily overlooked. Desiring more than just landmark status, the community leader Mary Yturria spearheaded local efforts to bring the National Park Service to Palo Alto. Her efforts languished, however, until the Brownsville native Walter Plitt returned from touring national parks at Civil War battle sites in 1972. Inspired by what he saw, Plitt made the preservation of the Palo Alto battlefield his mission. He joined forces with Yturria, the local Chamber of Commerce, and historical organizations to found the Palo Alto National Park Committee with the express purpose of having the site dedicated as a federal facility. In spite of Brownsville's early reluctance to remember the U.S.–Mexican War, the committee touted the proposal as a way to heal racial and ethnic rifts in the community. The idea proved to be popular, and Yturria and Plitt soon attracted supporters from both sides of the border.[46]

The National Park Service experienced unprecedented growth in the decades after the Second World War. Mission 66 provided increased accessibility for automobile tourists to visit the growing number of parks throughout the nation. By the 1970s visiting national parks had become the cornerstone of the American family vacation. In this environment the Palo Alto National Park Committee was optimistic that the Department of Interior would accept their proposal. Accordingly, on November 10, 1978, Congress made a small purchase of land in Brownsville and established the Palo Alto Battlefield National Historic Site as the country's 302nd national park. Lawmakers failed, however, to allocate funds for staff or improvements, and local optimism soon vanished when it became clear that the park existed in name only.[47]

Undeterred, the Palo Alto National Park Committee lobbied local, state, and national politicians to have their site made operational. Even modest achievements proved difficult for the group. In the mid-1980s Plitt approached the Texas Department of Transportation for permission to clean up the area around the monument established in 1936. The highway superintendent grudgingly gave him permission to renovate the memorial but scolded him, declaring, "[You] ought to be ashamed of it." In spite of such setbacks the committee persevered in its self-appointed mission. Having no significant landholdings, staff, buildings, or budget, however, the Palo Alto battlefield continued to lie fallow until 1992.[48]

While preservation-minded Texans struggled at Palo Alto, the Church of Jesus Christ of Latter-day Saints continued its ever-expanding commemoration of the Mormon Battalion. In 1981 the church dedicated another monument at Fort Leavenworth, Kansas, where the unit mustered for its march toward Santa Fe. The Latter-day Saints invited President Ronald Reagan to speak at the dedication, but he declined to attend, instead sending Special Assistant Stephen M. Studdert to deliver a personal message to the crowd. After recounting Hubert Howe Bancroft's description of the Mormon Battalion, Studdert read a personal message from the president: "Nancy and I are very proud to extend our greetings and congratulations to your ceremonies. The dedication of this historical marker reminds us all once more of the great sacrifices exacted of our ancestors as they struggled to win the freedoms we enjoy today. It will memorialize for generations to come the sense of duty and special faith of these brave men and their loved ones." The president's words were revealing on two levels. First, Reagan referred to the battalion as "our ancestors," explicitly including the Mormons in the mainstream of America's pioneers. Such a pronouncement from the U.S. president validated the historical struggles of the Latter-day Saints and confirmed the modern value of the battalion's memory. Second, in calling the U.S.–Mexican War a struggle to win freedom Reagan ignored the real nature of the conflict, namely, that it was an invasion, and reclassified it as a defensive battle for democracy. Not surprisingly, the conservative president embraced a conservative interpretation of the war that ran parallel to his interventionist foreign policy in Latin America.[49]

As the Latter-day Saints continued to build memorials to the Mormon Battalion, older monuments to the U.S.–Mexican War came under physical attack. In 1940 the Sons of the Utah Pioneers had erected a monument to the Mormon Battalion along a stretch of El Camino Real adjacent to the San Felipe Indian Reservation. As the roadway became part of the interstate highway system, the Sons of the Utah Pioneers expanded the original monument and added a large bronze plaque describing the accomplishments of the battalion. Particularly offensive to neighboring members of the San Felipe Nation was the use of the word *savages* in an army report quoted on the monument. An unknown individual succeeded in obscuring the racist slur on the plaque by defacing it with a hammer.[50]

Other monuments met their demise during this period. In northern California thieves stole a marker placed in 1962 to commemorate the Battle of Santa Clara from a busy street corner. In Los Angeles construction crews demolishing old buildings for a new train yard destroyed the large stone and bronze memorial to the Battle of La Mesa. Monuments honoring the suppression of the Taos Revolt and the march of Kearny's army south of Santa Fe likewise disappeared. While it is impossible to know with certainty what motivated such destruction, the loss of the monuments nonetheless challenged the memories of the groups that had erected them.[51]

As memorials to the U.S.–Mexican War disappeared, other reminders of the conflict reemerged in the public imagination. After decades in storage, Santa Anna's wooden leg made a rare public appearance. First, the Illinois National Guard used the prosthetic in a traveling recruitment effort during the Vietnam War. Then, in 1976, as part of the U.S. bicentennial celebration, it was displayed in the National Guard Heritage Gallery in Washington. There, amid artifacts of the nation's wars, the prosthesis was one of the exhibition's most popular attractions. The publicity surrounding the leg eventually reached Texans, who again became enthralled with the unique trophy. In 1985 a Fort Worth radio station began a statewide campaign to convince the Illinois National Guard to loan the leg to Texas for the sesquicentennial of the Revolution of 1836. Much to the disappointment of the Lone Star State, officials in Springfield declined the request.[52]

Memory of Santa Anna's leg would not rest. The following year, Sen. Phil Gramm of Texas began a dialogue with the Mexican government for the return of the most coveted artifact of the Texas Revolution—the battle flag of the New Orleans Greys. This volunteer ensign was the only flag known to have survived the siege of the Alamo. After his victory, Santa Anna sent the trophy to Mexico City, where it resided in the National Museum of History at Chapultepec. The congressional press aide Larry Neal described Gramm's negotiations as being a "fairly delicate, quasi-diplomatic situation. There are very strong emotions attached to the flag on both sides of the border." Clearly, the Texans needed extra leverage in their dialogue with Mexico.[53]

As Gramm's negotiations stalled, a Houston attorney named Andrew L. Payne conceived an even more ambitious scheme, namely, to trade the flag of the New Orleans Greys for Santa Anna's prosthetic leg. Asserting that "the leg is necessary to Texas as a bargaining tool in order to retrieve the Alamo flag back from Mexico," Payne wrote to the Illinois state officials proposing the donation or sale of the artifact to interested parties in Texas. Rumors swirled as newspapers around the nation printed stories about the possible exchange. The adjutant general of the Illinois National Guard refused to yield to pressure and declared that the "leg must remain in the custody of the State of Illinois."[54]

The excitement over Santa Anna's prosthesis even inspired competing claims in the state. During the 1980s another wooden leg appeared at the Governor Olgesby Mansion in Decatur, a privately funded house museum that honored Richard James Oglesby, a former U.S. senator, governor of Illinois, and confidant of Abraham Lincoln. As a young man Oglesby had fought with the Illinois Volunteers in the U.S.–Mexican War, and family folklore alleged that Oglesby brought Santa Anna's leg home from Mexico. When docents who were cleaning out one of the governor's former residences found a wooden leg hidden in a closet they displayed it in the museum as yet another authentic relic of Santa Anna's crippling wound. The Oglesby limb failed to impress the public, however, since it was a cheaply manufactured peg leg unbecoming of the Napoleon of the West. Apparent dubiousness aside, the leg remained proudly on display as an amusing exhibit for volunteers and visitors alike.[55]

Why did Santa Anna's prosthetic leg capture the imagination of the American public? As explored earlier, the baby boom generation grew up with images of the villainous Mexican dictator slaughtering the brave defenders of the Alamo. The public display of such a personal extension of Santa Anna's body therefore allowed Americans to humiliate the murderer of Davy Crockett beyond the peace normally granted by the grave. Like the lifted scalp of an enemy, the bodily trophy became a totem signifying America's power over its Mexican enemies. Illinois's tenacious grip on the relic also suggested that it held particular significance to the state's honor. As long as Americans remained fascinated by the leg they would remember that soldiers from Illinois had fought bravely in defense of the nation.

As illustrated by the actions of Illinoisans, Texans, Californians, and Mormons, the scholarly writings of the 1970s and 1980s, which condemned the United States for initiating the U.S.–Mexican War, did not reflect the group memories of the nation at large. These monographs had mirrored the academy's support of the antiwar and civil rights movements, not the beliefs of America's silent majority. Scholarly publications often alienated the white population which did not appreciate this iconoclastic approach to its history. Such alienation did not mean that Anglo-Americans remained devoted to the racist system of the past, but the attention drawn toward white privilege made the recipients of such benefits increasingly uncomfortable with the portrayal of their heritage. This proved a threat to cherished group memories of white struggle and inspired a conservative backlash.[56]

The resurgence of interest in commemorating the U.S.–Mexican War was but one manifestation of this social and political reaction. Another way Anglo-Americans reasserted control of the memory of the conflict was through historical reenacting, or living history. The phenomenon of men and women donning period costumes and manners to recreate the past surged during the centennial of the Civil War. In the decades following the commemoration, thousands of Americans flocked to former battlefields to reenact the conflict that had originally overshadowed the U.S.–Mexican War. Aficionados of these recreations made a clear distinction between reenactors, who fought in mock battle performances, and living historians, who provided visual demonstrations of everyday life at historic sites or events. As tensions developed between the battlefield thespians and those more didactically inclined, some individuals decided to leave the Civil War in search of new opportunities.[57]

The production of the popular television miniseries *North and South* in 1985 opened up a new world of possibilities for the wayward living historians. The program, based on the best-selling novel by John Jakes, followed the lives of two young men through their schooling at West Point, service in Mexico, and then their engagement in combat on opposite sides during the

Civil War. Largely avoiding the politics of the conflict, the Emmy Award–winning miniseries recreated the Battle of Churubusco and introduced American television audiences to the U.S.–Mexican War for the first time. The image of the dashing Patrick Swayze in the uniform of a soldier fighting in the Mexican War exposed living historians to the aesthetics of the era and inspired an alternative for Civil War reenactors.[58]

Steven Abolt of Fort Worth was among the first to take up the light blue uniform of the Mexican War soldier. Disturbed by the academic revisions of the sixties and seventies, the self-described flag waver decided to adopt the U.S.–Mexican War for his living history demonstrations. As Texas approached its sesquicentennial celebration in 1986 he was able to recruit a number of former Civil War reenactors to join him. Abolt built a network of similar groups that had formed independently in the West and Midwest. A retired United States Army colonel named William E. Laybourn, an entrepreneurial-minded West Point graduate, re-created uniforms and gear for this new movement. Soon Abolt had enough uniformed men to organize Company A, Seventh U.S. Infantry Living History Association.[59]

In the late 1980s the Seventh Regiment presented exhibitions at historic sites around the West, including the national parks at Bent's Old Fort in Colorado and Fort Scott in Kansas. Dressing as a U.S.–Mexican War soldier allowed Abolt to express his love for the United States and its heritage. In the face of academic attacks on America's war in Mexico, living history also gave Abolt an opportunity to "teach a balanced version of history" to the visitors at the historic sites where he performed. Living history exhibitions have long been a popular draw and granted their practitioners an authority to create and frame memory for their audiences. Many living historians of this era had conservative political views, and their activities gave them a unique soapbox for expressing them.[60]

To brand living historians of the Mexican War as merely political or racial reactionaries, however, misses their broader meaning. A number of the men who donned the uniform of 1846, in fact, empathized with the Mexican soldiers they feigned to fight, and many understood the injustice of Manifest Destiny, which they embodied in their historical recreations. Interestingly, the majority of the living historians were drawn to this era not because they wished to attack Mexicans but because they were reacting to the Confederate Civil War reenactors who dominated the field of living history. The neo-Confederates' perceived exuberance for violence and racist politics repulsed those interested in the more academic applications of living history. Individuals who left Civil War reenactment for the U.S.–Mexican War often rejected the glorification of the Lost Cause commonly espoused around Confederate campfires during the 1980s.[61]

In spite of their ties to Civil War commemorations, the reenactments of the era were not exclusively white affairs. On December 6, 1986, the 140th anniversary of the Battle of San Pasqual, Anglo members of the San Diego Old Town Boosters Association mounted horses to engage in mock battle with the Mexican American Charro Riders Association of Escondido. The sounds of swords crashing against lances once again echoed in the San Pasqual Valley. After several charges and feigned deaths, the uniformed and costumed men retired from the field to the thrilled applause of the audience. The annual event proved so popular that it soon attracted hundreds of tourists to the state park.[62]

The reenactments at San Pasqual allowed for good-natured catharsis as Mexican Americans celebrated their greatest victory in a war otherwise marked by defeat. The spectacle also had a strong didactic function. After the third annual reenactment, Ben Cueva, the chairman of the Charro Riders Association, stated that he was especially interested in educating new residents of the area who might not understand the critical role Mexicans played in the early history of California. He stated that the newcomers "don't realize Mexicans developed . . . mining, roads, agriculture and ports. They named Rancho Bernardo, San Diego and Los Angeles. . . . It's important that people realize the history of Mexican people in this area." Cueva's sentiments echoed those of early California and New Mexico heritage societies which used their commemorations of the U.S.–Mexican War to establish primacy in the face of waves of immigration. Ultimately, living history became yet another means of creating and defending collective memory in a rapidly diversifying nation.[63]

On May 13, 1989, Steven R. Butler convened the first meeting of the Descendants of Mexican War Veterans in Dallas. Some years earlier Butler's genealogical research had located a progenitor who had fought in the conflict. His search for a corresponding heritage society led him to the Aztec Club of 1847. During the late twentieth century, however, the organization had dwindled to a handful of elderly men who jealously guarded their exclusivity. Spurned by the Aztec Club, Butler decided to establish a society for the descendants of the many enlisted men who fought in the conflict. The four elderly gentlemen who responded to his initial posting in the *Dallas Morning News* hardly seemed a promising beginning, yet Butler persevered and eventually recruited several hundred fellow descendants for his heritage organization.[64]

The heritage craze of the post–civil rights era highlighted white Americans' desire to validate their own historical struggles. In the coming decade, as the United States and Mexico attempted to redefine their official public memories in light of the pending North American Free Trade Agreement, Butler positioned himself at the center of the memory debate. After being confronted with the many perspectives of the U.S.–Mexican War, however, he found himself questioning his sense of history and remembrance. Indeed, the turn of the millennium would again force Americans and Mexicans alike to challenge cherished myths and memories as a means of fostering political and economic cooperation.[65]

The years between 1966 and 1989 were marked by yet more battles to control collective memory in the United States. Unlike the international disputes of previous decades, this struggle was largely a domestic affair that pitted Chicano against Anglo, liberal against conservative, and academic against layman. The strong emotions tied to this fight evinced the high stakes of this rivalry. To defend their positions Americans added new weapons to their memory arsenal, including government parks, historical reenactors, and heritage groups devoted to the war. All sides achieved victories in this struggle, resulting in a fractured and at times contradictory sense of memory. The experiences of this turbulent era demonstrated that an ethnically diverse nation will, by its very nature, host a variety of memories serving many masters. This was true above all in the United States, where the federal government exerted little control over the nation's public remembrance. The 1990s brought an end to the neglect the United States showed toward Mexico. With the collapse of the Soviet Union and the termination of the Cold War, the United States turned again to its southern neighbor. This time the motivation would be not continental security but continental commerce.

10 Remembrance and Free Trade

THE UNITED STATES AND MEXICO, 1990–2008

❖

ON MAY 22, 1990, President Carlos Salinas de Gortari addressed the Mexican Senate. Standing beneath a gold-lettered motto that read, La Patria es Primero (The Fatherland Is First), he proclaimed that Mexico would seek "free trade with the United States and Canada." The declaration pleased the senators, who had previously encouraged the president to take radical steps to end Mexico's economic stagnation. Garnering legislative support was only the beginning of Salinas de Gortari's challenges. For decades a lingering anti-Americanism had seeped into the culture of Mexico. Generations of textbooks had defined national identity and patriotism in terms of resistance to the United States. The government had used the scheming gringo as a foil for the patriotic Mexican, making the North Americans a convenient scapegoat for the ills of the country. Salinas de Gortari knew he had to do more than just gain the confidence of his northern neighbor; he also had to convince his people that the United States could be a trusted ally and friend.[1]

Free trade flows in two directions, however, and the U.S. government, too, needed to change popular attitudes toward Mexico to encourage support for the economic alliance. The nation's intellectual elites had long adopted the belief that their country was to blame for the U.S.–Mexican War. Far from engendering popular sympathy for Mexico, such attitudes alienated many Americans. These private citizens tenaciously fought to reassert control over the remembrance of the war through a number of means. As the countries discussed free trade they had to contend with the looming sesquicentennial of this divisive war. Alone and in tandem, the two governments attempted to shape the memory of the conflict to forward their political and economic agendas.

At the beginning of the twenty-first century, both the United States and Mexico sought to harness the power of memory to bring their nations together. Although popular remembrances of the war had previously rein-

forced suspicions of one another, individuals and agencies from both countries attempted to find common ground during the creation of the Palo Alto
Battlefield National Historic Site and while producing an ambitious documentary film series. These enterprises enjoyed some success, but people on
both sides of the border were not always willing to accept the governments'
authority over memory. In Mexico, rejection manifested itself as strikers
forced the government to embrace once again discarded symbols of the past.
North Americans likewise eschewed the political correctness of the new
federally fostered memory and found ways to continue recollecting the war
according to their individual and group needs. As the 160th anniversary of
the Treaty of Guadalupe Hidalgo approached in 2008 the familiar question
arose once more: How would the conflict be remembered?

After Salinas de Gortari announced that his nation was interested in
reaching a continental free trade agreement, Mexico and the United States
began the difficult process of negotiating an appropriate treaty. In light of
this new arrangement Mexico took the first step toward changing attitudes
about the War of North American Intervention. Official government positions were not always in harmony with popular Mexican views of the
United States, particularly those held by authors. Ernesto Zedillo Ponce de
León, secretary of education, had the unenviable task of modifying Mexico's textbooks to reflect the government's new stance. Zedillo was raised on
the Mexican border with California and had earned a doctoral degree at
Yale University. Although his record of public service identified him as a
consummate patriot, his lifelong exposure to the United States made him
sympathetic toward his northern neighbor. The free textbook system had
not been revised in twenty years, and Zedillo hoped to change the attitudes
of the rising generation of Mexicans toward the United States.[2]

In September of 1992 the Secretaría de Educación Pública (SEP) sent
sample copies of the new textbooks to select educators for assessment. The
new editions had several significant modifications that shocked the review-
ers. They rehabilitated the reputation of Porfirio Díaz and for the first time
since the Revolution presented his rule in a positive light. The books also
addressed the massacre of striking students at Tlatelolco in 1968. Finally,
contradicting decades of nationalistic rhetoric, Zedillo downplayed the role
of Mexico's revolutionary *caudillos* and the Boy Heroes of Chapultepec.[3]

Word of these changes sparked angry demonstrations. Political opponents attacked Salinas de Gortari's administration for "rewriting the country's history to suit its political needs." A Mexican attorney exclaimed,
"What is in dispute is the very essence of the nation." One of the creators of
the textbooks defended the work, declaring that the "myths that the country and the world have left behind have yet to be demolished in political

speech and public education. . . . Today, when what is conventional academic wisdom passes into the public debate, it seems like sacrilege." The controversy threatened the SEP's authority and unnerved President Salinas de Gortari.[4]

In the midst of this controversy the government hosted its annual commemoration of the Boy Heroes at Chapultepec Park on September 13. Reporters surrounded Salinas de Gortari following the ceremony and asked him about the legacy of the Boy Heroes. The president appeared to be wavering in his commitment to the SEP when he declared, "We will always be willing to promote the remembrance of this historical act, of that glorious memory, to our children and our children's children."[5]

Two nights later Salinas de Gortari presided over the Independence Eve celebration in Mexico City. Traditionally, Mexico's president stood on the balcony of the National Palace to give the Grito de Dolores (Cry of Dolores) in ritual reenactment of Father Miguel Hidalgo y Costilla's call to arms in the town of Dolores, Guanajuato, at the beginning of the War of Independence.

As Salinas de Gortari looked out across the crowded Plaza de la Constitución he could see banners challenging his new textbooks, including one that read, "The Boy Heroes—An Essential Part of Our History." In addition to the traditional cries of "Long live independence!" and "Long live Mexico!" the president added for the first time "Long live the Boy Heroes!" With this act of capitulation, the battle over the martyred cadets was over. Realizing that he was unable to win the fight for the nation's memory, Salinas de Gortari ordered Zedillo to recall 6.8 million of the divisive textbooks.[6]

Popular support for the Boy Heroes had an immediate impact on federal policy. Months after the Zedillo controversy the national mint in Mexico City added the cadets' images to the fifty-peso coin. The five-thousand-peso bill showing the Boy Heroes had quietly disappeared from circulation on the eve of free trade negotiations, but this act restored the iconic youths to the currency of the nation. When the SEP published its final, revised textbooks in 1994 the Boy Heroes had returned to their place of honor, although with minor modifications. After describing the Battle of Chapultepec and the deaths of the cadets, the book stated, "We venerate the memory of this defense in the form of the Boy Heroes: Juan de la Barrera, Juan Escutia, Francisco Márquez, Agustín Melgar, Fernando Montes de Oca, and Vicente Suárez." The illustrations included an oil painting of Juan Escutia, but the caption failed to perpetuate the myth of his jump. The legendary story, however, was kept alive by individual schools and teachers who defiantly hosted annual reenactments of the Battle of Chapultepec. To this day, little children dressed in paper hats, leap from chairs wrapped in their fatherland's tricolored flag (see fig. 28).[7]

While the Mexican government attempted to regain control of the nation's memory, the United States undertook a major federal project that also attempted to frame public remembrance of the war. From its beginnings in the 1970s the Palo Alto National Park Committee had united the citizens of Brownsville with those of its sister city of Matamoros in a quest to establish a national park dedicated to the U.S.–Mexican War in South Texas. The National Park Service, as noted, had previously identified the battlefield as a site of historical significance, but it had not yet purchased any significant land or provided funding for staff or interpretation.[8]

The driving force behind the national park movement during the 1980s and 1990s, as we have seen, was Walter Plitt, the president of the Palo Alto National Park Committee. Plitt had grown up in a Brownsville family whose members felt that the study of history was an important component of patriotism and good citizenship. Frustrated with the condemnation of the United States coming from the academy, Plitt hoped that visitors to Palo Alto would learn the "American side" of the conflict. He found loyal supporters in Steven Butler's newly organized Descendants of Mexican War Veterans, whose membership wholeheartedly agreed with his vision. Other individuals within his organization, however, challenged Plitt's conservative views. At a conference in Corpus Christi in 2002, for example, a Mexican historian who was a member of the committee deviated from his prepared talk and insisted that the United States pay war reparations to Mexico. Chicanos in the audience then demanded immigration reform as a discouraged Plitt tried in vain to regain control of the meeting. Ironically, the closer he came to achieving his goal of a fully functioning national park at Palo Alto, the less influence he would have over the historical interpretation of the war.[9]

Not letting internal dissension stop its work, the Palo Alto National Park Committee persevered and eventually gained the support of Sen. Lloyd Bentsen Jr., Gov. Ann Richards, and President George H. W. Bush. In January of 1992 Congress finally allocated money to purchase portions of the original battlefield and fund a modest full-time National Park Service staff. Tom Carroll, a veteran ranger nearing retirement, initially took the helm of the fledgling national park. Carroll struggled, however, as there was no budget to build offices or a visitors' center, and the three park rangers worked in a cramped rental space several miles from the battlefield.[10]

Among Carroll's duties was evaluating popular support for the park along both sides of the lower Rio Grande. He commissioned the local anthropologist Antonio Zavaleta to conduct seventy-six interviews among the citizens of Brownsville and Matamoros. The interviews offer insight into the group memories of the U.S.–Mexican War among Anglos, Mexican Americans, and Mexicans during the formative period of this national park.

Interestingly, the interviews revealed that none of the respondents recalled any oral traditions related to their families' participation in the battles of Palo Alto or Resaca de la Palma. Nonetheless, most had strong opinions about how the engagements should be remembered. All three groups overwhelmingly supported the establishment of the national park at Palo Alto: 96 percent of Mexican Americans, 91 percent of Anglos, and 83 percent of Mexicans backed the proposal. When asked why they supported the park, most respondents cited their belief in preserving local history, but there were some subtle differences.[11]

Mexican Americans most often expressed an interest in the national park being a place where they could tell the history of "how this area was before the United States took possession of it." While several of those interviewed affirmed their pride in being citizens of the United States, they were very aware of the perceived injustices of the U.S.–Mexican War. Maria Champion Henggler, for example, declared, "I am a loyal American, but I can see that the Mexicans were taken for a ride." Miguel Antonio Lopez echoed these sentiments, stating that the park was an important means of "identify[ing] who we are and where we've been," although he cautioned that visitors should remember that the site was the result of "one country actually stealing land from another country." Denise Saenz Blanchard considered the national park an opportunity to celebrate the genesis of the Mexican American people and reminded the interviewer that "the fastest growing population in the United States is the Hispanic people and culture, and yet we have nothing to signify where it all began." The national park could potentially be that place.[12]

Anglo-Texans likewise supported the park but in doing so made clear their own set of concerns. Several respondents worried that the war might be portrayed negatively as an imperialist land grab. Bruce Aiken insisted that interpretive programs should focus exclusively on the battle and not "push the morality or immorality of it." Two Anglos who lived through the Second World War cited the recent controversy over the display of the *Enola Gay* at the Smithsonian National Air and Space Museum as reason to carefully monitor how the federal government depicted the conflict. Several other white residents of Brownsville hoped the park would be a place to celebrate their peaceful coexistence with their Mexican neighbors. Using phrases such as "bury the hatchet" and "let bygones be bygones," they believed preserving the battlefield would ultimately "put that war behind us." Given that Anglos made up less than 8 percent of Brownsville's population, it served their social, political, and economic interests to downplay the ethnic violence of the past.[13]

Although slightly less enthusiastic about the national park than their northern neighbors, most Mexican respondents approved of the plan. Still, many of them worried that the park might not adequately portray their perspective of the war. Manuel Robledo Treviño, for example, agreed with the proposal "as long as it is given [with] the correct point of view, and [does] not hurt feelings—especially on the Mexican side." Clemente Rendón de la Garza warned that the United States should not "justify the past with lies and half-truths." He hoped the National Park Service would portray the invasion correctly, that is, as "an act of intervention and not the other way around." A park detractor named Antonio Rivera Yzaguirre lamented, "We live so close and yet things get distorted. . . . What happened at the Alamo is a total lie, and if the same thing happens here, it will be a serious problem." Another critic, Rosalia Sanchez Cárdenas, fatalistically replied, "We don't want to be reminded of our failures. . . . With or without our opinion, the United States will establish their park."[14]

In spite of their varied desires and concerns, the people of the southernmost U.S.–Mexican border largely welcomed the National Park Service to Brownsville. Individual ethnic and national groups all preferred their histories to be highlighted at the site, yet most retained the hope that Palo Alto could be a peaceful place for all visitors. In keeping with this spirit, less than one-third of Anglo and one-half of Mexican and Mexican American respondents thought that battle reenactments, like those seen at Civil War battlefields, would be appropriate at the site. The consensus among these diverse critics was that it would "rub salt into old wounds" and threaten the peaceful interethnic and international relations of the region. The National Park Service would soon find, however, that satisfying its multiple constituencies without disturbing this peace would prove to be nearly an impossible task.[15]

While Superintendent Carroll began the difficult task of interpreting the national memory of the U.S.–Mexican War at Palo Alto, KERA-TV, a Public Broadcasting Service (PBS) affiliate in Dallas, announced the production of a documentary miniseries about the conflict. The veteran PBS producer Sylvia Komatsu first conceived the idea for the series in 1989 while visiting an exhibition of U.S.–Mexican War lithographs and daguerreotypes at the Amon Carter Museum in Dallas. Realizing the visual potential of the subject matter, Komatsu successfully drafted a proposal for the series.[16]

Any program created by KERA-TV, a federally funded entity, carried the tacit approval of the U.S. government and, like the National Park Service, had the potential authority to shape the public memory of the war. Understanding the importance of her responsibility, Komatsu vowed to comply with the PBS mandate of "strict adherence to objectivity and balance." With development money provided by the Corporation for Public Broadcasting, Komatsu sought the assistance of the Clements Center for Southwest Studies at Southern Methodist University in Dallas, widely recognized as being among the leading centers supporting the academic study of the American West. Working with faculty and staff at the institution, Komatsu organized an advisory board that included some of the most important American, Chicano, and Mexican scholars of the war.[17]

While these intellectuals were familiar with each other's research, few had had the opportunity to meet in person. The initial congeniality of the group gave little indication of the contentious, emotional debates in which they would soon engage. From their first gathering, however, it became clear that each had his or her own ideas about how the film should unfold. Although the academic writings of this era closely paralleled those of the 1970s and 1980s, which overwhelmingly faulted the United States for inciting the war, the nuances of causation remained one of the hotly contested issues among the scholars. Over a quarter of American books published during this period alleged that while the United States pressed for war on the Rio Grande, the action was principally a boundary dispute. The debate, therefore, centered on whether Polk's war was a premeditated "land grab" or if the territorial conquest was incidental to the defense of Texas's southern boundary. Mexican and Chicano historians, for example, agreed that the war was an aggressive act to acquire land. American scholars, on the other hand, recognized that Polk had provoked the war, but some felt that the land grab claim was an oversimplification of a more complex political situation. The Mexican historian Josefina Zoraida Vázquez later described the academic sparring as being "very hot." Nonetheless, Komatsu considered the debates to be healthy and constructive for the development of the project.[18]

Particularly taxing for the board was overcoming the divergent collective memories of both nations. Unlike that of the United States, Mexico's public memory of the war was an important component of civic and political life. As the more liberal Mexican scholars compromised with the Americans on points challenging the established narrative, their conservative countrymen felt a personal betrayal akin to treason. The Americans, although less encumbered by public memory, also had group remembrance to address. This was manifested in various tangential tales of the war that they wanted to be highlighted in the program. These included stories of obscure campaigns, forgotten players, and political contexts not usually associated with the traditional narrative. Komatsu moderated these debates in search of a cohesive story that best represented the varied perspectives.[19]

While the advisory board sought common ground, Komatsu searched for production funds. Typically, PBS affiliates solicited grants from the National Endowment for the Humanities and private foundations to finance their programs. While a seasoned producer at a major PBS station could usually expect to raise sufficient money for a high-profile historical film, Komatsu found herself caught in the middle of free trade politics. In the midst of the negotiations over the North American Free Trade Agreement (NAFTA), many foundations were reluctant to disrupt international goodwill with memories of a devastating and divisive war. Komatsu was persuasive, however, and eventually raised the money necessary to produce the four-hour miniseries, which she entitled *The U.S.–Mexican War, 1846–1848*. She also formed a partnership with Once TV México (Mexican Eleven TV), Mexico's state-run television network, turning the program into a binational project. With the final planning and financial elements in place, Komatsu quietly labored on the lengthy process of completing the series. The nine-year project slipped from public view until its premiere in 1998.[20]

As Komatsu and her board of scholars debated the meaning of the U.S.–Mexican War, diplomats from the two nations completed their negotiations on the continental trade treaty. Over the objections of organized labor and environmentalists, U.S. and Mexican legislators ratified NAFTA at the end of 1993. American critics feared that the accord would lead to the loss of manufacturing jobs and further pollute the environment. Mexican skeptics worried that NAFTA would lead to the Americanization of their culture. The opposition was defeated, and the treaty went into effect on January 1, 1994, lowering existing tariffs and granting corporations in the United States greater financial participation in Mexican industry. Although he was unable to alter significantly his nation's public memory, Salinas de Gortari had nonetheless achieved his goal of instituting continental free trade.[21]

Following the textbook debacle of 1992, political observers assumed that Ernesto Zedillo's public career was over. The assassination of Salinas's heir apparent, Luis Colosio, in the spring of 1994, however, thrust Zedillo into the spotlight again. Mexican law forbade incumbent federal officials from running for president, but Zedillo had resigned his post shortly after the textbook controversy and was one of the few high-ranking officials in the dominant Partido Revolucionario Institutional (PRI) eligible to run. Zedillo's nomination assured his victory in the presidential election, and in the winter of that year he assumed leadership of the Mexican government. Unfortunately for the new president, he reaped the bitter harvest of his predecessor's faulty domestic policies. While Salinas de Gortari successfully negotiated NAFTA, he had artificially overvalued the nation's currency. Within weeks of Zedillo's assumption of the office, concerned foreign investors began removing their capital from Mexico. This had an immediate impact on the inflated peso, which crashed in the foreign exchange market.[22]

Attempting to thwart a Latin American currency meltdown, President Bill Clinton proposed an emergency fifty-billion-dollar aid package for Mexico to buttress the beleaguered peso. The president encountered immediate bipartisan resistance in Congress and was forced to use his executive authority and influence with the International Monetary Fund to make the necessary loans. Many Americans, believing that Clinton was ignoring domestic needs, resented the Mexican bailout. Others worried that Mexico's financial disaster would curb American imports or cause a flood of illegal immigrants to cross into the United States. Realizing that they were now inextricably tied to the social and economic welfare of Mexico, however, most Americans grudgingly accepted the president's plan.[23]

Supported by the international aid package of 1995, Mexico's economy stabilized, and Latin America averted the feared currency disaster. Clinton's act seemed to have an immediate effect on Mexico's public memory of the U.S.–Mexican War: the image of the Boy Heroes disappeared from the fifty-peso coin, making it an instant numismatic rarity. Not wanting to appear to be dependent on the United States, Zedillo focused on repaying the loan ahead of schedule. The bailout of the Mexican economy was all the more interesting because it occurred as both nations prepared to celebrate the 1996–98 sesquicentennial of their war.[24]

The first group to commemorate the 150th anniversary was the Descendants of Mexican War Veterans. After years of negotiations with the City of Brownsville, President Butler arranged for a memorial on the site of the original Fort Brown (Fort Texas) on May 4, 1996. All that remained of the fortress were some low-lying earthen walls that served as the backstop of a nearby golf course driving range. Believing that such an ignominious fate was unbefitting of this important historical site, the Descendants of Mexican War Veterans purchased a flagpole to return a measure of patriotic dignity to the ruins. Nearly three hundred supporters marked the sesquicentennial of Mexico's artillery barrage on the fort by attending the flagpole dedication. The Seventh U.S. Infantry Living History Association attended the event, wearing period uniforms and firing a cannon to honor the memory of the siege that began the war.[25]

The flagpole raising at Fort Brown was a politically conservative event supported by private groups such as the Palo Alto National Park Committee and the Descendants of Mexican War Veterans. Government authorities, however, could not afford to promote such partisan displays. Instead, a number of state and federal institutions from both Mexico and the United States sponsored a commemoration more befitting of their close economic partnership. On May 8, 1996, the sesquicentennial anniversary of the outbreak of hostilities at Palo Alto, dozens of scholars gathered across from Fort Brown in Matamoros for a two-day academic symposium named "Reflections Around the 150th Anniversary of the U.S.–Mexican War." In lieu of reenactments or battlefield tributes, the internationally respected historians of the

U.S.–Mexican War Josefina Zoraida Vázquez and David Edmonds sparred over the finer points of the causes and results of the conflict. Vázquez and Edmonds were then serving as advisers for the KERA-TV documentary, giving their academic disagreements a public forum outside of their board meetings. Aside from events on the lower Rio Grande, however, both the United States and Mexico seemed content to allow the anniversary of the beginning of the war to pass unnoticed.[26]

Although most Americans ignored the sesquicentennial of the early campaigns of the war in 1996, the Church of Jesus Christ of Latter-day Saints erected a monument in Tucson honoring the Mormon Battalion's arrival in the city 150 years earlier. The ceremonies included battalion reenactors, a parade of Mormon missionaries, and the presence of the church's prophet, Gordon B. Hinckley. The orators at the dedication stressed the nonviolent nature of the Tucson occupation, describing it as a peaceful, friendly encounter. Latter-day Saint speakers recounted that Mexican residents fed the beleaguered battalion after its march through the Sonoran desert. Descendants of both battalion members and original Mexican settlers helped unveil a large bronze statue portraying a Mexican Tucsonan, a Mormon Battalion volunteer, and an officer of the regular army engaged not in battle but in trade. Like other memorials to the Mormon Battalion, the Tucson monument commemorated peace rather than combat and further linked the Latter-day Saints to the early history of the American West. The bicultural nature of the celebration reflected the larger national trend of using such events to bring Americans and Mexicans together in common purpose. The participation of Mormon missionaries reconfirmed the proselytizing goals of such events.[27]

On January 15, 1997, President Clinton announced that Mexico had repaid its debt to the United States three years ahead of schedule. The proclamation thrilled Mexicans and restored a feeling of national honor and dignity to the country. In addressing his people, President Zedillo declared that the ability of the debt to "infringe our sovereignty" was no longer a concern. When Mexicans learned that they had paid over five hundred million dollars in interest to the United States, they also felt a sense of financial independence from their traditional rival. This renewed pride manifested itself in the ways in which Mexico celebrated the remainder of the sesquicentennial of the War of North American Intervention.[28]

Excitement over the commemoration became apparent when President Clinton made a state visit to Mexico City on May 7, 1997. Clinton expected to meet with President Zedillo to discuss illegal immigration and the drug trade, but he found himself in the middle of a remembrance which he little understood. Although Zedillo had earlier attempted to purge the Boy Heroes from Mexico's civic myth, he nonetheless suggested that Clinton visit the

Altar to the Fatherland in Chapultepec Park and lay a wreath in homage to the slain cadets. While Zedillo hoped to re-create the success of President Truman's visit fifty years earlier, the U.S. delegation was concerned that this reference to the U.S.–Mexican War might increase tensions between the nations. Mexican officials replied that the gesture was "just a sign of respect, part of the protocol." Assured that the observance would be a simple ceremony, Clinton agreed to the wreath laying. Accordingly, he stood silently next to Zedillo while cadets from the Military College paid their ritual honors to their fallen comrades. While the homage lacked the spontaneous sincerity of Truman's visit, it drew immediate comparisons to the earlier event in the media of both countries. In words reminiscent of 1947, one journalist wrote that Clinton's "single gesture of respect did more to restore the confidence and trust of the Mexican people than any agreement between heads of state could have."[29]

Clinton's presence did not soothe all ill feelings, however, and emotions simmered beneath the surface of Mexican society as they had for 150 years. Alejandro Bolaños, a fifteen-year-old resident of Mexico City, expressed the lingering anger many Mexicans still had of the American invasion. He stated to a reporter, "It infuriates me to read about it. . . . Mexico had no stable government. We were fighting each other, and you Americans invaded and took advantage." Other Mexicans remained suspicious of NAFTA. Julio Faesler, a politician, claimed that the "popular view in Mexico is that the United States is forcing Mexico to carry out America's economic agenda." A street sweeper named Juan Dominguez concluded bitterly, "Sure, Clinton bailed us out, but we're still poor."[30]

Ironically, Clinton's rescue of the peso soothed Mexican anger only during the time Mexico actually owed money to the United States. Once that debt was paid, relations returned to their former state. In assessing Clinton's visit to Chapultepec, the political analyst Delal Baer observed the growing tension between the two countries following repayment. He noted, "This whole trip was about symbols. Since January we had been in a downward spiral with accusations and recriminations coming from both sides. This visit was the circuit breaker." Clinton's journey to Mexico proved to be yet another short-term solution to the two nations' perpetually strained relations. Indeed, it was merely another thin strip of Yankee gauze meant to stem a hemorrhage of Mexican pride, memory, and nationalism.[31]

Three weeks after Clinton's visit the Mexican government again focused on its most important symbol of defiance—the Boy Heroes. On May 28, 1997, the secretary of the interior announced the formation of the Comisión Organizadora de los Homenajes del CL Aniversario de los Niños Héroes

(Organizing Committee for the Tribute to the 150th Anniversary of the Boy Heroes). The committee's first accomplishment was the publication of *In Defense of the Fatherland,* an oversized, illustrated history of the war. Including images and documents from the nation's archives and essays written by some of Mexico's most eminent scholars, the book claimed to "offer an integral vision of the war Mexico survived during the difficult years of nation building." The highlight of the book was Vázquez's essay "An Unjust Invasion," which followed the example of earlier Chicano literature by documenting the oft-overlooked Mexican resistance in California and New Mexico. A companion website likewise reaffirmed Mexico's traditional memory of the war. Earlier questions raised by President Zedillo when he was serving as secretary of education had no place in the sesquicentennial.[32]

To fulfill its stated objectives the commission also published a volume entitled *Historical Documents of the Defense of Chapultepec.* In addition to editorials praising the actions of the young cadets, the book served as a documentary history of the Boy Heroes and their celebrated defense of the Military College. Large color facsimiles of handwritten accounts and legal records supported the legitimacy of Mexico's commemoration of its young martyrs. Notwithstanding their impressive appearance, the documents inadvertently highlighted some weaknesses of the Boy Heroes myth. Official paperwork concerning Juan de la Barrera, for example, showed him to be a recently commissioned lieutenant rather than a cadet. More troubling was that there was no documentation proving that the flag-saving Juan Escutia had ever attended the Military College. The book merely reprinted a petition from 1947 submitted by a woman who claimed to be his niece and who desired a government pension based on the sacrifice of her famous relative. While later historians would acknowledge that Escutia was a regular soldier in the San Blas Battalion and not a cadet, such details would only diminish the goals of the sesquicentennial commission and its celebration.[33]

The commemorations of 1997 in Mexico predictably focused on the anniversaries of the Battles of Churubusco and Chapultepec. The observances at Churubusco, however, had little to do with the United States and instead celebrated positive diplomatic relations with Ireland. To mark the sesquicentennial of the battle Mexico and Ireland jointly issued a postage stamp honoring the Batallón San Patricio that had fought for Mexico during the war. Although the unit was composed of United States Army deserters of many national origins, Mexicans portrayed them as being almost exclusively Irish. During the 1950s expatriates of Eire living in Mexico recast the entire battalion as their freedom-fighting compatriots. This connection became all the more important when the two countries finally established full

diplomatic relations in 1992. On August 20, 1997, members of the Irish legation and the Mexican government met at Churubusco to dedicate a plaque
honoring the men who died at the former convent.[34]

Among those at the celebration was a newly organized pipe and drum
band formed in Mexico City for the anniversary of the battle. The Banda de
Gaitas del Batallón de San Patricio (Bagpipe Band of the Saint Patrick's Battalion) claimed its purpose was to "promote Highland bagpipe music in
Mexico and honor the members of the Saint Patrick's Battalion that died far
away from their land of birth defending their newly adopted country." In yet
another odd twist in the memory of this foreign legion, Mexicans now associated the group with Scottish Highland culture rather than that of Ireland.
The Banda de Gaitas remains a fixture at civic functions honoring the San
Patricios and the Battle of Churubusco. It continues to perform a monthly
tattoo at the Museum of Interventions to honor the presence of the Saint
Patrick's Battalion at the convent.[35]

Mexico's federal government also honored the legacy of the Saint Patrick's
Battalion at the annual commemoration of their mass execution on September 12, 1997. At the Plaza San Jacinto, President Zedillo presided over a ceremony attended by Ambassador Daniel Dultzin Dubin of Ireland that honored both the San Patricios and the diplomatic relations between Mexico and
Ireland. The Mexican legislature would eventually engrave the name of the
Batallón San Patricio on the walls of the congressional Cámara de Diputados
(Chamber of Deputies). Celebrated in ceremony and stone, the legacy of the
battalion remains the prime symbol of Mexican–Irish friendship.[36]

The day after the San Patricio celebration, President Zedillo led the annual commemoration of the Boy Heroes at Chapultepec. In addition to his
tribute to the cadets Zedillo used the event to promote unity within his federal government. Since 1989 the leftist Partido de la Revolución Democrática
(PRD) had threatened the hegemony of the president's institutional party. As
Zedillo prepared to present his wreath at the Altar to the Fatherland he
turned to Porfirio Muñoz Ledo, a member of the PRD and the president of
the Chamber of Deputies, and said, "Please, take it." In a show of solidarity,
the chief executive and his political challenger laid the wreath together. The
act offended some members of the Zedillo government and nearly created a
scandal within his party. In spite of being included in the ceremony, Muñoz
Ledo criticized what he considered to be a bland event. In an interview later
that day he characterized the celebration as being "ordinary, nothing special,
like it has always been. It was missing any deep reflections, or remorse or
vengeance. But the United States remains a central theme that cannot be forgotten." With his battle over the memory of the Boy Heroes blotting his
public record, Zedillo appeared out of step with his rivals, who did not

hesitate to use the commemoration as a pronouncement against the United States.[37]

Although such events garnered attention because of the sesquicentennial anniversary, they were modest affairs when compared to the spectacle of 1947 involving the cadets' remains. It seemed that the power of the Boy Heroes myth may have been slowly losing its hold on Mexicans' imagination. Beginning with an iconoclastic master's thesis written by María Elena García Muñoz and Ernesto Fritsche Aceves in 1989, Mexican scholars began questioning the legend of the slain cadets. The thesis, entitled "The Boy Heroes: From the Reality to the Myth," was written at the National Autonomous University of Mexico and traced the creation of the patriotic tale to its late nineteenth-century origins. In the days leading up to the 150th anniversary commemoration at Chapultepec, Mexico's intellectual elite addressed the veracity of the story in local newspapers. The federal government, however, elected to stay out of the academic debate for another decade.[38]

As Mexicans dedicated the summer of 1997 to official remembrances of the War of North American Intervention, private organizations in the United States continued to use the sesquicentennial for their own purposes. In a novel twist on living history, Latter-day Saints began a new tradition involving the memory of the Mormon Battalion. The church had recently opened the Mormon Handcart Visitors' Center at Martin's Cove, Wyoming. This historic site honored immigrant Mormon pioneers who pushed two-wheeled handcarts hundreds of miles over the Great Plains to the Utah Territory between 1856 and 1860. Church leaders encouraged their youth to reenact a portion of the trek as a means of strengthening their personal devotion and ties to their self-sacrificing ancestors.[39]

Wherever Mormon youth perform this ritual reenactment of their forebears they follow certain scripted elements. Principal among these is an anachronistic reference to the Mormon Battalion. Just before the youths ascend a large hill with their heavy wooden carts, a group of uniformed men representing the United States Army stop the handcart company. After announcing that the United States is at war with Mexico the soldiers command the young men to step forward and volunteer for the Mormon Battalion. After the boys march off the young women are left to push their handcarts over the steep hill alone (see fig. 29).[40]

The so-called women's pull is a highlight of the handcart reenactments. Relying on their physical strength and drawing upon a faith in the power of their ancestors to intercede, the young women haul the heavy-laden carts to the top of the hill. After performing this act of endurance the Mormon youth pause to discuss the spiritual lessons of the experience and commit themselves to avoiding drugs, alcohol, and sexual impurity. This spiritual rite of passage is made more interesting by the fact that the Mormon Battalion was drafted from wagon trains in 1846, not from the handcart companies of the 1850s. In the case of these modern handcart trekkers, however, memory is the servant of faith and not beholden to historical fact. The ritual of the Mormon Battalion women's pull continues to be reenacted by thousands of Latter-day Saint youth each summer.[41]

The Mormons were not the only North American group interested in the sesquicentennial of the U.S.–Mexican War. Under the leadership of Richard Hoag Breithaupt Jr., the Aztec Club of 1847 experienced a renaissance during the 1990s. The group had declined steadily during the twentieth century until it had a mere handful of active members. When Breithaupt took the reins of the organization in 1995 he began a recruiting campaign that added three hundred descendants of Mexican War officers to the club roster. As the 150th anniversary of the founding of their organization approached, the Aztec Club of 1847 planned a tour of the battlefields between Veracruz and Mexico City.[42]

In 1972 members of the club had visited the Mexican capital but were not well received as they adopted the bearing of returning conquerors. Breithaupt was not interested in repeating the mistakes of the past and instead proposed the theme of "150 years of peace." When President Zedillo learned of the trip he issued an official invitation to the Aztec Club to visit Chapultepec and committed to attend a formal banquet with the members. When U.S. Secretary of State Madeleine Albright heard about the quasi-state visit she asked the Aztec Club to reconsider its plans. Albright expressed concern for the group's physical safety, but the members believed she was more worried about the diplomatic implications of the descendants of Mexico's conquerors roaming the capital followed by the foreign press. Thirty members of the club ignored the State Department's warnings, however, and departed for Mexico City on October 7, 1997.[43]

When the Aztec Club contingent arrived in the capital, Mexican officials asked Breithaupt to address the media at a nearby hotel. The members were stunned to find the room filled with news cameras and reporters anxious to learn the intentions of these North Americans. As Breithaupt sat alone at a table a reporter fired the first question: "Why are you here?" The president carefully considered his words before answering, "We are here to celebrate 150 years of peace and commemorate the sacrifices made by both sides in the war." He explained that the group intended to lay a wreath to honor the memory of the Boy Heroes at Chapultepec.[44]

The next day the Aztec Club assembled at the Altar to the Fatherland alongside Mexican officials and a band from the Military College. Breithaupt gave a brief speech in which he said, "We hope in some small way to be an emissary, educating our families, friends, neighbors, and our nation, about the many important things that should unite us, so that we may enter the next millennium stronger, closer, and more prosperous." His oration was translated and broadcast through the park's public address system to the curious onlookers. After laying a wreath at the monument, Breithaupt was surprised as an official stepped forward with Mexico's national "Book of Honor" for him to sign. He leafed past President Clinton's signature before leaving his own message of goodwill.[45]

Accustomed to symbolic acts of reconciliation, the Mexican press was curious why the U.S. State Department neglected to participate in this important event. The next day a local newspaper headline read, "Important Visit—Missed Opportunity." The article praised the magnanimous gesture of the Aztec Club of 1847 while criticizing the State Department for failing to support the club's mission and to send a representative.[46]

The visit by the Aztec Club was not without its unscripted gaffes. When the men arrived at Churubusco for a personal guided tour the director of the Museum of the Interventions, Laura Herrera Serna, asked if they intended to honor the Saint Patrick's Battalion. One member replied sternly, "The San Patricios were traitors to our ancestors, and they are traitors to us!" Breithaupt hurried the club through the gate of the museum before the press could follow up on the remark. Once they were inside, a reporter from Reuters asked the group members their thoughts about Antonio López de Santa Anna. Before Breithaupt could judiciously address the question one of his comrades shouted out, "Best general the Americans ever had!" Minor diplomatic pitfalls aside, the Aztec Club demonstrated how unofficial ambassadors of group remembrance could nonetheless create transnational understanding.[47]

The final milestone of the sesquicentennial observances was the commemoration of the Treaty of Guadalupe Hidalgo in 1998. To Mexicans this anniversary was a bittersweet reminder of the ultimate cost of their defeat. The diplomats who signed the treaty could not be cast as anything but traitors. It was, in short, an event to forget, not remember. Neglecting that anniversary might have been easier had it not been for the binational public television production *The U.S.–Mexican War, 1846–1848*. The miniseries premiered in both the United States and Mexico over two nights in September. The program's four episodes—*Neighbors and Strangers, War for the Borderlands, The Hour of Sacrifice,* and *The Fate of Nations*—cautiously tiptoed through the political minefields of the war. Scholars from both countries made points and counterpoints to each other's claims. Viewers heard the voices of Mexican officers, politicians, and common soldiers as frequently as those of their U.S. counterparts. Significantly, when the program aired in Mexico the only thing that changed was the language of the narration. The content was identical in both countries.[48]

KERA-TV and its partners received considerable praise from both sides of the border. The series won a national Emmy for nonfiction programming as well as garnering numerous other awards. Not everyone was happy with the results, however. Some Mexicans argued that the program pandered to American audiences. In the United States some letters to PBS accused the program of being "another example of a left-leaning public television project trying to make Americans ashamed of their history." Individuals and groups who felt their version of memory had been threatened by the series contacted the producers to voice their emotional critiques.[49]

One of the project's first critics was Steven Butler, who attended a special test screening held in Dallas months prior to the premiere of the documentary. As the founder of the highly nationalistic Descendants of Mexican War Veterans, Butler took a defensive stance from the beginning. He became especially enraged when the film quoted a Mexican soldier who described the invading Americans in disparaging terms. Rather than ignore Butler's complaint Komatsu wrote him a letter explaining the importance of understanding Mexico's perspective of what it perceived to be an unprovoked invasion. Butler described this letter as an epiphany that changed his perspective on history and memory. He began an academic exploration that challenged his former views and led him to a deeper, more conflicted view of the war. Butler eventually earned a doctoral degree in U.S. history and resigned his presidency of the Descendants of Mexican War Veterans.[50]

What lessons can be learned from such major public media programs? For the American filmmakers there was no government-sanctioned public memory from which to draw, only the charge from PBS to consider multiple perspectives. This left critical decisions about content in the hands of private citizens, not public officials. Filmmakers, not scholars, dominated this world. When documentary producers allow historians to influence their work, as Komatsu did, powerful new voices and new forms of memory emerge. Still, a filmmaker less dedicated to historical analysis could have taken the project in an entirely different direction.

Considering the relative dearth of previous films and television programs about the U.S.–Mexican War, the turn of the new millennium represented a boom in visual media. The motion picture *One Man's Hero* (1998) was perhaps the most popular historical movie addressing the war. The Mexican filmmaker Lance Hool directed this film about the San Patricios in the English language, casting the popular American actor Tom Berenger as the Irish American leader of the battalion. This highly fictionalized motion picture demonized American soldiers and presented a nationalistic Mexican perspective of the war. While not a box office smash, the film was widely broad-cast on cable television and distributed internationally on home video. It became a television staple in Mexico. Known as *El Batallón de San Patricio,* the film is broadcast annually to commemorate the Battle of Churubusco.[51]

One Man's Hero had a considerable impact on the rehabilitation of the San Patricios in the United States. For 150 years Americans had branded the members of the batallion as traitors. The film, which billed itself as "a story of faith, devotion, and the fight for freedom," appealed to a growing sense of Irish ethnic identity in the United States. Rather than being turncoats who killed their former comrades, the San Patricios were Irish freedom fighters who defended religious liberty. The film ultimately posited that the Irish had been denied the white privilege of Anglo-Americans and had toiled as hard as any ethnic or racial group to survive in the United States.[52]

Shortly after the film's release William O'Brien, a seventy-six-year-old rancher, founded the social organization San Patricios de Arizona to honor the ill-fated battalion. O'Brien was a well-known Irish American activist in Phoenix who had previously helped establish the Irish Cultural Center and the An Gorta Mór (Great Hunger) Monument. He described his affinity for Mexico in terms of his Irish heritage. According to O'Brien, Ireland and Mexico "are two separate cultures that like the same things—values, music, dancing, drinking, and fighting. The good things in life." His organization attracted hundreds of members, many of whom continue to march in the Saint Patrick's Day Parade in Phoenix and gather for an annual fiesta cele-brating Irish–Mexican friendship. O'Brien and the San Patricios de Arizona make no apologies for the deserters and indeed celebrate them as heroes. They even launched a campaign (which ultimately was unsuccessful) to se-cure presidential pardons for the members of the battalion.[53]

In 2008 *USA Today* ran an article which explored the growing legend of the Saint Patrick's Battalion in the United States. The author noted, "Recently, Americans have begun to pay more attention to the battalion." Bernard Bren-nan, a tourist from San Francisco who was visiting Churubusco, said, "As an Irish-American, I'm proud of them. . . . Sometimes you have to stand up and say, 'What my country is doing is wrong.' I think they're heroes, heroes of conscience." The reputation of the group has changed so drastically that to-day the majority of the visitors to the Mexico City National Cemetery be-lieve they are viewing the mass grave of the San Patricios. To appease the disappointed guests the American caretaker regularly shows a documentary film about the Batallón San Patricio in the visitors' center. South of the bor-der America's traitors have become Mexico's heroes.[54]

While *One Man's Hero* shaped the Irish American remembrance of war, another program reintroduced the United States to one of the conflict's greatest symbols. On March 15, 1998, Fox Broadcasting Company aired a new episode of its popular animated series *King of the Hill.* The program followed the lives of a socially and politically conservative family in Texas. The episode, entitled *The Final Shinsult,* involved the fictional return of Santa Anna's wooden leg to Mexico. Upon hearing that the prosthesis was to be repatriated along with a "letter of apology signed by our Commander-in-Chief," Cotton Hill, the cantankerous family patriarch, exclaimed, "That draft dodger! He can't do that! The Japanese blew my shins off. When am I going to get them back?" Hill disrupted the formal return ceremony by stealing Santa Anna's "walking log" and replacing it with an imposter from a middle school reenactment. The tale ended with Hill secretly giving the leg to Mexican authorities in exchange for a driver's license—a perk denied the nearly blind man in the United States.[55]

Although intentionally farcical, the episode ended with a hint of verisimilitude. As the closing credits rolled, a narrator stated, "The story you have just seen is based on a true event. At the battle of Cerro Gordo in 1847, the Illinois Volunteer Infantry captured the artificial leg of Mexican General Antonio López de Santa Anna, while the General and his men feasted on a lunch of roasted chicken. Unfortunately, Santa Anna's leg still resides in an Illinois museum. If you would like to join the movement to help return the leg to the Mexican people, write Illinois Senator Richard J. Durbin. Thank you, and good night." With that statement a new generation of Americans was introduced to the story of Santa Anna's lost limb. While intended as a lark, the episode generated controversy regarding the return of the prosthesis. News agencies around the nation called Senator Durbin's office regarding his attempt to have the leg repatriated. After receiving some good-natured teasing from his colleagues, Durbin explained that the entire situation was a joke. The Fox Broadcasting Company likewise confirmed that the episode "was all in fun" and that there was no concerted effort to return the limb to Mexico. The media exposure, however, boosted the fame of the Illinois State Military Museum, where the prosthetic became the most popular attraction.[56]

Santa Anna's maimed leg was also a central theme of a Mexican motion picture made two years later. *Su Alteza Serenísima* (His Most Serene Highness) documented the dictator's final days. The film showed the housebound octogenarian doting over an enormous armoire filled with prosthetics like the one held in Illinois. Symbolically, the phantom pains from his missing limb caused him such agony that he was forced to take laudanum to escape his suffering. In the context of the film Santa Anna's multiple prostheses represented the dying dictator's vanity. They also served to demystify and trivialize the lone leg on display in the United States. Americans viewed their trophy as having intrinsic value and authority, but through the film Mexicans demonstrated that the leg was meaningless to them.[57]

Perhaps the most novel cinematic approach to the U.S.–Mexican War was the horror film *Ravenous* (1999). Set against the backdrop of the invasion of California by the United States, the film dealt with American soldiers cannibalizing each other at a fictitious fort in the Sierra Madres. The eating of human flesh bestowed near immortality upon the men but left them with insatiable appetites for their fellow human beings. Toward the end of the movie the fort's man-eating commander delivered a monologue while another soldier butchered an unfortunate victim of the bloodlust. Staring out across the mountains, he mused, "Manifest Destiny, westward expansion . . . this country is seeking to be whole, stretching out its arms and consuming all it can, and we merely follow." The association of cannibalism with the conquest of the Southwest was an unusual social and political statement about the U.S.–Mexican War.[58]

While fictional films about the U.S.–Mexican War kept the conflict alive in popular culture, the National Park Service focused on creating a visitors' center and museum at the Palo Alto Battlefield National Historic Site. To silence the complaints of heritage organizations that there was no federal monument honoring veterans of the war, Congress allocated funds for the building of an interpretive center on the battlefield. Since the country had no officially sanctioned public memory, Congress merely mandated that the park staff consider "the perspective of Mexico" in the park's presentations. While an idealistic goal, lawmakers had neglected to ask the Mexican government if it wanted to participate in America's commemoration of its devastating loss. Furthermore, Congress failed to clarify which Mexican perspective the National Park Service should consider, which agencies or individuals it should consult, or what matters required transnational collaboration. Essentially the federal government left Park Superintendant Carroll and his small staff to work out the details.[59]

Control of the memory of Palo Alto would eventually fall into the hands of the park's chief of interpretation, Douglas A. Murphy, a recent graduate of the doctoral history program at the University of North Carolina at Chapel Hill. After opening their offices in Brownsville in 1993, Carroll and Murphy attempted to form a binational planning team. The survey they commissioned in 1995 revealed popular support for the park in Matamoros. What it failed to show was the local government's antagonism to the plan. When Murphy organized a Palo Alto academic conference in neighboring Matamoros, for example, the mayor accused him of celebrating Mexican defeat. To thwart the event in his city, he threatened to arrest Murphy for disturbing the peace. At another conference a Mexican journalist invited the historian to step outside and defend his views with his fists. Immigration activists berated Murphy as a tool of an oppressive and racist system. Nonetheless, Carroll, Murphy, and the small park staff weathered the opposition and eventually found a handful of independent scholars across the border willing to assist in the project.[60]

Working under few official constraints, Carroll and Murphy sought out the ideas of individuals and groups in the United States and Mexico. The park rangers also solicited input through newspaper advertisements and by holding community meetings. At times they sat alone in rented conference rooms waiting for someone to appear. Yet their efforts did produce results. Preparatory to the opening of the visitors' center, the park's planning committee immersed itself in community feedback from both sides of the Rio Grande and emerged with a specific idea for park interpretation and programs. The subsequent strategy was not a closed-door, federal plan to control the public memory of the war. Instead, the committee's work represented a series of compromises that included ideas from several groups.[61]

On January 24, 2004, the visitors' center at Palo Alto Battlefield National Historic Site opened its doors. Guests learned about Manifest Destiny, which drove American settlers to covet Mexican lands. They also read about disputed borders and Mexico's political instability. In park programming, President James Polk postured belligerently while the American public cautiously supported his agenda. On wayside plaques lining the pathways through the battlefield American soldiers distinguished themselves with their superior training and discipline, and Mexican soldiers remained gallant and brave in the face of defeat. Rather than dictate an official script to visitors, the National Park Service hoped that the displays would instead promote dialogue about the war. Essentially, the park's middle-of-the-road interpretation was intended to provoke more questions than it answered.[62]

In avoiding offense, however, Palo Alto has left some visitors feeling conflicted. The entries in the Register of National Park Visitors at the center's front desk give some indication of the public's experience at Palo Alto. These short comments also document the larger conflicts of memory occurring daily in the park. For example, Alice Sanderson from Wattersville, Georgia, wrote, "The U.S. are such bullies!!!" A later guest crossed out her remark. Local residents Anthony and Vivian Salas wrote, "This is only history according to Anglos. Let's hear it according to original Texanos." Daniel Lopez Elizando of Tamaulipas, Mexico, simply added the nationalistic battle cry, "Viva México!" Pablo Ramos Benitez of Nuevo León, Mexico, on the other hand, wrote "Excellent place—good information." Ruben Martinez of Edinburg, Texas, asserted that "Mexican soldiers love it!!" A resident of Austin named Aurora Flores-Staples claimed that the park was "very informative and fairly balanced." The mixed response was predictable given the en-during divisiveness of the war.[63]

How are these patrons receiving such divergent messages? Although the park staff has labored over its battlefield markers, the wayside plaques do not have much impact in shaping memory. Of the handful of daily visitors only a few walk the mile-long path to read the various texts. A sizable number of guests visit only during the three-day commemoration of peace held each March. Dozens of busses deliver thousands of public school chil-dren who restlessly listen to park rangers discuss the history of the battle and the contemporary ramifications of the war. The obligatory lectures finished, the teachers lead the students to the ever-popular living history exhibits.[64]

Although these costumed U.S. and Mexican soldiers are not allowed to reenact the battle, their live-fire cannon and muskets are a powerful attrac-tion (see fig. 30). One such living historian is Christopher Fischer, a middle school teacher from San Antonio. Participating in past living history events at Palo Alto, he has attempted to give equal time to the Mexican perspective of the battle. Fischer is in the minority, however, noting that most reenactors "want to portray themselves as the heroes and not the villains." During the mid-2000s living historians performed before Brownsville's student popu-lation, which was 98 percent Hispanic and included children who de-scended directly from men who fought for Mexico at Palo Alto. Most of the actors, speaking in first-person impressions of Texas Rangers and American soldiers, do not dwell on the complex political intricacies that led to hostili-ties; rather they explain that they are in Palo Alto to defend the southern boundary of Texas from Mexico. The impact of such statements is tempered by the fact that over 40 percent of the students in Brownsville have only limited proficiency in English. For balance, guests can visit the Mexican camp and hear the opposing position in Spanish.[65]

Even though it received federal funding and support, the Palo Alto Battle-field National Historic Site was never intended to dictate a monolithic memory of the U.S.–Mexican War. While the National Park Service has an obvious influence, it is but one of several voices at the site. Volunteers from the Palo Alto National Park Committee often teach their personal versions of the battle to guests at the visitors' center. Walter Plitt, the cofounder of the park committee, has reasserted his conservative influence over the site's interpretation by leading private tours of the battlefield for politicians and other distinguished guests. The park's bookstore exposes readers to more critical accounts of America's role in the conflict, and living history perfor-mances given by amateur historians introduce even more complexity. The U.S. government, unlike that of Mexico, largely remains out of memory making, allowing these disparate agendas to contend freely. Ultimately, Palo Alto is disputed territory—a battlefield of memory.

While the National Park Service negotiated remembrance at Palo Alto, another federal agency delved into the memory of the U.S.–Mexican War. In 2004 the Smithsonian National Museum of American History launched a website commemorating the military legacy of the United States. As part of this virtual exhibit the museum displayed a small number of images of weapons, uniforms, lithographs, and other artifacts from the campaigns in Mexico. The accompanying text stated that "America went to war to gain territory from Mexico and expand the nation's boundary from Texas to California." There was no discussion of border disputes, politics, or failed diplomacy. The war was simply the result of America's ambition. Predictably, the much larger exhibits about the Civil War and the Second World War dwarfed the Mexican War section. Nonetheless, for the curators at the Smithsonian there was no disputing that the nation should accept blame for the invasion of Mexico.[66]

By the mid-2000s the war was again demonstrating its ability to adhere to issues regarding U.S.–Mexican relations. In January 2004 the *New York Times* columnist Tim Weiner explored the deeper implications of the conflict vis-à-vis diplomacy. His article, "Of Gringos and Old Grudges: This Land Is Their Land," began by observing that in the United States "almost no one remembers the war," but in Mexico "almost no one has forgotten." With the assistance of scholars who had worked on the KERA-TV documentary Weiner explained the lingering resentments over the war and how Mexico was "reoccupying its former property" in the American Southwest. Indeed, illegal immigration dragged the war once again into the backdrop of a contemporary political issue.[67]

Four weeks after the article was published, Mexico's animosity toward the United States was made painfully apparent at the Olympic Men's Soccer qualifying tournament in Guadalajara. Near a massive monument to the Boy Heroes, local fans jeered and booed the U.S. team during the American national anthem and throughout the entire match. As the defeated North Americans left the field, some Mexicans continued their chants of "Osama! Osama!" One soccer fan, Diego González, explained that Mexico's victory was vital to the nation's self-confidence, adding that "we need to show what Mexicans are made of." This display superseded sporting rivalries, however, and demonstrated the complex relationship between memory, politics, and diplomacy.[68]

Such hostility was not limited to Americans who were visiting Mexico. By the mid-2000s more than ten million Mexicans were living in the United States, as many as half of them undocumented. As the debate over immigration reform and amnesty heated up during the administration of George W.

Bush, the war was evoked to justify unrestricted immigration into the American Southwest. A masked protester at a rally, for example, carried a sign that summed up the feelings of many activists: "Hey Gringo dumbfucks, we are all standing in Mexico here. Remember 1846–1848?" Supporters of immigration turned to the rhetoric of earlier Chicano writers, declaring that Aztlán was still the birthright of Mexicans in spite of it being "stolen" by the United States.[69]

The immigration debate also drew upon the memory of the Mormon Battalion. During a protest in Los Angeles on May 1, 2006, Tony Valdez, a KTTV news reporter, debated immigration opponents on KFI Radio. As protestors shouted "Viva México!" in the background, Valdez expressed his contempt for Manifest Destiny, saying, "Here in California there's a monument to the Mormon Battalion, the great heroes who killed a lot of Mexicans, enough Mexicans so that this part of the world could be taken by force, by force by the United States." Members of the Church of Jesus Christ of Latter-day Saints were immediately outraged that their noncombatant ancestors had been accused of these violent acts and called for the reporter to apologize. Valdez refused, although his station did offer a clarification of his statements. Given all of the many monuments and tributes to the Mormon Battalion throughout the American Southwest, it was little wonder that such confusion could occur.[70]

Educational television also found itself in the midst of the immigration debate. In 2006 the History Channel aired a two-hour special entitled *The Mexican American War*. In spite of its interviews with prominent historians, the program was a superficial treatment of the subject. Blaming Polk for the war, the program lacked the nuance of the PBS miniseries, and critics of the documentary posted angry accusations of anti-Americanism on the History Channel's website:

> This is one of the biggest one-sided propaganda pieces I ever watched.
> The hate American crowd really did a good job on this one.
> The problem with that documentary was that it was completely anti-American and 110% one-sided.

One comment reached the core of the issue, declaring that the documentary was "an obvious attempt to give American citizens a guilty conscience to endorse amnesty for millions of illegals." Both sides of the immigration issue were equally capable of wielding the memory of the U.S.–Mexican War as a weapon in their political arsenal.[71]

As Mexico and the United States approached the 160th anniversary of the signing of the Treaty of Guadalupe Hidalgo, the link between the war and immigration came to a head. In February 2008 the Swedish makers of

Absolut vodka launched a new Latin American billboard campaign displaying a pre-1836 map of Mexico with the slogan "In an Absolut World." The advertisement earned laughs from Mexicans but enraged many people north of the border. Political conservatives decried the campaign as being anti-American and called for a boycott of Absolut products. Supporters saw the advertisement as humorous and encouraged greater consumption of the vodka. After two months the company removed the offending billboards and officially apologized to the United States.[72]

The Absolut controversy touched a nerve in the United States and sparked an international argument that raged through news agencies and the Internet for months. The debate consistently returned to illegal Mexican immigration. A spokesperson for the vodka maker addressed this issue in his apology, stating that the campaign was not "meant to offend or disparage, nor does it advocate an altering of borders, nor does it lend support to any anti-American sentiment, nor does it reflect immigration issues." Eduardo Caccia, a Mexican advertising executive explained that the advertisement "basically taps into a very painful episode of Mexico's history, so the cultural code for understanding that [for Mexicans] is 'We were robbed.' . . . For the U.S. it's different. The understanding for that episode is 'We bought some land. We made a deal.' The same event, but with different meanings." After 160 years of shifting memories, the "different meanings" of the U.S.–Mexican War continued to haunt both nations.[73]

On September 13, 2008, President Felipe Calderón of Mexico stood before a handpicked crowd of civilians and military officials at the Altar to the Fatherland in Chapultepec Park. One hundred sixty years had passed since the United States ended its occupation of the capital, yet symbols such as the Boy Heroes continually reminded Mexicans of the war that deprived them of half their territory. In spite of the stoic facade presented by Calderón and his officials, more immediate conflicts wracked the national conscience. Hours earlier the Mexican media had announced the discovery of the mutilated bodies of twenty-four men, the latest victims in the nation's drug war.[74]

Ingrid Berenice Martínez Manguía represented the Military College at the somber ceremony. Her face taut with rage, the young cadet turned the routine homage to the Boy Heroes into an emotional tirade against the "new traitors to the fatherland." Martínez condemned the "perverse, treacherous, bloodthirsty cowards" who slaughtered their fellow citizens in a bid to get wealthy from the illicit drug trade. Shaking her clenched fist she demanded, "What do they know of mourning and suffering if they cannot feel their own darkness? Are they not ashamed when they arrive at their homes? Where do they find feelings to love their own families? How do they justify this to themselves?" Cadet Martínez's oration highlighted collective memory's ability to serve any number of masters. It is this versatility that allows the remembrance of the U.S.–Mexican War to be the dynamic social and political force it remains to this day.[75]

In 1990 President Carlos Salinas de Gortari offered greater economic co-operation with the United States, an offer President George H. W. Bush accepted, thereby ushering in a new era in U.S.–Mexican relations. For the plan to succeed, both nations had to change the prejudicial attitudes each harbored about the other. Reshaping the memory of the U.S.–Mexican War was an important component of that process. Although they attempted high-profile collaborations, the two countries were forced to address their memories of the past. Salinas de Gortari attempted to rein in the officially sanctioned myth of the Boy Heroes while the U.S. government established a long-anticipated national park and supported the production of a binational public television program about the war.

Government agencies on both sides of the border learned, however, that their hold on public memory was more tenuous than they knew. Mexicans were unwilling to surrender their Boy Heroes and forced the government to return to its former policy. Americans also challenged the memory offered through PBS and the National Park Service. Motion pictures, heritage societies, religious commemorations, anniversary celebrations, and the Internet empowered individuals and groups who promoted their agendas through the remembrance of the conflict. After 160 years of experimentation and struggle, memory remains the domain of the federal government in Mexico and the territory of private groups in the United States. Memory, however, cannot remain static, and each generation will continue to recast the remembrance of the U.S.–Mexican War according to its own time and needs.

Conclusion

PUTTING THE SKELETONS TO REST

✤

IN 2009 Walter Plitt labored earnestly on a new project involving the U.S.–Mexican War. Mexican officials had recently announced that they had uncovered the graves of U.S. soldiers near Monterrey, Nuevo León. Plitt proposed that the United States exchange the Mexican skeletons found at Resaca de la Palma in 1967 for the newly unearthed Americans. Plitt, a seasoned veteran of the struggle to establish a national park at Palo Alto, found himself facing an insurmountable wall of bureaucracy and diplomatic red tape. The Mexican bones had been deposited in Austin for over forty years, safeguarded by the Texas Archeological Research Laboratory, which would return them only to Mexico's federal government. Much to Plitt's disappointment, neither nation showed interest in the proposed exchange. The fallen warriors of 1846 remained in political limbo—the victims of forces they unwittingly unleashed over 160 years earlier.[1]

Before the ink had dried on the Treaty of Guadalupe Hidalgo, Americans and Mexicans had sought to find a deeper significance in the war. That meaning varied depending on who wielded the remembrance of the conflict and under what circumstances. Scholars of the past twenty years have attempted to better understand the nature and mechanisms of this collective memory. They have been particularly interested in delineating the differences between history and memory. Throughout this book I have characterized history as an academic discipline that uses critical analysis to interpret and explain the past. Memory, on the other hand, is the socially negotiated reconstruction of past events to correspond with the needs of groups in the present. History often challenges popular assumptions about the past, while memory regularly enshrines them and grants them contemporary relevance.[2]

The semantic differences between history and memory are less important than their symbiotic relationship. There is considerable overlap between them, making them nearly indistinguishable at times. History, by its very

240

nature, is synthesized from the remembered past. It mines the depths of memory for sources to evaluate and interpret. Once historians have crafted their analysis, however, their work becomes yet another element shaping memory. History and memory therefore select and choose from one another those elements that best fulfill their respective needs. In this way, each supports and sustains the other.

This relationship, though vital for mutual survival, is far from peaceful. The tension between history and memory is largely the consequence of their differing methods and goals. The rigors and standards of the profession demand that historians challenge memory's sacred stories. Groups and individuals whose remembrance is threatened by historical revisions find ways to resist this unwelcome trespass. Monuments, museums, heritage organizations, and popular culture are some of the weapons in their arsenal of memory. The result is a perpetual friction between history and memory that is a hallmark not just of the war between the United States and Mexico but of all recollection. The rivalry between history and memory is only a part of these dynamics, however. There is also an internal struggle within each. Historians contend vigorously with one another about their varied interpretations of the past. Similarly, groups that have a vested interest in promoting one memory over another will fight for dominance. The stakes in this struggle are particularly high, as those who successfully control the past are endowed with the authority to define the present and shape the future.

But what is it about war that makes it so important to the understanding of memory? Over the past two decades scholars have argued that the remembrance of war is critical to the formation of a national identity. No act promotes social cohesion or demarcates group boundaries more dramatically than war. Memory delineates insiders from outsiders by bestowing greatness upon ancestral warriors and vilifying foreign foes. The recalling of former conflicts establishes a lineage of heroism which promotes nationalism, teaches children to be patriotic, and celebrates the greatness of the present. This remembrance is so critical to national morale that rulers have learned to recast even defeats into victories. The malleable nature of memory also allows each generation to reinterpret past warfare to satisfy a wide variety of contemporary needs.[3]

If the conflict in Mexico is indeed America's "forgotten war," then what lessons can be learned by analyzing its memory? Foremost is the question of why peoples and nations neglect some wars while celebrating others. The U.S.–Mexican War demonstrates that victory or defeat has little consequence on the ultimate power that a conflict has over a nation's memory. Although America's triumph over Mexico greatly expanded the boundaries of the United States, it did not have the same impact on the nation as the

Civil War or the Second World War. In that fewer than two hundred American troops were killed on even its bloodiest days, the war in Mexico lacked the massive casualties of these subsequent conflicts. There was neither serious threat of foreign invasion nor compulsory drafting of civilians for military service. The later conflicts, by contrast, immersed American society in total war and dramatically redefined national identity. Since the U.S.–Mexican War did not touch the lives of most Americans it failed to capture permanently the imagination of the country or contribute significantly to the formation of its identity.

Although the War of North American Intervention may have fallen from the national consciousness of the United States, it has always been very much a part of Mexico's public memory. Unlike its northern neighbor, Mexico was engaged in total warfare during the invasion by the United States. Aside from the opening battles, which were fought in disputed territory, the war was waged on Mexican soil. The conflict threw the political and economic systems of the country into chaos and sparked domestic violence and civil unrest. In addition, the needs of national defense required the forced conscription of civilians. The Treaty of Guadalupe Hidalgo furthermore bisected the nation and made foreigners of the Mexican citizens who were living in the north. The United States brought war to the average Mexican's doorstep and threatened his hearth and home.

American amnesia and Mexican memory suggest a correlation between the level of public sacrifice and the lasting influence of war on remembrance. The recollections of the people are the building blocks of group memory. Traumatic or profound individual remembrances therefore create more powerful group memories. In the case of the U.S.–Mexican War, victory and defeat were secondary to the impact the conflict had on the lives of the citizens of the respective nations. To Americans, the exceptional territorial gains of 1848 could not compete with the weighty sacrifices of the Civil War thirteen years later. To Mexicans, intense suffering and loss superseded the humiliation of defeat and found potent expression through memorialization and commemoration.

The collective memories of both nations have taken interesting and distinctive trajectories. In 1848 many Americans celebrated the conquest of northern Mexico as their greatest accomplishment since the War of Independence. One hundred and sixty years later, the conflict was perceived as an embarrassment that most Americans chose to forget. In Mexico the opposite has occurred. The decades immediately following the invasion saw its memory suppressed as a shameful event. In 2008, however, Mexicans celebrated their past defeat as a victorious symbol of independence and valor. This evolution was a gradual process, at times inconsistent and unpredictable, but nonetheless the passage of time witnessed the simultaneous evolution of the two nations' memories in directions antithetical to one another.

What explains these unusual paths? To some Americans the invasion of Mexico contradicted a much older and cherished memory of the United States as an honorable republic that observed the rule of law. To these people the war seemed an aberration, a denial of their nation's idealistic goals. This incongruity continues to challenge Americans and forces them to confront dark episodes in their history. Throughout the past 160 years and more, a number of groups have reinforced this sense of guilt. Not everyone has been willing to accept such a critical memory, however, and there has been a consistent backlash against the critics of the war. Yet, while ideologues continue to debate the deeper meaning of the conflict, many Americans have chosen to forget it altogether.

Mexico's memory arc fits within a larger tradition of nations that celebrate their valiant defeats alongside their victories. According to this convention, a devastating loss proves the mettle of a warrior with more certainty than a victory. Mortal suffering similarly allows a people to demonstrate how they choose to behave in the face of death. As a result, the names Masada, the Alamo, Gettysburg, and Nanjing resonate with both historic and modern political meaning. Much of that meaning has been superimposed over vague or little-known actions, allowing the ideological heirs of the conflicts to define their present in terms of a mythologized past. To Mexicans the Battle of Chapultepec remains a central focus of national memory. The skirmishes fought throughout the American Southwest serve that same purpose for Chicanos. Like the Confederate Lost Cause, Mexico's "glorious defeat" has a hold over the popular imagination of a people whose ancestral struggles continue to bolster a contemporary sense of identity and purpose.[4]

The divergent memories of the United States and Mexico must also be understood in terms of the sociopolitical environments in which they have been framed. In the absence of official sanction or control, the means of making memory in the United States have remained principally in the hands of private groups, creating a capitalism of memory. Like economic capitalism, American remembrance is consumer-driven. Those elements that best serve the group are preserved and perpetuated, while those that do not are neglected and forgotten. Visitors to the Palo Alto Battlefield National Historical Park, for example, are able to sample and select those elements of remembrance that best suit their needs. They are also free to reject and discard those aspects that challenge their group memories or sense of self-identity.

Mexico has operated under a highly different system. Since the reign of Santa Anna the federal government has largely dominated the remembrance of the War of North American Intervention. Through a deliberate process of manipulating symbols and past events, Mexico's rulers have consciously molded memory to serve the needs of the nation. Initially this official remembrance weakened the political power of the Catholic Church and inspired loyalty to Mexico's dictatorial leaders. After the Revolution the government utilized these same memories to support the building of the modern state. Public money in Mexico continues to fund the monuments, museums, and commemorations that shape the nation's remembrance of the war.

In 2009 the Instituto Nacional de Estudios Históricos de las Revoluciones de México posted an article on its government-sponsored website entitled "For the Honor of Mexico." The essay, written by the director of the institute, José Manuel Villalpando, began with a question: "Did the Boy Heroes actually live?" Villalpando then proceeded to supply the answer, stating that six young men had indeed died at Chapultepec but that much of what Mexicans understood about them was myth. The director explained that the six so-called boys were in fact considered adults under Mexican law of the time. He claimed that two of the supposed cadets were not enrolled at the Military College when they died. One of these, Juan Escutia, was actually a twenty-year-old member of the San Blas Battalion sheltering at the Military College with the cadets. Rather than having jumped from Chapultepec wrapped in the Mexican flag, Villalpando explained, Escutia was killed as he and several cadets tried to escape from the castle. His most shocking revelation was that there was no evidence that the bones entombed at the Altar to the Fatherland belonged to the cadets. He declared that the scientists who certified the bones "committed a grave and unpardonable sin" by deceiving the Mexican people.[5]

Villalpando's iconoclasm signals that changes are again in store for Mexico's public memory. What these modifications will mean for Mexico and the United States remains to be seen. Regardless of the outcome, this phenomenon is not surprising given the flexible nature of collective memory and the innate need of human beings to manipulate their past to understand and define their present. If history is any indicator, however, remembrance of the U.S.–Mexican War will continue to be driven by the social and political agendas of influential groups in the United States and by governmental power structures in Mexico.

At the dawn of this new era, three individuals with vastly disparate perspectives on the U.S.–Mexican War answered a query I posed about how the remembrance of the conflict might be utilized to promote a more equitable relationship between peoples and nations in the future. Josefina Zoraida Vázquez, Mexico's premiere historian of the War of North American Intervention, believed that the United States must not just recall the war but seek to understand the conflict's deeper implications for Mexicans. She stated,

"For us the war is always present. . . . A change of view in the United States will improve our relations." Vázquez appropriately believes the war will continue to be an important component of Mexican memory. Nevertheless, she recognized a potentiality that the United States might make amends to Mexico through its use of memory. In that there is no central authority over American remembrance, however, it is unlikely that a satisfactory change of view will occur in the near future.[6]

José Ángel Gutiérrez, the Chicano activist and cofounder of the Mexican American Youth Organization and La Raza Unida Party, thought it impossible that the memory of the war would ever unite Anglos with Chicanos and Mexicans. He declared, "They stole my land and they have got to give it back. They're not going to, so that's the remembrance we are going to have." Short of the creation by the United States of a Chicano homeland from the territory lost in the Treaty of Guadalupe Hidalgo, he felt the war's symbolism was largely exhausted. Gutiérrez looked forward to 2010 and the bicentennial of the Mexican War of Independence and centennial of the Mexican Revolution. He believed that these conflicts have "shaped Chicano memory even more" and will provide stronger role models and symbols for the rising generation. Perhaps the commemorations of these two important events will inspire Mexico to place an even greater emphasis on its triumphs.[7]

Douglas Murphy, the historian for the Palo Alto Battlefield National Historical Park, has likewise reflected on the question. Standing daily at the front lines of the nation's memory of the war, he asserted, "If recollection is simply used to support old prejudices, grievances, and rhetoric, memory of this war will always drive a wedge between the two countries." Murphy believed that if Mexicans and Americans can "set aside accusations and finger pointing and focus on how both countries strayed from their ideals and into conflict, it is possible to chart a course to avoid this type of confrontation in the future." Maybe in days to come memory will serve these idealistic goals. For now, however, it appears that the multifaceted memories of Mexicans, Chicanos, and Anglos will remain divisive.[8]

There is another, possibly more essential result of my study. The dynamics of memory provide further insight into the complex and often confusing relationship between the United States and Mexico. They reveal how the conflict is an oft-neglected but ever-present component of diplomacy. Although Americans have chosen to overlook the forgotten war, Mexicans have elected a different approach to an event that is unlikely to ever be forgotten. Politicians and diplomats from the United States must be sensitive to the profound and enduring influence that Mexico's devastating territorial losses have had on the national psyche. Past conciliatory gestures have failed to have a lasting effect on Mexico, as Yankee arrogance always negates their impact. On the other hand, Mexico's leaders must realize that blaming and disparaging the United States to deflect attention from domestic ills may prove detrimental to their nation's best interests. These changes will require both countries to make enormous ideological transformations. Yet if the United States and Mexico are ever able to move forward in a spirit of true mutual respect and solidarity, then perhaps the skeletons of the U.S.–Mexican War may at last be put to rest.

NOTES

Introduction

1. The square mileage excluded Texas, which the United States had already annexed. Donald S. Frazier, ed., *The United States and Mexico at War: Nineteenth-Century Expansion and Conflict* (New York: Simon and Schuster Macmillan, 1998), s.v. "Treaty of Guadalupe Hidalgo."

2. American athletes had a similar reception while competing in the Pan American Games in Mexico in 1975. "Politics Brief Helps in Tour Abroad," *Dallas Morning News,* December 14, 1975.

3. "Gloves Come off When USA, Mexico Meet," *USA Today,* February 10, 2004; "The U.S. Is Vanquished by Taunts and Mexico," *New York Times,* February 11, 2004; "U.S. Men's Olympic Bid Ends," *USA Today,* February 11, 2004.

4. "U.S. Men's Olympic Bid Ends," *USA Today,* February 11, 2004.

5. "Mexican Honor and Olympics on Line vs. U.S.," *New York Times,* February 10, 2004.

6. "U.S. Inexperience Ends Olympic Soccer Dream," *New York Times,* February 12, 2004; "Back of the Book," *O'Reilly Factor,* FOX, February 11, 2004. When reporters asked him if he would file a grievance with the Mexican Soccer League, the American coach Glenn Myernick stated, "The world's a political place. There are inherent jealousies between Mexico and the United States, and some people choose sports to make that their platform. . . . I don't know what any formal complaint would do." "Mexico Has Nothing to Jeer About," *USA Today,* February 12, 2004.

7. For an excellent survey of the U.S.–Mexican War, see K. Jack Bauer, *The Mexican War, 1846–1848* (Lincoln: University of Nebraska Press, 1992). There are two encyclopedias of the conflict: Frazier, *The United States and Mexico at War,* and Mark Crawford, David Stephen Heidler, Jeane T. Heidler, eds., *Encyclopedia of the Mexican-American War* (Oxford: ABC-Clio, 1999).

8. Fort Texas was renamed Fort Brown after its commander, Jacob Brown, who was killed in the siege. For specifics on the Thornton Affair, see Crawford, *Encyclopedia,* s.v. "Carricitos Ranch, Skirmish at."

9. Charles M. Haecker and Jeffrey G. Mauck, *On the Prairie of Palo Alto: Historical Archaeology of the U.S.–Mexican War Battlefield* (College Station: Texas A&M University Press, 1997), is a comprehensive study of the battle using both documentary sources and archaeology.

10. Bauer, *The Mexican War,* 59–63.

11. Throughout this book I refer to Palo Alto Battlefield as a National Historic Site. In 2010 the National Park Service expanded the site to include the battlefields of Resaca de la Palma and the siege of Fort Texas, thereby granting Palo Alto National Historical Park status. There are nearly four hundred units within the National Park System.

12. Maurice Halbwachs, *On Collective Memory,* trans. and ed. Lewis A. Coser (Chicago: University of Chicago Press, 1992); Michael Kammen, *Mystic Chords of Memory: The Transformation of Tradition in American Culture* (New York: Alfred A. Knopf, 1991), 3; see also G. Kurt Piehler *Remembering War the American Way* (Washington: Smithsonian Institution Press, 1995), Jacques Le Goff, *History and Memory,* trans. Steven Rendall and Elizabeth Claman (New York: Columbia University Press, 1992), and Marita Sturken, *Tangled Memories: The Vietnam War, the AIDS Epidemic, and the Politics of Remembering* (Berkeley: University of California Press, 1997).

13. A fundamental problem in memory literature results from a lack of consistency in the use of such terms as "individual memory," "collective memory," "popular memory," "cultural memory," "public memory," and others. Owing to the interdisciplinary nature of the study of memory, scholars use terminology in different and sometimes contradictory ways. While most agree that collective memory essentially pertains to "group memory," few have sought to define the limitations of "group." The result is a casualness in using the term to define everything from a family unit to an entire country. The definitions in this book are more in keeping with David Glassberg's *Sense of History: The Place of the Past in American Life* (Amherst: University of Massachusetts Press, 2001), 9–10.

14. Pierre Nora, *Realms of Memory: Rethinking the French Past,* trans. Arthur Goldhammer, 2 vols. (New York: Columbia University Press, 1996), 1:3; Fredrik Barth, *Ethnic Group and Boundaries: The Social Organization of Culture Difference* (Boston: Little, Brown, 1969). Kammen pits "popular memory" (populist folk history) against "collective memory" (dominant civic culture). In this book I agree with this use but adopt the terms "group memory" and "public memory" instead. Alan Gordon, *Making Public Pasts: The Contested Terrain of Montreal's Public Memories, 1891–1930* (Montreal: McGill-Queen's University Press, 2001), 17.

15. Of particular importance is the work of Edward Tabor Linenthal. See his *Sacred Ground: Americans and Their Battlefields* (Urbana: University of Illinois Press, 1991) and *Preserving Memory: The Struggle to Create America's Holocaust Museum* (New York: Viking, 1995). Linenthal also co-edited, with Tom Englehardt, *History Wars: The Enola Gay and Other Battles for the American Past* (New York: Metropolitan Books, 1996). See also Piehler, *Remembering War;* David Thelen, ed., *Memory and American History* (Bloomington: Indiana University Press, 1990); Roy Rosenzweig and David Thelen, *The Presence of the Past: Popular Uses of American History in American Life* (New York: Columbia University Press, 1998); Michael Kammen, *In the Past Lane: Historical Perspectives on American Culture* (New York: Oxford University Press, 1997); Glassberg, *Sense of History;* John Bodnar, *Remaking America: Public Memory, Commemoration and Patriotism in the Twentieth Century* (Princeton:

Princeton University Press, 1992); Arthur G. Neal, *National Trauma and Collective Memory: Major Events in the American Century* (New York: M. E. Sharpe, 1998).

16. Richard R. Flores, *Remembering the Alamo: Memory, Modernity, and the Master Symbol* (Austin: University of Texas Press, 2002); David W. Blight, *Race and Reunion: The Civil War in American Memory* (Cambridge: Harvard University Press, 2001); David W. Blight, *Beyond the Battlefield: Race, Memory, and the American Civil War* (Amherst: University of Massachusetts Press, 2002); Jim Weeks, *Gettysburg: Memory, Market, and an American Shrine* (Princeton: Princeton University Press, 2003); Thomas A. Desjardin, *These Honored Dead: How the Story of Gettysburg Shaped American Memory* (Cambridge: Da Capo Press, 2003); Timothy B. Smith, *This Great Battlefield of Shiloh: History, Memory, and the Establishment of a Civil War National Military Park* (Knoxville: University of Tennessee Press, 2004); Linenthal and Englehardt *History Wars;* Nicolaus Mills, *Their Last Battle: The Fight for the National World War II Memorial* (New York: Basic Books, 2004); Patricia A. Rooney, "Re-Presenting World War II, Reviving Neo-Classicism, Reaffirming Super Power in a Post-9/11 Era: The Anomalous 2004 American National World War II Memorial" (Ph.D. diss., Saint Louis University, 2008); Thomas D. Beamish, Harvey Molotch, and Richard Flacks, "Who Supports the Troops? Vietnam, the Gulf War, and the Making of Collective Memory," *Social Problems* 42, no. 3 (August 1995): 344–60; Sturken, *Tangled Memories;* Jerry Lembcke, *The Spitting Image: Myth, Memory, and the Legacy of Vietnam* (New York, 1998); Marc Gallicchio, "What Were We Fighting For? Myth, Memory and the Vietnam War in American Politics," *Nanzan Review of American Studies* 27 (2005): 15–25.

17. John S. D. Eisenhower, *So Far from God: The U.S. War with Mexico, 1846–1848* (New York: Random House, 1989), xvii. Examples of the "forgotten war" sentiment can also be found in the prefaces of many works about the U.S.–Mexican War. See James M. McCaffrey, *Army of Manifest Destiny: The American Soldier in the Mexican War, 1846–1848* (New York: New York University Press, 1992), xii; Cecil Robinson, trans. and ed., *The View from Chapultepec: Mexican Writers on the Mexican American War* (Tucson: University of Arizona Press, 1989), x; Frazier, *The United States,* ix.

18. Ilene V. O'Malley, *The Myth of the Revolution: Hero Cults and the Institutionalization of the Mexican State, 1920–1940* (New York: Greenwood Press, 1986); Charles Weeks, *The Juárez Myth in Mexico* (Tuscaloosa: University of Alabama Press, 1987).

19. Important works include Pedro Santoni, "'Where Did the Other Heroes Go?' Exalting the *Polko* National Guard Battalions in Nineteenth-Century Mexico," *Journal of Latin American Studies* 34 (2002): 807–44; Enrique Plasencia de la Parra, "Conmemoración de la hazaña épica de los niños heroes: su origin, desarrollo y simbolismos," *Historia Mexicana* 45, no. 2 (October–December 1995): 241–79; Maria Elena García Muñoz and Ernesto Fritsche Aceves, "Los Niños Héroes, de la realidad al mito" (M.A. thesis, Universidad Nacional Autónoma de México, 1989).

20. Of particular significance in this research are two works that have considered the U.S.–Mexican War in American memory: Robert W. Johannsen, *To the Halls of*

the Montezumas: The Mexican War in American Imagination (New York: Oxford University Press, 1985), and Shelley Streeby, *American Sensations: Class, Empire, and the Production of Popular Culture* (Berkeley: University of California Press, 2002). Johannsen's work documented how the press romanticized and popularized the war for Americans. Drawing from contemporary popular culture, he demonstrated how mid-nineteenth-century Americans viewed victory over the Mexicans as the triumph of Anglo-Saxonism and republicanism. Streeby's book explored the introduction of inexpensive, mass-produced literature and the role it played in politics and culture in 1848. Both of these books are exceptional studies, but they largely confine their analysis to the antebellum period, leaving decades of postwar memory unexplored. More recently, Jaime Javier Rodríguez's *The Literatures of the U.S.–Mexican War: Narrative, Time, and Identity* (Austin: University of Texas Press, 2010) documented the constructed meanings of the conflict's narratives for Americans, Mexicans, and Mexican Americans over time. While not a study of memory, it is useful to understanding how these written accounts have influenced national and ethnic identities.

21. My book utilizes a wide variety of sources, including newspapers, motion pictures, music, artwork, monuments, museums, oral history interviews, historic sites, state and national park archives, and Internet websites. It also draws upon a survey of over five hundred books written since 1848 that address the U.S.–Mexican War. One-quarter of these books originate in Mexico, while the rest are from the United States. Many of these publications are a part of the Jenkins Garrett Collection at the Special Collections of the University of Texas at Arlington. Along with its assemblage of rare newspapers, maps, lithographs, broadsides, sheet music, and pamphlets, the Jenkins Garrett Collection is the best single repository of works related to the war. See Jenkins Garrett, *The Mexican American War of 1846–1848: A Bibliography of the Collection of the Holdings of the Libraries, The University of Texas at Arlington,* ed. Katherine Goodwin (College Station: Texas A&M University Press, 1995). A selected bibliography is available online at scholarworks.umass.edu/umpress/.

1. Victory and Dissolution

1. Theodore Parker, *A Sermon of the Mexican War: Preached at the Melodeon, On Sunday, June 25th,* 1848 (Boston: Coolidge and Wiley, 1848), 26, 32.

2. Parker gave at least two antiwar speeches during the conflict. Dean Grodzins, *American Heretic: Theodore Parker and Transcendentalism* (Chapel Hill: University of North Carolina Press, 2002), 498.

3. For Parker's radical abolitionism, see Edward J. Renehan Jr., *The Secret Six: The True Tale of the Men Who Conspired with John Brown* (New York: Crown, 1995).

4. The experience prompted Thoreau to publish the essay *Resistance to Civil Government* three years later. Elizabeth P. Peabody, ed., *Aesthetic Papers* (Boston: Elizabeth P. Peabody, 1849), 189–211.

5. For a catalogue of the holdings of the Jenkins Garrett Collection at the University of Texas at Arlington, see Jenkins Garrett, *The Mexican American War of 1846–*

1848: A Bibliography of the Collection of the Holdings of the Libraries, The University of Texas at Arlington, ed. Katherine Goodwin (College Station: Texas A&M University Press, 1995).

6. Donald S. Frazier, ed., *The United States and Mexico at War: Nineteenth-Century Expansion and Conflict* (New York: Simon and Schuster Macmillan, 1998), s.v. "Monterrey, Mexico, Battle of."

7. Frazier, *The United States,* s.v. "Buena Vista, Battle of."

8. *A Review of the Life, Character and Political Opinions of Zachary Taylor* (Boston: Eastburn's Press, 1848), 4; *A Brief Review of the Career, Character and Campaigns of Zachary Taylor* (Washington: J. and G. S. Gideon, 1848), 7. See also *The Taylor Text-Book or Rough and Ready Reckoner* (Baltimore: Samuel Sands, 1848), 6; Robert W. Johannsen's *To the Halls of the Montezumas: The Mexican War in American Imagination* (New York: Oxford University Press, 1985) is an exhaustive study of antebellum literature about the U.S.–Mexican War. Rather than repeat Johannsen's research, this section highlights the important works that framed memory after the conflict itself had ended. Another important study of this literature is Shelley Streeby's *American Sensations: Class, Empire, and the Production of Popular Culture* (Berkeley: University of California Press, 2002).

9. *A Short Statement of the Causes which Led to the War with Mexico: Showing the Inconsistent Course of the Whig Party on the Subject* ([Washington?], 1848), 8.

10. *The Democratic Text Book, Being a Compendium of the Principles of the Democratic Party* (New York: Burgess, Stringer, 1848), 7.

11. Thomas D. Anderson, *A Funeral Oration Delivered Before the City Government and Citizens of Roxbury, on the Occasion of Paying Funeral Honors to Zachary Taylor, Late President of the United States, July 31, 1850* (Roxbury, Mass.: Northfolk County Journal Press, 1850), 14. Abraham Lincoln, a critic of the war, also chose to remain vague as to the causes of the war in his eulogy. See Abraham Lincoln, *The Life and Public Service of General Zachary Taylor,* 1850, reprint (Boston: Houghton Mifflin, 1922), 35–36, 39.

12. J. T. Headley, *The Lives of Winfield Scott and Andrew Jackson* (New York: Charles Scribner, 1852), 74.

13. Abiel Abbott Livermore, *The War with Mexico Reviewed* (Boston: American Peace Society, 1850), v.

14. Ibid., 15, 215, 283. Another submission for the competition made similar claims. See William Jay, *A Review of the Causes and Consequences of the Mexican War* (Boston: Benjamin B. Mussey, 1849), 90, 269.

15. Livermore, *The War,* 8. See also Jay, *A Review of the Causes,* 176, 254.

16. Johannsen, *To the Halls of the Montezumas,* 253–55, 272.

17. Roswell Sabine Ripley, *The War with Mexico,* 2 vols. (New York: Harper and Brothers, 1849), 1:49, 73. See also J. B. Robinson's *Reminiscences of a Campaign in Mexico; By a Member of "The Bloody-First"* (Nashville: John York, 1849), 48; John S. Jenkins, *History of the War between the United States and Mexico From the Commencement of Hostilities to the Ratification of the Treaty of Peace* (Auburn, Ala.: Derby, Miller, 1848), 21–27, 499; Edward D. Mansfield, *The*

Mexican War: A History of its Origins, 10th ed. (New York: A. S. Barnes and Burr, 1850), 20–25.

18. Livermore, *The War,* 126; Robinson, *Reminiscences,* 148–49; Anderson, *Funeral,* 7; George L. Prentiss, *Eulogy on the Life and Character of Gen. Zachary Taylor, Late President of the United States . . .* (New Bedford, Mass.: Benjamin Lidsey, 1850), 32; James Henry Carleton, *The Battle of Buena Vista, with the Operations of the "Army of Occupation" for One Month* (New York: Harper and Brothers, 1848), 149–50.

19. Henry W. Harrison, *Battles of the Republic, By Sea and Land, From Lexington to the City of Mexico* (Philadelphia: Porter and Coates, 1858), 339; also published under the title *Battle-Fields and Naval Exploits of the United States, From Lexington to the City of Mexico* (Philadelphia: Peck and Bliss, 1858). See also Varina Howell Davis, *Jefferson Davis: Ex-President of the Confederate States of America,* 2 vols. (New York: Belford, 1890), 1:346.

20. Carleton, *The Battle of Buena Vista,* 62; Albert G. Brackett, *History of the United States Cavalry, from the Formation of the Federal Government to the 1st of June 1863,* (1865; repr., New York: Greenwood Press, 1968), 83. See also Franklin Tuthill, *The History of California* (San Francisco: H. H. Bancroft, 1866), 154; John Charles Frémont, *Memoirs of My Life* (1886; repr., New York: Cooper Square Press, 2001), 578.

21. Brackett, *History of the United States Cavalry,* 53.

22. John Scott, *Encarnacion, or the Prisoners in Mexico* (Louisville: G. H. Monsarrat, 1848), 8; Jenkins, *History of the War,* 232; George Ballentine, *The Autobiography of an English Soldier in the United States Army* (New York: Stringer and Townsend, 1853), 258; see also Teresa Griffen Vielé, *Following the Drum: A Glimpse of Frontier Life* (New York: Rudd and Carleton, 1858), 101.

23. George B. McClellan, *The Mexican War Diary of George B. McClellan,* ed. William Starr Myers (Princeton: Princeton University Press, 1917), 11–12.

24. Jay, *A Review of the Causes,* 223.

25. Luther Giddings, *Sketches of the Campaign in Northern Mexico in Eighteen Hundred Forty-Six and Seven, by an Officer of the First Regiment of Ohio Volunteers* (New York: George P. Putnam, 1853), 53–54.

26. Amy S. Greenberg, *Manifest Manhood and the Antebellum American Empire* (New York: Cambridge University Press, 2005).

27. Charles A. Averill, *The Secret Service Ship, or, The Fall of San Juan D'Ulloa: A Thrilling Tale of the Mexican War* (Boston: F. Gleason, 1848), 100.

28. Seymour Conner's sampling of 766 books written between 1846 and 1970 noted that 23 percent of all sources were published between 1846 and 1849. This dropped to only 14 percent from 1850 to 1899. My sample included books written between 1848 and 2008, of which only 10 percent were written during the 1848–65 time period—half of those were published in 1848–49. Both samplings demonstrate the considerable decline in publishing on the U.S.–Mexican War within a few years of the end of the conflict. Seymour V. Conner, "Changing Interpretations of the Mexican War, 1846–1970," in Odie B. Faulk and Joseph A. Stout Jr., eds., *The Mexi-*

can War: Changing Interpretations (Chicago: Swallow Press, 1973), 204–5. Exceptions published during the Civil War included Winfield Scott, *Memoirs of Lieut.-General Scott, L. L. D., Written by Himself* (New York: Sheldon, 1864), and Ashbel Woodward, *Life of General Nathaniel Lyon* (Hartford, Conn.: Case, Lockwood, 1862). Scott was a popular general at the end of his life, and Lyon was the first Union general killed in the conflict.

29. The best collections of U.S.–Mexican War lithographs and woodcuts are found at the Amon Carter Museum, University of Texas at Arlington, Yale University, and the Library of Congress. Examples have been drawn from all four of these archives. A complete catalogue of Currier's prints shows forty-two specifically under the Mexican War category; see Harry T. Peter, *Currier and Ives: Printmakers to the People*, 2 vols. (1929, repr., New York: Arno Press, 1976), 1:237–38. Johannsen found an additional forty-three placed in other categories, *To the Halls of the Montezumas*, 225. Donald H. Mugridge and Helen F. Conover, *An Album of American Battle Art* (1947, repr., New York: Da Capo, 1972), 128–30; Ronnie C. Tyler, *The Mexican War: A Lithographic Record* (Austin: Texas State Historical Association, 1973), 8–11; Martha A. Sandweiss, Rick Stewart, and Ben W. Huseman. *Eyewitness to War: Prints and Daguerreotypes of the Mexican War, 1846–1848* (Washington: Smithsonian Institution Press, 1989), 1–3.

30. "Death of Lieut. Col. Henry Clay Jr." by N. Currier, Library of Congress Prints and Photographs Division (hereafter LOC); "Death of Lieut. Col. Clay," by R. Magee, LOC; "Death of Col. Clay" by Kellogg, LOC.

31. Johannsen also studied the music and artwork of the antebellum period. This portion of the chapter reviews some of the most important postwar work. Johannsen, *To the Halls of the Montezumas*, 225; "Storming of the Castle of Chapultepec" by T. H. Matteson, University of Texas at Arlington Special Collections (hereafter UTA).

32. George Wilkins Kendall and Carl Nebel. *The War between the United States and Mexico, Illustrated . . .* (New York: D. Appleton, 1851). Interest in the work has been great enough that the Texas State Historical Association reprinted the full-size bound portfolio in 1994. For a detailed history of the portfolio including the *Boston Atlas* quote, see Ron Tyler's "Introduction" in the 1994 reprint, vii–xxviii; see also Sandweiss, *Eyewitness to War*, 13, 36–39; Tyler, *The Mexican War*, 2, 18–20, 81–83; Mugridge, *An Album*, 142.

33. "Scott's Entrance into Mexico" in Kendall, *The War between the United States and Mexico*. Not all copies of the book contained this print, as Frost employed two illustrators for his volume of 1849. See Sandweiss, *Eyewitness to War*, 34–35, 98, 346; Tyler, *The Mexican War*, 62, 81–83.

34. The painting was moved to the Marine Corps Museum at the Washington Navy Yard. United States Senate, "U.S. Senate: Art and History—The Battle of Chapultepec," www.senate.gov/artandhistory. Mugridge, *An Album*, 140.

35. The University of Texas at Arlington and the Library of Congress Music Division both contain important collections of Mexican War sheet music. Examples are drawn from both of these collections. See also Elise K. Kirk, "Sheet Music Related to

the United States War with Mexico (1846–1848) in the Jenkins Garrett Library, University of Texas at Arlington," *MLA Notes* (September 1980): 14–22. Johannsen made a thorough study of wartime sheet music and its impact on American society. See Johannsen, *To the Halls of the Montezumas*, 118, 120, 125, 128, 142, 230–40.

36. Jesse Hutchinson Jr., *Eight Dollars a Day* (Boston: Oliver Ditson, 1848), Library of Congress Music Division (hereafter LOCMD); Scott Gac, *Singing for Freedom: The Hutchinson Family Singers and the Nineteenth-Century Culture of Reform* (New Haven: Yale University Press, 2007), 219, 223–25, 231.

37. J. W. Hewitt, *The Maid of Monterey* (Baltimore: F. D. Benteen, 1848), LOCMD; Kirk, *Sheet Music*, 17. This musical score came on the heels of a popular wartime novel by Ned Buntline entitled *The Volunteer: or, The Maid of Monterey, A Tale of the Mexican War* (Boston: F. Gleason, 1847). The heroine of Buntline's book bears little resemblance to the woman of the song except for her bravery and love of American men. To read "The Angels of Buena Vista," see Burton Egbert Steveson, ed., *Poems of American History* (Boston: Houghton Mifflin, 1908), 366–68.

38. *Gen. Taylor's Rough and Ready Almanac 1848* (1848, repr., Dallas: Highlands Historical Press, 1947), 8, 16, 20; Fayette Robinson, *California and Its Gold Regions . . .* (New York: Stringer and Townsend, 1849), 69; Robinson, *Reminiscences of a Campaign in Mexico,* 90, 116, 122, 177, 180–81, 256; Benjamin F. Scribner, *A Campaign in Mexico by "One Who Was Thar"* (Philadelphia: James Gihon, 1850), 29, 63–68. For another perspective, see Scott, *Encarnacion,* 9–10.

39. Streeby, *American Sensations,* 84, 120; Andrea Tinnemeyer, *Identity Politics of the Captivity Narrative after 1848* (Lincoln: University of Nebraska Press, 2006), xx, 64–66. See also Averill, *Secret Service.*

40. Sandweiss, *Eyewitness to War,* 3.

41. David W. Lloyd, *Battlefield Tourism: Pilgrimage and the Commemoration of the Great War in Britain, Australia and Canada, 1919–1939* (Oxford: Berg, 1998), 1–2. For an analysis of how American soldiers became Mexico's first tourists from the United States, see Andrea Boardman, "The U.S.–Mexican War and the Beginnings of American Tourism to Mexico," in Dina Berger and Andrew Grant Wood, eds. *Holiday in Mexico: Essays on Tourism and Tourist Encounters* (Durham: Duke University Press, 2009).

42. Giddings, *Sketches of the Campaign in Northern Mexico,* 41.

43. Samuel Ryan Curtis, *Mexico under Fire: Being the Diary of Samuel Ryan Curtis, 3rd Ohio Volunteer Regiments during the American Military Occupation of Northern Mexico 1846–1847,* ed. Joseph E. Chance (Fort Worth: Texas Christian University Press, 1994), 52–54. McCulloch's Texas Rangers also visited Resaca de la Palma on their way to the frontier. See Cornelius C. Smith Jr., *William Sanders Oury: History-Maker of the Southwest* (Tucson: University of Arizona Press, 1967), 67.

44. Reprinted in the *Niles' National Register,* June 27, 1846.

45. Frazier, *The United States,* s.vv. "Encarnación, Hacienda de," "Goliad Massacre;" *Encarnacion Prisoners: Comprising an Account of the March of the Kentucky Cavalry from Louisville to the Rio Grande . . .* (Louisville, Ky.: Prentice and Weissner, 1848), 16.

46. James Henry Carleton, *The Battle of Buena Vista, with the Operations of the "Army of Occupation" for One Month* (New York: Harper and Brothers, 1848), v–vi.

47. Lew Wallace, *Lew Wallace: An Autobiography*, 2 vols. (New York: Harper and Brothers, 1906), 1:164.

48. George Rutledge Gibson, *Over the Chihuahua and Santa Fe Trails 1847–1848, George Rutledge Gibson's Journal*, ed. Robert W. Frazer (Albuquerque: University of New Mexico Press, 1981), 10–11.

49. Richard Coulter and Thomas Barclay, *Volunteers: The Mexican War Journals of Private Richard Coulter and Sergeant Thomas Barclay, Company E, Second Pennsylvania Infantry*, ed. Allan Peskin (Kent, Ohio: Kent State University Press, 1991), 201–2; Lucius H. Vermilya, *The Battles of Mexico, from the Beginning to the End of the War, with a Sketch of California* ([Prattsville?]: John L. Mackstaff, 1850), 10, 19; Israel Uncapher, *Diary*, September 17, 1847, UTA; Johannsen, *To the Halls of the Montezumas*, 156–57.

50. Melinda Rankin, *Texas in 1850* (Boston: Damrell and Moore, 1850), 192–93; *Dallas Morning News*, May 9, 1893.

51. Vielé, *Following the Drum*, 100–102. See also Nahum Capen, *The Republic of the United States of America: Its Duties to Itself, and Its Responsible Relations to Other Countries* (New York: D. Appleton, 1848), 149.

52. American soldiers began collecting trophies and souvenirs from dead Mexican troops the morning after the battle of Palo Alto. See Charles M. Haecker and Jeffrey G. Mauck, *On the Prairie of Palo Alto: Historical Archaeology of the U.S.–Mexican War Battlefield* (College Station: Texas A & M University Press, 1997), 51.

53. Today the flag resides at the Missouri History Museum. Mott Porter, "A History of Battery 'A' of St. Louis, with an Account of the Early Artillery Companies from Which It Descended," *Missouri Historical Society Collections* 2, no. 4 (March 1905): 1–48; William Elsey Connelley, *Doniphan's Expedition and the Conquest of New Mexico and California* (Topeka: 1907), fn 375; Ralph Emerson Twitchell, *The History of the Military Occupation of the Territory of New Mexico from 1846 to 1851 by the Government of the United States* (Denver: Smith-Brooks, 1909), 106.

54. *New York Times*, April 8, 1894.

55. Ernest R. Dupuy, *The Compact History of the United States Army* (New York: Hawthorne Books, 1956), 98, and Fairfax Downey, *Texas and the War with Mexico* (New York: American Heritage, 1961), 123. Today the cannon guard the front of the administration building. See Peter F. Stevens, *Rogue's March: John Riley and the St. Patrick's Battalion* (Dulles, Va.: Potomac Books, 2005), 298.

56. Samuel Bigger McCartney, *Illinois in the Mexican War* (Evanston: Northwestern University Press, 1939), 78. The final disposition of the cannon is unknown. Richard Colton (Springfield Armory National Historic Site) to the author, May 18, 2010.

57. Porter, "A History of Battery 'A'," 17; Johannsen, *To the Halls of the Montezumas*, 141; Federal Writers' Program of the Work Projects Administration for the State of Kansas, *Kansas: A Guide to the Sunflower State* (New York: Hastings House, 1949), 341, 484. "Old Sacramento" is currently on display at the Watkins Community

Museum of History in Lawrence, Kansas. Cannon collecting nearly derailed the career of one officer in Mexico. Gen. Gideon Pillow was second only to Gen. Winfield Scott during the assault on Mexico City. Pillow was a jealous man who tried to undermine the authority of his commander by writing anonymous letters to American newspapers. In the midst of this intrigue Pillow attempted to secret two small howitzers from Chapultepec Castle to send to his home in Tennessee. Arrested for his insubordination to Scott, he surrendered the cannons lest he face additional charges in their theft. See Edward S. Wallace, *General William Jenkins Worth: Monterey's Forgotten Hero* (Dallas: Southern Methodist University Press, 1953), 169; Frazier, *The United States,* s.v. "Pillow, Gideon."

58. Joseph E. Chance, *Jefferson Davis's Mexican War Regiment* (Jackson: University Press of Mississippi, 1991), 109.

59. Robert Anderson, *An Artillery Officer in the Mexican War 1846–7: Letters of Robert Anderson, Captain 3rd Artillery, U. S. A.,* ed. Eba Anderson Lawton (New York: G. P. Putnam's Sons, 1911), 324.

60. George Ballentine, *The Autobiography of an English Soldier in the United States Army* (New York: Stringer and Townsend, 1853), 197.

61. J. Jacob Oswandel, *Notes of the Mexican War 1846–47–48,* rev. ed. (Philadelphia, 1885), 224–25; Illinois State Military Museum, "Illinois in the Mexican-American War," www.il.ngb.army.mil; *New York Herald,* June 26, 1847; Neil Harris, *Humbug: The Art of P. T. Barnum* (Boston: Little, Brown, 1973), 62; James Lutzweiler to Col. William L. Holland, September 4, 1996, Santa Anna Leg Collateral Files, Illinois State Military Museum (hereafter ISMM).

62. Point Isabel is today Port Isabel, Texas. Ulysses S. Grant to Julia Dent, May 11, 1846, in Ulysses S. Grant, *The Papers of Ulysses S. Grant,* vol. 1: *1837–1861,* ed. John Y. Simon (Carbondale: Southern Illinois University Press, 1967), 84–87; Theodore F. Rodenbough, *From Everglade to Cañon with the Second Dragoons (Second United States Cavalry)* (New York: D. Van Nostrand, 1875), 112; Scribner, *A Campaign in Mexico,* 20; *Daily Picayune,* May 26, 1846; Alexander Corbin Pickett, *A. C. Pickett's Private Journal of the U.S.–Mexican War,* ed. Jo Blatti (Little Rock, Ariz.: Butler Center Books, 2011), 78–79. Ringgold was mortally wounded at the Battle of Palo Alto.

63. *Harper's Weekly,* "Sketches of the Metropolitan Fair," April 23, 1864.

64. Glassberg, *Sense of History,* 27.

65. Davis, *Jefferson Davis,* 1:358.

66. Francis F. McKinney, *Education in Violence: The Life of George H. Thomas and the History of the Army of the Cumberland* (Detroit: Wayne State University Press, 1961), 47; Ernest McPherson Lander Jr., *Reluctant Imperialists: Calhoun, the South Carolinians, and the Mexican War* (Baton Rouge: Louisiana State University Press, 1980), 173; Jack Allen Meyer, *South Carolina in the Mexican War: A History of the Palmetto Regiment of Volunteers, 1846–1917* (Columbia: South Carolina Department of Archives and History, 1996), 120–25; *Reports of the Special Committees Appointed to Make Suitable Arrangements for Bringing on from Mexico the Bodies of the Officers of the New York Regiment of Volunteers . . .* (New York: McSpedon and Baker, 1850), 93–103; Wallace, *Lew Wallace,* 1:193–95.

67. *Charleston Mercury,* July 13, 1848; Meyer, *South Carolina in the Mexican War,* 120–25.

68. *The Taylor Text-Book,* 4; Holman Hamilton, *Zachary Taylor: Soldier in the White House* (Indianapolis: Bobbs-Merrill, 1951), 13; Scott, *Memoirs of Lieut.-General Scott,* 386; C. W. Upham, *Life Explorations and Public Services of John Charles Fremont* (Boston: Ticknor and Fields, 1856), 268–70; Wallace, *General William Jenkins Worth,* 168–69; J. Robert Moskin, *The U.S. Marine Corps Story* (New York: McGraw-Hill, 1977), 135; Frazier, *The United States,* s.v. "Pierce, Franklin"; Jay P. Altmayer, *American Presentation Swords: A Study of the Design and Development of Presentation Swords . . .* (Mobile: Rankin Press, 1958).

69. *Life of Maj. Gen. Winfield Scott: Sketch of All His Battles and Personal Anecdotes* (Boston: Skinner's Publication Room, [1852?]), 15.

70. McKinney, *Education in Violence,* 46–47; Virginia Historical Society, "Museum Collection Overview," www.vahistorical.org.

71. *Lays of Churubusco; with Hints toward the Formation of a State Cemetery* (Augusta, Ga.: Chronicle and Sentinel, 1847), 21; Meyer, *South Carolina in the Mexican War,* 128–32, 143–51; Michael O'Brien, *Conjectures of Order: Intellectual Life and the American South, 1810–1860,* 2 vols. (Chapel Hill: University of North Carolina Press, 2004), 1:343.

72. Glassberg, *Sense of History,* 25–57.

73. Fort Brown was formerly known as Fort Texas. It was renamed after its commander, Jacob Brown, who was killed during the siege of May 1846. Curtis, *Mexico under Fire,* 52–54; U.S. Corps of Topographical Engineers, "Jacob Edmund Blake," www.topogs.org; Florence Johnson Scott, *"Old Rough and Ready" on the Rio Grande,* rev. ed. (Waco: Texian Press, 1969), 93–94.

74. Abraham Robinson Johnston, Marcellus Ball Edwards, and Philip Gooch Ferguson, *Marching with the Army of the West, 1846–1848,* ed. Ralph P. Bieber (Glendale, Calif.: Arthur H. Clark, 1936), 28 fn 25; Red Reeder, *The Story of the Mexican War* (New York: Meredith Press, 1967), 110; Richard Bruce Winders, *Mr. Polk's Army: The American Military Experience in the Mexican War* (College Station: Texas A&M University Press, 1997), 165.

75. John Cabell Breckinridge, *An Address on the Occasion of the Burial of the Kentucky Volunteers, Who Fell at Buena Vista . . .* (Lexington: Observer and Reporter, 1847).

76. Ibid., 13–14.

77. Ibid., 1, 13–14; James C. Klotter, *The Breckinridges of Kentucky* (Lexington: University Press of Kentucky, 1986), 103.

78. G. N. Allen, *Mexican Treacheries and Cruelties: Incidents and Sufferings in the Mexican War; with Accounts of the Mexicans, Battles Fought, and Success of American Arms . . .* (Boston, 1847), 20–24.

79. Scott, *Memoirs,* 452–54.

80. James Davie Butler and Frederick W. Hopkins, *Discourses at Norwich, Vermont, during the Obsequies of Truman B. Ransom, Colonel of the New-England*

Regiment, February Twenty-Second, 1848 (Hanover: Dartmouth and Journal Press, 1848), 15–16, 18, 20–21, 25–27.

81. Ibid., 21–32; South Carolina and other states also hosted elaborate state funerals after the war, although the texts of the eulogies have not survived. See Meyer, *South Carolina,* 125–26. Tragically for the Ransom family, memories quickly faded in the years after the war. Promises of pensions and land grants failed to materialize, and his widow and children lived in poverty. Ransom's son Thomas, a boy of fourteen when his father died, initially sought an academic career. At the outbreak of the Civil War, however, the younger Ransom volunteered for military service and raised a volunteer infantry unit in Illinois. Like his father, he died far from home and was greatly mourned by his community. William Tecumseh Sherman, *The Vermont Boy Who Volunteered in 1861, Served Bravely, Was Wounded Grievously, and Died for the Union, Eulogy of General T. E. G. Ransom given before Ransom Post No. 131, Grand Army of the Republic, St. Louis, Missouri, June 20, 1884* (Washington: National Tribune, 1884).

82. *Reports of the Special Committees,* 29, 44; Eric Foner, *Free Soil, Free Labor, Free Men: The Ideology of the Republican Party before the Civil War* (New York: Oxford University Press, 1995), 61, 124–25. In spite of plans to erect a memorial to the memory of the officers at the cemetery, the remembrance of the men seemed short-lived. In 1899 one New Yorker publicly decried the "deplorable state of neglect" of the forgotten gravesite. *New York Times,* November 4, 1899.

83. *New York Times,* November 26, 1857. Worth Square is bounded by Broadway, Fifth Avenue, and 25th Street. The monument was vandalized during the twentieth century and finally restored in 1991. Texas State Historical Association *Handbook of Texas Online,* "Worth, William Jenkins," www.tshaonline.org.

84. Cenotaphs were erected in Lawrenceburg and Frankfort, Tennessee; Cynthiana and Paris, Kentucky; and Platte City, Missouri. *San Diego Union,* January 18, 1990; Wallace, *Lew Wallace,* 1:193.

85. American Battle Monuments Commission, *American Memorials and Overseas Military Cemeteries* (Arlington, Va.: 2006), 30; G. Kurt Piehler, *Remembering War the American Way* (Washington: Smithsonian Institution Press, 1995), 41–43, 184; additional information from the files of the Mexico City National Cemetery.

86. Douglas A. Murphy, "The March to Monterey (Tennessee) and the View From Chapultepec (Wisconsin): American Community Names and the Commemoration of the Mexican War," *Military History of the West* 40 (2010): 1–26; Murphy's pioneering work was the first study of place names associated with the U.S.–Mexican War. His research became the basis for a temporary exhibit at the Palo Alto Battlefield National Historic Site Visitors' Center from 2001 to 2009.

87. John Rydjord, *Kansas Place-Names* (Norman: University of Oklahoma Press, 1972), 6; Murphy, "The March to Monterey," 2, 8.

88. George R. Stewart, *Names on the Land* (New York: Random House, 1945), 254; Ronald L. Baker, *From Needmore to Prosperity: Hoosier Place Names in Folklore and History* (Bloomington: Indiana University Press, 1995), 94–95, 320; Frank R. Abate, *Omni Gazetteer of the United States of America,* 10 vols. (Detroit: Omni-

graphics, 1991), 10:263, 1468; Bill Earngey, *Missouri Roadsides: The Traveler's Companion* (Columbia: University of Missouri Press, 1995), 260; Michael A. Beatty, *County Name Origins of the United States* (Jefferson, N.C.: McFarland, 2001), 63, 114, 121, 141, 162, 234, 293, 496; Walter Prescott Webb, ed., *The Handbook of Texas*. 2 vols. (Austin: Texas State Historical Association, 1952), 1:278–81, 620–34.

89. Beatty, *County Name Origins of the United States,* 107–23; Baker, *From Needmore to Prosperity,* 80–81.

90. Robert M. Rennick, *Kentucky Place Names* (Lexington: University Press of Kentucky, 1984), 201; Murphy, "The March to Monterey," 13–14.

91. Rennick, *Kentucky,* 201; Murphy, "The March to Monterey," 12–13; Hannah Kimble Swain, "Hildreth–Rio Grande," *Cape May County New Jersey Magazine of History and Genealogy* (1987): 68; John Anthony Gutowski, "American Folklore and the Modern American Community Festival: A Case Study of Turtle Days in Churubusco, Indiana" (Ph.D. diss., Indiana University, 1977), 29–30.

92. Baker, *From Needmore to Prosperity,* 80–81, 90, 145, 319, 333; Earngey, *Missouri Roadsides,* 12, 260; Rennick, *Kentucky Place Names,* 40, 186, 251.

93. Earngey, *Missouri Roadsides,* 255.

94. Stewart, *Names on the Land* and *American Place Names: A Concise and Selective Dictionary for the Continental United States of America* (New York: Oxford University Press, 1970); Rennick, *Kentucky Place Names,* x.

95. Larry L. Miller, *Ohio Place Names* (Bloomington: Indiana University Press, 1996), 35, 54, 56, 158, 203, 206; Rennick, *Kentucky Place Names,* x–xi, 55; Frazier, *The United States,* s.vv. "Camargo," "Cerralvo." Also see the varied origins of "Resaca" in Kenneth K. Krakow, *Georgia Place-Names* (Macon: Winship Press, 1975), 190.

96. Their postbellum activities will be explored in later chapters. Richard Hoag Breithaupt Jr., *Aztec Club of 1847: Military Society of the Mexican War, Sesquicentennial History, 1847–1997* (Universal City, Calif.: Walika Publishing, 1998), 4–10. This expansive volume serves as both a documentary history and a narrative history of the organization.

97. William B. Reed, *Oration Delivered at Philadelphia by William B. Reed, February 22, 1849* (Philadelphia: Crissy and Markley Printers, 1849); Roy Franklin Nichols, *Franklin Pierce: Young Hickory of the Granite Hills* (Philadelphia: University of Pennsylvania Press, 1931), 286; Meyer, *South Carolina in the Mexican War,* 133–34, 182–84; Breithaupt, *Aztec Club of 1847,* 22–23.

98. Ulysses S. Grant, *Personal Memoirs of U. S. Grant,* 2 vols. (New York: Charles L. Webster, 1892), 1:53, 54–56.

99. Ibid., 2:490.

2. In the Shadow of Defeat

1. The titles of Mexican books are translated into English in the text but are retained in Spanish in the footnotes. Ramón Alcarez et al., *Apuntes para la historia de la Guerra entre México y los Estados Unidos* (1848, repr., Mexico City: Editora

Nacional, 1952); Maria Elena García Muñoz and Ernesto Fritsche Aceves, "Los Niños Héroes, de la realidad al mito" (Thesis, Universidad Nacional Autónoma de México, 1989), 49.

2. Alcarez, *The Other Side,* 1. The English translations are from Ramón Alcarez et al. *The Other Side: or Notes for the History of the War between Mexico and the United States,* trans. Albert C. Ramsey (New York: John Wiley, 1850). While assisted at times by scholars and native speakers, I am responsible for the translations in this book. Anyone working in multiple languages will attest to the challenges of a literal, word-for-word translation. To preserve the original or intended meaning of a quotation, I have taken minor liberties occasionally with the English text of the translations.

3. For the Mexican underclass the shame of defeat coupled with widespread illiteracy among the poor served to silence the memories of the conscripts and enlisted men who filled the ranks of the Mexican army and National Guard. Mexican vernacular folk expressions, such as the narrative "corrido" ballad, might have preserved the oral traditions of the poor, but the delay in collecting such examples until the mid-twentieth century has resulted in a dearth of these materials. Consequently, Mexico's early collective memory was framed by elites and then filtered down over time to the nation's lower classes. Américo Paredes, *A Texas-Mexican Cancionero: Folksongs of the Lower Border* (Austin: University of Texas Press, 1995), 21.

4. Antonio López de Santa Anna, *Detalle de las operaciones ocurridas en la defensa de la capital de la República, atacada por el ejército de los Estados-Unidos del Norte, año de 1847* (Orizaba, Mexico: Imprenta de la Amistad, 1848), 3–6. Similar vindications and blame seeking followed Mexico's loss of Texas in 1836. See James E. Crisp, *Sleuthing the Alamo: Davy Crockett's Last Stand and Other Mysteries of the Texas Revolution* (New York: Oxford University Press, 2005), 88.

5. Anastasio Parrodi, *Memoria sobre la evacuación militar, del puerto de Tampico de Tamaulipas* (San Luis Potosí, Mexico: Imprenta del Estado en Palacio, 1849); Pánfilo Barasoda, *Pedimentos presentados a la Exma. Primera Sala del Supremo Tribunal de la Guerra y Marina . . . contra las órdenes expresas del supremo gobierno* (Mexico City: Impresa de Lara, 1849); *Fallo definitivo del Supremo Tribunal de la Guerra, al examinar la conducta militar del exmo. sr. General D. Mariano Arista, en las acciones de guerra que sostuvo al principio de la invasión Americana* (Mexico City: Imprenta de Vicente García Torres, 1850); Benjamín Laurent, *Vindicación que hacen Benjamín y Tomas Laurent, confutando la esposición que dirigió al Exmo. Sr. General en gefe del ejército norte-americano . . .* (Mexico City: Vicente G. Torres, 1848); *Memoria del Secretario del Estado y del Despacho de Guerra y Marina, leída en la cámara de diputados el día 9, y en la de senadores el 11 de enero de 1849* (Mexico City: Imprenta de Vicente García Torres, 1849), 9; Ramón de Ceballos, *XXIV Capítulos en vindicación de Méjico* (Madrid: M. Rivadeneyra, 1856).

6. Ramón Gamboa, *Impugnación al Informe del Señor General Santa-Anna, y constancias en que se apoyan las ampliaciones de la acusación del Sr. Diputado Gamboa* (Mexico City: Imprenta de Vicente García Torres, 1849), 3, 7–16, 28–29.

7. Antonio López de Santa Anna, *Apelación al buen criterio de los nacionales y estrangeros* (Mexico City: Imprenta de Cumplido, 1849); Antonio López de Santa Anna, *The Eagle: The Autobiography of Santa Anna,* trans. and ed. Ann Fears Crawford (Austin: Pemberton Press, 1967), 116.

8. Donald S. Frazier, ed., *The United States and Mexico at War: Nineteenth-Century Expansion and Conflict* (New York: Simon and Schuster Macmillan, 1998), s.v. "Paredes y Arrillaga, Mariano"; Mariano Aniceto de Lara, *Historical Summary of the Most Notable Deeds of the York, Scotch and Santanista Parties in Mexico,* trans. Claude Kennard (1852), 31. Typescript at the University of Texas at Arlington Special Collections (hereafter UTA).

9. Mexican reactions are in keeping with David W. Blight's findings about memory of defeat. Blight noted that former Confederates rewrote their history to absolve themselves of starting the Civil War. See David W. Blight, *Race and Reunion: The Civil War in American Memory* (Cambridge: Harvard University Press, 2001), 259; *Dictamen de la comisión de la cámara de senadores del Congreso General sobre la aprobación del tratado celebrado por el gobierno de la Republica con el de los Estados-Unidos de Norte* (Querétaro, Mexico: Imprenta de J. M. Lara, 1848), 4; *Esposición dirigida al supremo gobierno por los comisionados que firmaron el tratado de paz con los Estados-Unidos* (Matamoros, Mexico: Antonio Castañeda, 1848), 3, 6. The reports echoed *Notes for the History of the War between Mexico and the United States,* which stated, "It is sufficient to say that the insatiable ambition of the United States, favored by our weakness, caused it." See Alcarez, *The Other Side,* 2.

10. *Observaciones al mensage del Presidente de los Estados-Unidos* (Mexico City: Imprenta de Vicente García Torres, 1848), 6, 11; Manuel Crescencio Rejón, *Observaciones del diputado saliente Manuel Crecencio Rejón, contra el tratado de paz, firmado en la ciudad de Guadalupe el 2 del próximo pasado febrero, precedidas de la parte histórica relativa a la cuestion originaria* (Querétaro, Mexico: Imprenta de J. M. Lara, 1848), 3, 13–14, 17–18, 23, 25; Alcarez, *The Other Side,* 1–2.

11. Antonio Rodríguez, *Calendario de Antonio Rodríguez para el año bisiesto de 1848* (Mexico City, 1848), 43, 47–48; Alcarez, *The Other Side,* 405.

12. *Dictamen de la comisión de la cámara,* 21; Gamboa, *Impugnación,* 34.

13. Alcarez, *The Other Side,* 375–79.

14. *Manifiesto del ayuntamiento a los habitantes de la capital . . .* (Mexico City: Imprenta de Mariano Arevalo, 1848), 8. See also *Protesta que dirigió el ecsmo. sr. Gobernador del Estado . . .* (Toluca, Mexico: Imprenta de Juan Quijano, 1848), 5.

15. Rejón, *Observaciones,* 32, 61; *Esposición dirigida,* 25–26; *Dictamen de la comisión,* 6.

16. Alcarez, *The Other Side,* 45–48, 210, 242.

17. Parrodi, *Memoria sobre la evacuación militar,* 6. Both the United States and Mexico were also prone to exaggerate the number of enemy soldiers they faced; *Documentos relativos a la reunión en esta capital de los gobernadores de los estados . . .* (Mexico City: Imprenta de J. M. Lara, 1851), 5–6. See also Luis G. Cuevas, *Memoir of the Minister of Interior and Exterior Relations, Don Luis G.*

Cuevas, trans. J. C. Gardiner (Washington: Office of the Globe, 1849), 16; *Observaciones al mensage del Presidente de los Estados-Unidos* (Mexico City: Imprenta de Vicente García Torres, 1848), 4–5; *Esposición,* 3.

18. *Observaciones al mensage,* 5.

19. *Fallo definitivo del Supremo Tribunal de la Guerra,* 16–17.

20. K. Jack Bauer, *The Mexican War, 1846–1848* (Lincoln: University of Nebraska Press, 1992), 209–18.

21. Rodriguez, *Calendario,* 57–58; Lara, *Historical Summary,* 33–34; Jenkins, *History of the War,* 237–39; Santa Anna, *The Eagle,* 93; Alcarez, *The Other Side,* 123–35, 141.

22. Alcarez, *The Other Side,* 360–63.

23. *Observaciones al mensage,* 5; Roswell Sabine Ripley, *The War with Mexico,* 2 vols. (New York: Harper and Brothers, 1849), 2:423.

24. Alcarez, *The Other Side,* 356.

25. Gamboa, *Impugnación,* 52–54; García Muñoz, "Los Niños Héroes," 47–48.

26. Joaquín Rangel, *Parte de las operaciones ejecutadas por la Tercera Brigada de Ynfanteria del Ejército Mexicano en los días 12 y 13 de septiembre de 1847* (1847, repr., Mexico City: M. Murguia, 1856), 1–2.

27. Ibid.

28. As the Mexican art historian Isidro Vizcaya Canales explained, "This is not one of our favorite eras." Ronnie C. Tyler, *The Mexican War: A Lithographic Record* (Austin: Texas State Historical Association, 1973), 11–12; Mexico's "golden age" of lithography was between 1836 and 1862. W. Michael Mathes, *Mexico on Stone: Lithography in Mexico, 1826–1900* (San Francisco: Book Club of California, 1984), 17.

29. Tyler, *The Mexican War,* 39, 53; Martha A. Sandweiss, Rick Stewart, and Ben W. Huseman. *Eyewitness to War: Prints and Daguerreotypes of the Mexican War, 1846–1848* (Washington: Smithsonian Institution Press, 1989), 294, 306–7, 313–15, 324–25.

30. Sandweiss, *Eyewitness to War,* 320–25, 340–41.

31. Julio Michaud y Thomas, *Álbum Pintoresco de la República Méxicana* (Mexico City: Estampería de Julio Michaud y Thomas, 1850). See also Sandweiss, *Eyewitness to War,* 297.

32. Text at the Museo Nacional de Historia claims the paintings were completed in 1849. This date is unlikely since the cult of the Boy Heroes would not develop for several more years. Miraculous rescue during combat has proven a popular theme throughout the history of votive painting both in Mexico and in Catholic Europe. The example I refer to is housed in the Museum of International Folk Art in Santa Fe. For additional information on Mexican ex-voto paintings, see Gloria Fraser Giffords, *Mexican Folk Retablos* (Albuquerque: University of New Mexico Press, 1992).

33. The anthropologist Charles M. Carrillo believed such corridos may have existed in New Mexico. Charles M. Carrillo, interview by the author, Santa Fe, July 15, 2007; National Anthems Info, "Mexico: 'Mexicanos, al grito de guerra,' (Mexicans, to the War Cry)," http://david.national-anthems.net. The Mexican American folklorist Américo Paredes unsuccessfully searched for U.S.–Mexican War corridos

along the Texas–Mexico border. He believed they may have existed but had disappeared in the century before he began his work. Paredes, *Texas-Mexican Cancionero,* 21.

34. *National Anthems of the American Nations* (Washington: Organization of American States, 1972), 88–89; Frazier, *The United States,* s.v. "Gadsden Purchase."

35. *National Anthems,* 88–89.

36. France invaded Mexico in 1838 and 1862.

37. Fernando Iglesias Calderón, *Rectificaciones históricas* (Mexico City: Tip. Literaria de F. Mata, 1901), 4; "Recuerdo de la Guerra con los Estados Unidos," lithograph by Espasa y Compañía (ca. 1890), UTA.

38. For an excellent study of war commemorations held in Mexico City in 1848 and their political uses, see Pedro Santoni, "'Where Did the Other Heroes Go?' Exalting the *Polko* National Guard Battalions in Nineteenth-Century Mexico," *Journal of Latin American Studies* 34 (2002): 818; Frank W. Grove, *Medals of Mexico* (Guadalajara, Jalisco: Frank W. Grove, 1974), 3:66–73. Examples of the medals are displayed at the Museo de las Intervenciones and the Museo Nacional de Historia in Mexico City.

39. Robert Ryal Miller, *Shamrock and Sword: The Saint Patrick's Battalion in the U.S.–Mexican War* (Norman: University of Oklahoma Press, 1989), 82–88; Santoni, "Where Did the Other Heroes Go?," 807–44; Frazier, *United States,* s.v. "Herrera, José Joaquín de."

40. Santoni's "Where Did the Other Heroes Go?" is the definitive study of Mexico's postwar celebration of the National Guard.

41. Ibid., 818 –21.

42. Peñúñuri led an ill-fated bayonet charge against the North American assault on Churubusco, while Balderas was killed during the defense of Molino del Rey. Ibid., 820–33. Local and federal governments also passed laws memorializing the dead. Mexico City's town council wrote the names of the district's deceased defenders on an honor roll displayed in their conference room. Congress likewise decreed that a national Escalafón del Ejército (Army Roster) should be created with the names of fallen officers inscribed along with the place and date of their deaths. See Iglesias Calderón, *Rectificaciones históricas,* 3, 44; Domingo Ibarra, *Un Recuerdo en memoria de los Mexicanos que murieron en la Guerra contra los norte americanos en los años de 1836 á 1848* (Mexico City: Tip. de Reyes Velasco, 1888), 12; Santoni, "Where Did the Other Heroes Go?," 817.

43. Vargas Rea, ed., *A los grandes hombres que murieron en el Valle de México en tiempo de la invación norte Americana, la patria agradecida les tributó un justo homenaje a sus virtudes el 17 de septiembre de 1848* (1848, repr., Mexico City: Biblioteca Aportación Histórica, 1946), 17–18, 34; *El coronel Felipe Santiago Xicoténcatl y la Batalla de Chapultepec, 1847–1947* (Tlaxcala, Mexico: Publicaciones de la Dirección de Bibliotecas, Museos e Investigaciones Históricas, 1947), 18–24. This would not be the last funeral for Lieutenant Colonel Xicoténcatl, who was again exhumed in 1879. In 1952 he was reburied in the Altar of the Fatherland a few hundred yards from where he fell at Chapultepec.

44. García Muñoz, "Los Niños Héroes," 48; Santoni, "Where Did the Other Heroes Go?," 839; María Elena Salas Cuesta et al., *Molino del Rey: historia de un monumento* (Mexico: Instituto Nacional de Antropología e Historia, 1988), 59.

45. Rangel, *Parte de las operaciones,* 2; Iglesias Calderón, *Rectificaciones históricas,* 3, 44; Santoni, "Where Did the Other Heroes Go?," 841.

46. The monument at Molino del Rey was moved to accommodate a rail line in 1985. The Instituto Nacional de Antropología e Historia conducted a full survey of the site. Their official report is found in Salas Cuesta, *Molino del Rey.*

47. Rangel, *Parte de las operaciones,* 1. See also Alcarez, *The Other Side,* 75.

48. *El Soldado mexicano 1837–1847, The Mexican Soldier, organización—vestuario—equipo—Organization—Dress—Equipment* (Mexico City: Ediciones Nieto, Brown, Hefter, 1958), 53; Ibarra, *Un Recuerdo,* 12; *Memoria del Secretario del Estado,* 17.

49. Juan N. Chávarri, *El Heroico Colegio Militar en la historia de México* (Mexico City: Editorial B. Costa-Amic, 1960), 222–23; García Muñoz, "Los Niños Héroes," 46–47. Only two of the six were actually minors. The controversy surrounding the actual ages of the cadets is addressed below.

50. Chávarri, *El Heroico Colegio Militar,* 222–23; García Muñoz, "Los Niños Héroes," 47.

51. Michael C. Meyer and William L. Sherman. *The Course of Mexican History* (New York: Oxford University Press, 1979), 379–91.

52. This persistence also demonstrates that memory is never static but constantly evolves according to the needs of the people it serves. John Bodnar, *Remaking America: Public Memory, Commemoration, and Patriotism in the Twentieth Century* (Princeton: Princeton University Press, 1992), 170.

3. Old Soldiers and New Wars

1. To Grant's frustration, Congress refused to ratify the free trade treaty. Mark Perry, *Grant and Twain: The Story of a Friendship that Changed America* (New York: Random House, 2004), 76–80; Jean Edward Smith, *Grant* (New York: Simon and Schuster, 2001), 70–71, 463, 618, 621; William S. McFeely, *Grant* (New York: W. W. Norton, 1981), 486–88, 493, 503.

2. Ulysses S. Grant, *Personal Memoirs of U. S. Grant,* 2 vols. (New York: Charles L. Webster, 1892), 2:53, 54–56. For Grant's earlier criticism of the war, see Perry, *Grant and Twain,* 21, 117–18.

3. Works addressing the organization of Mexican War veterans include Wallace E. Davies, "The Mexican War Veterans as an Organized Group," *Mississippi Valley Historical Review* 35, no. 2 (September 1948): 221–38, and Steven R. Butler, "Alexander M. Kenaday and the National Association of Veterans of the Mexican War," *Mexican War Quarterly* 1, no. 2 (winter 1992): 11–21. My book differs from these two in that it focuses less on how the veterans organized and more on the debate in Congress to win support for their pensions. See also Michael Scott Van Wagenen, "U.S.–Mexican

War Veterans and the Congressional Pension Fight," *Military History of the West* 40 (2010): 27–51.

4. National Association of Veterans of the Mexican War (hereafter NAVMW), *Origin and Progress of the National Association of Veterans of the Mexican War* (Washington, 1887), 3–5.

5. Ibid., 6.

6. Ibid.

7. Ibid.; United States Department of Defense, "U.S. Soldiers' and Airmens' Home (USSAH) Washington DC," www.defenselink.mil; Alexander M. Kenaday, *Proceedings of the National Convention of the Veterans of the Mexican War, Held in the City of Washington, February 22d and 23d, 1875* (Washington: John H. Cunningham, 1875), 12.

8. NAVMW, *Origin and Progress,* 6. The House of Representatives eventually impeached Belknap. See Asher C. Hinds, *Hind's Precedents,* 5 vols. (Washington: United States Congress, 1907), 3:902–47.

9. NAVMW, *Origin and Progress,* 6; Kenaday, *Proceedings 1874,* 4.

10. Kenaday, *Proceedings 1874,* 4; NAVMW, *Origin and Progress,* 2, 6; United States Congress, "Biographical Directory of the United States Congress—Negley, James Scott," http://bioguide.congress.gov/. Negley would spend half of his congressional career serving on the board of the National Home for Disabled Volunteer Soldiers, a federal institution which cared for invalid volunteers of the Civil War. United States Department of Veterans Affairs, "National Home for Disabled Volunteer Soldiers," www.va.gov.

11. NAVMW, *Origin and Progress,* 3–6; the most recent biography of Denver is Edward Magruder Cook, ed., *Justified by Honor: Highlights in the Life of General James William Denver* (Falls Church, Va.: Higher Education, 1988).

12. NAVMW, *Origin and Progress,* 6–7; Kenaday, *Proceedings 1874,* 5–8.

13. Kenaday, *Proceedings 1874,* 5–7, 21–22.

14. These goals evolved over the organization's first year but are easily synthesized from their early literature. See Kenaday, *Proceedings 1874,* 21–22, 30; Kenaday, *Proceedings 1875,* foreword, 29–30, 36.

15. Kenaday was in contact with President Grant as early as 1868 regarding his proposed soldiers' home. See Ulysses S. Grant, *Ulysses S. Grant Papers,* Microform, 32 reels, Washington: Library of Congress, 19:324; Kenaday, *Proceedings 1874,* 4–29; Kenaday, *Proceedings 1875,* 17. For examples of invitations extended to Grant by Civil War veterans, see *Grant Papers,* 23:95–96, 173, 246, 288–89.

16. The bill was submitted as H.R. No. 577; Kenaday, *Proceedings 1874,* 21–22, 30; NAVMW, *Origin and Progress,* 6–7; Kenaday, *Proceedings 1875,* 10–13, 15, 18; U.S. Congress, *Congressional Record,* 43d Congress, 2d session, 1874, 3:922; *Annual Report of the Commissioner of the General Land Office for the Fiscal Year Ending June 30, 1878* (Washington: Government Printing Office, 1878), 83–84. Logan had been a Democrat before the Civil War but switched parties during the conflict. There remains some controversy as to whether or not the Committee on Invalid Pensions

exaggerated these numbers. In 1884 it still claimed that 36,550 veterans remained alive. U.S. Congress, *Congressional Record,* 48th Congress, 1st session, 1884, 15:4506. Exact numbers of survivors are hard to assess. Justin Smith found that some 90,000 men (31,000 regulars and 59,000 volunteers) served in the U.S. forces, but that approximately 32,000 died, deserted, or were discharged early. See Justin H. Smith, *The War with Mexico,* 2 vols. (New York: Macmillan, 1919), 2:318–19. Historians have criticized Smith's overt racism and imperialism, but his statistical data on U.S. forces remain an important contribution to the field. Winders similarly counted 88,000 regular and volunteer troops combined. See Richard Bruce Winders, *Mr. Polk's Army: The American Military Experience in the Mexican War* (College Station: Texas A&M University Press, 1997), 11. Federal records show that the largest number of veterans on pension rolls amounted to 17,158 in 1890. See William H. Glasson, *Federal Military Pensions in the United States* (New York: Oxford University Press, 1918), 119.

17. Records show that the defiant New Yorkers remained in arrears with the organization; Kenaday, *Proceedings 1874,* 21–22, 30; NAVMW, *Origin and Progress,* 6–7; Alexander M. Kenaday, *"Centennial Reunion" of the National Association of Veterans of the Mexican War, Third Annual Session, Philadelphia July 4, 1876* (Washington: Cunningham and Brashears, 1876), 3, 24–26, 28–29.

18. Kenaday, *Proceedings 1875,* 29–30; *The Vedette,* vol. 6, no. 10, October 1885.

19. In 1876 Col. Robert Klotz of the Scott Legion in Philadelphia organized a trip to retrace the U.S. invasion from Veracruz to Mexico City. The proposed eight-week excursion was to take participants by rail to New Orleans, then by steamship to Veracruz. The five-hundred-dollar cost of the so-called pleasure excursion would prove prohibitive to all but the wealthiest of veterans, and it remains unclear if the trip ever took place. Regardless, the plans themselves speak to the impulse of the veterans to retrace the steps of their glorious youths. Kenaday, *Centennial Reunion,* 27–28. *The Vedette,* vol. 1, no. 1, October 1879.

20. Ibid.

21. Ibid.; NAVMW, *Origin and Progress,* 7; Kenaday, *Proceedings 1875,* 29–30.

22. The monument to Winfield Scott is the centerpiece of Scott Circle at the intersection of Massachusetts Avenue, Rhode Island Avenue, and 16th Street in North West Washington, D.C. The Native American family is part of the *Progress of Civilization* pediment on the Senate wing of the capitol. Kirk Savage, *Monument Wars: Washington, D.C., the National Mall, and the Transformation of the Memorial Landscape* (Berkeley: University of California Press, 2009), 64, 82, 89–90.

23. The California and Utah monuments are covered in greater detail in chapter 5. Details regarding the construction of the Harrisburg memorial are found in Pennsylvania Capitol Preservation Committee, "Mexican War Monument," http://cpc.state.pa.

24. Kenaday was himself falsely accused of being an imposter, James W. Denver to William G. Mosely, April 15, 1878, Mrs. Moore Murdock Papers, Texas State Library and Archives (hereafter TSLA). The decoration consisted of a bronze shield suspended from a red, white, and blue ribbon. The shield itself bore the names of all major battles as well as scenes of a cannon, warship, cactus, and maguey plant stamped in bas-relief.

The actual minting of the awards was conducted at the U.S. Mint in Philadelphia in early 1876; Kenaday, *Proceedings 1875*, 30–31; *The Vedette*, vol. 1, no. 1, October 1879; Kenaday, *Centennial Reunion*, 1, 7–8, 24–26, 34. In 1893 newspapers like the *St. Louis Globe-Democrat* and the *Dallas Morning News* debated the extent of pension fraud in the nation. The latter blamed unscrupulous agents for padding the roles with undeserving pretenders; see *Dallas Morning News*, June 29, 1893.

25. NAVMW, *Origin and Progress*, 7. For examples of these state petitions, see Legislature of the State of Texas, *Pensions of the War with Mexico, Joint Resolution of the Legislature of Texas* (Austin?, 1875); Legislature of the State of Kentucky, *Resolution of the Legislature of Kentucky in Relation to Pensions to Soldiers of the Mexican War* (n.p. 1876); *Mr. Cockrell presented the following memorial and resolutions of the Mexican Veteran Volunteer Association of the state of Missouri* (Washington?, 1898); U.S. Congress, *Congressional Record*, 47th Congress, 2d session, 1883, 14:2137.

26. For examples, see U.S. Congress, *Congressional Record*, 45th Congress, 2d session, 1878, 7:1043; and compare to U.S. Congress, *Congressional Record*, 45th Congress, 2d session, 1878, 7:1039; U.S. Congress, *Congressional Record*, 45th Congress, 3d session, 1879, 8:1627–28.

27. Kenaday, *Proceedings 1875*, 15–16, 27. For examples of the these appeals, see U.S. Congress, *Congressional Record*, 45th Congress, 1st session, 1877, 6:429; U.S. Congress, *Congressional Record*, 45th Congress, 2d session, 1878, 7:1038–39; U.S. Congress, *Congressional Record*, 46th Congress, 2d session, 1879–80, 10:2384; U.S. Congress, *Congressional Record*, 46th Congress, 2d session, 1879–80, 10:3960–61; U.S. Congress, *Congressional Record*, 48th Congress, 1st session, 1884, 15:50.

28. Jefferson Davis, *The Address on the Mexican War and Its Results, as Delivered by the Hon. Jefferson Davis, Before the Louisiana Associated Veterans of the Mexican War, at Exposition Hall, New Orleans, Tuesday, March 7th, 1876* (New Orleans: L. McGrane, 1876), 4, 15.

29. *The Vedette*, vol. 1, no. 1, October 1879.

30. U.S. Congress, *Congressional Record*, 45th Congress, 1st session, 1877, 6:222–23; U.S. Congress, *Congressional Record*, 45th Congress, 2d session, 1878, 7:1039.

31. Ibid., 7:1043–44.

32. Bureau of Pensions to the National Association of Mexican War Veterans, September 22, 1902, TSLA. In 1890 there were still over seventeen thousand veterans on pension rolls; Glasson, *Federal Military Pensions*, 119. The youngest veteran uncovered in this research was William J. Wilkinson, who claimed to have been discharged following the Battle of Buena Vista at the age of fifteen, Web Jarvis to David R. Francis, September 13, 1904, TSLA. The life expectancies were collected by the University of Oregon, "Mapping History—Life Expectancy Graphs," www.uoregon.edu.

33. *The Vedette*, vol. 4, no. 12, December 1883.

34. In 1877 the Mexican War pension was part of H.R. No. 2283 "granting pensions to certain soldiers and sailors of the Mexican, Florida, Black Hawk wars." The

legislation remained linked to these wars intermittently throughout the next decade. U.S. Congress, *Congressional Record,* 44th Congress, 2d session, 1877, 5:428.

35. NAVMW, *Origin and Progress,* 6–7; *The Vedette,* vol. 1, no. 1, October 1879; Mary R. Dearing, *Veterans in Politics: The Story of the G.A.R.* (Baton Rouge: Louisiana State University Press, 1952), 337; Kenaday, *Centennial Reunion,* 30–32. Slaveholding states did, in fact, provide a disproportionate number of volunteers, and Democrats dominated the ranks of the officer corps. See Smith, *The War with Mexico,* 2:319; Winders, *Mr. Polk's Army,* 75–80.

36. U.S. Congress, *Congressional Record,* 45th Congress, 2d session, 1878, 7:1316, 1320. Examples of sectionalism are common throughout the debate. For examples, see U.S. Congress, *Congressional Record,* 45th Congress, 2d session, 1878, 7:1044–46, 1315–20, 1386; U.S. Congress, *Congressional Record,* 46th Congress, 2d session, 1879–80, 10:4481–83.

37. U.S. Congress, *Congressional Record,* 45th Congress, 2d session, 1878, 7:1046, 1316, 1425. For antebellum praise of Davis, see Carleton, *Battle of Buena Vista,* 74–79.

38. Jacob K. Neff, *The Army and Navy of America . . .* (Philadelphia: John H. Pearsol, 1866), 639–42; Horatio O. Ladd, *Fighting in Mexico* (New York: Dodd, Mead, 1883), 33; J. J. Grindall, *The Battle of Buena Vista* (Baltimore: Press of Isaac Friedenwald, 1882), 8.

39. U.S. Congress, *Congressional Record,* 45th Congress, 2d session, 1878, 7:1425.

40. United States Congress, "Biographical Directory of the United States Congress—Shields, James," http://bioguide.congress.gov. Ezra J. Warner, *Generals in Blue: Lives of the Union Commanders* (Baton Rouge: Louisiana State University Press, 1992), 444–45.

41. U.S. Congress, *Congressional Record,* 45th Congress, 3d session, 1879, 8:1627.

42. Ibid., 8:1627–28.

43. Ibid., 8:1628; Wilcox, *History of the Mexican War,* 2, 236; Joseph E. Chance, *Jefferson Davis's Mexican War Regiment* (Jackson: University Press of Mississippi, 1991), 89; Frémont, *Memoirs,* 546; Philip St. George Cooke, *The Conquest of New Mexico and California in 1846–1848: An Historical and Personal Narrative* (1878, repr., Chicago: Rio Grande Press, 1964), 222; John Watts De Peyster, *Personal and Military History of Philip Kearny, Major-General United States Volunteers* (New York: Rice and Gage, 1869), 140.

44. U.S. Congress, *Congressional Record,* 45th Congress, 3d session, 1879, 8:1628.

45. NAVMW, *Origin and Progress,* 2, 6–7; *The Vedette,* vol. 1, no. 1, October 1879. Instead of supporting the Mexican War veterans, the senators voted to increase the pension for disabled Union veterans of the Civil War. There was one small victory that session when Congress approved an act that paid service bonuses promised to some soldiers and sailors in 1848.

46. NAVMW, *Origin and Progress*, 7; *The Vedette*, vol. 1, no. 1, October 1879. The poem is printed in its entirety on the front page with the author listed only as "Veteran." "Vedette" means a sentinel or sentry. The most complete collections of *The Vedette* are in the Special Collections of California State University Long Beach and in the Mrs. Moore Murdock Papers, TSLA.

47. To read the poem in its entirety, see F. M. Finch, "The Blue and the Gray," in J. W. Keene, *Selections for Reading and Elocution: A Handbook for Teachers and Students*, 2d ed. (Boston: Willard Small, 1879), 236–37.

48. *The Vedette*, vol. 1, no. 1, October 1879; Kenaday, *Proceedings 1875*, 10, 16.

49. Kenaday, *Proceedings 1875*, 22.

50. David W. Blight, *Beyond the Battlefield: Race, Memory, and the American Civil War* (Amherst: University of Massachusetts Press, 2002), 103, 127.

51. Davies, "Mexican War Veterans," 229–31; Dearing, *Veterans in Politics*, 211–12, 336–37; NAVMW, *Origin and Progress*, 7; Butler, "Alexander M. Kenaday," 13; *The Vedette*, vol. 8, no. 12, February 1888. In the early years of the national association a small group of men attended the meetings specifically to harass Kenaday and challenge his war record. The claims worried James Denver enough that he surreptitiously wrote a letter to Kenaday's commanding officer asking for details of his service record. While the contents of the reply remain unknown, Denver was satisfied enough to put his full faith behind his comrade; James W. Denver to Colonel William G. Mosely, April 15, 1878, TSLA.

52. Democrats were likewise guilty of playing politics with war pensions. In a bit of congressional quid pro quo, many southern Democrats opposed Republican legislation granting pensions to Civil War veterans since these annuities would be awarded exclusively to Union soldiers. NAVMW, *Origin and Progress*, 6–7; Dearing, *Veterans in Politics*, 336–37; *Dallas Morning News*, October 3, 1894; United States Congress, "Biographical Directory of the United States Congress—Hoar, George Frisbee," http://bioguide.congress.gov; U.S. Congress, *Congressional Record*, 48th Congress, 1st session, 1884, 15:1570–71.

53. U.S. Congress, *Congressional Record*, 46th Congress, 2d session, 1879–80, 10:2384–85, 4431–32, 4474–76.

54. Benjamin F. Van Meter, *Genealogies and Sketches of Some Old Families Who Have Taken Prominent Part in the Development of Virginia and Kentucky . . .* (Louisville: John P. Morton, 1901).

55. U.S. Congress, *Congressional Record*, 46th Congress, 2d session, 1879–80, 10:3960–61.

56. Ibid., 10:3962–63; Williams delivered a similar speech in 1884, U.S. Congress, *Congressional Record*, 48th Congress, 1st session, 1884, 15:4510–12.

57. U.S. Congress, *Congressional Record*, 47th Congress, 1st session, 1882, 13:1336; U.S. Congress, *Congressional Record*, 48th Congress, 1st session, 1884, 15:5519–20.

58. U.S. Congress, *Congressional Record*, 48th Congress, 1st session, 1884, 15:4613.

59. Ibid., 15:4516.

60. Ibid., 15:4516–17; Warner, *Generals in Blue*, 524–25.

61. U.S. Congress, *Congressional Record*, 47th Congress, 2d session, 1883, 14:2137; U.S. Congress, *Congressional Record*, 48th Congress, 1st session, 1884, 15:5519–20; U.S. Congress, *Congressional Record*, 48th Congress, 2d session, 1884–85, 16:101, 428, 456, 1035, 1049, 1278, 2326.

62. U.S. Congress, *Congressional Record*, 48th Congress, 1st session, 1884, 15:1571, 4511.

63. *The Kentucky Encyclopedia*, John E. Kleber, ed. (Lexington: University Press of Kentucky, 1992), 963; U.S. Congress, *Congressional Record*, 49th Congress, 1st session, 1885–86, 17:1878.

64. Associated Veterans of the Mexican War, *History of the Joint Anniversary Celebration at Monterey, Cal.* (San Francisco: Fraternal Publishing Company, 1886), 20.

65. NAVMW, *Origin and Progress*, 2, 7–8; Butler, "Alexander M. Kenaday," 13; *Dallas Morning News*, August 15, 1897; Glasson, *Federal Military Pensions*, 119.

66. Davies, "The Mexican War Veterans," 224–25.

67. Richard Hoag Breithaupt Jr., *Aztec Club of 1847: Military Society of the Mexican War, Sesquicentennial History, 1847–1997* (Universal City, Calif.: Walika, 1998), 163–64.

68. A photograph of the meeting held in 1873 shows only sixteen original members in attendance. The membership medal was to be worn by living members of the club and passed to their descendants upon their deaths. This way a family could have tangible proof of the gallant exploits of their ancestor in the Mexican War. The decoration was a gold and enamelwork Maltese cross suspended from a red, white, and green ribbon. To control access to the award, the medal and the recipients were recorded in a master list kept by the club treasurer. In 1897 the club also issued a bronze fiftieth anniversary medal minted by Tiffany and Company; Breithaupt, *Aztec Club of 1847*, 25–30, 33, 69, 72. The organization continues as a hereditary society to this day. Ibid., 39–41, 45–46; finding his organization in a similar predicament during the 1890s, Kenaday also began granting membership in the national association to "blood relatives." *The Vedette*, vol. 1, no. 1, October 1879, and vol. 11, no. 1, April 1893.

69. *The Vedette*, vol. 1, no. 1, October 1879; Louisiana Associated Veterans of the Mexican War, *Memorial to the Honorable Senators and Representatives of the General Assembly, State of Louisiana* (New Orleans, 1886); Associated Veterans, *History*, title page; Association of the Soldiers of the Mexican War of the State of Texas, *Proceedings of the Annual Meeting Association of the Soldiers of the Mexican War of the State of Texas,* (Austin: J. D. Logan, 1875); Grindall, *The Battle of Buena Vista;* Kenaday, *Proceedings 1875,* 17; *Eureka Daily Sentinel*, May 23, 1873.

70. *Harper's Weekly*, June 17, 1893; *Dallas Morning News*, May 12, 1895;

71. Kenaday died in 1897. It remains unclear how many veterans belonged to the organization during its existence. Estimates vary from five thousand to seventeen thousand. *The Vedette*, vol. 11, no. 1, April 1893; Alexander M. Kenaday to Repre-

sentative Benton McMillin, February 6, 1897, TSLA; Butler, "Alexander M. Kenaday," 14; Davies, "The Mexican War Veterans," 223–24.

72. Between 1866 and 1897 North Americans wrote only a handful of histories specifically about the war. Cadmus M. Wilcox, *History of the Mexican War* (Washington: Church News, 1892), 1; Odie B. Faulk and Joseph A. Stout Jr., eds., *The Mexican War: Changing Interpretations* (Chicago: Swallow Press, 1973), 203–5.

4. Creating Heroes

1. The Battle of Molino del Rey occurred on the south side of Chapultepec on September 8, 1847. It remains unclear what role, if any, the cadets played in that battle. The Battle of Chapultepec was fought five days later. Asociación del Heroico Colegio Militar, *Chapultepec* (Mexico City: Secretaría de la Defensa Nacional, 1960), 9; Juan N. Chávarri, *El Heroico Colegio Militar en la historia de México* (Mexico City: Editorial B. Costa-Amic, 1960), 223–25; Maria Elena García Muñoz and Ernesto Fritsche Aceves, "Los Niños Héroes, de la realidad al mito" (Thesis, Universidad Nacional Autónoma de México, 1989), 50–52; Antonio Fernández del Castillo, *A Cien años de la epopeya 1847–1947* (Mexico City, 1947), 41–47.

2. *El Siglo XIX*, September 9, 1871; Chávarri, *El Heroico Colegio Militar*, 224; Fernández del Castillo, *A Cien años*, 42; Enrique Plasencia de la Parra, "Conmemoración de la hazaña épica de los niños heroes: su origen, desarrollo y simbolismos," *Historia Mexicana* 45, no. 2 (October–December 1995): 242.

3. William H. Beezley, Cheryl English Martin, and William E. French, eds., *Rituals of Rule, Rituals of Resistance: Public Celebrations and Popular Culture in Mexico* (Wilmington, Del.: Scholarly Resources, 1994), xiii.

4. Fernando Iglesias Calderón, *Rectificaciones históricas* (Mexico City: Tip. Literaria de F. Mata, 1901), 3, 44; Domingo Ibarra, *Un Recuerdo en memoria de los Mexicanos que murieron en la Guerra contra los norte americanos en los años de 1836 á 1848* (Mexico City: Tip. de Reyes Velasco, 1888), 12; Joaquín Rangel, *Parte de las operaciones ejecutadas por la Tercera Brigada de Ynfanteria del Ejército Mexicano en los días 12 y 13 de septiembre de 1847* (1847, repr., Mexico City: M. Murguia, 1856).

5. Robert J. Knowlton, *Church Property and the Mexican Reform, 1856–1910* (DeKalb: Northern Illinois University Press, 1976), 205; Pedro Santoni, "'Where Did the Other Heroes Go?' Exalting the *Polko* National Guard Battalions in Nineteenth-Century Mexico," *Journal of Latin American Studies* 34 (2002): 841.

6. C. José Maria Lafragua, *Discurso pronunciado el día 20 de agosto de 1871 por el C. José Maria Lafragua en conmemoración de la batalla de Churubusco* (Mexico City: Imprenta del Gobierno, en Palacio, 1871), 45.

7. *El Siglo XIX*, August 20, 1874.

8. The plantation building in Virginia where Thomas "Stonewall" Jackson died was also dedicated as a shrine to the Confederacy. David W. Blight, *Race and Reunion: The Civil War in American Memory* (Cambridge: Harvard University Press, 2001), 255–56; Richard R. Flores, *Remembering the Alamo: Memory, Modernity, and the Master Symbol* (Austin: University of Texas Press, 2002).

9. Antonio López de Santa Anna, *The Eagle: The Autobiography of Santa Anna,* ed. Ann Fears Crawford (Austin: Pemberton Press, 1967), 251. A search of the larger newspapers in Mexico City failed to locate any such letters, making it unlikely that they were published.

10. The Porfiriato refers to the years 1876–80 and 1884–1911. Beezley, *Rituals,* xiii, xvi–xvii; Barbara A. Tenenbaum, "Streetwise History: The Paseo de la Reforma and the Porfirian State, 1876–1910," in Beezley, *Rituals,* 127–50; Ibarra, *Un Recuerdo,* 14; Alfonso Teja Zabre, *Chapultepec* (Mexico City: Talleres de Impresión de Estampillas y Valores, 1938), 41–42.

11. Laurens Ballard Perry, *Juárez and Díaz: Machine Politics in Mexico* (DeKalb: Northern Illinois University Press, 1978), 205–6, 295–97; Paul Garner, *Porfirio Díaz* (London: Pearson Education, 2001), 110–15; José F. Godoy, *Porfirio Díaz: President of Mexico, the Master Builder of a Great Commonwealth* (New York: G. P. Putnam's Sons, 1910), 120.

12. *El Siglo XIX,* September 9, 1871; Asociación del Heroico Colegio Militar, *Chapultepec,* 9; Chávarri, *El Heroico Colegio Militar,* 223–25.

13. Moctezuma I is the great-grandfather of Moctezuma II, who was killed during the Spanish conquest of Mexico. García Muñoz, "Los Niños Héroes," 50–52; H. B. Nicholson, "The Chapultepec Sculpture of Motecuhzoma Xocoyotzin," *El México Antiguo* 11 (1961): 379–423; Enrique Krauze, *Mexico: Biography of Power, A History of Modern Mexico, 1810–1996* (New York: Harper Collins, 1997), 27.

14. *El Siglo XIX,* September 8, 9, 1871.

15. Fernández del Castillo, *A Cien años,* 41–47; Chávarri, *El Heroico Colegio Militar,* 225; Guillermo Vigil y Robles, *La Invasión de México por los Estados Unidos en los años de 1846, 1847 y 1848* (Mexico City, 1923), 61–62; Plasencia de la Parra, "Conmemoración," 253.

16. Díaz's papers are at the Universidad Iberoamericana in Mexico City. Unfortunately, the speeches he gave at Chapultepec are not part of the catalogued collection, and their whereabouts remain unknown. His words at these commemorations survive only in contemporary newspaper accounts. Maria Eugenia Ponce to the author, June 26, 2008; Teja Zabre, *Historia de México,* 41–42; José María Roa Bárcena, *Recuerdos de la invasión norteamericana, 1846–1848* (1883, repr., Veracruz, Mexico: Colección Rescate Universidad Veracruzana, 1986), 483 fn 2.

17. Teja Zabre, *Historia de México,* 41–42; Roa Bárcena, *Recuerdos,* 483; Tenenbaum, "Streetwise," 141. The Association of the Heroic Military College continues to hold its commemorations at the obelisk on September 8 instead of at the much larger celebration at the Altar to the Fatherland on September 13. The reasons for this are discussed in chapter 6.

18. *El Siglo XIX,* September 9, 1871; *New York Times,* September 9, 1899; Plasencia de la Parra, "Conmemoración," 253–54; Beezley, *Rituals,* xiii–xvii, 127–50.

19. David W. Blight's study of Confederate memory following the Civil War found that "all great mythologies . . . changed with succeeding generations and shifting political circumstances." Blight, *Race and Reunion,* 258. The most important

works about the evolution of the Boy Heroes myth are García Muñoz's and Fritsche Aceves's thesis "Los Niños Héroes" and Plasencia de la Parra's "Conmemoración."

20. *El Siglo XIX,* September 9, 1871; García Muñoz, "Los Niños Héroes," 51–53; Rafael Echenique, *Catálogo alfabético y cronológico de los hechos de armas que han tenido lugar en la República Mexicana desde su independencia hasta nuestros días* . . . (Mexico City: Oficina Tipográfica de la Secretaría de Fomento, 1894), 282; Departamento del Distrito Federal, *El Asalto al Castillo de Chapultepec y los Niños Héroes* (Mexico City: Colección Conciencia Cívica Nacional, 1983), 79.

21. A Mexican burial party recovered this flag from Xicoténcatl's body after the battle. The bloodstained banner is on display at the Museo de las Intervenciones in Churubusco. García Muñoz, "Los Niños Héroes," 53; Donald S. Frazier, ed., *The United States and Mexico at War: Nineteenth-Century Expansion and Conflict* (New York: Simon and Schuster Macmillan, 1998) s.v. "Flags."

22. Emilio de Castillo Negrete, *Invasión de los norte-americanos en México,* 4 vols. (Mexico City: Imprenta del Editor, 1890), 1:x–xi; García Muñoz, "Los Niños Héroes," 56; Asociación, *Chapultepec, 72.*

23. Today the national flag is flown from the tower. Given the geography of Chapultepec, the only possibility would have been for Escutia to have taken a flag from the roof of the east wing of the castle. A small flag flies there today, although this appears to be part of Maximilian's later renovation of the building. Carl Nebel's portrayal of Chapultepec is perhaps the most accurate, as he had lived in Mexico City and witnessed the battle. In two lithographs he placed the flag over the main entrance. See "Storming of Chapultepec—Pillow's Attack" and "Storming of Chapultepec—Quitman's Attack" in George Wilkins Kendall and Carl Nebel, *The War between the United States and Mexico, Illustrated* . . . (New York: D. Appleton, 1851). General Pillow's battle report stated that Thomas Hart Seymour, the future governor of Connecticut, cut down the Mexican national flag; Nathan Covington Brooks, *A Complete History of the Mexican War: Its Causes, Conduct, and Consequences* (Philadelphia: Grigg, Elliot, 1849), 416. The account was reconfirmed by an additional witness in *New York Times,* July 4, 1883. Modern apologists have speculated that Escutia rescued a National Guard unit flag from the east wing and jumped. While this is the only realistic scenario, it would seem that such a dramatic feat would have been recorded in the historical record prior to 1890. García Muñoz, "Los Niños Héroes," 55.

24. Ramón Alcarez et al. *The Other Side: or Notes for the History of the War between Mexico and the United States,* trans. Albert C. Ramsey (New York: John Wiley, 1850), 360–63; *Observaciones al mensage del Presidente de los Estados-Unidos* (Mexico City: Imprenta de Vicente García Torres, 1848), 5; R. S. Ripley, *The War with Mexico.* 2 vols. (New York: Harper and Brothers, 1849), 2:423. While histories of the war written during this era generally documented the heroism and death of the cadets, they did not popularize the legend of Escutia's jump until after the Revolution. Important books that do not discuss Escutia's jump include D. Bernardo Reyes, *El Ejército Mexicano* (Mexico City: J. Ballesca y C. A. Sucessor,

Editor, 1901), 34; Vigil, *La Invasión,* 55–57; Juan Manuel Torrea, José Osorio Mondragón, and José Maria Álvarez, *Apuntes de geografía é historia militares escritos para uso de los alumnos del Colegio Militar por los profesores en la material* (Mexico City: Sociedad de Edición y Librería Franco-Americana, 1924), 253–55; Alfonso Toro, *Compendio de historia de México: La Revolución de Independencia y México independiente* (Mexico City: Sociedad de Edición y Librería Franco-Americana, 1926), 430.

25. The ages were confirmed through records in the Family History Library in Salt Lake City. They correspond with the ages displayed at the Museo Nacional de Historia at Chapultepec, except that Suárez is listed as being fifteen. In 1852 the director of the Military College began the tradition of referring to the slain cadets as boys. *El Siglo XIX,* September 9, 1874; García Muñoz, "Los Niños Héroes," 44.

26. Departamento del Distrito Federal, *El Asalto,* 47–58, 89–93.

27. García Muñoz, "Los Niños Héroes," 53–55; Departamento del Distrito Federal, *El Asalto,* 81–85.

28. Teja Zabre, *Chapultepec,* 107–13; Chávarri, *El Heroico Colegio Militar,* 146–59; Leopoldo Martínez Caranza, *La Intervención norteamericana en México, 1846–1848: Historia político-militar de la pérdida de gran parte del territorio mexicano* (Mexico City: Panorama Editorial, 1981), 190–97.

29. García Muñoz, "Los Niños Héroes," 59.

30. José Juan Tablada, *La Feria de la vida* (Mexico City: Consejo Nacional para la Cultura y las Artes, 1991), 82–83.

31. Powell Clayton to John Sherman, June 2, 1897, in United States Department of State, *Despatches from United States Ministers to Mexico, Volume 130, January 4–June 30, 1897* (Washington: National Archives Microfilm Publications, 1934); *Mexican Herald,* May 30, 1897; "Memorial Day in Mexico," *New York Times,* June 1, 1897.

32. Clayton to Sherman; *Mexican Herald,* May 30, 1897; William H. Burnside, "Powell Clayton: Ambassador to Mexico, 1897–1905," *Arkansas Historical Quarterly* 38, no. 4 (winter 1979): 328–44; William H. Burnside, *The Honorable Powell Clayton* (Conway: University of Central Arkansas Press, 1991).

33. Ibarra, *Un Recuerdo,* 13–14. It is unclear if the building was ever constructed.

34. Ibid. Sometime prior to 1904 the organization moved its headquarters to Puebla. See Asociación de Defensores de la República Mexicana de 1836 a 1848 to the National Association of Mexican War Veterans, September 11, 1904, Mrs. Moore Murdock Papers, Texas State Library and Archives.

35. Ibarra, *Un Recuerdo,* 13–15.

36. Ulysses S. Grant, *Personal Memoirs of U. S. Grant,* 2 vols. (New York: Charles L. Webster, 1885), 1:169. In 1899 the *New York Times* reported on the Chapultepec commemorations for the first time. *New York Times,* September 9, 1899.

37. Garner, *Porfirio Díaz,* 145–49.

38. Will Fowler, *Santa Anna of Mexico* (Lincoln: University of Nebraska Press, 2007), 337–41; Santa Anna, *The Eagle,* 4.

39. Santa Anna, *The Eagle,* xii, 248–49. The manuscript found a larger audience when it was translated and published in English in 1967. Will Fowler, *Santa Anna of Mexico* (Lincoln: University of Nebraska Press, 2007), 337–41.

40. Roa Bárcena, *Recuerdos;* Manuel Balbontín, *La Invasión americana, 1846 á 1848* (Mexico City: Tip. de Gonzalo A. Esteva, 1883); Eduardo Paz, *La Invación norte americana en 1846* (Mexico City: Imprenta Moderna de Carlos Paz, 1889), i; Emilio de Castillo Negrete, *Invasión de los norte-americanos en México,* 4 vols. (Mexico City: Imprenta del Editor, 1890), i:x–xi; Echenique, *Catálogo alfabético,* 5–6.

41. Balbontín, *La Invasión,* 135–37; Roa Bárcena, *Recuerdos,* ii, 630.

42. Lafragua, *Discurso,* 9; Ibarra, *Un Recuerdo,* 15; Paz, *La Invación,* 7–8, 13, 26; Javier F. Gaxiola, *La Invasión norteamericana en Sinaloa,* 2d ed. (Mexico City: Cargo de Antonio Rosas, 1891), 37; Balbontín, *La invasion,* 75–79; Garner, *Porfirio Díaz,* 113–24, 173–86.

43. Ibarra, *Un Recuerdo,* 3, 7–11; Echenique, *Catálogo alfabético,* 278; Juan de Marin, *El 20 de agosto de 1847; "Churubusco" glorioso recuerdo histórico por el Capitán 10 de Caballería Juan de Marin* (Mexico City: Imprenta de Guillermo Veranza, 1887), 9.

44. Charles Weeks, *The Juárez Myth in Mexico* (Tuscaloosa: University of Alabama Press, 1987), 71–73.

45. Frederick Starr, *Mexico and the United States: A Story of Revolution, Intervention, and War* (Chicago: Bible House, 1914), 33–38.

46. The font came from the small village of Cuitzeo, Guanajuato. As of 2008 it remained in the possession of the Museo Nacional de Historia in Mexico City. Starr, *Mexico,* 39–42.

47. Secretaría de Guerra y Marina, *El Colegio Militar: A la eterna memoria de sus héroes* (Mexico City: Talleres del Departamento de Estado Major, 1910), 18.

48. In addition to having a distinguished military career, Otis was the president of the Times-Mirror Company. *New York Times,* September 9, 1910; Starr, *Mexico,* 43.

49. Alan Knight, *The Mexican Revolution,* 2 vols. (Cambridge: Cambridge University Press, 1986).

50. The president received the diploma at the Military College on September 7. *El Pais,* September 8, 9, 1911; Plasencia de la Parra, "Conmemoración," 258.

51. The one deviation was Madero's laying of a wreath at the nearby monument to the Battle of Molino del Rey. *El Pais,* September 9, 1912; Knight, *Mexican Revolution,* 1:247–490.

52. Rangel, *Parte de las operaciones,* 2; Iglesias Calderón, *Rectificaciones históricas,* 3, 44; *El Pais,* August 20, 1913; Oscar Arriola to the author, December 1, 2008.

53. *El Pais,* August 21, 1913.

54. *El Pais,* September 9, 1913; Michael C. Meyer and William Beezley, eds., *The Oxford History of Mexico* (Oxford: Oxford University Press, 2000), 449–50; Knight, *Mexican Revolution,* 1:488–90, 2:1–171.

55. American forces occupied the city for seven months. Beezley, *Oxford History,* 449–50; Fredrick B. Pike, *The United States and Latin America: Myths and*

Stereotypes of Civilization and Nature (Austin: University of Texas Press, 1992), 210–11; Knight, *Mexican Revolution,* 2:150–57.

56. *New York Times,* June 7, 1914; Jack Sweetman, *The Landing at Veracruz: 1914* (Annapolis: Naval Institute Press, 1987), 71–72, 77–79; Secretaría de Marina de México, "Marinos Ilustres," www.semar.gob.mx.

57. *El Siglo XIX,* September 9, 1875; Sweetman, *The Landing,* 77.

58. Cristóbal Martínez Perea and Andrés Montes Cruz were not cadets but young civilians killed while fighting alongside military forces. *New York Times,* September 9, 1915; Sweetman, *The Landing,* 73–74, 86.

59. *New York Times,* September 9, 1915; Plasencia de la Parra, "Conmemoración," 259; Anita Brenner, *The Wind that Swept Mexico: The History of the Mexican Revolution of 1910–1942* (Austin: University of Texas Press, 1984), 46–48, Knight, *Mexican Revolution,* 2:162–71; Josefina Zoraida Vázquez and Lorenzo Meyer, *The United States and Mexico* (Chicago: University of Chicago Press, 1985), 113.

60. Krauze, *Mexico,* 328–30, 368; *New York Times,* March 1, 1917, March 3, 1917, March 4, 1917, September 14, 1914; Knight, *Mexican Revolution,* 2:329, 347–54; Vázquez, *United States,* 116–22.

61. The current commander of the Asociación del Heroico Colegio Militar twice denied my requests for interviews or access to the group's archives. The modern association is considered part of the Mexican army and does not allow foreigners to view their records. Manuel V. Larics served as president in 1914–20. Asociación, *Chapultepec,* 8; Plasencia de la Parra, "Conmemoración," 259–60; Juan Manuel Torrea, *La Vida de una institución gloriosa: el Colegio Militar 1821–1930* (Mexico City: Talleres Tip. Centenario, 1931), 116–20; Edwin Lieuwen, *Mexican Militarism: The Political Rise and Fall of the Revolutionary Army, 1910–1940* (Westport, Conn.: Greenwood Press, 1981), 15, 20–21, 47.

62. Krauze, *Mexico,* 302–3, 367, 370–73.

5. Empire and Exclusion

1. *New York Times,* June 22, 1902, June 19, 1904; *Dallas Morning News,* June 19, 1904; Charles Burr Todd, *A General History of the Burr Family* (New York: Knickerbocker Press, 1902), 506; Illinois State Historical Society, *Transactions of the Illinois State Historical Society for the Year 1906* (Springfield: Illinois State Journal, 1906), 184–85; Genealogy Trails, "Pensions Granted in the State of Illinois for the Week Ending July 16, 1887," www.genealogytrails.com; Rootsweb, "Miron Laban Burr / Elizabeth Austin Gould," http://freepages.genealogy.rootsweb.ancestry.com; Illinois State Military Museum, "Illinois in the Mexican-American War," www.il.ngb .army.mil.

2. In 1896 there were 11,800 pensioned veterans alive. That number dropped by more than half by 1904. William H. Glasson, *Federal Military Pensions in the United States* (New York: Oxford University Press, 1918), 119.

3. "Mormon Battalion Members 1896" (photograph), Historical Department of the Church of Jesus Christ of Latter-day Saints (hereafter LDS); R. G. M. Dunovant,

The Palmetto Regiment: South Carolina Volunteers, 1846–48, part 2 (Charleston: Walker, Evans and Cogswell, 1897); D. C. Allen, *A Sketch of the Life and Character of Col. Alexander W. Doniphan* (Liberty, Mo.: Advance Office, 1897), preface. For another perspective of the semicentennial anniversary of the war, see Amy S. Greenberg, "1848/1898: Memorial Day, Places of Memory, and Imperial Amnesia," *Publications of the Modern Language Assocation of America* 124, no. 5 (October 2009): 1869–73.

4. "Anglo" is the common term for all non-Hispanic whites in the American Southwest. "Hispano" is a popular term of self-definition for New Mexicans of Spanish descent. While perhaps anachronistic for 1846, the word is frequently used in historical literature to describe New Mexicans of the time. Donald S. Frazier, ed., *The United States and Mexico at War: Nineteenth-Century Expansion and Conflict* (New York: Simon and Schuster Macmillan, 1998), s.v. "Taos Revolt;" Ramón A. Gutiérrez, *When Jesus Came, the Corn Mothers Went Away: Marriage, Sexuality, and Power in New Mexico, 1500–1846* (Stanford: Stanford University Press, 1991), 167.

5. Charles Montgomery, "Becoming 'Spanish American': Race and Rhetoric in New Mexico Politics, 1880–1928, *Journal of American Ethnic History* 20, no. 4 (Summer, 2001), 79; Charles Montgomery, "The Trap of Race and Memory: The Language of Spanish Civility on the Upper Rio Grande," *American Quarterly* 52, no. 3 (September 2000), 478–513. The *Santa Fe New Mexican* and the *Albuquerque Morning Democrat* failed to mention the events. *Santa Fe New Mexican,* August 18, 1896, August 22, 1896, February 3, 1897, February 4, 1897; *Albuquerque Morning Democrat,* August 18, 1896.

6. See *San Antonio Express, Houston Daily Post,* and *Dallas Morning News* for the week of May 8, 1896; *Dallas Morning News,* February 11, 1896, February 20, 1896, March 6, 1896, September 13, 1897.

7. Sonoma's actual anniversary was June 14, but the city held the commemoration on the thirteenth because the original date fell on a Sunday. R. A. Thompson, *Conquest of California: Capture of Sonoma by Bear Flag Men June 14, 1846, Raising the American Flag in Monterey by Commodore John D. Sloat, July 7, 1846* (Santa Rosa, Calif.: Sonoma Democrat, 1896), 1–2, 7, 8, 11, 13; Associated Veterans of the Mexican War, *History of the Celebration of the Fiftieth Anniversary of the Taking of Possession of California and Raising of the American Flag at Monterey, Cal. by Commodore John Drake Sloat, U.S.N., July 7th, 1846 . . .* (Oakland, Calif.: Carruth and Carruth, 1896), 3, 7–10.

8. Four Bear Flaggers survived, but only two could travel to the anniversary. A photo of the two men is reprinted in Thompson, *Conquest,* 1–2, 7, 8, 11, 13; Associated Veterans, *History of the Celebration,* 7–11.

9. "Nuevo Mexico" and "Alta California" refer to the Mexican states prior to annexation to the United States by the Treaty of Guadalupe Hidalgo in 1848. After that time they are referred to as New Mexico and California. K. Jack Bauer, *The Mexican War, 1846–1848* (Lincoln: University of Nebraska Press, 1992), 183–96; Carol and Thomas Christensen, *The U.S.–Mexican War: A Companion to the Public Television Series* (San Francisco: Bay Books, 1998), 99–104; Mark Crawford, David

Stephen Heidler, Jeane T. Heidler, eds., *Encyclopedia of the Mexican American War* (Oxford: ABC-Clio, 1999), s.vv. "California," "Frémont, John C." A Califorñio is a Hispanicized native Californian from the Spanish or Mexican periods. It is sometimes used as a term of self-definition by their descendants. Donald S. Frazier, ed., *The United States and Mexico at War: Nineteenth-Century Expansion and Conflict* (New York: Simon and Schuster Macmillan, 1998), s.v. "California."

10. Associated Veterans, *History of the Celebration,* 12–17. The details of this monument are addressed later in this chapter.

11. The roster of the Associated Veterans shows more than 250 members. Apparently only 150 were fit to march in the parade. Associated Veterans, *History of the Celebration,* 17–18, 49–51. A smaller celebration was held to mark the fortieth anniversary of the Monterey landing. See Associated Veterans of the Mexican War, *History of the Joint Anniversary Celebration at Monterey, Cal.* (San Francisco: Fraternal Publishing Company, 1886).

12. Associated Veterans, *History of the Celebration,* 4–5, 16–18, 21, 34–36.

13. Ibid., 20–21.

14. Ibid., 21.

15. Ibid. A reporter at the association's reunion in 1905 wrote, "Although all show the effects of age, they still give evidence of the virility of the manhood of this country at the time they were in their prime. Some of them are giants in size; few of them require the support of a cane, and only two use crutches." *Dallas Morning News,* May 23, 1905. See also *Dallas Morning News,* February 20, 1898 and October 16, 1912; Texas Association of Mexican War Veterans, *Proceedings 1903,* 8.

16. Associated Veterans, *History of the Celebration,* 34–37.

17. Ibid., 37–40.

18. Ibid., 44.

19. Ibid., 41.

20. Dicie May Graves was the granddaughter of the American soldier William J. Graves and great-granddaughter of the Califorñio commander, Jesus Jose Pico. She was also the distant cousin of Major Pico, who spoke at the commemoration at San Francisco. Associated Veterans, *History of the Celebration,* 44. For the "male–female" treatment of U.S.–Mexican relations see chapter 1 of this book and Shelley Streeby, *American Sensations: Class, Empire, and the Production of Popular Culture* (Berkeley: University of California Press, 2002), 84, 120.

21. In Texas the arrival of the railroad and the solidification of Anglo political and social control in the 1880s weakened the Tejano community. Matt S. Meier and Feliciano Rivera, *Dictionary of Mexican American History* (Westport, Conn.: Greenwood Press, 1981), s.vv. "New Mexico," "Texas"; David Montejano, *Anglos and Mexicans in the Making of Texas, 1836–1986* (Austin: University of Texas Press, 1987), 92–95; Nadine Ishitani Hata, *The Historic Preservation Movement in California, 1940–1976* (Sacramento: California Department of Parks and Recreation Office of Historic Preservation, 1992), 1.

22. At the San Francisco commemoration a reporter noted that "the yellow-skinned Mongolians peered down upon the crowds below. They were there, no part

of the picture they framed—a barbaric setting to the glory of American civilization."
Associated Veterans, *History of the Celebration,* 35. During the fortieth-anniversary
celebrations at Monterey in 1886, the president of the Associated Veterans of the
Mexican War referred to the "Mongolian pollution which is poisoning our land."
Associated Veterans, *History of the Joint Anniversary Celebration,* 21. David Glass-
berg, *Sense of History: The Place of the Past in American Life* (Amherst: University
of Massachusetts Press, 2001), 170; Meier and Rivera, *Dictionary,* s.v. "California";
Kevin Starr, *California: A History* (New York: Modern Library, 2005), 118; Walter
J. Stein, *California and the Dust Bowl Migration* (Westport, Conn.: Greenwood
Press, 1973), 35–37; Roger Daniels and Spencer C. Olin Jr., eds., *Racism in California: A Reader in the History of Oppression* (New York: Macmillan, 1972), 35–37,
181–84; Allyn C. Loosley, *Foreign Born Population of California* (San Francisco:
R and E Research Associates, 1971).

23. Richard Hofstadter, *The Age of Reform: From Bryan to F.D.R.* (New York:
Alfred A. Knopf, 1955), 135–38, 147; Michael McGerr, *A Fierce Discontent: The
Rise and Fall of the Progressive Movement in America, 1870–1920* (New York:
Oxford University Press, 2003), 3–6; William B. Friedricks, *Henry Huntington and
the Creation of Southern California* (Columbus: Ohio State University Press, 1992);
David Igler, *Industrial Cowboys: Miller & Lux and the Transformation of the Far
West, 1850–1920* (Berkeley: University of California Press, 2001); Robert M. Fogel-
son, *The Fragmented Metropolis: Los Angeles, 1850–1930* (Berkeley: University of
California Press, 1993), 43–62.

24. Hofstadter, *Age of Reform,* 138–39 fn 8; Fogelson, *Fragmented Metropolis,*
188–89; David M. Wrobel, *Promised Lands: Promotion, Memory, and the Creation
of the American West* (Lawrence: University Press of Kansas, 2002), 104–7, 121–28,
140. For an excellent study of the role of heritage organizations in the larger battle
for memory in the West, see David M. Wrobel, "The Politics of Western Memory," in
Jeff Roche, ed., *The Political Culture of the New West* (Lawrence: University Press
of Kansas, 2008), 332–63.

25. The University of California at Berkeley named its Bancroft Library after
him. *New York Times,* July 20, 1891; John Walton Caughey, *Hubert Howe Bancroft: Historian of the West* (Berkeley: University of California Press, 1946), 67–85,
100–101, 301; Society of California Pioneers, *Proceedings of the Society of California Pioneers in Reference to the Histories of Hubert Howe Bancroft* (San Francisco:
Stenett Printing, 1894), 3; Edwin A. Sherman, *The Life of the Late Rear-Admiral
John Drake Sloat of the United States Navy* (Oakland: Carruth and Carruth, 1902),
8; Hubert Howe Bancroft, *The Works of Hubert Howe Bancroft,* 39 vols. (San Francisco: A. J. Bancroft, 1885); Glassberg, *Sense of History,* 171.

26. *New York Times,* July 20, 1891; Bancroft, *Works,* 13:307.

27. *The Vedette,* vol. 6, no. 10, October 1885; Caughey, *Hubert Howe Bancroft,*
vii, 299, 330–31.

28. The society produced a thirty-seven-page indictment of Bancroft. See Society,
Proceedings. Stockton was Sloat's replacement in California following the initial occupation. Sutter was a Swiss national who aided in the overthrow of the Mexican

government in California, although he is mostly remembered for owning the mill where gold was discovered in 1848. Caughey, *Hubert Howe Bancroft,* 330–48; Bancroft, *Works,* 20:747–49, 22:735, 738–40; *New York Times,* July 20, 1891; Sherman, *The Life,* 8–9.

29. Society, *Proceedings,* 6; Associated Veterans, *History of the Celebration,* 3.

30. Thompson, *Conquest,* 1–2, 7, 8, 11, 13; Associated Veterans, *History of the Celebration,* 8.

31. Bancroft, *Works,* 22:213, 237, 249, 254 fn 48; Associated Veterans, *History of the Celebration,* 13. The battle against Bancroft continued long after his death in 1918. In 1936 Ernest A. Wiltsee, a member of the exclusive Pacific-Union Club, wrote a biography of John C. Frémont entitled *The Truth about Frémont: An Inquiry.* Upset that Bancroft had called Frémont a filibuster, Wiltsee claimed that "Bancroft had enough facts in front of him to show at least the dubiousness of his theory. But whatever may have been Bancroft's reason for his attitude, we can dismiss them as of no consequence." See Ernest A. Wiltsee, *The Truth about Frémont: An Inquiry* (San Francisco: John Henry Nash, 1936), 1.

32. Caughey, *Hubert Howe Bancroft,* 345–46.

33. Edward L. Ayers, *The Promise of the New South: Life after Reconstruction* (New York: Oxford University Press, 1992), 334.

34. For a detailed treatment of Murdock's life, see Steven R. Butler, "Mrs. M. Moore Murdock: Angel of the Veterans," *Mexican War Journal* 3, no. 3 (spring 1994): 18–33. Murdock preferred to be called Mrs. Moore Murdock and is known as such in all archival material. The Associated Veterans' stationery bore evidence of their misfortune, as they had lost their building in San Francisco and had moved into a rented room in city hall. Handwritten corrections on their letterhead bore further witness to their financial troubles. Associated Veterans of the Mexican War to William McKinley, May 16, 1901, William McKinley Presidential Papers, Library of Congress (hereafter WMPP). For details of the reorganization of the National Association of Mexican War Veterans, see Louis F. Beeler to John L. Bromley, June 14, 1906, Mrs. Moore Murdock Papers, Texas State Library and Archives (hereafter TSLA).

35. Associated Veterans of the Mexican War to William McKinley, May 18, 1901, WMPP. See also correspondence arriving at the White House on August 30, 1901, series 3, reel #80, WMPP. High elected officials often turned down offers to attend Mexican War reunions. See Associated Veterans, *History of the Joint Anniversary,* 6; C. N. Farr to Thomas H. Taylor, February 4, 1881, in possession of the author (hereafter MSVW).

36. Butler, "Mrs. M. Moore Murdock," 18; *Dallas Morning News,* July 4, 1911.

37. Isaac George, *Heroes and Incidents of the Mexican War* (Greensburg, Pa.: Review Publishing, 1903), 274–80.

38. TAMWV, *Proceedings 1904,* 5; James C. Carlton to Porfirio Díaz, February 16, 1904, TSLA; James C. Carlton to Ambassador Powell Clayton, February 16, 1904, TSLA; Porfirio Díaz to James C. Carlton, April 27, 1904, TSLA. The last Díaz correspondence had the headline and article (from an undated and unidentified local newspaper) glued to the letter.

39. Asociación de Defensores de la República Mexicana de 1836 a 1848 to the National Association of Mexican War Veterans, September 11, 1904, TSLA.

40. David W. Blight, *Beyond the Battlefield: Race, Memory, and the American Civil War* (Amherst: University of Massachusetts Press, 2002), 103, 125–27.

41. TAVMW, *Proceedings 1903*, 10; Blight, *Race and Reunion*, 290–91; Ayers, *The Promise*, 334–38. For the Confederate influence on Mexican War reunions, see TAVMW, *Proceedings 1903*; TAVMW, *Proceedings 1904*; *Dallas Morning News*, April 15, 1899, May 24, 1899, May 23–25, 1905. The issue of May 24 shows a photograph of Abe Harris, the president of the Texas association, wearing his Confederate officer's uniform.

42. Associated Veterans, *History of the Celebration*, 8; *Dallas Morning News*, May 24, 1905; Wrobel, "Politics of Western Memory."

43. *Dallas Morning News*, May 4, 1900; Jason B. Baker to George Finlay, May 20, 1905, TSLA; Jamestown Exposition Company to the National Association of Mexican War Veterans, January 11, 1906 and February 16, 1906, TSLA; Convention Bureau Division of the Chicago Commercial Association to the National Association of Mexican War Veterans, February 9, 1906, TSLA; Gulf, Colorado and Santa Fe Railroad Company to Abe Harris, May 20, 1909, TSLA.

44. The War Department concluded its investigation in April 1908. Hilton died in January 1910, leaving relatively little time for a thorough exposé. *Dallas Morning News*, November 5, 1905, December 28, 1905, January 12, 1910; Louis F. Beeler to John L. Bromley, June 14, 1906, TSLA; War Department to John N. Garner, April 11, 1908, TSLA; Bureau of Pensions to John N. Garner, April 11, 1908, TSLA.

45. *Dallas Morning News*, May 9, 1909, September 21, 1909; Frazier, *United States*, 461.

46. Aztec Club of 1847, *Constitution of the Aztec Club of 1847 (Military Society of the Mexican War) and List of Members*, 1928; Richard Hoag Breithaupt Jr., *Aztec Club of 1847: Military Society of the Mexican War, Sesquicentennial History, 1847–1997* (Universal City, Calif.: Walika, 1998), 81.

47. "Charter of the Dames of 1846," TSLA.

48. "Dames of 1846 Constitution and By-Laws," TSLA.

49. After the Dames ceased meeting in 1910, Murdock devoted the remaining years of her life to serving the United Daughters of the Confederacy. Membership applications and "Dames of 1846 Constitution and By-Laws," TSLA; Officers of the United Sons of Confederate Veterans to Whom It May Concern, September 27, 1909, TSLA; Butler, "Mrs. M. Moore Murdock," 19–22.

50. The Dames grew to fourteen camps, or chapters. Butler, "Mrs. M. Moore Murdock," 19–23; Glasson, *Federal Military Pensions*, 119; *Dallas Morning News*, January 4, 1906; Texas Association of Mexican War Veterans, *Proceedings of the Eighth Annual Reunion of the Texas Association of Mexican War Veterans* (Austin: Gammel-Statesman, 1903), 12; Silas Han to J. C. Carlton, March 16, 1904, TSLA; W. R. Smith to J. G. Starks, February 27, 1905, TSLA.

51. James L. Slayden to James T. McCuistion, September 12, 1905, TSLA.

52. Butler, "Mrs. M. Moore Murdock," 27–28.

53. *Dallas Morning News,* May 23–25, 1905; Texas Association of Mexican War Veterans, *Proceedings of the Ninth Annual Reunion of the Texas Association of Mexican War Veterans* (Austin: Gammel-Statesman, 1904), 3–4; Butler, "Mrs. M. Moore Murdock," 25, 29.

54. In 1901 there were 7,568 veterans surviving versus 8,109 widows. This margin continued to grow over the following years. In 1916 there were 513 veterans compared to 3,785 widows living. Murdock was aware of this change, as she had a Bureau of Pensions report from 1902 in her possession. Bureau of Pensions to the National Association of Mexican War Veterans, September 22, 1902, TSLA; Glasson, *Federal Military Pensions,* 119; Fanny Pettit to Mrs. Pruyn, February 6, 1906, TSLA.

55. Carlton family information is found in the *1880 United States Census,* 19th Ward, Indianapolis, Marion County, Indiana. Mattie Carlton to Mrs. Moore Murdock, July 13, 1905, TSLA.

56. Guadalupe Club of 1848, *Constitution Guadalupe Club* ([Washington?], 1906); Guadalupe Club of 1848, *List of Members Guadalupe Club* ([Washington?], 1913); "President and Mrs. Wilson on Golf Links—French Ambassador and Mme. Jusserand Entertain—General Gibson Celebrates Birthday," *Washington Times,* May 22, 1918; Daughters of the American Revolution, *Proceedings of the Thirtieth Continental Congress of the National Society of the Daughters of the American Revolution* (Washington: Hayworth, 1921), 149–50; "Women Will Hear Legion Commander," *New York Times,* January 25, 1931.

57. Mrs. John J. to Mrs. L. Dilts, August 16, 1913, MSVW.

58. For studies of gendered memory, see Lori D. Ginzberg, *Women and the Work of Benevolence: Morality, Politics, and Class in the Nineteenth-Century United States* (New Haven: Yale University Press, 1990); Marla Miller and Anne Digan Lanning, "Common Parlors: Women and the Recreation of Community Identity in Deerfield, Massachusetts, 1870–1920," *Gender and History* (November 1994): 435–55; Patricia West, *Domesticating History: The Political Origins of America's House Museums* (Washington: Smithsonian Institution Press, 1999); Karen L. Cox, *Dixie's Daughters: The United Daughters of the Confederacy and the Preservation of Confederate Culture* (Gainesville: University Press of Florida, 2003); Cynthia Mills and Pamela H. Simpson, eds., *Monuments to the Lost Cause: Women, Art, and the Landscapes of Southern Memory* (Knoxville: University of Tennessee Press, 2003); and Caroline E. Janney, *Burying the Dead but Not the Past: Ladies' Memorial Associations and the Lost Cause* (Chapel Hill: University of North Carolina Press, 2008).

59. Steven R. Butler, *Historic Sites of the Mexican War in the United States, Part One: Texas* (Richardson, Tex.: Descendants of Mexican War Veterans, 1997), 64–65.

60. Anna Geil Andresen, *Historic Landmarks of Monterey, California: A Brief Sketch of the Landmarks of Monterey, with a Resume of the History of Monterey . . .* (Salinas, Calif.: Native Daughters of the Golden West, 1917), 11–14. For an example of one of these stone-laying ceremonies, see *Dallas Morning News,* December 28, 1905.

61. The money for the building was endowed by Maj. Gen. George W. Cullum, the onetime director of the academy. Breithaupt, *Aztec Club,* 72–73; United States

Military Academy, "Cullum Hall History," www.usma.edu; West-Point.org: The West Point Connection, "Bugle Notes: Learn This!" www.west-point.org.

62. "Dames of 1846 Constitution and By-Laws," TSLA; *Dallas Morning News,* April 24, 1905, May 25, 1905, May 18, 1907, May 22, 1908, May 26, 1910; Butler, "Mrs. Moore Murdock," 26, 29; Butler, *Historic Sites,* 64–65.

63. *Dallas Morning News,* December 2, 1912. An excellent study of the DAR is found in Francesca Morgan, *Women and Patriotism in Jim Crow America* (Chapel Hill: University of North Carolina Press, 2005).

64. The DAR required initiates to order in numerical importance the European people who came to America prior to the Revolution. Predictably, much of their literature celebrated the Anglo-Saxon's role in U.S. history. United States Senate, *Seventh Report of the National Society of the Daughters of the American Revolution,* 58th Congress, 3rd Session, Document no. 193 (Washington: Government Printing Office, 1905), 92, 304–5; Morgan, *Women and Patriotism,* 70, 83–84; Peggy Anderson, *The Daughters: An Unconventional Look at America's Fan Club— The DAR* (New York: St. Martin's Press, 1974), 8–11.

65. *Dallas Morning News,* October 4, 1921; Butler, *Historic Sites,* 6, 18–19, 49; Florence Johnson Scott, *"Old Rough and Ready" on the Rio Grande,* rev. ed. (Waco: Texian Press, 1969), 90–91; "San Pasqual Battlefield State Historic Park" (undated outline of park history), San Pasqual Battlefield State Historic Park (hereafter SPB); George Walcott Ames Jr., *Battlefield of San Pascual* (Berkeley: Works Progress Administration and the State of California Department of Natural Resources Division of Parks, 1936), 1; Hata, *Historic Preservation,* 8; Morgan, *Women and Patriotism,* 63–65; The Kearny marker is in San Diego and the Taylor marker is in Corpus Christi.

66. The modern Native Sons and Daughters no longer subscribe to the racist agendas of the group's founders. Hata, *Historic Preservation,* 1; Native Daughters of the Golden West, *Native Daughters of the Golden West, 1886–1986* (Fresno: Pioneer Publishing, 1986); Associated Veterans, *History of the Celebration,* 7; Glassberg, *Sense of History,* 179–83, 193–94; Robert Alan Goldberg, *Hooded Empire: The Ku Klux Klan in Colorado* (Urbana: University of Illinois Press, 1981), vii, 4, 178; Charles C. Alexander, *The Ku Klux Klan in the Southwest* (Norman: University of Oklahoma Press, 1995), 7–8, 15–17, 161–62. For a comparison of the agendas of the Native Sons of the Golden West and the KKK, see Clarence M. Hunt, "Grizzly Growls," *Grizzly Bear* 36 (April 1925), and contrast with pamphlets: H. W. Evans, "The Attitude of the Knights of the Ku Klux Klan toward the Roman Catholic Hierarchy (Ku Klux Klan, ca. 1920)", and Ku Klux Klan, "The Klan Today" (Atlanta: American Printing and Manufacturing, 1928).

67. Carey McWilliams, *North from Mexico: The Spanish-Speaking People of the United States* (Philadelphia: J. B. Lippincott, 1949), 35–47; Natalia Molina, *Fit to Be Citizens: Public Health and Race in Los Angeles, 1879–1939* (Berkeley: University of California Press, 2006), 119. Chinese Americans in California founded an alternative society named the Native Sons of the Golden State. Roger Daniels, *Asian America: Chinese and Japanese in the United States since 1850* (Seattle: University

of Washington Press, 1988), 98–99; Yong Chen, *Chinese San Francisco, 1850–1943: A Trans-Pacific Community* (Stanford: Stanford University Press, 2000), 209.

68. "Program for the Battle of La Mesa Dedication," California State Library; "San Pasqual Battlefield State Historic Park" (undated outline of park history), SPB; Lois Ann Woodward., *La Mesa Battlefield* (Berkeley: Works Progress Administration and the State of California Department of Natural Resources Division of Parks, 1936), 1; Glassberg, *Sense of History,* 179; Richard S. Kimball and Barney Noel, *Native Sons of the Golden West* (Charleston, S.C.: Arcadia, 2005), 61; Wrobel, "Politics of Western Memory"; Fogelson, *Fragmented Metropolis,* 188–89.

69. Glassberg, *Sense of History,* 193.

70. Twenty-one Mormons and one Missourian died in the violence. Leonard J. Arrington and Davis Bitton, *The Mormon Experience: A History of the Latter-day Saints* (New York: Alfred A. Knopf, 1979), 45; Stephen C. LeSueur, *The 1838 Mormon War in Missouri* (Columbia: University of Missouri Press, 1990). For a comprehensive treatment of the Mormon Battalion, see Norma B. Ricketts, *The Mormon Battalion: U.S. Army of the West, 1846–47* (Logan: Utah State University Press, 1996); Sherman L. Fleek, *History May Be Searched in Vain: A Military History of the Mormon Battalion* (Spokane: Arthur H. Clark, 2006).

71. Frazier, *The United States,* s.v. "Mormon Battalion"; Arrington and Bitton, *The Mormon Experience,* 95–105; Ricketts, *The Mormon Battalion,* viii, 277.

72. Joseph G. Dawson, *Doniphan's Epic March: The 1st Missouri Volunteers in the Mexican War* (Lawrence: University of Kansas Press, 1999); Frazier, *The United States,* s.v. "Doniphan's March"; Ricketts, *The Mormon Battalion,* 20, 55, 149, 242, 323 fn 10.

73. This monument is on the grounds of the Clay County Courthouse in Richmond, Missouri.

74. Roberts also underestimated the length of the Missourians' march from Santa Fe to Matamoros by approximately four hundred miles. B. H. Roberts, *The Mormon Battalion: Its History and Achievements* (Salt Lake City, Deseret News, 1919), 2–4.

75. "Minutes Book," Utah Mormon Battalion Monument Commission Papers, 1917–27, LDS; *Deseret News,* May 30–31, 1927; for an overview of early Mormon historical preservation, see Paul L. Anderson, "Heroic Nostalgia: Enshrining the Mormon Past," *Sunstone* 5, no. 4 (July–August 1980): 47–55. The reflecting pool has been filled in with earth to make a flower garden.

76. *Deseret News,* May 30–31, 1927. The changes included altering hymn lyrics and temple rituals that challenged the authority of the United States. See David John Buerger, *The Mysteries of Godliness: A History of Mormon Temple Worship* (Salt Lake City: Signature Books, 2002), 37, 139–40.

77. For further historiographical studies of this period, see Peter T. Harstad and Richard W. Resh, "The Causes of the Mexican War: A Note on Changing Interpretations," *Arizona and the West* (winter 1964): 296; Odie B. Faulk and Joseph A. Stout Jr., eds. *The Mexican War: Changing Interpretations* (Chicago: Swallow Press, 1973), 204–5.

78. The number of books blaming the United States for the war dropped to under 14 percent. Half the works of the time chose not to assign blame for the conflict. Webb's *The Texas Rangers in the Mexican War* was typical in stating that the "causes of the war, the justice of it, and the results are left largely to the ambitious historian, the tender moralist, and the thoughtful philosopher." Walter Prescott Webb, *The Texas Rangers in the Mexican War* (1920, repr., Austin: Jenkins Garrett Press, 1975), 1.

79. Henry Hutchins Morris, *Thrilling Stories of Mexican Warfare including Intervention and Invasion by the United States* (n.p., 1914), 44–45, 74, 235, 306–11. See also T. J. Schoonover, *The Life and Times of Gen. John A. Sutter,* rev. ed. (Sacramento: Press of Bullock–Carpenter Printing Company, 1907), 80.

80. Thomas B. Gregory, *Our Mexican Conflicts: Including a Brief History of Mexico from the Sixth Century to the Present Time* (New York: Hearst's International Library, 1914), 54–56, 71, 109, 117–18; Herbert Ingram Priestly, *The Mexican Nation, A History* (New York: Macmillan, 1924), 299–300, 315–16; Thomas H. Russell, *Mexico in Peace and War* (Chicago: Reilly and Britton, 1914), 97.

81. Frederick Starr, *Mexico and the United States: A Story of Revolution, Intervention, and War* (Chicago: Bible House, 1914), 435–38.

82. Robert H. Howe, *How We Robbed Mexico in 1848* (New York: Latin American News Association, 1916), 2–8.

83. Germany's Zimmerman Telegram of 1917 offered to return portions of the American Southwest to Mexico and helped thrust the United States into the First World War. Curiously, it played no significant role in the historiography of the U.S.–Mexican War. Perhaps the coming of the war with Germany so soon after its publication muted the impact. Faulk found that twentieth-century wars led to increased interest in publications about the U.S.–Mexican War. Faulk, *The Mexican War,* 204–5; Justin H. Smith, *The War with Mexico,* 2 vols. (New York: Macmillan, 1919), 1:82–88, 105, 149–50, 188; *New York Times,* December 7, 1919, June 13, 1920; the Chicano historian Rodolfo Acuña later claimed that Smith was "rewarded for relieving the Anglo-American conscience." Rodolfo Acuña, *Occupied America: The Chicano's Struggle toward Liberation* (San Francisco: Canfield Press, 1972), 22.

84. Smith, *War with Mexico,* 1:3–6, 10–11.

85. Ibid., 1:4–5, 14.

86. For later works inspired by Smith, see Nathaniel W. Stephenson, *Texas and the Mexican War: A Chronicle of the Winning of the Southwest* (New Haven: Yale University Press, 1921); Priestly, *The Mexican Nation;* J. Fred Rippy, *The United States and Mexico* (New York: Alfred A. Knopf, 1926); Herbert Bashford and Harr Wagner, *The Story of John Charles Frémont* (San Francisco: Harr Wagner, 1927).

87. *Dallas Morning News,* November 2, 1928, November 16, 1928, June 17, 1929, September 4, 1929; *New York Times,* November 3, 1928, June 17, 1929, September 4, 1929; Bill Earngey, *Missouri Roadsides: The Traveler's Companion* (Columbia: University of Missouri Press, 1995), 203.

88. In the twentieth century, veterans' groups tried to prolong their inevitable decline by opening membership to their descendants or encouraging heritage societies.

Aside from the Aztec Club of 1847, all of these attempts failed. *Dallas Morning News*, November 29, 1908; TAMWV, *Proceedings 1904*, 5–7.

6. Rituals of the State

1. José Vasconcelos, *A Mexican Ulysses: An Autobiography*, trans. W. Rex Crawford (Bloomington: Indiana University Press, 1963), 146–48; Luis A. Marentes, *José Vasconcelos and the Writing of the Mexican Revolution* (New York: Twayne Publishers, 2000), 13, 33–34; Mary Kay Vaughan, *The State, Education, and Social Class in Mexico, 1880–1928* (DeKalb: Northern Illinois University Press, 1982), 134; Enrique Krauze, *Mexico: Biography of Power, A History of Modern Mexico, 1810–1996* (New York: Harper Collins, 1997), 253, 349, 393.

2. Josefina Zoraida Vázquez and Lorenzo Meyer, *The United States and Mexico* (Chicago: University of Chicago Press, 1985), 155; Alan Riding, *Distant Neighbors: A Portrait of the Mexicans* (New York: Alfred A. Knopf, 1985), 295–97; Ilene V. O'Malley, *The Myth of the Revolution: Hero Cults and the Institutionalization of the Mexican State, 1920–1940* (New York: Greenwood Press, 1986), 119–20; Anne T. Doremus, *Culture, Politics, and National Identity in Mexican Literature and Film, 1929–1952* (New York: Peter Lang, 2001), 1.

3. Vaughan, *The State*, 172; Gregorio Torres Quintero, *La Patria mexicana: Elementos de la historia nacional*, 10th ed. (Mexico City: Herrero Hermanos Sucesores, 1922), prologue.

4. Torres Quintero, *La Patria Mexicana*, 296, 300–302, 305, 307–8; for additional examples of this image, see Jose María Bonilla, *La evolución del pueblo mexicano: Elementos de historia patria* (Mexico City: Herrero Hermanos Sucesores, 1932), 254; Jorge de Castro Cancio, *Historia patria* (Mexico City: Editorial Patria, 1935), 198; Longinos Cadena, *Elementos de historia general y de historia patria: Para el Segundo año de instrucción primaria superior*, 13th ed. (Mexico City: Herrero Hermanos Sucesores, 1937), quoted in Carmen Castañeda García, Luz Elena Galván Lafarga, and Lucía Martinez Moctezuma, eds., *Lecturas y lectores en la historia de México* (Mexico City: Historias Ciesas, 2004), 172–73; *La Epica tragedia de Chapultepec* (Mexico City: Ediciones de Campaña Pro-Civismo e Historia, 1946), front cover. The account of U.S. soldiers displaying their rosaries and begging for their lives originally appeared in Heriberto Frías, *Episodios militares mexicanos* (Mexico City: Librería de la Vida de Ch. Bouret, 1901), 92.

5. Alfonso Toro, *Compendio de historia de México: La Revolución de Independencia y México independiente* (Mexico City: Sociedad de Edición y Librería Franco-Americana, 1926), 398–99, 434–36.

6. Toro, *Compendio*, 430; Edward Deering Mansfield, *The Mexican War: A History of its Origins*, 10th ed. (New York: A. S. Barnes and Burr, 1850), 298–99.

7. Departamento del Distrito Federal, *El Asalto al Castillo de Chapultepec y los Niños Héroes* (Mexico City: Colección Conciencia Cívica Nacional, 1983), 121; Enrique Plasencia de la Parra, "Conmemoración de la hazaña épica de los niños héroes: su origen, desarrollo y simbolismos," *Historia Mexicana* 45, no. 2 (October–

December 1995): 259; Asociacíon del Heroico Colegio Militar, *Chapultepec* (Mexico City: Secretario de la Defensa Nacional, 1960), 8; Edwin Lieuwen, *Mexican Militarism: The Political Rise and Fall of the Revolutionary Army, 1910–1940* (Westport, Conn.: Greenwood Press, 1981), 15–16, 20–21, 47, 70.

8. Plasencia de la Parra, "Conmemoración," 259–60.

9. *El coronel Felipe Santiago Xicoténcatl y la Batalla de Chapultepec, 1847–1947* (Tlaxcala, Mexico: Publicaciones de la Dirección de Bibliotecas, Museos e Investigaciones Históricas, 1947), 50–51; Krauze, *Mexico,* 396–99; Lieuwan, *Mexican Militarism,* 92–93.

10. Marentes, *José Vasconcelos,* 146–47; Krauze, *Mexico,* 396–99.

11. Krauze, *Mexico,* 397; Plasencia de la Parra, "Conmemoración," 259–60; Lieuwan, *Mexican Militarism,* 92–93.

12. Obregón was assassinated before his second inauguration. Lieuwan, *Mexican Militarism,* 85–86, 92–93; Plasencia de la Parra, "Conmemoración," 261–62; Krauze, *Mexico,* 403.

13. Ilene V. O'Malley's *The Myth of the Revolution* is a fascinating study of the use of the memory of the Revolution to support postrevolutionary power.

14. Juan Manuel Torrea, *La Vida de una institución gloriosa: el Colegio Militar 1821–1930* (Mexico City: Talleres Tip. Centenario, 1931), 58.

15. Two proposed motion pictures about the Niños Héroes focused on the story of Agustín Melgar. See Alfonso Teja Zabre, *Murió por la patria: Los Niños Héroes de Chapultepec* (Mexico City: Ediciones Botas, 1938) and *El Cementerio de las Aguilas,* motion picture. Directed by Luis Lezama (Producciones Cinematográficas Aztla, 1939). The former was never made. The latter, however, visually portrayed Escutia's suicide and popularized the legend in Mexicans' public memory. Torrea, *La Vida,* 49.

16. *El Colonel,* 50–51; Plasencia de la Parra, "Conmemoración," 261–62. The flag has undergone extensive restoration and remains in the custody of the Instituto Nacional de Antropología e Historia; "Restaura INAH bandera del batallón activo de San Blas," *El Universal,* February 23, 2006.

17. Anita Brenner, *The Wind that Swept Mexico: The History of the Mexican Revolution of 1910–1942* (Austin: University of Texas Press, 1984), 90; Krauze, *Mexico,* 438–90; Dirk Raat and William H. Beezley, eds., *Twentieth-Century Mexico* (Lincoln: University of Nebraska Press, 1986), 152–53. For a wider treatment of the Cárdenas presidency, see Friedrich E. Schuler, *Mexico between Hitler and Roosevelt: Mexican Foreign Relations in the Age of Lázaro Cárdenas, 1934–1940* (Albuquerque: University of New Mexico Press, 1998), and Carlos Alvear Acevedo, *Lázaro Cárdenas: El hombre y el mito* (Mexico City: Editorial Jus, 1972).

18. Krauze, *Mexico,* 448–49; Patricia Hurtado Tomás, "Los libros de texto oficiales en las escuelas primarias durante la educación socialista en el Estado de México"; Luz Elena Galván Lafarga, "Arquitipos, mitos y representaciones en libros de historia patria (1934–1939," in Carmen Castañeda García, Luz Elena Galván Lafarga, and Lucía Martinez Moctezuma, eds., *Lecturas y lectores en la historia de México* (Mexico City: Historias Ciesas, 2004), 143–76.

19. Castro Cancio, *Historia patria,* 193–201. For a treatment of the use of Christian iconography to support Mexican state building, see O'Malley, *Myth,* 130–33.

20. Krauze, *Mexico,* 472–75.

21. Lázaro Cárdenas, *Apuntes,* 4 vols. (Ciudad Universitaria: Universidad Nacional Autónoma de México, 1973), 1:356; Plasencia de la Parra, "Conmemoración," 262–63; Krauze, *Mexico,* 475; Raat, *Twentieth-Century,* 186–88.

22. Alfonso Teja Zabre, *Chapultepec* (Mexico City: Talleres de Impresión de Estampillas y Valores, 1938). Although he was unable to have the script produced, he did have it published; see Teja Zabre, *Murió por la patria.*

23. *El Cementerio de las Águilas.*

24. In her study of borderland folk religion Monica Delgado Van Wagenen found that the motion picture *Las Rosas del Milagro* influenced how Mexicans and Mexican Americans remembered and interpreted the appearance of the Virgin of Guadalupe. *The Cemetery of the Eagles* likewise shaped Mexican memory of the War of North American Intervention. See Monica Delgado Van Wagenen, "The Sacred and the Mundane: Images of Deity in Ordinary Objects in the Lower Rio Grande Valley of Texas" (MAIS thesis, University of Texas at Brownsville, 2001), 85–86 fn 80.

25. Torrea, *La Vida,* 49.

26. A film reviewer for the *New York Times* gave *The Cemetery of the Eagles* a strong recommendation. *New York Times,* September 2, 1939.

27. "Press Unanimous on Avila Camacho," *New York Times,* December 3, 1940; "Embassy Proposed Idea for Tribute by Truman," *New York Times,* March 5, 1947; "Mexican Child Heroes of 1847 Were Honored by U.S. Naval Detachment 42 Years Ago," *New York Times,* March 16, 1947; Stephen R. Niblo, *Mexico in the 1940s: Modernity, Politics, and Corruption* (Wilmington, Del.: Scholarly Resources, 1999), 86–88; Schuler, *Mexico between Hitler and Roosevelt,* 195–96.

28. *General Pedro María Anaya, Héroe de la patria* (Mexico: Departamento del Distrito Federal–Dirección de Acción Social, 1942); "Sobrevivirá a nuestras autoridades?" *Diario de Morelos,* July 21, 2010; D. Enrique Olavarría y Ferrari, *México: A través de los siglos,* 4 vols. (Mexico: Ballescá, 1880), 4:679–70; "Memorias de la ciudad / effigies errantes," *La Jornada,* June 10, 2004.

29. *El Universal,* September 14, 1941; Plasencia de la Parra, "Conmemoración," 263.

30. Krauze, *Mexico,* 503.

31. "War Board Visits Mexico," *New York Times,* September 14, 1942; "Mexico Fetes Defense Body," *New York Times,* September 15, 1942; Cárdenas, *Apuntes,* 2:89; Vázquez, *United States,* 158–59.

32. Alfonso Taracena, *La Vida en México bajo Ávila Camacho,* 2 vols. (Mexico City: Editorial Jus, 1976), 2:85–88; Krauze, *Mexico,* 504; Vázquez, *United States,* 155–62; Plasencia de la Parra, "Conmemoración," 263; Robert A. Pastor and Jorge Castañeda, *Limits to Friendship: The United States and Mexico* (New York: Alfred A. Knopf, 1988), 315; Eduardo Obregón Pagán, *Murder at the Sleepy Lagoon: Zoot Suits, Race, and Riot in Wartime L.A.* (Chapel Hill: University of North Carolina Press, 2003), 193–94.

33. Taracena, *La Vida en México*, 2:191; Plasencia de la Parra, "Conmemoración," 264.

34. *El Nacional*, September 14, 1944, quoted in Plasencia de la Parra, "Conmemoración," 264–65; Vázquez, *United States*, 157–62; Krauze, *Mexico*, 504.

35. Francisco Escuerdo Hidalgo, *La Guerra de los Pasteles en 1838 y la invasión norteamericana en 1847; Lecturas históricas para alumnos de primaria y secundaria, tomadas de mi libro 'Historia de México'* (Mexico City, 1943); *Defensores de la patria* (Mexico City: Ediciones de la Secretaría de Educación Pública, 1943); Tomas Sánchez Hernández, *Los Niños Héroes* (Mexico City: Ediciones de la Secretaría de Educación Pública, 1944); *La Épica tragedia de Chapultepec*.

36. *El Coronel*, 50–51; "Museo Nacional de Historia," Instituto Nacional de Antropología e Historia (http://mnh.inah.gob.mx); for a color image of the mural, see Instituto Nacional de Antropología e Historia, *Los Niños héroes y el asalto al castillo de Chapultepec* (Mexico City: Servicios Gráficos de Morelos, 2003).

37. More recently the museum installed an exhibit dedicated to the memory of the Niños Héroes.

38. Plasencia de la Parra, "Conmemoración," 244, 265–66.

39. "La República Entera Rindió Ayer Homenaje a los Niños Héroes," *Excelsior*, September 14, 1947; Instituto Nacional de Antropología e Historia, *Chapultepec en la guerra con los Estados Unidos* (Mexico City: Museo Nacional de Historia, 1947); Instituto Nacional de Antropología e Historia, *Churubusco en la acción militar del 20 de agosto de 1847* (Mexico City: Museo Histórico de Churubusco, 1947); Jesús Eduardo García Olvera, *La Leyenda y la historia de Chapultepec, 1847–2000, la noble terquedad de Juan Manuel Torrea Higuera* (Mexico City: Revisión Histórica, 2001), 6, 61, 72; Plasencia de la Parra, "Conmemoración," 244, 265–66; "News of the World of Stamps," *New York Times*, September 21, 1947; Maria Elena García Muñoz and Ernesto Fritsche Aceves, "Los Niños Héroes, de la realidad al mito" (Thesis, Universidad Nacional Autónoma de México, 1989), 6, 61, 72; Frank W. Grove, *Medals of Mexico* (Guadalajara, Jalisco: Frank W. Grove, 1972), 2:110. Examples of these medals are found in Mexico City museums and in the personal collections of Royd Riddell and Rod Bates.

40. Francisco Castillo Nájera, *Invasión norteamericana: Efectivos y estado de los ejércitos beligerantes, consideraciones sobre la campaña* (Mexico City: Congreso Mexicano de Historia, 1947); Vicente Fuentes Diaz, *La Intervención norteamericana en México [1847]* (Mexico City: Imprenta Nuevo Mundo, 1947); José C. Valadés, *Breve Historia de la guerra con los Estados Unidos* (Mexico City: Editorial Patria, 1947); Francisco Castillo Nájera, *El Tratado de Guadalupe . . .* (Mexico City: Ponencia al Congreso, 1947); Julio Luelmo, *Los Antiesclavistas norteamericanos: La Cuestión de Texas y la guerra con México* (Mexico City: Secretaría de Educación Pública, 1947), and James Knox Polk, *Diario del presidente Polk [1845–1849]*, trans. Luis Cabrera (Mexico City: Antigua Librería Robredo, 1948).

41. *La Epica tragedia de Chapultepec;* Instituto Nacional de Antropología e Historia, *Chapultepec en la guerra con los Estados Unidos* (Mexico City: Museo Nacional de Historia, 1947); Colonel Miguel A. Sánchez Lamego, *El Colegio Militar*

y la defensa de Chapultepec en septiembre de 1847 (Mexico City, 1947); Carlos A. Echanove Trujillo, *Juan Crisóstomo Cano, Héroe de Chapultepec, 1847* (Mexico City: Editorial Cultura, 1947); Antonio Fernández del Castillo, *A Cien años de la epopeya 1847–1947* (Mexico City, 1947); Arturo Sotomayor, *Nuestros Niños Héroes: Biografía de una noticia* (Mexico City: T. G. de la N., 1947).

42. Alemán delayed construction of the monument until after the visit of President Harry S. Truman in March of 1847. "Truman Bolsters Ties With Mexico" and "Mexico Is Touched as Truman Honors Her Heroes of 1847," *New York Times,* March 5, 1947; Plasencia de la Parra, "Conmemoración," 265–66.

43. Gen. Juan Manuel Torrea championed the movement to find the cadets' remains as early as 1921, when he published a pamphlet entitled "A Mausoleum Where There Are No Remains." See Departamento del Distrito Federal, *El Asalto al Castillo de Chapultepec y los Niños Héroes* (Mexico City: Colección Conciencia Cívica Nacional, 1983), 123–26. Accounts of the excavation process can be found in two reports: Sotomayor, *Nuestros Niños Héroes,* and Fernández del Castillo, *A Cien años,* 7–32.

44. Alemán also suspended public discussion of the new Altar to the Fatherland during Truman's visit. "Truman Charms Mexico," *Life,* March 17, 1947, 47–50; "Truman, Aleman Find Some Discord" and "Mr. Truman at Chapultepec," *New York Times,* March 6, 1947.

45. "Truman Bolsters Ties With Mexico" and "Mexico Is Touched as Truman Honors Her Heroes of 1847," *New York Times,* March 5, 1947; *Harry S. Truman 1947 Diary,* March 4, 1947, Harry S. Truman Library and Museum (hereafter HST).

46. "Truman Bolsters Ties with Mexico" and "Mexico Is Touched as Truman Honors Her Heroes of 1847," *New York Times,* March 5, 1947; "The Presidency: Fiesta," *Time* 49, no. 11 (March 17, 1947): 19–20.

47. "Truman Bolsters Ties with Mexico" and "Mexico Is Touched as Truman Honors Her Heroes of 1847," *New York Times,* March 5, 1947.

48. Cárdenas, *Apuntes,* 2:234.

49. Headlines quoted in "Truman Is Hailed as Noble Leader," *New York Times,* March 7, 1947.

50. Torrea, *La Vida,* 50–51, 66; Fernández del Castillo, *A Cien años,* 9–12, 17.

51. Fernández del Castillo, *A Cien años,* 15–18; Sotomayor, *Nuestros Niños Héroes,* 16–17; García Muñoz, "Los Niños Heróes," 92.

52. "Fueron Localizados los Restos de los Niños Héroes del 74," *La Prensa,* March 26, 1947.

53. Sotomayor, *Nuestros Niños Héroes,* 13–17.

54. "Depositaron los Restos de los Niños en el Altar de la Patria," *Excelsior,* September 13, 1947; Sotomayor, *Nuestros Niños Héroes,* 16–17, 67–69; Fernández del Castillo, *A Cien años,* 21.

55. Sotomayor, *Nuestros Niños Héroes,* 16–17, 80; Thomas Benjamin, *La Revolución: Mexico's Great Revolution as Memory, Myth, and History* (Austin: University of Texas Press, 2000), 134; Liturgy Office of England and Wales, *Rite of Dedication of a Church and an Altar* (United Kingdom: International Committee on English

in the Liturgy, 1978), 5–6. Juan N. Chávarri noted that Melgar's body was found in the form of a cross in *El Heroico Colegio Militar en la historia de México* (Mexico City: Editorial B. Costa-Amic, 1960), 139, 175.

56. "Homenaje de Escolares a los Héroes," *Excelsior*, September 12, 1947; "Honor a los Niños Héroes," *La Prensa*, September 13, 1947; "Mexico Fetes Castle Heroes," *Dallas Morning News*, September 14, 1947.

57. "La República Entera Rindió Ayer Homenaje a los Niños Héroes," *Excelsior*, September 14, 1947; "Todo México Exalta a sus Inmortales," *El Universal Gráfico*, September 13, 1947; "Mexico Fetes Castle Heroes," *Dallas Morning News*, September 14, 1947.

58. "La República Entera Rindió Ayer Homenaje a los Niños Héroes," *Excelsior*, September 14, 1947; "Todo México Exalta a sus Inmortales," *El Universal Gráfico*, September 13, 1947; "En Chapultepec Vibraron esta Mañana Himnos de Epopeya y de Glorificación," *El Universal Gráfico*, September 13, 1947; additional information drawn from the "Epopeya de Chapultepec 1847–1947" commemorative medal in the collection of Royd Riddell.

59. "La Inmortalidad de los Niños Héroes, Consagrada Ayer en el Altar de la Patria," *Excelsior*, September 15, 1947.

60. "Hoy, Hace Cien Años, Murieron por la Patria," *Excelsior*, September 13, 1947; "La Inmortalidad de los Niños Héroes, Consagrada Ayer en el Altar de la Patria," *Excelsior*, September 15, 1947; Pope Benedict XIV uttered the quote from Psalm 147 after viewing the image of Guadalupe left on the man's cloak. This image has shaped and defined Mexico's spiritual identity for nearly five centuries and is often appropriated by civil authorities. See Archbishop's Column of the St. Louis Review Online, "Am I not here, I who am your Mother?" www.stlouisreview.com.

61. Héctor Espinoza, *Mexicanos al grito de Guerra!* (Mexico City, [1947?]), in possession of the author. The tract was collected along with a newspaper from 1947 covering the centennial celebration. The graphics and printing style are consistent with the time period.

62. Monuments to the Boy Heroes may be found in Toluca, Veracruz, San Juan Teotihuacan, and many other locations. A small town in Puebla named itself Xochitlán de Vicente Suárez after one of the cadets.

63. In anticipation of the celebrations in Mexico City, a banner headline declared, "The Entire Nation Will Give Homage to the Boy Heroes Tomorrow." Beneath it in much smaller print was the announcement, "One Hundred Years Ago Today the City Suffered a Cannonade by the Invader." While not entirely ignoring the somber meaning behind the anniversary, the newspaper placed it in a minor context. See *Excelsior*, September 12 and 14, 1947.

64. U.S. Congress, *Congressional Record*, 81st Congress, 2d session, 1950–1951, 96:1127; American Legion Post 11, "Mount Holly Legion Unites Nations with Carranza Memorial," www.post11.org; "Mexican Flags Returned," *New York Times*, September 13, 1950; "Meeting with the President, January 9, 1950," HST; "Memorandum of Conversation with the President, January 23, 1950," HST; Roger W. Jones to William J. Hopkins, August 4, 1950, HST.

65. "Mexico Gets Back Banners in Colorful Presentation," *San Antonio Express,* September 17, 1950; "Mexican Flag Move Sped," *New York Times,* August 6, 1950; "Mexican Flags Returned," *New York Times,* September 13, 1950; "1847 Flags Returned to Mexican Hands," *New York Times,* September 14, 1950.

66. The returned colors were later included in an extensive catalogue of historic Mexican flags prepared by the museum and the Instituto Nacional de Antropología e Historia. Museo Nacional de Historia, *Banderas: Catálogo de la Colección de Banderas* (Mexico City: Secretaría de Gobernación, 1990). While creating exhibits at the Palo Alto Battlefield National Historic Site, Douglas Murphy, the park historian, contacted the Museo Nacional de Historia about the flags. The museum staff claimed they were undergoing extensive restoration and were unavailable to researchers. Douglas Murphy, interview by the author, Brownsville, May 15, 2006.

67. In an odd twist to the memory of the event, all official Mexican sources list the dedication as occurring on September 27, 1952. This includes the sign in front of the monument. Six million pesos were worth $693,641 at the time. "Foreign Exchange," *New York Times,* November 27, 1952; "Inauguran hoy el Monumento a los Niños Héroes," *Excelsior,* November 27, 1952; "Fue Inaugurado el Monumento a los Niños Héroes," *Excelsior,* November 28, 1952.

68. "4 Killed in Mexico in Post Election Riot," *New York Times,* July 8, 1952; "Mexicans Charge Many Died in Riot," *New York Times,* July 10, 1952; "Rains Nearly Paralyze Mexico City Area," *New York Times,* July 25, 1952; "Complaints Delay Mexican Returns," *New York Times,* July 29, 1952; "Aid Flown to 200,000 in Mexican Floods," *New York Times,* September 27, 1952; "43 Dead in Mexican Flood," *New York Times,* October 16, 1952; "Mexican Flood Again Rises," *New York Times,* October 19, 1952; "Inauguran hoy el Monumento a los Niños Héroes," *Excelsior,* November 27, 1952; "Fue Inaugurado el Monumento a los Niños Héroes," *Excelsior,* November 28, 1952.

7. Good Neighbors and Bad Blood

1. Francisco E. Balderrama and Raymond Rodriguez, *Decade of Betrayal: Mexican Repatriation in the 1930s* (Albuquerque: University of New Mexico Press, 2006), 57–59.

2. Juan F. Perea, ed., *Immigrants Out! The New Nativism and the Anti-Immigrant Impulse in the United States* (New York: New York University Press, 1996), 193–94; Balderrama, *Decade of Betrayal.*

3. George J. Sánchez, *Becoming Mexican American: Ethnicity, Culture and Identity in Chicano Los Angeles, 1900–1945* (Oxford: Oxford University Press, 1993), 122–23; Balderrama, *Decade of Betrayal,* 64, 118–19.

4. Robert A. Pastor and Jorge Castañeda, *Limits to Friendship: The United States and Mexico* (New York: Alfred A. Knopf, 1988), 52–54; Josefina Zoraida Vázquez and Lorenzo Meyer, *The United States and Mexico* (Chicago: University of Chicago Press, 1985), 141–46.

5. The text of the legislation is found in National Park Service, *Federal Historic Preservation Laws: The Official Compilation of U.S. Cultural Heritage Statutes* (Washington: U.S. Department of Interior, 2006), 12–19. A list of Depression-era national parks is found in Barry Mackintosh, *The National Parks: Shaping the System,* 3d ed. (Washington: U.S. Department of Interior, 2005), 44–45.

6. These battlefields included Rio San Gabriel (1944), Dominguez Ranch (1945), Mule Hill (1950), Natividad (1958), and San Pasqual (1962). Site observations revealed that each marker credited the private organizations that partnered with the state. Nadine Ishitani Hata, *The Historic Preservation Movement in California, 1940–1976* (Sacramento: California Department of Parks and Recreation Office of Historic Preservation, 1992), 16–18, 111–15; James L. Lindgren, "'A Spirit that Fires the Imagination:' Historic Preservation and Cultural Regeneration in Virginia and New England, 1850–1950," in Max Page and Randall Mason, eds., *Giving Preservation a History: Histories of Historic Preservation in the United States* (New York: Routledge, 2004).

7. Pat M. Neff, Walter F. Woodul, and L. W. Kemp, *Monuments Erected by the State of Texas to Commemorate the Centenary of Texas Independence: The Report of the Commission of Control for the Texas Centennial Celebrations* (Austin: Commission of Control for the Texas Centennial Celebrations, 1938), 9, 123, 132, 138, 145, 153. Unknown individuals have since removed the marker at Fort Brown. The removal may have happened within two years, as the Daughters of the American Revolution erected a replacement marker at Fort Brown in 1938. There were several sites in Texas that could have been included in 1936, including Camp Crockett, Camp Marcy, Landmark Inn, Old Bayview Cemetery, Rio Nueces crossing site, Rio Colorado crossing site, Fort Polk, Fort Belknap, and Brazos Island Depot.

8. Warren A. Beck, *New Mexico: A History of Four Centuries* (Norman: University of Oklahoma Press, 1962), 283, 299; today the Mormon Battalion Monument is visible near Exit 257 on Interstate 25.

9. The petrachrome mural, pioneered by the southern California WPA director, Stanton Macdonald-Wright, was a popular style in southern California. "TLC for a Mural," *Los Angeles Times,* January 11, 2004; "Mormons' President, City, Army, Navy Leaders Pay Tribute to Famous Battalion," *San Diego Union,* January 29, 1940; WPA Art Project, "New Deal Art during the Great Depression," www.wpamurals.com. Latter-day Saints temples were much larger than the many meetinghouses they had already built around the state. They are used for sacred rituals and hold a place of special reverence and devotion in the religion. In 1984 the Mormons finally built their temple in San Diego.

10. Vázquez, *United States,* 152, 157–58; Enrique Krauze, *Mexico: Biography of Power, A History of Modern Mexico, 1810–1996* (New York: Harper Collins, 1997), 503.

11. Vázquez, *United States,* 160–62.

12. "State House Static: Some Leg Pulling," a newspaper clipping ca. 1942 from Santa Anna Leg Collateral Files, Illinois State Military Museum (hereafter ISMM).

For an interesting account of the fate of Santa Anna's actual and prosthetic legs, see Alan Knight, "The Several Legs of Santa Anna: A Saga of Secular Relics," *Past and Present* 206, supplement 5 (2010): 227–55.

13. Carter Jenkins to Frank H. Tolbert, October 11, 1971, ISMM. It is unclear how old Jenkins was when he wrote the letter, although by the context it seems likely he was born in the early twentieth century. Jenkins claimed that the poem was several stanzas in length, but he could recall only this one. In 1929 Ripley's syndicated column "Believe It or Not" dedicated a feature to facts about Mexico, including an illustration of a soldier swinging a "peg leg." Underneath it was the caption "American soldiers played baseball with the wooden leg of General Santa Anna who was captured during the Mexican War by the Fourth Illinois Regiment, 1847. The leg is now in the Springfield Memorial Hall." "Believe It or Not," *San Francisco Chronicle,* May 1929, ISMM.

14. "Santa Anna's Cork Leg: Loans and Loan Requests"; John J. Gill to Carlos E. Black, August 29, 1939, ISMM; L. V. Regan to John J. Gill, September 9, 1939, ISMM.

15. Jennie A. Russ to Carlos E. Black, July 18, 1935, ISMM; John J. Gill to Carlos E. Black, August 29, 1939, ISMM; L. V. Regan to John J. Gill, September 9, 1939, ISMM; J. B. Koraday to Illinois Secretary of State, January 24, 1941, ISMM; Leo M. Byle to J. B. Korrady, January 28, 1941, ISMM; *Chicago Tribune,* undated clippings, ISMM; Knight, "Several Legs," 244.

16. "Mexicans Puzzled Over U.S. Drafting," *New York Times,* October 29, 1942; "Mexico's Fliers Hailed," *New York Times,* July 22, 1944; "Washington Praises Mexico's War Aid," *New York Times,* December 31, 1944; "Mexicans to Fight in Philippines," *New York Times,* February 24, 1945; "Mexican Unit Joins MacArthur," *New York Times,* April 12, 1945; Vázquez, *United States,* 157–62; Krauze, *Mexico,* 504.

17. *Latin America and College Teaching Materials* (Washington: American Council on Education, 1944); James Truslow Adams, *The Epic of America* (Garden City, N.Y.: Garden City, 1933), 179; John Spencer Bassett, *A Short History of the United States, 1492–1938,* 3d ed. (New York: Macmillan, 1939), 446. Editions of Bassett's work were available since 1921.

18. *Latin America in School,* 55.

19. See the online selected bibliography for the American monographs surveyed from this era (UMass URL to be announced).

20. Vázquez, *United States,* 163–64; Dirk Raat and William H. Beezley, eds., *Twentieth-Century Mexico* (Lincoln: University of Nebraska Press, 1986), 62–63.

21. See *San Antonio Express,* May 7–9, 1946; *Houston Chronicle,* May 7–9, 1946; *Los Angeles Times,* May 7–9, 1946; *San Francisco Chronicle,* May 7–9, 1946; *Santa Fe New Mexican,* May 7–9, 1946; *Washington Post,* May 7–9, 1946; *Dallas Morning News,* May 7–9, 1946; *New York Times,* May 7–9, 1946; *Brownsville Herald,* May 12–14, 1946.

22. *Washington Post,* May 12, 1946; *Dallas Morning News,* February 2, 1948. See also *San Antonio Express,* May 12–14, 1946, February 1–3, 1948; *Houston Chronicle,* May 12–14, 1946, February 1–3, 1948; *Los Angeles Times,* May 12–14,

1946, February 1–3, 1948; *San Francisco Chronicle,* May 12–14, 1946, February
1–3, 1948; *Santa Fe New Mexican,* May 12–14, 1946, February 1–3, 1948; *Dallas
Morning News,* May 12–14, 1946; *New York Times,* May 12–14, 1946, February
1–3, 1948; *Brownsville Herald,* May 12–14, 1946, February 1–3, 1948; *Albuquerque Tribune,* February 2–3, 1948.

23. *Dallas Morning News,* October 16, 1946; *Santa Fe New Mexican,* August 15,
1946. The Historical Society of New Mexico was established in 1859 and is the first
state historical society founded west of the Mississippi River. See the Historical Society
of New Mexico, "About the Historical Society of New Mexico," www.hsnm.org.

24. "DAR Commemorates Kearny's Entry at Public Program Monday," *Santa Fe
New Mexican,* August 13, 1946; "Kearny Exhibition Goes Up in Palace of Gover-
nors Aug. 18," *Santa Fe New Mexican,* August 15, 1946; "DAR Commemorates
Kearny Entrada," *Santa Fe New Mexican,* August 20, 1946.

25. "DAR Commemorates Kearny Entrada," *Santa Fe New Mexican,* August 20,
1946; "Centennial of Good Will," *Santa Fe New Mexican,* August 19, 1946.

26. Beck, *New Mexico,* 242, 283–87.

27. Seymour V. Conner and Odie B. Faulk, *North America Divided: The Mexican
War, 1846–1848* (New York: Oxford University Press, 1971), v–vi.

28. Alfred Hoyt Bill, *Rehearsal for Conflict: The War with Mexico, 1846–1848*
(New York: Alfred A. Knopf, 1947), vi–viii, 57–61, 79, 92–93.

29. Vázquez, *United States,* 163–64.

30. "Truman Bolsters Ties With Mexico" and "Mexico Is Touched as Truman
Honors Her Heroes of 1847," *New York Times,* March 5, 1947; "Truman, Aleman
Find Some Discord" and "Mr. Truman at Chapultepec," *New York Times,* March 6,
1947; "Truman is Hailed as Noble Leader," *New York Times,* March 7, 1947; "Truman Wins Triumph as a Good-Will Envoy," *New York Times,* March 9, 1947;
"Truman Termed New Champion," *Dallas Morning News,* March 5, 1947; Harry S.
Truman, *Memoirs,* 2 vols. (Garden City, N.Y.: Doubleday, 1956), 2:104; *Harry S. Truman 1947 Diary,* March 4, 1947, HST. See Senator Hatch's assessment of the "unos-
tentatious" act in U.S. Congress, *Congressional Record,* 80th Congress, 1st session,
1947, 93: part 14, 1680.

31. Merwin L. Bohan (Counselor of Embassy for Economic Affairs, Mexico
City, 1945–49), interview by Richard D. McKinzie, Dallas, Tex., June 15, 1974,
HST; "Embassy Proposed Idea for Tribute by Truman," *New York Times,* March 5,
1947; the official photograph of the event shows both Truman and Thurston posing
at the obelisk, see photo 59–72–44, HST.

32. "Truman Termed New Champion," *Dallas Morning News,* March 5, 1947;
U.S. Congress, *Congressional Record,* 80th Congress, 1st session, 1947, 93: part 14,
1680; *Harry S. Truman 1947 Diary,* March 4, 1947, HST.

33. Compare the original nineteenth-century marker as seen in National Archives photograph (92-CA-30A-1) to the one used today. "Executive Order 9873,"
Executive Orders 1945–1953, HST.

34. U.S. Congress, *Congressional Record,* 81st Congress, 2d session, 1950–
1951, 96:1127; American Legion Post 11, "Mount Holly Legion Unites Nations

with Carranza Memorial," www.post11.org; *New York Times,* "Mexican Flags Returned," September 13, 1950.

35. U.S. Congress, *Congressional Record,* 81st Congress, 2d session, 1950–1951, 96:1127; U.S. House of Representatives, *Report No. 2515,* 81st Congress, 2d Session, 1950–1951; U.S. Senate, *Report No. 1199,* 81st Congress, 1st Session, 1949–1950; "Would Return Flags to Mexico," *New York Times,* September 30, 1949; "Return of Mexican Flags Is Approved by Congress," *New York Times,* July 28, 1950. The State Department gave a similar endorsement, see Jack K. McFall to Frederick J. Lawton, August 1, 1950, HST.

36. Frank Pace, Jr. to Frederick J. Lawton, August 2, 1950, HST.

37. Vázquez, *United States,* 166; Jeff Broadwater, *Eisenhower and the Anti-Communist Crusade* (Chapel Hill: University of North Carolina Press, 1992), xi, 11–13.

38. It is unclear if these negotiations also included the handful of Texas colors captured during the War of Independence. "Meeting with the President, January 9, 1950"; "Memorandum of Conversation with the President, January 23, 1950"; Roger W. Jones to William J. Hopkins, August 4, 1950, HST; for information on flags held by Mexico, see Secretaría de Gobernación, *Banderas: Catálogo de la Colleción de Banderas* (Mexico City: Museo Nacional de Historia INAH, 1990).

39. "Mexican Flag Move Sped," *New York Times,* August 6, 1950; "Mexican Flags Returned," *New York Times,* September 13, 1950; "1847 Flags Returned to Mexican Hands," *New York Times,* September 14, 1950.

40. "1847 Flags Returned to Mexican Hands," *New York Times,* September 14, 1950; Vázquez, *United States,* 166; "Thinking Out Loud: Seeing Red," *Dallas Morning News,* September 25, 1950.

41. Daniel H. Ludlow, ed., *Encyclopedia of Mormonism,* 4 vols. (New York: Macmillan, 1992), s.vv. "Grant, Heber J.," "Smith, George Albert."

42. Mary Lambert Taggart, *Modern Day Trek of the Mormon Battalion* (Sugar House, Utah: D. James Cannon, 1955); "Scrapbook 1950–1958," Helen Carter Warr Papers, Historical Department of the Church of Jesus Christ of Latter-day Saints (hereafter LDS).

43. "Scrapbook 1950–1958," Helen Carter Warr Papers, LDS; Taggart, *Modern Day Trek,* 43–51; *Sons of the Utah Pioneers Trek 1950,* 16mm film, LDS.

44. The journal of William Wallace Casper detailed the battalion's lack of shoes and proper clothing; see typescript in "Russell R. Casper Biography of William Wallace Casper," Brigham Young University Special Collections; "Scrapbook 1950–1958," Helen Carter Warr Papers, LDS; *Sons of the Utah Pioneers Trek 1950,* 16mm film, LDS. Images of the SUP members in uniform are found throughout Taggart, *Modern Day Trek.*

45. "Scrapbook 1950–1958," Helen Carter Warr Papers, LDS.

46. Juan Ramón García, *Operation Wetback: The Mass Deportation of Mexican Undocumented Workers in 1954* (Westport, Conn.: Greenwood Press, 1980), 169–71, 183–96, 202, 227. García believed these statistics were inflated but did not offer revised numbers.

47. For an overview of "Crockettmania," see Michael Barnes's interview with Heather Brand at the Bob Bullock Texas State History Museum, *Abilene Reporter News*, March 2, 2002.

48. The baby boom generation is generally defined as children born between 1946 and 1964. Jack Patton and John Rosenfield, *Texas History Movies: 400 Years of Texas History and Industrial Development Portrayed by Action Cartoons*, rev. ed. (Dallas: Mobile Oil, 1943); "Movies Comic Gets New Look," *Dallas Morning News*, June 3, 2007.

49. Classics Illustrated Special #144A, *Blazing the Trails West* (New York: Gilberton, June 1958).

50. The World Around Us #11, *The Illustrated Story of the Marines* (New York: Gilberton, July 1959).

51. *The Robin Hood of El Dorado,* motion picture. Directed by William A. Wellman (Metro-Goldwyn-Mayer, 1936). For a review, see *New York Times*, March 14, 1936. Other films about the Texas War of Independence include *The Fall of the Alamo* (1935), *The Heroes of the Alamo* (1937), *The Alamo: Shrine of Texas Liberty* (1938), *Man of Conquest* (1939), *The Man from the Alamo* (1953), *The Last Command* (1955), *The First Texan* (1956), *The Adventures of Jim Bowie* (1958), and John Wayne's *The Alamo* (1960).

52. Los Angeles County Arts Commission, "Fort Moore Pioneer Monument," www.lacountyarts.org.

53. *Church News,* July 5, 1958, clipping in "Scrapbook 1950–1958," Helen Carter Warr Papers, LDS.

54. Paul P. Parker, "The Battle of Salinas," manuscript, Monterey County Historical Society (hereafter MHS); Robert B. Johnston, "The Place Called Natividad," manuscript, MHS.

55. "Bronze Monument to Mark Site of Battle of Natividad," *Salinas Californian,* November 15, 1958; "Battle Site Plaque Is Unveiled," *Salinas Californian,* November 17, 1958; Program of the "Dedication of the Plaque for the Battle of Natividad," MHS.

56. For a comprehensive study of the Civil War centennial, see Robert J. Cook, *Troubled Commemoration: The American Civil War Centennial, 1961–1965* (Baton Rouge: Louisiana State University Press, 2007).

57. "7 Historic Texas Sites Recognized Nationally," *Dallas Morning News*, December 20, 1960; "The War and Other Attractions for 1961," *Dallas Morning News,* January 8, 1961; "San Pasqual Battlefield State Historic Park" (undated outline of park history), San Pasqual Battlefield State Historic Park. The Armistice Oak Tree Site on the Santa Clara Battlefield was Registered Historical Landmark Number 260.

58. Arthur M. Schlesinger Jr., *A Thousand Days: John F. Kennedy in the White House* (Boston: Houghton Mifflin, 1965), 172, 178, 191, 250–97, 781, 779.

59. There was some debate at the time as to his exact words. See "Robert Kennedy Remark on Mexican War Irks Daniel," *Dallas Morning News*, February 15, 1962; "Bobby Riles Texans," *Dallas Morning News,* March 2, 1962; and compare to

Grady McWhiney and Sue McWhiney, eds., *To Mexico with Taylor and Scott, 1845–1847* (Waltham, Mass.: Blaisdell, 1969), viii.

60. "Texas History Sent R. Kennedy," *New York Times,* February 20, 1962; "Robert Kennedy Remark on Mexican War Irks Daniel," *Dallas Morning News,* February 15, 1962; "Robert Kennedy Shocks Texans by Questioning Mexican War," *Dallas Morning News,* February 17, 1962; "Kennedy Stirs Texas Twister With War Quip," *Dallas Morning News,* February 17, 1962; "Texas vs. Robert Kennedy," *Dallas Morning News,* February 18, 1962; "A Newsman Looks at the World's Week," *Dallas Morning News,* February 18, 1962; "Formby Says LBJ Seeks Stranglehold," *Dallas Morning News,* February 22, 1962; "Letters from Readers" *Dallas Morning News,* February 26, 1962, March 7, 1962, March 23, 1962.

61. "Robert Kennedy Shocks Texans by Questioning Mexican War," *Dallas Morning News,* February 17, 1962; "Texas vs. Robert Kennedy," *Dallas Morning News,* February 18, 1962; "Letters from Readers" *Dallas Morning News,* February 26, 1962, March 7, 1962. As I stood transcribing the Bear Flag Monument in Sonoma Plaza on June 30, 2006, I overheard a baby boomer ask a friend, "So is this the business that started at the Alamo?"

62. "Presidents to Meet at Border, Mark End of Dispute," *Dallas Morning News,* September 24, 1964; "Johnson Says U.S. Won't Spark War," *New York Times,* September 26, 1964.

63. For a detailed treatment of the dispute, see Sheldon B. Liss, *A Century of Disagreement: The Chamizal Conflict, 1864–1964* (Washington: University Press of Washington, D.C., 1965); Alan C. Lamborn and Stephen P. Mumme, *Statecraft, Domestic Politics, and Foreign Policy Making: The El Chamizal Dispute* (Boulder: Westview Press, 1988); see also Vázquez, *United States,* 86, 98–99, 109, 174.

64. "Mexico Seems Sure to Win Chamizal," *Dallas Morning News,* March 9, 1963; Liss, *Century of Disagreement,* 95.

65. Cárdenas, *Apuntes,* 2:234.

8. Resisting the Gringos

1. "Conmovedor Homenaje Rindió México a los Niños Héroes de Chapultepec," *Excelsior,* September 14, 1953; Enrique Plasencia de la Parra, "Conmemoración de la hazaña épica de los niños héroes: su origen, desarrollo y simbolismos," *Historia Mexicana* 45, no. 2 (October–December 1995): 268. The same basic format continues to be used in the twenty-first century.

2. Dirk Raat and William H. Beezley, eds., *Twentieth-Century Mexico* (Lincoln: University of Nebraska Press, 1986), 63–66.

3. Charles Weeks, *The Juárez Myth in Mexico* (Tuscaloosa: University of Alabama Press, 1987), 107; Thomas Benjamin, *La Revolución: Mexico's Great Revolution as Memory, Myth, and History* (Austin: University of Texas Press, 2000), 124, 125, 137.

4. Plasencia de la Parra, "Conmemoración," 268–69. The dagger presentations remain an important part of the present-day commemoration.

5. The definitive history of the Batallón San Patricio is Robert Ryal Miller, *Shamrock and Sword: The Saint Patrick's Battalion in the U.S.–Mexican War* (Norman: University of Oklahoma Press, 1989).

6. Patricia Cox, *Batallón de San Patricio* (Mexico City: Editorial Stylo, 1954); Martin Foley, (former head of the Batallón San Patricio Memorial in Mexico City) interview by the author, September 12, 2007; Miller, *Shamrock and Sword*, 179.

7. Foley, interview; Miller, *Shamrock and Sword*, 182–83; September 12 was chosen to coincide more closely with the large executions carried out during the Battle of Chapultepec on the thirteenth.

8. Miller, *Shamrock and Sword*, 179–84.

9. Dermot Brangan (Irish ambassador to Mexico), interview by the author, September 12, 2007; Foley, interview; Miller, *Shamrock and Sword*, 179–84; the website for the Mexican embassy in Ireland contains the diplomatic history of the two nations along with an account of the Batallón San Patricio, see Secretería de Relaciones Exteriores, "Embajada de México en Irlanda," http://portal.sre. gob.mx.

10. Ana Cristina Ávila and Virgilio Muñoz, *Creación de la Comisión Nacional de Libros de Texto Gratuitos: La perspectiva escolar, 1958–1964* (Mexico City: Noriega Editores, 1999), 87–112; *La Jornada*, May 16, 1999; J. Jesús Cárabes Pedroza, *Mi Libro de Tercer Año: Historia y Civismo* (Mexico City: Comisión Nacional de los Libros de Texto Gratuitos, 1960), 2.

11. Ávila, *Creación*, 102, 105.

12. Illustration from *Mi cuaderno de trabajo de segundo año* reproduced in Josefina Vázquez de Knauth, *Nacionalismo y educación en México* (Mexico City: El Colegio de México, 1970), plate 11.

13. Cárabes Pedroza, *Mi Libro*, 16–17.

14. Amelia Monroy Gutiérrez, *Mi Libro de Quinto Año: Historia y Civismo* (Mexico City: Comisión Nacional de los Libros de Texto Gratuitos, 1964), 163.

15. "Héroes de México," *Nuevos Cuentos de Calleja* 1, no. 14 (August 15, 1959): 25–32. The comic *Epopeya* (Epic Poem), supported by the Secretaría de Educación Pública, also began operation in 1958.

16. Thelma González Sullivan, interview by the author, March 30, 2009; Adolfo Garcia Zamora, interview by the author, April 1, 2009; Sylvia Casares, interview by the author, Brownsville, April 1, 2009; Maritza Arrigunaga Coello, interview by the author, April 6, 2009.

17. Oscar Arriola, interviews by the author, September 10, 12, 2007, and additional personal communication.

18. Gobierno del Estado de Veracruz, *Mi libro y Cuaderno de Trabajo de tercer año: Historia de Veracruz Libro de Texto Gratuito* (Veracruz: Xalapa-Enriquez, 1966), 73.

19. Américo Paredes, "The Anglo-American in Mexican Folklore," in Ray B. Browne, Donald M. Winkelman, and Allen Hayman, eds., *New Voices in American Studies* (Lafayette: Purdue University Press, 1966), 124.

20. Gobierno de Jalisco, "Boletines: Dirección General de Comunicación Social," http://app.jalisco.gob.mx; Instituto Nacional de Antropología e Historia, "Museo Nacional de las Intervenciones," www.inah. gob.mx.

21. The most important work on the student movement in Mexico in 1968 is Elena Poniatowska's oral history, *Massacre in Mexico,* trans. Helen R. Lane (New York: Viking Press, 1975).

22. "Homenaje Escolar a Nuestros Héroes," "Exhorto al Estudio," "En Chapultepec . . . 13 de septiembre de 1847," *Excelsior,* September 13, 1968.

23. "Los Niños Héroes Exaltados Como Ejemplo de los Jóvenes," *Excelsior,* September 14, 1968.

24. Ibid.; Enrique Krauze, *Mexico: Biography of Power, A History of Modern Mexico, 1810–1996* (New York: Harper Collins, 1997), 470, 540, 570, 613–14, 641.

25. "Se Efectuó la Manifestacion del Silencio," *Excelsior,* September 14, 1968; Poniatowska, *Massacre,* 53–58; Krauze, *Mexico,* 711.

26. "Se Efectuó la Manifestacion del Silencio," *Excelsior,* September 14, 1968; Poniatowska, *Massacre,* 178–79; Casares, interview.

27. Poniatowska, *Massacre,* 200–323; Krauze, *Mexico,* 717–22; "Mexicans Honor 300 Victims of '68 Government Massacre," *San Antonio Express-News,* October 3, 1995.

28. *Epopeya: Los Niños Héroes* 12, no. 135 (August 1969).

29. Ibid.

30. Garcia Zamora, interview. Garcia Zamora, disillusioned that members of the Communist Party offered to pay him to participate in antigovernment rallies, left the student movement.

31. González Sullivan, interview.

32. Three editions of the book were published in three years. See Manuel Medina Castro, *El gran despojo: Texas, Nuevo México, California,* 3d ed. (Mexico City: Editorial Diogenes, 1974), 73–74, 78–79.

33. Ciro E. González Blackaller and Luis Guevara Ramírez, *Síntesis de historia de México* (Mexico City: Editorial Herrero, 1971), 323, 325.

34. Casares, interview; students in other parts of Mexico reported similar experiences; Jorge Chavez, interview with the author, April 6, 2009; Jose Chacon, interview by the author, April 16, 2009; Arrigunaga Coello, interview; Plasencia de la Parra, "Conmemoración," 270–72. A college textbook published in 1974 likewise downplayed the Boy Heroes, see Daniel Cosío Villegas et al., *Historia mínima de México,* 7th ed. (Mexico City: Colegio de México y HARLA, 1983), 101.

35. Dirk W. Raat, *Mexico and the United States: Ambivalent Vistas* (Athens: University of Georgia Press, 1992), 156–57.

36. Ángela Moyano Pahissa, *El Comercio de Santa Fe y la guerra del "47"* (Mexico City: Sep Setentas, 1976), 155–59, 165; Raat, *Mexico and the United States,* 185–87.

37. Gilberto López y Rivas, *La Guerra del 47 y la resistencia popular a la ocupación* (Mexico City: Editorial Nuestro Tiempo, 1976), 9. See also Cosío Villegas, *Historia,* 100–101.

38. Krauze, *Mexico,* 758–61; Raat, *Mexico and the United States,* 161–62.

39. Jorge Fernández Tomas, *México, historia de un pueblo: Tomo 8, Ahí vienen los del norte* (Mexico City: Secretería de Educación Pública, 1980).

40. The fort was actually under construction at the outbreak of the war. Carlos Rugiero Cázares (director of Museo Casa Mata) interview by the author, May 17, 2006; Milo Kearney and Anthony Knopp, *Boom and Bust: The Historical Cycles of Matamoros and Brownsville* (Austin: Eakin Press, 1991), 61; *El Soldado mexicano 1837–1847, The Mexican Soldier, organización—vestuario—equipo—Organization—Dress—Equipment* (Mexico City: Ediciones Nieto, Brown, Hefter, 1958), 49; Instituto Nacional de Antropología e Historia, *Churubusco en la acción militar del 20 de Agosto de 1847* (Mexico City: Museo Histórico de Churubusco, 1947).

41. Enriqueta Cabrera (museum director), interview by the author, September 7, 2007; Instituto Nacional de Antropología e Historia, "Museo Nacional de las Intervenciones," www.inah. gob.mx.

42. The note was planned in late 1980 but was not put into circulation until 1982. Banco de México, "Circular número 1861/80 del 2 de septiembre de 1980"; "Mexico Cuts Oil Prices by $4 a Barrel," *New York Times,* June 3, 1981; Raat, *Twentieth-Century Mexico,* 63–66.

43. Heriberto Frías, *Episodios militares mexicanos* (Mexico City: Librería de la Vida de Ch. Bouret, 1901); Heriberto Frías, *Episodios militares mexicanos* (Mexico City: Biblioteca del Oficial Mexicano, 1983); Heriberto Frías, *La Guerra contra los gringos* (Mexico City: Ediciones Leega/Jucar, 1984).

44. Frías, *La Guerra,* 7, 61.

45. Raat, *Mexico and the United States,* 161–65; Krauze, *Mexico,* 759–69.

46. "In Mexico, a Bold New President Is Surprising both Friends and Enemies," *New York Times,* March 28, 1989; "Mexico Makes Itself a Model Debtor," *New York Times,* April 19, 1989; "Mexican–U.S. Pact Reached on Trade and Investments," *New York Times,* October 4, 1989.

9. Contesting American Pasts

1. "Archeologists Are Working on Digs," *Brownsville Herald,* April 3, 1967; "University of Texas Archeologists . . . ," *Brownsville Herald,* April 4, 1967; Al B. Wesolowsky to Daniel Fox, September 14, 1982, Palo Alto Battlefield National Historical Park Archives (hereafter PAB); Eric Alan Ratliff, "Life and Death in the Mexican Army: An Analysis of Skeletal Remains from the Battle of Resaca de la Palma, May 9, 1846" (Thesis, University of Texas at Austin, 1993).

2. Coverage included two small articles in the English language section of the bilingual *Brownsville Herald* (April 3, 4, 1967); Ratliff, "Life and Death," 8–10; Douglas Murphy (Palo Alto Battlefield National Historical Park historian), interview by the author, May 15, 2006, and additional personal communication.

3. Josefina Zoraida Vázquez and Lorenzo Meyer, *The United States and Mexico* (Chicago: University of Chicago Press, 1985), 181–98.

4. Donald Barr Chidsey, *The War with Mexico* (New York: Crown Publishers, 1968), 10, 68–70, 86; Ernest R. Dupuy, *The Compact History of the United States Army* (New York: Hawthorne Books, 1956), 92; see also Otis A. Singletary, *The Mexican War* (Chicago: University of Chicago Press, 1960), 9–14; between 1966 and 1969 approximately one-third of those works ascribing culpability for the war continued to fault Mexico. See the online selected bibliography for the books surveyed from this era (UMass URL to be announced).

5. The American Presidency Project at the University of California at Santa Barbara, "Lyndon B. Johnson Press Conference November 17, 1967," www.presidency .ucsb.edu; "Fulbright Warns of Peril in Power," *New York Times,* April 22, 1966; "Take a New Look at Dissent, Johnson Admonishes Critics," *Dallas Morning News,* November 18, 1967; "Off in All Directions," *Dallas Morning News,* September 6, 1967; "Two Wars in Perspective," *Dallas Morning News,* November 28, 1967; "The Year that Failed to Turn," *New York Times,* December 30, 1968; "Stage: Thoreau in Jail," *New York Times,* November 2, 1970; The American Presidency Project at the University of California at Santa Barbara, "Gerald Ford Remarks at a Dinner in New York City Honoring Vice President Rockefeller," www.presidency.ucsb.edu.

6. This statistic is generated from a survey of books written between 1970 and 1979. See the online selected bibliography for the books surveyed from this era at scholarworks.umass.edu/umpress/. Samuel Eliot Morrison, Frederick Merk, and Frank Freidel, *Dissent in Three American Wars* (Cambridge: Harvard University Press, 1970); Seymour Martin Lipset, *Rebellion in the University* (Boston: Little, Brown, 1971), 12–13; "As American as Antiwar Dissent," *New York Times,* May 25, 1970; K. Jack Bauer, *The Mexican War, 1846–1848* (Lincoln: University of Nebraska Press, 1992), xxv–xxvi.

7. Soldiers with Hispanic surnames represented over 19 percent of the dead from those states while composing less than 12 percent of their population. United States Department of Defense, *Hispanics in America's Defense* (Washington: U.S. Department of Defense, 1989), 37–40; Manuel Gomez to the draft board of Temescal, California, December 8, 1969, reprinted in Elizabeth Sutherland Martinez and Enriqueta Longeaux y Vázquez, *Viva La Raza! The Struggle of the Mexican-American People* (New York: Doubleday, 1974), 287–89. See also Lorena Oropeza, *¡Raza Sí! ¡Guerra No! Chicano Protest and Patriotism during the Viet Nam Era* (Berkeley: University of California Press, 2005).

8. Ernest Barrios et al., *A Resource Guide for Teaching Chicano Studies in Junior and Senior High Schools* (San Diego: San Diego City Schools, 1969); the difference between textbooks and monographs can be seen by comparing Rodolfo Acuña, *A Mexican American Chronicle* (New York: American Book Company, 1971) to his later *Occupied America: The Chicano's Struggle toward Liberation* (San Francisco: Canfield Press, 1972).

9. John Tebbel and Ramón Eduardo Ruiz, *South by Southwest: The Mexican-American and His Heritage* (Garden City, N.Y.: Zenith Books, 1969), 96–104.

10. Julian Nava, *Mexican Americans: Past, Present, and Future* (New York: American Book Company, 1969), v, 61.

11. *Texas and the Mexican War,* motion picture. Directed by Rojer Tilton (Encyclopedia Britannica, 1966).

12. Mirta Vidal, *Chicano Liberation and Revolutionary Youth* (New York: Pathfinder Press, 1971), 3. Modern scholars in the field of ethnic studies use the term "Chicana/o" to explicitly include both men and women. I use the original "Chicano" in the understanding that the word historically implied both genders.

13. Acuña, *Occupied America,* 1. In 2007 the book went into its seventh revised edition and continues to be widely used as a college text. Acuña addressed his struggle against American historians in an essay published by the American Historical Association in 2007, "Why Become a Historian?" www.historians.org.

14. Armando B. Rendón, *Chicano Manifesto* (New York: Collier Books, 1972), 70.

15. Octavio Ignacio Romano, *Voices: Readings from El Grito, A Journal of Contemporary Mexican American Thought, 1967–1973* (Berkeley: Quinto Sol, 1973), 162; Matt S. Meier and Feliciano Rivera, *Dictionary of Mexican American History* (Westport, Conn.: Greenwood Press, 1981), s.v. "Romano-V, Octavio."

16. Vidal, *Chicano Liberation,* 1; for an analysis of Aztlán in Chicano literature, see Sheila Marie Contreras, *Blood Lines: Myth, Indigenism, and Chicana/o Literature* (Austin: University of Texas Press, 2008), 78–83. Chicano scholars now treat the period before 1846 more critically, especially regarding Spanish–indigenous interactions. Acuña, for example, has added a chapter about the Spanish conquest of Mexico to *Occupied America.* See Acuña, "The Occupation of Middle America," in *Occupied America: A History of Chicanos,* 7th ed. (New York: Longman, 2007). Brian DeLay presented a fascinating study of violence between indigenous peoples and Mexican settlers in Texas and New Mexico in *War of a Thousand Deserts: Indian Raids and the U.S.–Mexican War* (New Haven: Yale University Press, 2008).

17. Reprinted in Rendón, *Chicano Manifesto,* 336–37.

18. Acuña, *Occupied America,* 7; Nephtalí De León, *Chicanos: Our Background and Our Pride* (Lubbock, Tex.: Trucha Publications, 1972), 25, 31.

19. *Occupied America,* 25; Abiel Abbott Livermore, *The War with Mexico Reviewed* (Boston: American Peace Society, 1850), 126. For contemporary accounts of the artillery duel between Fort Texas and Matamoros, see Napoleon Jackson Tecumseh Dana, *Monterrey Is Ours! The Mexican War Letters of Lieutenant Dana, 1845–1847,* ed. Robert H. Ferrell (Lexington: University Press of Kentucky, 1990), 62; Nathan Covington Brooks, *A Complete History of the Mexican War: Its Causes, Conduct, and Consequences* (Philadelphia: Grigg, Elliot, 1849), 114; Benjamin F. Scribner, *A Campaign in Mexico by "One Who Was Thar"* (Philadelphia: James Gihon, 1850), 30; John R. Kenly, *Memoirs of a Maryland Volunteer: War with Mexico, in the Years 1846–7–8* (Philadelphia: J. B. Lippincott, 1873), 52; Donald S. Frazier, ed., *The United States and Mexico at War: Nineteenth-Century Expansion and Conflict* (New York: Simon and Schuster Macmillan, 1998), s.v. "Matamoros." In a footnote in the seventh edition of *Occupied America* Acuña addressed criticism of his allegation of the "incessant bombing of Matamoros." To support his claim he cited a congratulatory order written on behalf of Zachary Taylor which read, in

part, "The garrison left opposite Matamoros has rendered no less distinguished service, by sustaining a severe cannonade and bombardment for many successive days." In this context, however, "sustaining" meant "withstanding" or "suffering" as in "sustaining an injury." Acuña, *Occupied America*, 56 fn. 51. For the full text of Acuña's citation, see Brooks, *A Complete History of the Mexican War*, 151. Brooks covers the siege of Fort Texas in great detail, see pages 113–22.

20. Acuña, *Occupied America*, 25–27; see also Martínez, *Viva La Raza!*, 64.

21. David F. Gomez, *Somos Chicanos: Strangers in Our Own Land* (Boston: Beacon Press, 1973), 43–45; Martínez, *Viva La Raza!*, 65–67.

22. Ruiz, *South by Southwest*, 100; Nava, *Mexican Americans*, 61; American newspaper reports of President Truman's visit to Chapultepec in 1947 perhaps started the idea that multiple students had committed suicide, see *New York Times*, "Mr. Truman in Chapultepec," March 6, 1947.

23. De León, *Chicanos*, 32–33.

24. Acuña, *Occupied America*, 27–28; Matt S. Meier and Feliciano Rivera, *The Chicanos: A History of the Mexican Americans* (New York: Hill and Wang, 1972), 68–69; Gomez, *Somos Chicanos*, 44; Martínez, *Viva La Raza!*, 67–68.

25. David Sanchez wrote the early history of the organization in *Expedition through Aztlán* (La Puente, Calif.: Perspectiva Publications, 1978).

26. The march was originally limited to California. Inspired by the success of the operation, Sanchez extended the expedition throughout the Southwest. Sanchez, *Expedition*, 15–17, 53–54, 68, 83, 89, 162; "Beret Had Bayonet on Person," *Brownsville Herald*, July 20, 1972.

27. The Brown Berets erected at least seven monuments of various sizes and materials. Sanchez, *Expedition*, 75, 88, 123–24, 131, 136, 159, 160.

28. Ibid., 30, 51–53. Sanchez referred to his comrades as *soldados* (soldiers).

29. Ibid., 95–99.

30. The Thornton Skirmish is also known as the Thornton Affair. The small concrete monument was erected by the Brown Berets in Brownsville. Ibid., 159–60.

31. Sanchez, *Expedition*, 174–75, 180.

32. "Brown Berets Invade," *Dallas Morning News*, September 1, 1972; "Judge Asks Berets to Leave—They Do," *Los Angeles Times*, September 23, 1972; Sanchez, *Expedition*, 173–92.

33. "New Mexicans Thwart Police and Again Claim Forest Lands," *New York Times*, October 23, 1966; "150 Seize a Town in Land Dispute," *New York Times*, June 6, 1967; Library of Congress, "Bill Summary & Status, 94th Congress (1975–1976) S.68, CRS Summary," http://thomas.loc.gov; Richard Griswold del Castillo, *The Treaty of Guadalupe Hidalgo: A Legacy of Conflict* (Norman: University of Oklahoma Press, 1990), 132–38. Tijerina's memoirs of the events are found in Reies López Tijerina, *They Called Me "King Tiger": My Struggle for the Land and Our Rights,* trans. and ed. José Angel Gutiérrez (Houston: Arte Público Press, 2000). For New Mexican resistance to land confiscations in the 1880s and 1890s, see Amanda Taylor-Montoya, "'Under the Same Glorious Flag': Land, Race, and Legitimacy in Territorial New Mexico" (Ph.D. diss., University of Oklahoma, 2009).

34. Rendón, *Chicano Manifesto*, 81–83. For an interesting study on the importance of the document, see the chapter "The Chicano Movement and the Treaty" in Griswold del Castillo, *Treaty*, 131–53.

35. Contreras, *Blood Lines*, 37.

36. National Society of the Sons of the Utah Pioneers, "The Mormon Battalion Monument," Salt Lake City, [1969?], Historical Department of the Church of Jesus Christ of Latter-day Saints (hereafter LDS).

37. "Harold Bingham Lee Dedicatory Prayer—1972," LDS.

38. The Church of Jesus Christ of Latter-day Saints, "Mormon Battalion Memorial Visitors' Center: Commemorating the Longest Infantry March in the United States" (1975), LDS. The archive has copies of this pamphlet in both English and Spanish.

39. "Radio Advertisements—Mormon Battalion Memorial Visitors' Center," LDS.

40. "San Pasqual Battlefield State Historic Park" (undated outline of park history), San Pasqual Battlefield State Historic Park Archives (SPB); Ronald Hinrichs (vice president San Pasqual Battlefield Volunteer Association), interview by the author, San Diego County, Calif., June 10, 2006.

41. Hinrichs, interview; "San Pasqual Battlefield State Historic Park" (undated outline of park history), SPB; Juan F. Perea, ed., *Immigrants Out! The New Nativism and the Anti-Immigrant Impulse in the United States* (New York: New York University Press, 1996), 62–63; Raymond V. Padilla and Rudolfo Chávez Chávez, *The Leaning Ivory Tower: Latino Professors in American Universities* (New York: State University of New York Press, 1995), 169–70.

42. "San Pasqual Battlefield State Historic Park" (undated outline of park history), SPB; "Volunteers Restage Storied Battle of San Pasqual," *San Diego Union*, December 5, 1988; "(Nearly) Hidden History," unidentified newspaper clipping, SPB.

43. "San Pasqual Battlefield State Historic Park" (undated outline of park history), SPB; *San Diego Union*, "Volunteers Restage Stories Battle of San Pasqual," December 5, 1988; Hinrichs, interview; Martha K. Norkunas, *The Politics of Public Memory: Tourism, History, and Ethnicity in Monterey, California* (New York: State University of New York Press, 1993), 108–9.

44. Walter Plitt (Palo Alto National Park Committee founder), interview by the author, May 11, 2006; Pat M. Neff, Walter F. Woodul, and L. W. Kemp, *Monuments Erected by the State of Texas to Commemorate the Centenary of Texas Independence: The Report of the Commission of Control for the Texas Centennial Celebrations* (Austin: Commission of Control for the Texas Centennial Celebrations, 1938).

45. The National Park Service designated a total of nine sites under the theme "The Texas Revolution and the Mexican War." Barry Mackintosh, *The Historic Sites Survey and National Historic Landmarks Program: A History* (Washington: National Park Service, 1985), 33–40; National Park Service, "National Historic Landmarks Survey—Listing of National Historic Landmarks by State," Washington: U.S. Department of Interior, n.d.

46. "7 Historic Texas Sites Recognized Nationally," *Dallas Morning News*, December 20, 1960. Plitt, interview; Murphy, interview.

47. Paul S. Sutter, *Driven Wild: How the Fight against Automobiles Launched the Modern Wilderness Movement* (Seattle: University of Washington Press, 2002), 256–57; National Park Service, "National Park System Areas Listed in Chronological Order of Date Authorized Under DOI" (Washington: National Park Service, 2005); Plitt, interview.

48. Plitt, interview; Murphy, interview.

49. "Ronald Wilson Reagan—Message 1981," LDS.

50. Site examination; Mormon Battalion Association, "Dedication of the Mormon Battalion Monument," www.mormonbattalion.com.

51. The Santa Clara monument was recovered years later in a scrap yard. Information was gathered from site examination and oral history interviews: Tommy Purselley (Los Angeles Junction Railway), interview by author, June 15, 2006; Lori Garcia (Santa Clara Historical and Landmarks Commission), interview by the author, June 28, 2006; Marie Otto (Art History and Landmark Committee of the Native Daughters of the Golden West), interview by the author, July 23, 2006.

52. Mexico's reaction to this development, if any, is unknown. "Illinois Agrees to Loan Out General's Leg," *Bloomington Normal*, May 8, 1976; "Santa Anna's Cork Leg—Loans and Loan Requests," Santa Anna Leg Collateral Files, Illinois State Military Museum (hereafter ISMM); Major General Francis S. Greenlief to General John R. Phipps, October 10, 1978, ISMM; Warren Potash to Major General Harold Holesinger, August 6, 1985, ISMM; Alan Knight, "The Several Legs of Santa Anna: A Saga of Secular Relics," *Past and Present* 206, supplement 5 (2010): 227–55.

53. "Santa Anna Legacy Likely to Remain in State," *State Journal Register*, January 15, 1986.

54. "Santa Anna's Cork Leg—Loans and Loan Requests," ISMM; Andrew L. Payne to Colonel Carl O. Johnson, January 17, 1985, ISMM; Andrew L. Payne to Michael Madigan, January 28, 1986, ISMM; Major General Harold G. Holesinger to Andrew L. Payne, March 14, 1986, ISMM; "Santa Anna Legacy Likely to Remain in State," *State Journal Register*, January 15, 1986.

55. Joanne Forrest (historian and chair of the Restoration Committee, Richard Oglesby Mansion), interview by the author, January 15, 2008; "Santa Anna's Wooden Leg—Provenance Letter by Lynn Potter," Governor Oglesby Mansion; U.S. Congress, "Biographical Directory of the United States Congress—Oglesby, Richard James," http://bioguide.congress.gov.

56. Matthew Frye Jacobson, *Roots Too: White Ethnic Revival in Post–Civil Rights America* (Cambridge: Harvard University Press, 2006), 8–9.

57. An interesting study of Civil War memory and reenactors is Tony Horwitz, *Confederates in the Attic: Dispatches from the Unfinished Civil War* (New York: Vintage Books, 1999).

58. *North and South*, television series. Directed by Richard T. Hefron. American Broadcasting Company, 1985; John Jakes, *North and South* (New York: Harcourt Brace Jovanovich, 1982); Internet Movie Database, *North and South*, www.imdb.

com; Christopher Fischer (Texas-based living historian), interview by the author, June 30, 2007, and additional personal communication.

59. Steven Abolt, interview by the author, April 21, 2009; Richard Bruce Winders (historian and curator of the Alamo), interview by the author, April 22, 2009; Paul Donald Erickson (Colorado-based living historian), interview by the author, April 20, 2009; Fischer, interview.

60. Abolt, interview; Fischer, interview; Robert Moulder (Colorado-based living historian), interview by the author, April 19, 2009.

61. Abolt, interview; Fischer, interview; Erickson, interview; Moulder, interview; Rollie Schafer (Texas-based living historian) interview by the author, April 20, 2009; John Lemons (Colorado-based living historian), interview by the author, April 19, 2009.

62. "Volunteers Restage Storied Battle of San Pasqual," *San Diego Union*, December 5, 1988.

63. Ibid.; Joe Lopez (San Pasqual reenactor), interview by the author, June 10, 2006.

64. Steven R. Butler, interview by the author, Dallas, June 14, 2007; Richard Hoag Breithaupt Jr. (president emeritus, Aztec Club of 1847), interview by the author, April 22, 2009.

65. Jacobson, *Roots Too*, 4.

10. Remembrance and Free Trade

1. "Talking Business with Camacho Gaos, Mexican Official," *New York Times*, June 6, 1989; "Business Forum: Perestroika Goes South," *New York Times*, November 12, 1989; "Mexico Asks for Trade Pact," *New York Times*, May 23, 1990; Dirk W. Raat, *Mexico and the United States: Ambivalent Vistas* (Athens: University of Georgia Press, 1992), 193–95.

2. "Man in the News; An Uncertain Mandate: Ernesto Zedillo Ponce de León," *New York Times*, August 23, 1994; Thomas Benjamin, *La Revolución: Mexico's Great Revolution as Memory, Myth, and History* (Austin: University of Texas Press, 2000), 155; Zedillo currently lives in Connecticut and is the director of the Yale Center for Globalization.

3. *Caudillos* were authoritarian civil–military leaders in Mexico. "Mexicans Look Askance at Textbooks' New Slant," *New York Times*, September 21, 1992; "Reconciling Mexico's Past Entangles Its Present," *New York Times*, August 17, 1997; Emily Hind, "Historical Arguments: Carlos Salinas and Mexican Women Writers," *Discourse* 23, no. 2 (spring 2001): 82–100.

4. "Mexicans Look Askance at Textbooks' New Slant," *New York Times*, September 21, 1992; "Reconciling Mexico's Past Entangles Its Present," *New York Times*, August 17, 1997; Hind, "Historical Arguments," 82–100.

5. Enrique Plasencia de la Parra, "Conmemoración de la hazaña épica de los niños héroes: su origen, desarrollo y simbolismos," *Historia Mexicana* 45, no. 2 (October–December 1995): 274.

6. Ibid., 274–75; Benjamin, *La Revolución,* 155.

7. The coins circulated between 1993 and 1995. "Mexican Graduation Ceremonies Steeped in National Themes," *Houston Chronicle,* October 22, 1993; *Historia Sexto Grado,* 5th printing (Mexico City: Secretaría de Educación Pública, 2001), 36, 38; the video hosting site youtube.com has several videos of these reenactments posted by schools and individuals in Mexico. The variations within the programs demonstrate the autonomy these classes have in creating their versions of the story. Fausta Pilar Cruz Martinez, interview by the author, April 11, 2010. Cruz Martinez attended primary school in Oaxaca and recalled the importance of such displays in the early 1990s.

8. Walter Plitt, interview by the author, May 11, 2006, and additional personal communication; Douglas Murphy (Palo Alto Battlefield National Historic Park historian), interview by the author, May 15, 2006, and additional personal communication.

9. Plitt, interview; Steven R. Butler, interview by the author, June 14, 2007; Clemente Rendón (Matamoros city historian), interview by the author, May 10, 2006.

10. Plitt, interview; Murphy, interview.

11. The interviews are part of a larger study by Antonio N. Zavaleta at the University of Texas at Brownsville. Zavaleta intends to publish his findings from the original forty-six interviews at Brownsville and thirty at Matamoros in an upcoming ethnography. The transcribed interviews are currently in his possession.

12. The individual interviews were conducted by Rodolfo Flores. The transcripts are neither dated nor identified as to location. Additional records show that all interviews were conducted between January and May of 1995. See the following interviews, listed alphabetically in the files: Rudolfo Ruiz Cisneros, Maria Champion Henggler, Miguel Antonio Lopez, and Denise Saenz Blanchard.

13. See interviews with Bruce Ansel Aiken, Louis Raphael Cowan, Betty Pace Dodd, Larry Holzman, Lesley Gene Gloor, and Francis Elizabeth Wagner. Census data for 2000 was retrieved from *Houston Chronicle,* "Databases—Census 2010 in Texas," www.chron.com.

14. See interviews with Manuel Robledo Treviño, Clemente Rendón de la Garza, Antonio Rivera Yzaguirre, and Rosalia Sanchez Cárdenas.

15. See interviews with Manuel Robledo Treviño, Bruce Ansel Aiken, James Anthony John, and Francis Elizabeth Wagner for criticism of reenactments.

16. Sylvia Komatsu, interview by the author, June 28, 2007.

17. Komatsu, interview; Andrea Boardman (Clements Center executive director), interview by the author, June 29, 2007; Rob Tranchin (film producer and screenwriter), interview by the author, June 28, 2007; David Weber (Clements Center director), interview by the author, June 29, 2007; Center for Public Broadcasting, "Public Broadcasting Act of 1967, as amended," www.cpb.org. The board initially consisted of R. David Edmunds (Indiana University), Mario T. García (University of California, Santa Barbara), Deena J. González (Pomona College), Richard Griswold del Castillo (San Diego State University), Sam W. Haynes (University of Texas at Arlington), Robert W. Johannsen (University of Illinois Urbana-Champaign), Robert

Ryal Miller (California State University Hayward), David M. Pletcher (Indiana University), Miguel Soto (Universidad Nacional Autónoma de México), Ron Tyler (University of Texas at Austin), Josefina Zoraida Vázquez (El Colegio de México), Jesús Velasco-Márquez (Instituto Tecnológico Autónomo de México), and David Weber (Southern Methodist University).

18. This statistic is based on a review of books published between 1990 and 2008. For specific titles, see the online selected bibliography for the American monographs surveyed from this era at scholarworks.umass.edu/umpress/. Komatsu, interview; Boardman, interview; Josefina Zoraida Vázquez to the author, May 5, 2009; Miguel Soto to the author, May 6, 2009.

19. Komatsu, interview; Boardman, interview; Tranchin, interview.

20. Including the National Endowment for the Humanities, twenty-one organizations and individuals contributed to the project. For a complete list, see Public Broadcasting Service, "About the Show," www.pbs.org; Komatsu, interview; Andrea Boardman, interview by the author, Dallas, June 29, 2007; Tranchin interview; David Weber, interview by the author, Dallas, June 29, 2007.

21. Raat, *Mexico and the United States,* 200–201; "Tariffs Drop as Trade Agreement Kicks in with New Year's Arrival," *New York Times,* January 1, 1994; "A Promise of Employment Gains Is Not Forgotten," *New York Times,* January 1, 1994.

22. Enrique Krauze, *Mexico: Biography of Power, A History of Modern Mexico, 1810–1996* (New York: Harper Collins, 1997), 790.

23. Ultimately, the United States offered $20 billion in loans. Mexico used only $12.5 billion. "U.S. Is Fearful of Alien Surge," *New York Times,* January 18, 1995; "Aid to Mexico and Immigration Are Linked," *New York Times,* January 26, 1995; "Peso's Plunge May Cost Thousands of U.S. Jobs," *New York Times,* January 30, 1995; "Emergency Power: International Package of Aid Could Reach about $50 Billion," *New York Times,* February 1, 1995; "Two Views of the Peso Bailout: Wall Street vs. Main Street," *New York Times,* February 2, 1995; "Mexico Repays Bailout by U.S. Ahead of Time," *New York Times,* January 16, 1997; Krauze, *Mexico,* 790–92; Raat, *Mexico and the United States,* 203–4.

24. Raat, *Mexico and the United States,* 204; David C. Harper, ed., *2010 North American Coins and Prices: A Guide to U.S., Canadian, and Mexican Coins,* 19th ed. (Iola, Wis.: Krause Publications, 2009), 586–87.

25. The festivities were scheduled five days earlier to accommodate the weekend. "Soldiers Ready to Re-Enact Palo Alto Battle Today," *Brownsville Herald,* May 3, 1996; Butler, interview; Anthony Knopp, interview by the author, May 10, 2006.

26. Murphy, interview; Vázquez to author; "Simposio en Mats. de Guerra Mex.–EU," *Brownsville Herald,* May 8, 1996; "Dictan conferencia sobre el 150 aniversario de la Guerra entre EU y México, *El Bravo,* May 10, 1996; "Mexico Remembers Different Battle," *Brownsville Herald,* May 10, 1996.

27. "Video: Grand Encampment Celebration—1996," Historian's Office of the Church of Jesus Christ of Latter-day Saints (hereafter LDS); reenacting of the Mormon Battalion had grown in popularity since the Sons of Utah Pioneer Mormon Battalion Trek of 1950. John Bascom, interview by the author, September 23, 2008.

Latter-day Saints in Arizona had commemorated the Mormon Battalion as early as 1960, when church-sponsored Troop 34 of the Boy Scouts of America erected a small marker near Sierra Vista. The next year the Church of Jesus Christ of Latter-day Saints held a more modest celebration commemorating the battalion's march through Kern County, California. Gathered at the Fort Tejon State Historic Park north of Los Angeles, church leaders gave sermons and recognized the descendants of members of the battalion who were in the audience. "Video: Commemoration of the Passage of Members of the Mormon Battalion through Kern County," LDS.

28. "Mexico Repays Bailout by U.S. Ahead of Time," *New York Times,* January 16, 1997.

29. On Clinton itinerary: "Mexico City Counterpart of the Alamo," *New York Times,* May 6, 1997; "For Mexicans, Clinton's Visit Is a Serenade," *New York Times,* May 8, 1997; "Olviden Chapultepec," *Reforma,* May 12, 1997; "Countries Share a Mixed Heritage," *San Antonio Express-News,* May 10, 1997. A Freedom of Information Act request turned up no documents at the Clinton Presidential Library related to the president's visit to the monument. Dana Simmons to the author, December 21, 2009.

30. "Monument to War Heroes on Clinton Itinerary," *Fort Worth Star-Telegram,* May 6, 1997; "Clinton Visits Latin America," *Seattle Times,* May 8, 1997.

31. "Clinton Visits Latin America," *Seattle Times,* May 8, 1997.

32. "Organizan 150 Aniversario de Niños Héroes," *El Norte,* May 29, 1997; María Elena Ruiz Cruz, ed., *En defensa de la patria* (Mexico City: Archivo General de la Nación, 1997), introduction, 104–5; Universidad Nacional Autónoma de México, "En Defensa de la Patria, 1847–1997" http://biblioweb.dgsca.unam.mx.

33. Escutia's missing paperwork also proved to be a problem to the anonymous authors of *Chapultepec* (Mexico City: Asociación del Heroico Colegio Militar, 1960), 71. Comisión Organizadora de los Homenajes del CL Aniversario de los Niños Héroes, *Documentos históricos sobre la defensa de Chapultepec, 13 de septiembre de 1847* (Mexico: Archivo General de la Nación, 1997); Instituto Nacional de Estudios Históricos de las Revoluciones de México, "Por el Honor de México," www.inehrm.gob.mx.

34. The large bronze sesquicentennial plaque is installed on one of the convent's exterior walls; Dermot Brangan (Irish ambassador to Mexico), interview by the author, September 12, 2007; St. Patrick's Battalion, "Remembering the Irish Soldiers," http://stpatricksbattalion.org.

35. Banda de Gaitas del Batallón de San Patricio, "History," www.bandadegaitas.com.mx.

36. St. Patrick's Battalion, "Remembering the Irish Soldiers," http://stpatricksbattalion.org; Secretaría de Relaciones Exteriores, "Embajada de México en Irlanda," http://portal.sre.gob.mx.

37. "Tiempos Nuevos," *El Norte,* September 14, 1997.

38. Maria Elena García Muñoz and Ernesto Fritsche Aceves, "Los Niños Héroes, de la realidad al mito" (Thesis, Universidad Nacional Autónoma de México, 1989);

"Organizan 150 Aniversario de Niños Héroes," *El Norte,* May 29, 1997; "Niños Héroes," *Reforma* and *El Norte,* September 12, 1997; "¿Quién Aventó a Juan Escutia?" *La Jornada,* September 13, 1998.

39. Megan Sanborn Jones, "(Re)living the Pioneer Past: Mormon Youth Handcart Trek Re-enactments," *Theatre Topics* 16, no. 2 (2006): 113.

40. Ibid., 113–30; "Trials of the Trail," *San Diego Union-Tribune,* July 15, 2006.

41. Jones, "(Re)living the Pioneer Past," 119–22; "Trials of the Trail," *Pulling Toward Zion,* documentary film. Directed by Tom Michael Perry. Canyon Rim Stake, 2007.

42. Richard Hoag Breithaupt Jr., interview by the author, April 22, 2009.

43. Breithaupt, interview; Richard Hoag Breithaupt Jr., *Aztec Club of 1847: Military Society of the Mexican War, Sesquicentennial History, 1847–1997* (Universal City, Calif.: Walika, 1998), 129.

44. Breithaupt, interview.

45. Breithaupt, interview; Breithaupt, *Aztec Club,* 131–45.

46. Breithaupt, interview.

47. Breithaupt, interview; Breithaupt, *Aztec Club,* 129–61.

48. *The U.S.-Mexican War, 1846–1848,* television series. Directed by Ginny Martin. KERA-TV, 2008; Komatsu, interview; Boardman, interview; Tranchin, interview; Josefina Zoraida Vázquez to the author, May 5, 2009; Miguel Soto to the author, May 6, 2009.

49. Komatsu, interview; Boardman, interview; Tranchin, interview; Josefina Zoraida Vázquez to the author, May 5, 2009; Miguel Soto to the author, May 6, 2009. An in-depth review of the series is in James Yates, "Assessing Television's Version of History: The Mexican-American War and the KERA Documentary Series," in Peter C. Rollins and John E. O'Conner, eds., *Why We Fought: America's Wars in Film and History* (Lexington: University of Kentucky Press, 2008), 77–98.

50. Butler, interview; Komatsu, interview. Steven Ray Butler, "Away O'er the Waves: The Transatlantic Life and Literature of Captain Mayne Reid" (Ph.D. diss., University of Texas at Arlington, 2006). Reid was a Mexican War veteran, but that fact was only a small part of Butler's study.

51. *One Man's Hero,* motion picture. Directed by Lance Hool. Silver Lion Films, 1998; the film did not receive theatrical release until 1999; The Numbers: Box Office Data, Movie Stars, Idle Speculation, "One Man's Hero," www.the-numbers.com; Internet Movie Data Base, "One Man's Hero," www.imdb.com; Oscar Arriola, interviews by the author, September 10, 12, 2007, and additional personal communication.

52. *One Man's Hero,* 1998; for an insightful study of the Irish ethnic revival in the United States, see Matthew Frye Jacobson, *Roots Too: White Ethnic Revival in Post-Civil Rights America* (Cambridge: Harvard University Press, 2006).

53. Various correspondence between William O'Brien and the author; "San Patricios de Arizona Membership Certificate," in the possession of the author (hereafter MSVW); "San Patricios de Arizona News Letter—December 2008," MSVW;

"Mexico's Fighting Irish," *Phoenix New Times,* March 11, 2004; Arizona Highways Online, "The Luck of the Irish-Arizona Cowboy Bill O'Brien," www.arizonahighways.com; "Americans of Irish, Mexican Descent Share Deep Cultural Links," *Houston Chronicle,* March 8, 1998.

54. "Bagpipers Honor 600 Irish Who Fought for Mexico," *USA Today,* March 10, 2008; "Los San Patricios Honored in Mexico," *Arizona Daily Star,* March 16, 2008; Hector de Jesus (superintendant, American Cemetery, ABMC), interview by the author, September 7, 2007. In 2010 the American musician Ry Cooder and the Irish folk music group The Chieftains released an album titled "San Patricio" to honor the battalion. The release of the album prompted a heated political debate on a popular music review website. Amazon.com, "San Patricio Forum."

55. "The Final Shinsult," *King of the Hill* episode SE17, television series. Directed by Jack Dyer, Fox Broadcasting Company, 1998.

56. Richard Schachtsiek (assistant curator, Illinois State Military Museum), interview by the author, January 15, 2008; "Cartoon Show's Focus on Leg Relic Prompts Smiles, Officials Say No Need for Return to Mexico," *St. Louis Post-Dispatch,* March 23, 1998; "Santa Anna's Leg Took a Long Walk," Champaign, Illinois, *News-Gazette,* March 30, 1998; "Pulling Our Leg: King of the Hill Episode Was Just a Joke," Springfield, Illinois, *State Journal-Register,* undated clipping, Santa Anna Leg Collateral File, Illinois State Military Museum.

57. *Su Alteza Serenísima,* motion picture. Directed by Felipe Cazals. Serenísima Films, 2000.

58. *Ravenous,* motion picture. Directed by Antonia Bird. Heyday Films, 1999.

59. Murphy, interview; National Park Service, *General Management Plan—Palo Alto Battlefield National Historic Site—Texas* (Washington: U.S. Department of the Interior, 1998) Palo Alto Battlefield National Historic Park (hereafter PAB).

60. Murphy, interview.

61. Murphy, interview; Community Feedback File, PAB; "Dr. Antonio N. Zavaleta Ethnographic Data File."

62. Murphy, interview; Karen Weaver (National Park Service), interview by the author, May 16, 2006; additional details drawn from site observations.

63. "Register of National Park Visitors, NPS Form 10-144," PAB; Edward Tabor Linenthal, *Sacred Ground: Americans and Their Battlefields* (Urbana: University of Illinois Press, 1991), 1–6.

64. Christopher Fischer (living historian), interview by the author, June 30, 2007, and additional personal communication; Weaver, interview; Rolando Garza (National Park Service), interview by the author, Brownsville, May 16, 2006; Murphy, interview; additional details drawn from site observations.

65. Fischer, interview; Brownsville Independent School District, "Facts and Statistics," http://bisd.us.

66. Smithsonian National Museum of American History, "The Price of Freedom: Americans at War," http://americanhistory.si.edu.

67. "Of Gringos and Old Grudges: This Land Is Their Land," *New York Times,* January 9, 2004.

68. "The U.S. Is Vanquished in a Hostile Environment," *New York Times,* February 11, 2004; ESPN Soccer Net, "U.S. Coach Downplays Unfriendly Crowd," http://soccernet.espn.go.com.

69. "Mexico Hopes Cautiously after Proposal on Migrants," *New York Times,* January 8, 2004; WeHateGringos.com, "Flash Video"; "Deadly Crossing—Underground Network Offers Aid to Illegal Immigrants," *Houston Chronicle,* May 18, 2003; "Chicano Group Says It Is Misunderstood, Students Seek Opportunity, Autonomy," *Houston Chronicle,* March 30, 2002; "Anti-Immigration Forces Warn of Conspiracy to Retake the Southwest," Victoria, Texas, *Victoria Advocate,* September 8, 2008.

70. LA Observed, "John & Ken vs. Tony & Friends," www.laobserved.com; Free Republic, "Mormon Battalion Monument (the True Story vs. the Lies of KTTV Reporter Tony 'Reconquista' Valdez)," www.freerepublic.com; Bascom, interview.

71. *The Mexican-American War,* television program. Directed by Jim Lindsay. Jim Lindsay Productions, 2006; History Channel, "Mexican–American War Boards," http://boards.history.com.

72. "Absolut Vodka Ad Stirs a U.S.–Mexico Debate," *Los Angeles Times,* April 5, 2008; "Absolut Apologizes for Mexican Vodka Ad," *Los Angeles Times,* April 6, 2008.

73. For an example, see the conservative columnist Michelle Malkin, "Absolut Arrogance and the Advertising Agency behind the Reconquista Ad," http://michellemalkin.com; "Absolut Vodka Ad Stirs a U.S.–Mexico Debate," *Los Angeles Times,* April 5, 2008; "Absolut Apologizes for Mexican Vodka Ad," *Los Angeles Times,* April 6, 2008.

74. "Los Narcos, Nuevos Traidores a la Patria, Dice Una Cadete en Homenaje a los Niños Héroes," *La Jornada,* September 14, 2008.

75. This was the first time a female cadet was allowed to speak at the commemoration; "Los Narcos, Nuevos Traidores a la Patria, Dice Una Cadete en Homenaje a los Niños Héroes," *La Jornada,* September 14, 2008; "Pronuncia Discursa por Primera Vez Mujer Cadete," *El Universal,* September 13, 2008; a news segment of the speech is posted at www.youtube.com.

Conclusion

1. Plitt worked with James Mills, an instructor at the University of Texas at Brownsville, on the project. Walter Plitt, telephone interview by the author, May 18, 2009; "Hallan Reliquia de EU en NL," Monterrey, Nuevo León, *El Norte,* December 28, 2008; "Mexican Archeologists Have Found Remains of Four U.S. Soldiers," *American Eagle,* July 2008; Esther Garza to James Mills, August 20, 2008, in possession of James Mills (hereafter JM); James Mills to Congressman Solomon Ortiz, October 16, 2008, JM; Tom Hester to Rolando Garza, October 8, 2003, Palo Alto Battlefield National Historical Park (hereafter PAB); Senator John Cornyn to Frank Yturria, September 25, 2003, PAB; National Park Service memorandum, September 24, 2003, PAB; National Park Service memorandum, September 23, 2003, PAB;

"Historians Want Reburial for 1846 Battle Casualties," *San Antonio Express-News,* May 8, 1996.

2. There is no academic consensus on the differentiation of history and memory. Geoffrey Cubitt wrote that the two are interlocked in an "imagined relationship." He has synthesized the leading theories in *History and Memory* (Manchester, U.K.: Manchester University Press, 2007), 26–65; Pierre Nora argued in his essay "Between Memory and History: Les Lieux de Mémoire" that memory and history are in "fundamental opposition" to each other. His work is translated into English in Geneviéve Fabre and Robert O'Meally, eds., *History and Memory in African-American Culture* (New York: Oxford University Press, 1994), 284–300.

3. For an example, see G. Kurt Piehler, *Remembering War the American Way* (Washington: Smithsonian Institution Press, 1995), 8.

4. Nachman Ben-Yahuda, *The Masada Myth: Collective Memory and Mythmaking in Israel* (Madison: University of Wisconsin Press, 1995); Richard R. Flores, *Remembering the Alamo: Memory, Modernity, and the Master Symbol* (Austin: University of Texas Press, 2002); Jim Weeks, *Gettysburg: Memory, Market, and an American Shrine* (Princeton: Princeton University Press, 2003); Tony Horwitz, *Confederates in the Attic: Dispatches from the Unfinished Civil War* (New York: Vintage Books, 1999); Takashi Yoshida, *The Making of the "Rape of Nanking": History and Memory in Japan, China, and the United States* (New York: Oxford University Press, 2006). The historian of Mexico Timothy J. Henderson, coined this apt term for the U.S.–Mexican War for the title of his book *A Glorious Defeat: Mexico and Its War with the United States* (New York: Hill and Wang, 2007).

5. Instituto Nacional de Estudios Históricos de las Revoluciones de México, "Por el Honor de México," www.inehrm.gob.mx.

6. Josefina Zoraida Vázquez to the author, May 7, 2009.

7. José Ángel Gutiérrez, interview by Manuel Medrano, May 1, 2009.

8. Douglas A. Murphy to the author, May 13, 2009.

INDEX

Abolt, Steven, 211
Absolut vodka, 237–38
Acción Agraria de la Confederación
    Nacional de Campesina, 182–83
Acuña, Rodolfo, 196–99, 285n83
Aiken, Bruce, 218
Alamo, 5, 83, 158, 167–72, 209–10, 219,
    243
The Alamo (motion picture), 171
Albright, Madeline, 228
Alemán Valdes, Miguel, 142–44, 148–52,
    163–65
La Alianza Federal de Mercedes Libres, 202
Allen, Merton C., 110
*Alphabetical and Chronological Catalogue
    of the Feats of Arms That Have Taken
    Place in the Mexican Republic from
    Independence to the Present Time*
    (Echenique), 93
Alta California (Mexican territory), 3, 44,
    46, 103–6, 201. *See also* California
Altar to the Fatherland (Chapultepec), 53,
    143, 147, 179–80, 244; commemorations,
    174–75, 182–83, 223–24, 226–28, 238;
    dedication, 151–52
Amaro, Joaquín, 133
American Battle Monuments Commission,
    163
American Council on Education, Committee
    on the Study of Teaching Materials on
    Inter-American Subjects, 158–59
The American Invasion, 1846 to 1848
    (Balbontín), 93–94
American Legion, 163–64
American Museum, 6, 26
American Peace Society, 12–13
Americanization School, 120
amnesia, historical, 5–6, 242–43, 245
Anaya, Pedro María de, 137, 139
Anderson, Robert, 25–26

"The Angels of Monterey" (poem), 19–20
Anglo-Saxonism, 104–8, 113, 120–21,
    124–27
An Gorta Mór Monument (Phoenix), 231
*Appeal to the Good Judgment of Natives
    and Foreigners* (Santa Anna), 43
Appomattox Courthouse (Virginia), 39
Aragón Echegaray, Enrique, 143, 151
Arbenz, Jacobo, 167
Arista, Mariano, 3, 47, 192
The Army and Navy of America (Neff), 70
Army of the North, 3
Arriola, Oscar, 180
Artillery, U.S., 25
Artillery School of Mexico, 53
Asociación del Colegio Militar: archives,
    276n61; challenges, 100, 143; commemo-
    rations, 85–90, 131–32; founding, 80, 85
Asociación de Defensores de la República
    Mexicana de 1836 a 1848, 91–92, 112
Associated Veterans of the Mexican War, 77,
    79, 103–7, 111, 280n34
Association of Limb Manufacturers, 158
Association of the Soldiers of the Mexican
    War of the State of Texas, 79
Ateneo de la Juventud, 128
Austin, Stephen F., 177
Avalon (California), 202
Averill, Charles A., 16, 20
Ávila Camacho, Manuel, 138–41, 157–58
Ayer, Washington, 104, 110
Aztec Calendar Stone, 25–26
Aztec Club of 1847, 38–39, 78–79, 114,
    117, 270n68; as a heritage society, 79,
    212; monument, 119; revival, 228–29
Aztlán, 197, 200
Azueta, José, 98–99, 181

Badger, Charles Johnson, 114
Baer, Delal, 224

Balbontín, Manuel, 93–94
Balderas, Lucas, 55, 263n42
"The Ballad of Davy Crocket" (song), 167
Ballentine, George, 15
Bancroft, Hubert Howe, 108–11, 207, 280n31
Banda de Gaitas del Batallón de San Patricio (musical group), 226
Barnum, P. T., 6, 26
Barrera, Juan de la, 87–89, 225
Bastin, Ferdinand, 51
Batallón de San Blas, 87, 134, 141, 151, 199–200, 225, 244
Batallón de San Patricio: commemoration, 142, 175–77, 225–26, 230–31; diplomacy, 176–77, 225–26; execution of, 87; monument, 176; mythologizing, 177, 187–88, 230–31; service in war, 54, 229. See also Churubusco: Battle of; One Man's Hero
Batallón Independencia, 55
"The Battle of Buena Vista" (song), 70
The Battle of Chapultepec (painting), 19
battlefield tourism, 21–24, 27
battlefields. See specific names of battles
Battles of the Republic (Harrison), 14
El Batallón de San Patricio (Cox), 176
El Batallón de San Patricio (motion picture). See One Man's Hero
Bauer, K. Jack, 194
Bear Flag Revolt, 103, 109–10; monuments, 118, 121, 298n61
Beeson, Henry, 103
Belknap, William Worth, 61, 65
Bentsen, Lloyd, Jr., 217
Bent's Old Fort (Colorado), 211
Beteta, Ramón, 144
Bierce, Ambrose, 109
Bill, Alfred H., 161–62
Bin Laden, Osama, 2, 236
Blaine, James G., 74
Blake, Jacob Edmund, 30–31
Blazing the Trails West (comic book), 168
Blight, David W., 73, 272n19
"The Blue and the Gray" (poem), 72–73
Bolaños, Alejandro, 224
Bonfil, Alfredo, V., 182–83
Boston, 9, 32
Boston Atlas, 18
Boy Heroes. See Niños Héroes
"The Boy Heroes: From the Reality to the Myth" (García and Fritsche), 227
Bracero Agreement, 140, 157

Brackett, Albert, 14
El Brazito, Battle of, 24, 36
Breckinridge, John C., 31–32
Brennan, Bernard, 231
Breithaupt, Richard Hoag, Jr., 228–29
Brief History of the War with the United States (Valadés), 142
A Brief Review of the Career, Character and Campaigns of Zachary Taylor, 11
Brooke, Walter, 206
Brother Jonathan, 17
Brown, John, 10
Brown, John H., 31
Brown Berets, 200–202
Browne, Thomas, 76–77
Brownsville (Texas), 3, 37, 118, 164, 206, 217–19, 222, 235
Bucareli Accords, 132, 135; repudiation of, 135–36, 138, 140
Buckner, William F. T., 127
Buena Vista: battlefield, 22–23, 111–12; Battle of (La Angostura), 11, 13, 17, 24–25, 28, 39, 70, 176, 179, 189; bodies recovered, 31–32; Mexican perspective, 47, 189–90; namesakes, 35–37; trophies taken, 53, 164
Buena Vista (Kentucky), 37
Bureau of Pensions, 64, 68, 71
Burr, Daniel Gould, 101
Bush, George H. W., 190, 217, 239
Bush, George W., 236–37
Butler, James Davie, 33
Butler, Steven R., 212, 217, 222, 230

Caccia, Eduardo, 238
Calderón, Felipe, 238
California, 103–11, 121, 155–56, 169–71, 196, 199–202, 205–6; centennial, 166–67; Chicano activism, 201–2. See also Alta California
California Gold Rush, 123
California Landmarks League, 121
California State Landmark Commission, 170
California State Park Commission, 171
Californios, 103–4, 170, 196, 199, 205, 212
Calles, Plutarco Elías, 132–33
Camargo (Tamaulipas), 38
Cano, Juan, 49, 55
Capitol, U.S., 19, 65, 114
Cárdenas, Lázaro, 134–38, 145, 173
Carleton, James Henry, 13–14, 22
Carlton, Mattie, 117
Carothers, A. G., 64–65

Carranza, Emilio, 163
Carranza, Venustiano, 99–100, 128, 133
Carroll, Tom, 217, 219, 233–34
Casares, Sylvia, 186
Castillo Nájera, Francisco, 142
Castillo Negrete, Emilio de, 87, 93
Castro Cancio, Jorge de, 135
Catholic Church: clergy, 129–30, 135;
    commemorations, 176–77; co-opting
    authority, 82–83, 97, 143, 146–47, 185,
    244; criticism, 126; secularization, 82–83,
    86
caudillos, 6, 133, 215
Caughey, John Walton, 196
Cazares, Anselmo, 2
El Cementerio de las Águilas (motion
    picture), 136–38
cemeteries: for U.S. soldiers, 30–36, 55–56,
    64–65, 80, 240
cenotaphs, 34, 85, 143, 258n84
centennial anniversary of the war: Mexico,
    142–50; U.S., 159–61
Centennial of Good Will (Santa Fe), 161
Central Intelligence Agency, 185
Ceralvo (Kentucky), 38
Cerralvo (Nuevo León), 38
Cerro Gordo: Battle of, 25–26, 50–51, 53,
    101, 176, 232; namesakes, 35–36
Chamberlain, Samuel E., 199
El Chamizal (Texas and Chihuahua), 172–73
Champion Henggler, Maria, 218
Chapultepec: Battle of, 19, 32, 47–49,
    87–88, 136–38, 179, 184, 188, 225,
    243–44; centennial, 147–49; commemora-
    tions, 49, 57, 81–92, 95–99, 128–29,
    131–35, 139–44, 147–49; mural, 181;
    reenactments, 216. See also Altar to the
    Fatherland; Niños Héroes; Obelisco a los
    Niños Héroes y al Honor Militar
Chapultepec (Teja Zabre), 136
Chapultepec in the War with the United
    States, 143
Charleston (South Carolina), 29–30
Chicano Manifesto (Rendón), 197, 203
Chicanos, 168, 243, 245; activism, 200–203,
    236–37, civil rights movement, 186–88,
    193, 195–203; genesis, 197–98; immigrant
    rights, 217, 236–38; scholars, 195–200,
    220
Chicanos: Our Background and Our Pride
    (De León), 198–200
Chidsey, Donald Barr, 193
The Chieftans (musical group), 312n54

Children of the American Revolution,
    160–61
China, 164, 186
Church of Jesus Christ of Latter-day Saints,
    6, 122–24, 156, 165–67, 169, 203–5,
    207–8, 223–28, 237. See also Mormon
    Battalion; Utah
Churubusco: Battle of, 39, 54, 60, 139, 179,
    211; centennial, 147; commemorations,
    54–56, 82–84, 97, 137, 225–26; museum,
    188–89; namesakes, 36–37; pilgrimage site,
    180, 231. See also Batallón de San Patricio
Churubusco (Indiana), 37
Cinco de Mayo (Battle of Puebla), 58
civil rights movement, 168, 193, 196. See
    also Chicanos
Civil War, 25, 27, 29, 39, 62, 113, 166, 236,
    242; battlefields, 170–71, 206–7;
    centennial, 170–71; Confederate veterans,
    67–71, 73, 79, 113, 115; overshadowing
    U.S.–Mexican War, 5, 63, 77; reconcilia-
    tion, 72–73, 77–79, 112–13; reenactments,
    210–11, 219; Union veterans, 65, 67,
    73–79, 104, 111
Clark, Meriwether Lewis, 24
Clay, Henry, Jr., 17
Clay County (Missouri), 122
Clayton, Powell, 90–91
Clements Center for Southwest Studies
    (Southern Methodist University), 219–20
Cleveland, Grover, 78
Clinton, Bill, 221–24, 229
Cochrane, Richard, 31
Cold War, 142–45, 162, 164–65, 173,
    186–87
collective memory. See memory
Colorful Album of the Mexican Republic
    (Michaud y Thomas), 51
Colosio, Luis, 221
Columbia (South Carolina), 29–30, 39
Columbus (New Mexico), 99
Comargo (Ohio), 38
comic books, 168–69, 179, 184, 187–88
Comisión Méxicano-Norteamerica de
    Defensa Conjunto. See Mexican-American
    Joint Defense Commission
Comisión Nacional de los Libros de Texto
    Gratuitos, 178–80, 215–16, 221
Comisión Organizadora de los Homenajes
    del CL Aniversario de los Niños Héroes,
    224–25
Comité Nacional Pro-Conmemoración
    Héroes 1846–1847, 142, 151

Committee on Invalid Pensions, 68
Committee on the Study of Teaching
    Materials on Inter-American Subjects
    (American Council on Education), 158–59
Communist Party, U.S., 165
Comonfort, Ignacio, 49–50, 56
The Compact History of the United States
    Army (Dupuy), 193
Compendium of Mexican History (Toro),
    130–31
Connally, Tom, 164
Congress, Mexican, 45, 54, 57, 165, 174,
    182, 214, 226
Congress, U.S., 110, 233; awards to officers,
    29; criticism, 9, 19; laws regarding Mexico,
    164; pension fight, 63–64, 66–78, 115–16
Conner, Seymour V., 161
Consejo Nacional de Huelga, 183–84
Constitution, U.S., 204
Contreras, Battle of, 36, 50
Cooder, Ry, 312n54
Cope, William, 172
Corbin, Alexander, 27
Corporation for Public Broadcasting, 219
Corpus Christi (Texas), 217
El Correo de México, 84
corridos, 52, 260n3
Cortina, Juan, 201
Council Bluffs (Iowa), 122
Covandonga, Spain, 86
Cox, Patricia, 176
Coyoacán (Mexico City), 147
Craven, William A., 205
Crescencio Rejón, Manuel, 44
Crockett, Davy, 167, 210; Crocketmania,
    167–69
Cuba, 10, 90, 171, 187
Cuéllar, José Tomás de, 84, 89
Cueva, Ben, 212
Cumplido, Ignacio, 51
currency, 189, 216
Currier, Nathaniel, 17, 51

Daily Picayune, 22
Dallas Morning News, 103, 160, 165, 172,
    212
Dames of 1846, 115–19
Daniel, Price, 171
Daniels, Josephus, 154
Daughters of the American Revolution
    (DAR), 117, 119–21, 160–61, 201, 205,
    283n64, 293n7
Daughters of the Mormon Battalion, 123

Davis, Jefferson, 28, 67–68, 70, 113
Davis, Varina Howell, 28
Davy Crockett, King of the Wild Frontier
    (television series), 167
Década Perdida, 189–90
Declaration of Independence, 204
The Definitive Failure of the Supreme
    Tribunal of War, 47
De León, Nephtalí, 198–200
Democratic Party, 33–34, 116, 171–72;
    criticism of, 10–11, 60, 194; support of
    Mexican Pension Bill, 68–78
The Democratic Text Book, 11
Denver, James W., 62–63, 65, 68
Department of Defense, 164
Descendants of Mexican War Veterans, 212,
    217, 222, 230
Detail of the Operations That Occurred in
    the Defense of the Capital of the Republic
    (Rangel), 56
Detail of the Operations That Occurred in
    the Defense of the Capital of the Republic
    (Santa Anna), 42
Deuell, Benjamin, 103
Díaz, Porfirio: and Boy Heroes, 89–91,
    95–96; at Chapultepec, 84–86, 95–96; at
    Churubusco, 56; modernization plans,
    94–95; president, 84, 93–95; rehabilita-
    tion, 215, 272n16; and veterans, 91
Díaz de la Vega, Rómulo, 42–43
Díaz Ordaz, Gustavo, 181–84
diplomacy. See U.S.–Mexican diplomacy
Dissent in Three American Wars (Morrison,
    Merk, and Freidel), 194
Dominguez, Juan, 224
Dominguez Ranch, Battle of, 103–4, 293n6
Doniphan, Alexander, 122–23
Dragoons, U.S., 22, 26–27, 60, 169, 181
drug trafficking, 223, 238
Dubin, Daniel Dultzin, 226
Dupuy, Ernest R., 193
Durbin, Richard J., 232

Eastford (Connecticut), 65–66
Echenique, Rafael, 93
Echeverría, Concepción, 95
Echeverría, Luis, 186
economic nationalism, 186
Edgar, Owen Thomas, 127
Edmonds, David, 223
Eight Dollars a Day (song), 19
Eisenhower, Dwight D., 167
Eisenhower, John S. D., 5

El Brazito, Battle of, 24, 36
El Chamizal (Texas and Chihuahua), 172–73
El Moviemiento. *See* Chicanos
El Paso (Texas), 172
elections (Mexico): of 1940, 139; of 1952, 151
elections (U.S.): of 1848, 10–11, 19; of 1852, 29; of 1856, 37; of 1880, 73–74; of 1884, 74
Enola Gay, 5, 218
Epic (comic book), 184
The Epic of America (Adams), 158
The Epic Tragedy of Chapultepec, 143
Episodes of the Mexican Military (Frías), 189–90
Escondido (California), 205–6, 212; Chamber of Commerce, 205
Escutia, Juan, 87–89, 134, 137, 180–81, 225, 244, 273n23, 273–74n24, 310n33
Eureka Association of Mexican War Veterans, 79
Eureka Typographical Union, 61
Evans, Sam, 113
Excelsior, 148, 182
Executive Order 9873, 163
ex voto, 51–52

Faesler, Julio, 224
Fairbanks, Avard, 166
Fairbanks, Cornelia Cole, 120
Faulk, Odie B., 161
Federal Bureau of Investigations, 139
Fighting in Mexico (Ladd), 70
films. *See* motion pictures
Finch, F. M., 72–73
First National Chicano Liberation Youth Conference (Denver), 198
Fischer, Christopher, 235
Fletcher, Frank F., 98
Flores García, Gabriel, 181
Flores-Staples, Aurora, 234–35
Foley, Martin, 176–77
Ford, Gerald, 194
Formby, Marshall, 171
Fort Brown (Texas), 3, 31, 37, 119, 171, 188, 198, 303–4n19; monuments, 155, 222; preservation of, 206
Fort Casa Mata (Matamoros), 188
Fort Leavenworth (Kansas), 207–8
Fort Moore Pioneer Monument, 169
Fort Polk (Texas), 24, 26
Fort Scott (Kansas), 211
Fort Tejon Historic Park, 309–10n27

Fort Texas. *See* Fort Brown
Fort Titus, Battle of, 25
Fort Worth (Texas), 37, 115, 209
Frankfort (Kentucky), 31–32
Free Soil Party, 19, 34
Freemasons, 104
Freidel, Frank, 194
Fremont, John C., 29, 37, 44–45, 103, 109
French Intervention in Mexico, 50, 53, 58, 81
Frías, Heriberto, 189
Frías y Soto, Hilarión, 83, 88
Fritsche Aceves, Ernesto, 227
Frontera, José, 55
Frost, John, 18
Fuentes Díaz, Vicente, 142
funerals, 30–34, 55

Gamboa, Ramón, 43, 45, 49
Garay, Francisco, 42–43
García Cuéllar, Samuel, 96
García Muñoz, María Elena, 227
García Zamora, Adolfo, 184
Garfield, James, 73–74
Garita de Belén (lithograph), 51
Garner, John Nance, 114
Garza, Ramón, 144
Gaxiola, Francisco Javier, 87
George, Isaac, 111–12
Germany, 139–40, 157, 198
Gesford, Henry C., 113
La Gesta Heroica de 1847 (mural), 181
Gettysburg, Battle of, 243
Gibson, George Rutledge, 23
Giddings, Luther, 15, 21
Glassberg, David, 30
Goliad (Texas), 22
Gomez, Juan, 144
Gomez, Manuel, 194–95
Goode, John, 70
Good Neighbor Policy, 154, 157–59, 167
González, Diego, 236
González, Thelma, 184–85
González Bocanegra, Francisco, 2, 52
Governor Olgesby Mansion (Decatur), 209
Gramm, Phil, 209
Grand Army of the Republic, 76, 78, 90, 111
Grant, Heber J., 156, 165
Grant, Ulysses S.: advocate for veterans, 63–64, 66, 78, 92; attitudes about U.S.–Mexican War, 59–60, 77, 109, 198–99; memoir, 59–60, 77; service in Mexico, 59

Graves, Dicie May, 106, 278n. 20
Great Depression, 153–56
The Great Plunder (Medina), 185
Greenberg, Amy S., 15–16
Gregory, Thomas B., 125
Grindall, John J., 70
Group of Patriotic Gratitude, 97
Guadalajara (Jalisco), 1, 149, 236
Guadalupe, Our Lady of, 149, 288n24, 291n60
Guadalupe Club of 1848, 117
Gual Vidal, Manuel, 151
Gutiérrez, José Ángel, 245

Haile, Christopher, 22
Haislip, Wade H., 150, 165
Halbwachs, Maurice, 4
Hancock, Winfield Scott, 73–74
Hardin, John J., 25
Harper's Weekly, 27
Harrison, Henry, 14
He Died for the Fatherland: The Boy Heroes of Chapultepec (screenplay), 136
Headly, J. T., 12
Herald of Freedom, 25
Here Come the Northerners (comic book), 187, 190
Heredia, Joaquín, 50
heritage societies, 103–4, 108–11, 113, 115–23, 212, 228–29, 231, 241
Hermanos Tangassi, 56
Hernández Dorantes, Saúl, 182
Hernández y Ayllón, Santiago, 51
Herrera, José Joaquín de, 42–43, 54–55
Herrera Serna, Laura, 229
Hewitt, J. W., 19–20
Hidalgo y Castilla, Miguel, 95, 97, 216
Hill, Ricardo, 153
Hilton, William H., 114
Hinckley, Gordon B., 223
His Most Serene Highness. See Su Alteza Serenísima
Historic Sites Act, 155
Historical Documents of the Defense of Chapultepec, 225
Historical Landmarks Committee, 121
Historical Society of New Mexico, 160
Historical Summary of the Most Notable Deeds of the York, Scotch and Santanista Parties in Mexico (Lara), 43, 47
historiography: Mexico, 41–50, 92–95, 129–36, 141–43, 178–81, 185–90, 216–25; U.S., 11–17, 59, 70, 80, 108–11,

124–27, 158–59, 161–62, 168–69, 194–200, 220, 252n28
History and Civics, 179
History Channel, 237
History of the Fatherland (Castro Cancio), 135
History of the Mexican War (Wilcox), 80
History of the United States Cavalry (Brackett), 14
History of the War between the United States and Mexico (Jenkins), 15
Hoar, George Frisbee, 74–75, 77
Hofstadter, Richard, 108
Hool, Lance, 230
Hoover, Herbert, 153–54
Hopkins, Frederick, W., 33
Horner, Henry, 157–58
House Committee on Pensions, 116
How We Robbed Mexico in 1848 (Howe), 125
Howard, Richard, 127
Howe, Robert H., 125
Howell, Charles, 164
Howell, William C., 79
Huerta, Adolfo de la, 132–33
Huerta, José Victoriano, 97–99
Huntington, Collis P. 108
Huntington, Henry, 108
Hutchinson, Jesse, Jr., 19
Hutchinson Family Singers, 19

Ibarra, Domingo, 94
Illinois, 26, 36, 122, 157–58, 210, 232
Illinois National Guard, 158, 208–10
Illinois Military and Naval Department, 157–58
Illinois State Military Museum, 232
Illinois Volunteers, 25–26, 101, 209, 232
The Illustrated Story of the Marines (comic book), 168–69
immigrants, 120; Chinese, 107, 153, 278–79n22, 283n67; illegal, 167, 187, 190, 200–203, 222–23, 236–38; Japanese, 107, 153; Mexican, 107, 153–54, 158, 167
Immigration and Naturalization Services, 153, 167
imperialism, 101, 124–27, 154, 193
Import Substitution Industrialization, 175
Impugnation of the Report of General Santa Anna (Gamboa), 43, 45, 49
In Defense of the Fatherland, 225
Indiana Volunteers, 28, 34–35

Ingalls, John, 77
Instituto Nacional de Antropología e
    Historia (INAH), 188
Instituto Nacional de Estudios Históricos de
    las Revoluciones de México, 244
Inter-American Treaty of Reciprocal
    Assistance, 162
International Monetary Fund, 222
Invasion of the North Americans in Mexico
    (Castillo), 93
Irish-Americans, 231
Irish Cultural Center (Phoenix), 231
Irish-Mexicans, 175–77, 225–26

J., Mrs. John, 117–18
Jakarta (Indonesia), 171
Jakes, John, 210
Jay, William, 13, 15
Jenkins, John, 15
Johannsen, Robert W., 250n20, 251n8
Johnson, Lyndon B., 172–73, 194
Jones, J. Harry, 148
Joyce, Charles, 69–70
Juárez, Benito, 50, 56, 58, 81–82, 85
*Judgment of the Commission of the
    Chamber of Senators,* 44–45

Kammen, Michael, 4
Kearney, Stephen Watts, 120, 160–61, 201,
    206; exhibition, 160; monument, 120, 161
Kenaday, Alexander M., 61–64, 66–78, 80,
    104, 111
Kendall, George Wilkins, 18
Kennedy, John F., 171–72
Kennedy, Robert F., 171–72
Kent State University, 185
Kentucky, 31, 36–37, 66
Kentucky Volunteers, 22, 32
KERA-TV (Dallas), 219–21, 223, 230, 236
KFI Radio (Los Angeles), 237
King, John Alsop, 34
King of the Hill (television series), 232
Kit Carson National Forest, 202
Komatsu, Sylvia, 219–21, 230
Korea, 165
KTTV (Los Angeles), 237
Ku Klux Klan, 120–21, 283n66

La Angostura, Battle of. *See* Buena Vista:
    Battle of
La Mesa: Battle of, 103–4; monument, 121,
    208
La Mesilla (Arizona), 189

Ladd, Horatio O., 70
Lama Rojas, José Antonio de la, 140–41
Lara, Mariano Aniceto de, 43, 47
Las Vegas (New Mexico), 201
Latin American intervention, 98–99, 124–25,
    167
Lawrence (Kansas): sacking of, 25
Laybourn, William E., 211
Lee, Harold B., 204
Lee, Robert E., 39
"The Leg I Left Behind Me" (song), 26
León de la Barra, Francisco, 96
León Toral, José de, 133
Lerdo de Tejada, Sebastián, 56, 82, 85
Life and Services of General Winfield Scott
    (Mansfield), 131
The Life of a Glorious Institution (Torrea),
    133–34, 137–38
Limón, Gilberto R., 146–47
Lincoln, Abraham, 194, 209, 251n11
Lincoln, George, 32
Lipset, Seymour Martin, 194
lithography, 17–19, 50–51, 253n29
Livermore, Abiel Abbott, 12–13
living history, 210–12, 223, 235
Lloyd, David W., 21
Logan, John A., 64
Lopez, Miguel Antonio, 218
Lopez Elizondo, Daniel, 234
López Mateos, Adolfo, 172, 175, 178
López y Rivas, Gilberto, 187
Los Angeles (California), 108, 122, 153, 166,
    169, 199, 237
Lost Cause, 5, 83, 211, 243
Loudenslager, Henry C., 116
Louisiana Associated Veterans of the
    Mexican War, 67
Louisiana Purchase Exposition, 112–13
Louisville (Kentucky), 66
Luelmo, Julio, 142
Lujan, Manuel, 161
Luttrell, John, 68
Lyon, Nathaniel, 65–66

MacArthur, Douglas, 165
Madero, Francisco I., 96–97, 133
Magee, R., 17
"The Maid of Monterey" (song), 19–20
Malkin, Elizabeth, 2
Manero, Vicente E., 91
Mangino, C. Manuel, 91
Manifest Destiny, 10, 13, 44, 105, 123, 188,
    195–96, 205, 211, 233–34

Manifestación del Silencio, 183
Manifesto of the Municipal Government of the Inhabitants of the Capital, 45
Mansfield, Edward O., 131
Marcha de la Reconquista, 200–201, 304n26
Marine Corps, U.S., 29, 104–5
Márquez, Francisco, 87–89
Martínez Manguía, Ingrid Berenice, 238–39
Martinez, Ruben, 234
Martino, Íñigo de, 136
Masada, 243
Matamoros (Tamaulipas), 188, 192, 198, 217–19, 233–34; occupation, 60, 122; siege, 3
Matteson, T. H., 17
Maximilian of Habsburg, 50, 81, 185
McAllister, A. A., 104–5
McKinley, William, 111
McWilliams, Carey, 121
medals: Mexico, 54, 134, 177, 263n38; U.S., 29–30, 66, 266–67n24, 270n68
Medina Castro, Manuel, 185
Melgar, Agustín, 49, 87–89, 134, 136–38
Melodeon Theater (Boston), 9
Memorial in Remembrance of the Mexicans That Died in the War against the North Americans in the Years 1836 to 1848 (Ibarra), 94
Memorial of the Military Evacuation of the Port of Tampico, Tamulipas (Parrodi), 42
Memories of the North American Invasion, 1846–1848 (Roa Bárcena), 93–94
memory (group), 4, 6, 210, 215, 234, 241, 248n13
memory (individual), 4, 215, 241, 248n13
memory (public), 4–5, 10, 248n13; in Mexico, 136, 175, 191, 214, 221, 242–44; in U.S., 215, 217, 234, 243, 245
memory: battlefields, 5; capitalism of, 243; defeat, 5–6, 47–48, 149–50, 241, 243; relationship to history, 240–41, 314n2; of war, 5
Mendez, H., 50–51
Merk, Frederick, 194
Mesa (Arizona), 166
Metropolitan Fair, 27
Mexican American Charro Riders Association, 212
Mexican-American Joint Defense Commission, 140, 157
The Mexican American War (television program), 237

Mexican American Youth Organization, 245
Mexican Americans (Nava), 195, 199
The Mexican Fatherland: Elements of National History (Torres), 130
Mexican Miracle, 175, 186
Mexican Pension Bill, 63–64, 66–78
Mexican Peso Crisis, 221–23; U.S. bailout, 221–24
Mexican Revolution, 95–101, 121, 124–28, 175, 178, 244–45
The Mexican War, 1846–1848 (Bauer), 194
Mexican War of Independence, 86, 95, 175, 178, 216, 245
Mexican War Survivors Act, 78
El Mexicano, 99
"Mexicanos al grito de guerra" (song), 1, 52–53, 178–79
Mexicans: effacing history of, 103–5, 121, 123, 169; racism toward, 14–16, 20, 120–27, 186–87; U.S. relations gendered, 16; women, 16, 19–20, 126
"Mexicans at the Cry of War" (religious tract), 149
"Mexicans at the Cry of War" (song). See "Mexicanos al grito de guerra"
Mexico 68 student movement, 175, 181–85
Mexico and the United States (Starr), 125
Mexico City: Americans living in, 90; Aztec Club visit, 228–29; Clinton visit, 223–23; commemorations, 143–49; Truman visit, 143–45, 162–63; U.S. occupation, 1, 18, 38, 45. See also Chapultepec
Mexico City National Cemetery, 35, 90, 163, 231
Michaud y Thomas, Julio, 51
Michigan State Association of Mexican Veterans, 79
Military College, 48–49, 55, 81, 84–90, 96, 130, 133, 162–63, 184; anniversary, 132; commemorations, 5, 175, 224–25, 238; Mexican Revolution, 96, 100. See also Asociación del Colegio Militar
The Military College and the Defense of Chapultepec in September of 1847, 143
The Military College: To the Eternal Memory of Your Heroes, 95
Miller, Henry, 108
Miller, Larry L., 38
Miller, Robert Ryal, 177
miscegenation: Anglo fear of, 20, 106–7; as acceptable, 16, 107
Mississippi Volunteers, 28, 70
Missouri History Museum, 255n53

Missouri-Mormon War of 1838, 122
Missouri Volunteers, 24–25, 102, 122–23; monument, 122
Moctezuma I, 85, 272n13
Molino, Ignacio, 89
Molino del Rey: Battle of, 15, 56, 177, 179; commemorations, 81–82, 85–86, 92, 142; monument, 56, 264n46
Monadnock, U.S.S., 104–5
Montemayor, García, Felipe, 146
Monterey (California), 77, 103–5, 108, 110, 199, 201; Old Customhouse, 104–5, 121, 155, 206; Sloat Monument, 113–14, 118–19
Monterey County Historical Society, 170
Monterrey (Nuevo León), 184–85; Battle of, 3, 10, 176; namesakes, 36; U.S. cemetery, 64–65, 240
Montes de Oca, Fernando, 49, 87–89
Montezuma Club, 39
monuments, 63, 65–66, 118–24; antebellum, 30–31, 34; Chicanos, 200–201; failure to erect, 24, 65, 80, 118–19; in Mexico, 56, 85, 129, 131, 185; twentieth-century movement, 101, 118–24, 155–56, 163, 165–67, 169–70. *See also* names of specific monuments
Moore, Walter B., 172
Morales, Francisco César, 132–33
Morgan, John Tyler, 75–76
Mormon Battalion, 102, 122–24, 237; commemorations, 165–67, 223, 227, 309–10n27; Memorial Visitors' Center, 203–5; monuments, 123–24, 156, 169, 203–4, 207–8, 223, 309–10n27
Mormon Handcart Trek, 227–28
Mormon Handcart Visitors' Center at Martin's Cove (Wyoming), 227
Morris, Henry Hutchins, 124–25
Morrison, Samuel Eliot, 194
motion pictures, 136–38, 169, 196, 230–33
Moyano Pahissa, Ángela, 186–87
Mule Hill, Battle of, 293n6
Muñoz Ledo, Porfirio, 226
Murdock, Mary Moore, 111, 115–18, 280n34, 281n49, 282n54
Murphy, Douglas A., 233–34, 245, 258n86, 292n66
Muse, E. B., 113
Museo Nacional de Historia (Chapultepec), 51, 134, 141, 147–48, 151, 185, 209
Museo Nacional de las Intervenciones (Churubusco), 188–89, 226, 229

museums, 4, 24, 26–27, 51, 53, 147–48, 150, 188, 241. *See also* names of specific museums
music, 19–21, 52–53
My Second Grade Workbook, 178
My Third Grade Text and Workbook: History of Veracruz, 180–81
"My Violets for the Cadets of Chapultepec" (poem), 95

El Nacional, 87
Nanjing Massacre, 243
Natchez (Mississippi), 28
National Association of Mexican War Veterans, 111–15
National Association of Veterans of the Mexican War: Bancroft controversy, 109–10; decline, 78, 111; founding, 62; medal, 66, 266–67n24; membership, 270–71n71; pension fight, 62–64, 72, 78, 104; reunions, 62–63, 69, 73, 78
National Cathedral (Mexico City), 148
National Cemetery at Alexandria (Louisiana), 31
National College of Mines, 91
National Commission of Free Textbooks. *See* Comisión Nacional de los Libros de Texto Gratuitos
National Endowment for the Humanitites, 220–21
National Guard Heritage Gallery, 208–9
National Guard of Mexico, 42, 54–57, 82–85, 97
National Historic Landmark Program, 206
National Museum of History. *See* Museo Nacional de Historia (Chapultepec)
National Palace (Mexico City), 1, 148, 150, 216
National Park Service, 3, 155, 170–71, 206, 219, 233–35; Mission 66, 206–7. *See also* Palo Alto Battlefield National Historic Site
National Society of the Colonial Dames in the State of Texas, 119
National World War II Memorial, 5
Native Americans, 188, 197–98, 205, 208; effacing history of, 103–5, 121, 123, 169
Native Daughters of the Golden West, 120–21, 155, 205, 283n66
Native Sons of the Golden West, 113, 120–21, 155, 283n66

Natividad: Battle of, 103–4, 293n6; monument, 170
nativism, 101, 120–21
Nava, Julian, 195, 199
Naval Military School (Veracruz), 98–99
Navy, U.S., 104–5, 119
Neal, Larry, 209
Nebel, Carl, 18, 188
Neff, Jacob K., 70
Negley, James S., 62, 64
Negrete, Jorge, 136
New England Regiment, 32–33
New Guinea, 171
New Mexico: conquest of, 102, 201; Chicano activism, 200–203; commemorations, 156, 160–61; Mexican territory, 46; monuments, 120, 156, 161, 208; shifting demographics, 161; statehood, 102
New Orleans Greys, 209
New Orleans (Louisiana), 28, 60, 116
New Tales of the Narrow Street (comic book), 179
New York City, 27–29, 33–34, 39, 78
New York Courier and Enquirer, 131
New York Herald, 26
New York Times, 2, 99, 126–27, 162, 236
New York Volunteers, 48, 61, 169, 258n82
Niños Héroes, 6, 81, 130; additional monuments, 236, 291n62; artistic representations, 51, 90, 130, 135, 141, 151, 181, 216, 262n32; challenges to, 215–16, 227, 239, 244; Chicanos, 199–200; commemorations (*see* Altar to the Fatherland; Chapultepec, Battle of; Obelisco a los Niños Héroes y al Honor Militar); currency, 189, 216; government use, 129, 135, 174, 179, 224–25; mythologizing, 86–90, 216; origins, 48–49; Protestants and, 149; as redeemers, 135, 139; reinterment, 143, 145–49; as role models for children, 175, 179–84; and Truman, 162
Noriega, Alfredo de, 136
The North American Abolitionists (Luelmo), 142
North American Free Trade Agreement (NAFTA), 190, 212, 214–15, 221, 239
The North American Intervention in Mexico (Fuentes Díaz), 142
North American Invasion (Castillo Nájera), 142
The North American Invasion in 1846 (Paz), 93

North and South (television miniseries), 210–11
Norwich (Vermont), 32
Notes for the History of the War between Mexico and the United States, 41, 44–45, 47–48
Nueces Strip, 3, 120, 126, 159

Obelisco a los Niños Héroes y al Honor Militar (Chapultepec), 85–86, 90–91, 99, 133, 139, 148; Truman's visit, 144, 162–63
Obregón, Álvaro, 128, 131–33
O'Brien, John Paul Jones, 24–25
O'Brien, William, 231
Observations (Crescencio), 44
Observations of the Message of the President of the United States, 44, 46, 48
Occupied America (Acuña), 196–99, 303n13, 303–4n19
"Of Gringos and Old Grudges" (Weiner), 236
Office of Historical Preservation (California), 155
Oglesby, Richard James, 209
Ohio Volunteers, 21
oil expropriation, 135–36, 138, 140
Olaguíbel, Juan Fernando, 139, 149
Old Sacramento (cannon), 25
Olympic Games: 1968, 182–84; 2004, 1–2, 236
Olympic Men's Soccer Qualifying Match (2004), 1–2, 236
Once TV México, 221
One Man's Hero (motion picture), 230–31
Operation Wetback, 167
O'Reilly, Bill, 2
Organization of American States, 162, 171
Otis, Harrison Gray, 96, 139
Our Boy Heroes, 143
Our Lady of Guadalupe, 149
Our Mexican Conflicts (Gregory), 125

Pace, Frank, Jr., 164
pacifism, 9–10, 28
paintings, 19, 51, 181, 216, 262n32
Palmetto Association, 39
Palmetto Regiment (South Carolina), 28–30, 102
Palo Alto: battlefield, 2–3, 21–24, 27, 30, 119; Battle of, 2–3, 42, 218, 222;

Mexican memory, 47, 218–19; monuments, 118, 155, 206–7; namesakes, 36
Palo Alto Battlefield National Historic Site, 3–4, 171, 206–7, 217–19, 233–36; historical park, 243, 245, 248n11
Palo Alto National Park Committee, 207, 217, 222, 235
Panteón de Santa Paula (Mexico City), 55
Parada Continental, 148
Paredes, Américo, 181
Paredes y Arrillaga, Mariano, 43
Paris (Illinois), 101
Parker, Fess, 167
Parker, Theodore, 9–10
Parrodi, Anastacio, 42
Partido de la Revolución Democrática, 226
Partido Revolucionario Institutional, 221
Payne, Andrew L., 209
Paz, Eduardo, 93
Pennsylvania Mexican War Monument (Harrisburg), 66
pensions: Mexican veterans, 57; U.S. veterans, 59–64, 66–78
Peñúñuri, Francisco, 55, 263n42
Pérez, Francisco, 55
Pershing, John, 124
Pettit, Fanny, 116
Philadelphia, U.S.S., 104–5
Phoenix (Arizona), 231
Pico, Andrés, 106–7
Pictorial History of Mexico and the Mexican War (Frost), 18
Pierce, Franklin, 12, 29, 39, 189
Pillow, Gideon, 256n57
Pino Suárez, José María, 97
Pioneers Trek, 166–67
Plan Espiritual de Aztlán, 197–98
Plasencia de la Parra, Enrique, 86
Plata, Manuel M., 145
Plaza de la Constitución, 1, 146, 148, 150, 183, 216
Plaza de las Tres Culturas, 183–84
Pliego, Antonio, 51
Plitt, Walter, 206–7, 217, 235, 240
Point Isabel (Texas), 26–27, 30, 44
Polk, James Knox, 3, 9, 12, 142, 158–59, 234
El Popular, 145
postage stamps, 142, 160, 225
Powers, Llewellyn, 68
La Prensa, 146
Preparatoria Número Uno (Monterrey), 184

Primaria Colegio México (Matamoros), 180
Primaria Franklin D. Roosevelt (Matamoros), 186
Public Broadcasting Service (PBS), 219, 230. See also KERA-TV
Pulitzer Prize, 126

Quiñones, Joel, 153

racism. See white supremacy
Rafael, Lorenzo, 176
Ramírez Garrido, José Domingo, 133
Ramsey, Albert C., 48–49
Rangel, Joaquín, 49–50, 56
Rankin, Melinda, 23
Ransom, Truman B., 32–33, 258n81
Ravenous (motion picture), 233
Rawlins, John Aaron, 61
Raygosa, Genaro, 83
La Raza Unida Party, 245
Reagan, Ronald, 207–8
Rebellion in the University (Lipset), 194
Reform War, 50, 178
Register of National Park Visitors, 234–35
Rehearsal for Conflict (Bill), 161–62
Reinaldo (engraver), 50
reinterments, 30–34, 55–56, 143, 145–49, 151–52
Rendón, Armando B., 197, 203
Rendón de la Garza, Clemente, 219
Rennick, Robert M., 38
Republican Party, 37, 116, 171–72; criticism of war, 60; opposition to Mexican Pension Bill, 68–78
Resaca de la Palma: battlefield, 21–24, 27, 171, 206; Battle of, 3, 42, 198; Mexican remains, 192, 240; monument, 155
A Review of the Causes and Consequences of the Mexican War (William), 13, 15
A Review of the Life, Character and Political Opinions of Zachary Taylor, 11
La Revista Universal, 84, 88
Revolution of Tuxtepec, 84
Reynosa, José, 97
Richards, Ann, 217
Ringgold, Samuel, 30, 36
Rio San Gabriel, Battle of, 103–4, 293n6
Ripley, Roswell Sabine, 13
Rivera Yzaguirre, Antonio, 219
Roa Bárcena, José María, 93–94
The Robin Hood of El Dorado (motion picture), 169

Roberts, Brigham H., 123
Robledo Treviño, Manuel, 219
Rock Island Arsenal (Illinois), 117–18
Rockefeller, John D., 108, 116
Rodríguez, Abelardo L., 134
Rodríguez, Antonio, 44, 47
Rodríguez Arangoity, Ramón, 85–86
Romano-V, Octavio Ignacio, 197
Romero, Matías, 59
Roosevelt, Franklin Delano, 135, 138–39,
    154–59, 167
Roosevelt, Theodore, 111, 116, 124
Roxbury (Massachusetts), 12
Ruelas, Miguel, 97–98
Ruiz Cortines, Adolfo, 174–75
Ruiz, Ramón Eduardo, 195, 199

Sacramento (California), 108, 201
Sacramento (Chihuahua): battlefield, 23,
    111–12; Battle of, 25
Sáenz, Aarón, 142, 151
Saenz Blanchard, Denise, 218
Saint Patrick's Batallion. See Batallón de San
    Patricio
Saint Patrick's Day Parade (Phoenix), 231
Salas, Anthony and Vivian, 234
Salinas (California), 170
Salinas de Gortari, Carlos, 190, 214–16,
    221, 239
San Ángel (Mexico City), 176–77
San Bernardino (California), 166
San Blas Battalion. See Batallón de San Blas
San Diego (California), 108, 122, 156, 166,
    199, 203–5
San Diego Old Town Boosters Association,
    212
San Felipe Indian Reservation (New
    Mexico), 156, 208
San Francisco (California), 61, 105–6, 108,
    199
San Francisco Chronicle, 160
San Luis Potosí, 53
San Pasqual: Battle of, 103–4, 199, 293n6;
    commemoration, 205; monuments,
    120–21; reenactments, 212
San Pasqual Battlefield State Historic Park,
    171, 205–6
San Pasqual Battlefield Volunteer Associa-
    tion, 206
San Patricio (Texas), 177
San Patricios de Arizona, 231
Sanchez, David, 200–202
Sanchez Cárdenas, Rosalia, 219

Sánchez Hernández, Tomás, 141, 151
Sanderson, Alice, 234
Santa Anna, Antonio López de: as author,
    42–43, 92–93; criticism of, 43, 135,
    189–90, 229; post-1848 political career, 2,
    83; prosthetic leg, 26, 101, 157–58,
    208–10, 232–33; suppression of com-
    memorations, 41, 55–57, 84–84; in
    U.S.–Mexican War, 10, 47, 75, 168–69,
    184
Santa Catalina Island (California), 201–2
Santa Clara: Battle of, 103–4, 171; monu-
    ment, 208, 306n51
Santa Fe (New Mexico), 102, 120, 122,
    160–61, 199, 201, 206–8
Santa Fe New Mexican, 161
The Santa Fe Trade and the War of '47'
    (Moyano), 186–87
Santiago de Querétero (Querétero), 41, 53
Savage, Kirk, 65
Scott, John, 14–15
Scott, Winfield: commander, 25–26, 45;
    honors, 29, 36, 65; monuments, 65, 156;
    presidential candidate, 12, 29
Scott Legion, 62, 266n19
Scott's Entrance into Mexico (lithograph), 18
Seaton, Fred A., 170–71
Secretaría de Educación Pública (SEP),
    128–30, 132–35, 141; commemorations,
    182–83, 186; publications, 174–75,
    178–80, 184, 187–88; textbook contro-
    versy, 215–16
The Secret Service Ship (Averill), 16, 20
semicentennial anniversary of the war,
    102–8
sesquicentennial anniversary of the war,
    222–29
Seventh U.S. Infantry Living History
    Association, 211
Sherman, Edwin A., 77, 109
Shields, James, 70–71, 75
A Short History of the United States
    (Bassett), 158–59
"A Short Statement of the Causes Which Led
    to the War with Mexico," 11
Siepp, Henry, 103
El Siglo XIX, 84, 99
Singleton, Ortho Robards, 70
slave conspiracy, 10, 12, 19, 135
Slayden, James Luther, 116
Slidell, John, 3
Sloat, John Drake, 103–4, 110; monument,
    104, 110, 113–14, 118–19

Sloat Monument Association, 104, 114, 118–19
Smith, George Albert, 165–66
Smith, Joseph, Jr., 204
Smith, Justin H., 126–27
Smithsonian National Air and Space Museum, 5, 218
Smithsonian National Museum of American History, 236
So Far From God (Eisenhower), 5
Social Darwinism, 124–25
Society of California Pioneers, 103–4, 109–10
Society of Veterans of 1846, 61
soldiers, Mexican: criticisms of, 14–15; cult of dead, 94; guerillas, 45; lancers, 14–15, 24–25, 51, 170; poor technology, 46, 94, 130, 135, 184, 189, 195; U.S. praise for, 14, 71–72, 75, 195. *See also* individual units by name
soldiers, U.S.: atrocities, 45, 185, 195, 197–99; praise, 13–14; receptions for, 27–29. *See also* individual units by name
soldiers' home, 57, 61–62, 111, 265n10
Solís, Manuel de Jesus, 146
Sonoma (California), 103, 110, 113, 118; monuments, 118, 121, 206
Sons of the American Revolution, 160–61, 165
Sons of the Utah Pioneers (SUP), 166–67, 203–4, 208
Sotomayor, Arturo, 147
South by Southwest (Ruiz and Tebbel), 195, 199
South Carolina, 28, 30
Southampton County (Virginia), 29
Soviet Union, 143, 164, 186
Spain, 105; fantasy heritage in the U.S., 102, 121
Spanish-American War, 91, 101, 111, 124
Special Commission on Guadalupe Hidalgo Land Rights, 202
Special Committee on Border Issues, 205
Springfield Armory (Massachusetts), 25
Standard Oil, 108, 116
Stanford, Leland, 108
State Department, U.S., 158, 228–29
St. Louis (Missouri), 25, 65–66, 112
"The Star-Spangled Banner" (song), 1
Starr, Frederick, 125
Statement Directed to the Supreme Government by the Commissioners That

Signed the Treaty of Peace with the United States, 44
The Statement of the Secretary of State, 42–43
status revolution, 108
Steward, George Rippey, 37
Stewart, Alice, 106
Stockton, Robert F., 37, 109
The Storming of the Castle of Chapultepec (lithograph), 17
Streeby, Shelley, 20, 250n20, 251n8
Studdert, Stephen M., 207–8
Su Alteza Serenísima (motion picture), 232–33
Suárez, Vicente, 49, 87–89, 199–200
Supreme Court, Mexican, 174, 182
Sutter, John A., 109
Swayze, Patrick, 211
swords, presentation, 29–30
Synthesis of the History of Mexico, 185–86

Tablada, José Juan, 90
Taft, William Howard, 96, 111
Talavera, Leonardo, 112
Tamariz, Ernesto, 151
Tampico (Illinois), 37
Tampico (Tamaulipas), 36, 42, 56, 98
Tampico Regiment, 26–27
Taos Revolt, 102, 161; monument, 208
Taylor, Zachary: honors, 29, 36, 66; monument, 66; presidential candidate, 11; Rio Grande Campaign, 3, 34, 47, 176, 192, 201
Tebbel, John, 195, 199
Teja Zabre, Alfonso, 136
Texas, 102–3, 107, 170–73
Texas and the Mexican War (motion picture), 196
Texas annexation, 3, 13, 44, 159, 193
Texas Archaeological Research Laboratory, 240
Texas Association of Mexican War Veterans, 111, 113–14
Texas Centennial Commission, 155–56
Texas History Movies (comic book), 168
Texas Rangers, 114, 235
Texas Republic, 3, 155–56, 167–69
Texas Semi-Centennial Exposition, 102–3
Texas War of Independence, 22, 43–44, 91, 167–69, 179, 188, 193, 209; centennial, 155; sesquicentennial, 209, 211
Thomas, George H., 28–29
Thompson, Robert A., 103–10

Thoreau, Henry David, 10
Thornton Affair, 3, 44–45, 155, 193; monument, 155, 201
Thrilling Stories of Mexican Warfare (Morris), 124–25
Thurston, Walter C., 144, 148, 162–63
Tijerina, Reies, 202–3
Tinnemeyer, Andrea, 20
Tlacaélel, 85
Tlatelolco Massacre, 183–84, 215
Toler, William P., 105
Tomb of the Unknown Soldier, 114
toponymy, 35–38
Toro, Alfonso, 130–31
Torrea, Juan Manuel, 133–34, 137–38, 145–46, 290n43
Torres Bodet, Jaime, 144, 178
Torres Quintero, Gregorio, 130
Tower, John G., 172
The Treaty of Guadalupe (Castillo Nájera), 142
Treaty of Guadalupe-Hidalgo: Chicanos, 201–3; failures, 194–95, 198, 201–3; Mexican Americans, 186; terms, 1, 45–46, 160, 172, 193, 242; U.S. gains, 67–68, 189
trophies, 24, 27; cannons, 24–25, 53, 66, 117–18, 225n57; flags, 24, 150–51, 163–65, 209, 292n66; taken by Mexicans, 25, 47, 53. *See also* Santa Anna, Antonio López de: prosthetic leg
Trophy Point (West Point), 24
Truman, Harry S., 143–45, 150, 161–65, 167
Tucson (Arizona), 122, 199, 223
Twiggs, David, 50, 139

United American Veterans, 79
United Confederate Veterans, 113
United Daughters of the Confederacy, 115, 281n49
El Universal, 139–40
Universidad de Nuevo León, 184–85
Universidad Nacional Autónoma de México (UNAM), 182–84, 227
University of North Carolina at Chapel Hill, 233
"An Unjust Invasion" (Vázquez), 225
Uribe, Virgilio, 98–99, 181
Urista, Alberto "Alurista," 197–98
U.S.–Mexican diplomacy, 7, 90–92, 132, 139, 153–54, 171–73, 223–24; challenges, 186–87; immigration, 153; military alliance, 140–41, 144–45, 150–51, 158,

162–65. *See also* Mexican Peso Crisis; North American Free Trade Agreement
The U.S.–Mexican War, 1846–1848 (television miniseries), 219–21, 223, 229–30, 236
U.S. Military Academy at West Point, 24–25, 148, 150, 211; Cullum Hall, 119; return of Mexican Flags, 163–65
USA Today, 231
Utah, 123–24, 165–67, 169
Utah Mormon Battalion Monument Commission, 123
Utah Pioneer Trails and Landmarks Association, 156, 165–66

Valadés, José C., 142
Valdez, Tony, 237
Van Buren, John, 34
Van Wagenen, Monica Delgado, 288n24
Van Wyck, Charles, 76
Vargas, Francisco, 91
Vasconcelos, José, 128, 132–33
Vázquez, Josefina Zoraida, 220, 223, 225, 244–45
Vázquez Colmenares, Gonzalo, 151
The Vedette, 72–73, 78, 109, 269n46
Velázquez de la Cadena, C. José, 91–92
Veracruz: Boy Heroes, 98–99, 135, 180–81; French Intervention, 58; namesakes, 36; Siege of, 16, 26, 98–99, 188; State of, 180; U.S. invasion of (1914), 98–99, 124, 135, 154, 178
veterans, Mexican: decline of, 94–95; organizations, 81–82, 84, 91–92; reunions, 81, 91, 112; role in commemorations, 85–90, 97
veterans, U.S.: decline of, 111–16, 127, 161; organizations, 39, 61–63, 77, 111–14; pension fight, 59–64, 66–78; political organization, 60–64, 66–78, 111; pretenders, 66, 114; reunions, 39, 61–64, 67, 69, 73, 77, 101, 103–7, 112–15; serving Confederacy, 60; vitality, 105, 278n15; youngest, 267n32
Vielé, Teresa Griffin, 24
Vietnam War, 5, 185, 193–95, 198, 200, 208
View of Cerro Gordo (lithograph), 50
View of Chapultepec and Molino del Rey (lithograph), 51
Villa, Francisco "Pancho", 99–100, 124, 133
Villalpando, José Manuel, 244
Virginia Association of Mexican Veterans, 79
Virginia Historical Society, 29

Voices: Readings from El Grito (Romano-V), 197
Voorsanger, Jacob, 104–5
Vorhees, Daniel, 74

Wakarusa War, 25
Wallace, Henry A., 139
Wallace, Lew, 22–23, 28, 34–35
Walker, James, 19
The War against the Gringos (Frías), 189–90
The War between the United States and Mexico, Illustrated (Kendall), 18
The War of '47 and the Popular Resistance to the Occupation (López y Rivas), 187
war reenactments. *See* living history
The War with Mexico (Chidsey), 193
The War with Mexico (Ripley), 13
The War with Mexico (Smith), 126–27
The War with Mexico Reviewed (Livermore), 12–13, 198
Warren, Earl, 166
Washington, D.C., 29, 65, 61–63, 190
Washington Post, 160
Wayne, John, 171
Weiner, Tim, 236
West Point. *See* U.S. Military Academy at West Point
"When There Are No Parties, Mexico Will Gain Immortality" (stage play), 54–55
Whig Party, 11, 12, 33–34, 60
White House of the Confederacy, 83
white supremacy, 5, 73, 101–2, 104, 113, 120–21, 124–27, 140, 154, 168, 196

Whittier, John Greenleaf, 19–20
Wilcox, Cadmus M., 80
Williams, John Stuart, 74–75
Wilson, Woodrow, 97, 124
Wingert, Chris, 2
Wolford, Frank Lane, 77
Wood, Fernando, 34
women: role in commemorations, 106–7, 111, 115–21, 123; war widows, 116–17
The Wonderful World of Disney (television series), 167
Worcester (Massachusetts), 32
The Works of Hubert Howe Bancroft (Bancroft), 109–11
Works Progress Administration, 156
World War I, 21, 30, 114, 126
World War II, 5, 138, 140–42, 156–60, 236, 242; Mexicans in U.S. military, 158; Mexico, 140–42
Worth, William Jenkins, 34, 37

Xicoténcatl, Felipe Santiago, 49, 87, 134, 151, 273n21; reinterment of, 55, 151–52

Yale University, 215
Yturria, Mary, 206–7

Zapata, Emiliano, 100, 133
Zavaleta, Antonio, 217, 308n11
Zedillo Ponce de León, Ernesto, 215–16, 221–28
Zimmerman Telegram, 99–100, 124, 285n83
Zoot Suit Riots, 140

MICHAEL SCOTT VAN WAGENEN is an assistant professor at Georgia Southern University, where he teaches courses in public history. He is the author of *The Texas Republic and the Mormon Kingdom of God* and co-editor of *Between Pulpit and Pew: The Supernatural World in Mormon History and Folklore*. He previously taught U.S.–Mexico borderlands history at the University of Texas at Brownsville. In addition to his scholarly research and writing, he is a national award–winning documentary filmmaker. His work has been screened at numerous film festivals and broadcast internationally on public and cable television.